Communications
in Computer and Information Science   1589

More information about this series at https://link.springer.com/bookseries/7899

Akram Bennour · Tolga Ensari ·
Yousri Kessentini · Sean Eom (Eds.)

Intelligent Systems and Pattern Recognition

Second International Conference, ISPR 2022
Hammamet, Tunisia, March 24–26, 2022
Revised Selected Papers

 Springer

Editors
Akram Bennour (ID)
Larbi Tebessi University
Tebessa, Algeria

Tolga Ensari (ID)
Arkansas Tech University
Russellville, AR, USA

Yousri Kessentini (ID)
Digital Research Centre of Sfax
Sakiet Ezzit, Tunisia

Sean Eom (ID)
Southeast Missouri State University
Cape Girardeau, MO, USA

ISSN 1865-0929   ISSN 1865-0937 (electronic)
Communications in Computer and Information Science
ISBN 978-3-031-08276-4   ISBN 978-3-031-08277-1 (eBook)
https://doi.org/10.1007/978-3-031-08277-1

This Springer imprint is published by the registered company Springer Nature Switzerland AG
The registered company address is: Gewerbestrasse 11, 6330 Cham, Switzerland

Preface

It gives us immense pleasure to introduce the proceedings of The Second International Conference on Intelligent Systems and Pattern Recognition (ISPR 2022) organized by the Laboratory of Mathematics, Informatics and Systems (LAMIS) at Larbi Tebessi University, Tebessa, Algeria, in collaboration with the Digital Research Center of Sfax, Tunisia, and the Artificial Intelligence and Knowledge Engineering Research Labs at Ain Sham University, Egypt. The event was aimed at providing an interdisciplinary forum of discussion to share the recent advancements in different areas of artificial intelligence and pattern recognition. It was endorsed by the International Association of Pattern Recognition (IAPR) and took place in Hammamet, Tunisia, during March 24–26, 2022.

This volume of proceedings contains the papers accepted and presented at the conference. A total of 91 papers in different areas of pattern recognition and artificial intelligence were submitted to ISPR 2022. The submissions were reviewed by renowned researchers in the respective fields from all over the world. After a thorough and competitive paper review and selection process, 36 papers were accepted for presentation at the conference yielding an acceptance rate of 40%. A total of 32 papers were registered and presented at the conference.

We would like to take this opportunity to thank the reviewers for their time and efforts in reviewing the papers and providing constructive feedback to the authors. We are also thankful to the keynote speakers, the authors, and the participants of the conference. We would also like to thank the authors whose papers did not meet the selection criteria for the conference and would like to encourage them to consider the next edition of ISPR for potential publication of their research. Our heartfelt gratitude goes to all members of the organizing committees for their big efforts in making this event a success. Finally, special thanks go to the International Association of Pattern Recognition (IAPR) as well as all the sponsors of the event.

We hope that ISPR 2022 provided valuable knowledge sharing and networking opportunities to the participants and we look forward to seeing you again at the next edition.

April 2022

Akram Bennour
Tolga Ensari
Yousri Kessentini
Sean Eom

Organization

General Chairs

Akram Bennour	Larbi Tebessi University, Algeria
Yousri Kessentini	Digital Research Center of Sfax, Tunisia

Program Committee Chairs

Akram Bennour	Larbi Tebessi University, Algeria
Tolga Ensari	Arkansas Tech University, USA
Yousri Kessentini	Digital Research Center of Sfax, Tunisia
Sean Eom	Southeast Missouri State University, USA

Publicity Chairs

Lotfi Chaari	INP Toulouse, France
Salma Jamoussi	University of Sfax, Tunisia
Nebras Gharbi	University of Kairouan, Tunisia
Tahar Mekhaznia	Larbi Tebessi University, Algeria

Steering Committee

Jerry Wood	Arkansas Tech University, USA
Lotfi Chaari	INP Toulouse, France
Akram Bennour	Larbi Tebessi University, Algeria
Brahim Hnich	University of Monastir, Tunisia
Abdel-Badeeh Salem	Ain Shams University, Egypt

Publication Chairs

Mustafa Ali Abuzaraida	Universiti Utara Malaysia, Malaysia
Takashi Matsuhisa	Russian Academy of Science, Russia
Tolga Ensari	Arkansas Tech University, USA

Program Committee

Mustafa Abuzaraida	Universiti Utara Malaysia, Malaysia
Hammad Afzal	National University of Sciences and Technology, Pakistan

Rossitsa Yalamova	University of Lethbridge, Canada
Nacereddine Zarour	Constantine 2 University, Algeria
Sam Zaza	Middle Tennessee State University, USA
Nadia Zeghib	Constantine 2 University, Algeria
Ehlem Zigh	INTTIC, Algeria

Contents

Computer Vision

3D Dense & Scaled Reconstruction Pipeline with Smartphone Acquisition 3
Quentin Thisse, Dominique Houzet, and Jérémy Adoux

A Genetic Model for Medical Images Reproduction 19
Karima Benhamza, Ines Guerziz, Amel Bentagine, and Hamid Seridi

A New Study of Needs and Motivations Generated by Virtual Reality
Games and Factor Products for Generation Z in Bangkok 29
Kawin Meksumphun and Chutisant Kerdvibulvech

A Hybrid Method for Window Detection on High Resolution Facade Images . . . 43
Kujtim Rahmani and Helmut Mayer

Neuro-Fuzzy Predictive Approach for Visual Analytics Evaluation
of Medical Data 51
Saber Amri and Med Lassaad Kaddachi

Improved Cerebral Images Semantic Segmentation Using Advanced
Approaches of Deep Learning 65
*Abderraouf Zoghbi, Maroua Benleulmi, Soraya Cheriguene,
Nabiha Azizi, Samira Lagrini, and S. Nadine Layeb*

Self-supervised Learning for COVID-19 Detection from Chest X-ray
Images 78
Ines Feki, Sourour Ammar, and Yousri Kessentini

Data Mining

Deep Learning-Based Segmentation of Connected Components in Arabic
Handwritten Documents 93
Takwa Ben Aïcha Gader and Afef Kacem Echi

Classifying the Human Activities of Sensor Data Using Deep Neural
Network 107
Hussein A. A. Al-Khamees, Nabeel Al-A'araji, and Eman S. Al-Shamery

Exploratory Analysis of Driver and Vehicle Factors Associated with Traffic
Accidents in Morocco 119
Hamza Khyara, Aouatif Amine, and Bouchra Nassih

Building a Multilingual Corpus of Tweets Relating to Algerian Higher
Education 132
  Asma Siagh, Fatima Zohra Laallam, and Okba Kazar

Recursive Feature Elimination Technique for Technical Indicators Selection ... 139
  Naik Nagaraj, B. M. Vikranth, and N. Yogesh

Document-Based Knowledge Discovery with Microservices Architecture 146
  Habtom Kahsay Gidey, Mario Kesseler, Patrick Stangl, Peter Hillmann,
  and Andreas Karcher

Pattern Recognition

Feature Selection for Credit Risk Classification 165
  Dalia Atif and Mabrouka Salmi

Parameter Identification and Validation of Multi-innovation Least Squares
Lithium Battery for Second-Order Battery Model 180
  Jie Wu, Huigang Xu, and Peiyi Zhu

Bat Echolocation Call Detection and Species Recognition by Transformers
with Self-attention 189
  Hicham Bellafkir, Markus Vogelbacher, Jannis Gottwald,
  Markus Mühling, Nikolaus Korfhage, Patrick Lampe, Nicolas Frieß,
  Thomas Nauss, and Bernd Freisleben

Scheduling Techniques for Liver Segmentation: ReduceLRonPlateau vs
OneCycleLR 204
  Ayman Al-Kababji, Faycal Bensaali, and Sarada Prasad Dakua

An Explainable Predictive Model for the Geolocation of English Tweets 213
  Sarra Hasni and Sami Faiz

Removing Redundancies in Binary Images 221
  Majid Banaeyan, Darshan Batavia, and Walter G. Kropatsch

Neural Machine Translation of Low Resource Languages: Application
to Transcriptions of Tunisian Dialect 234
  Abida Emna, Saméh Kchaou, and Rahma Boujelban

SPIRAL: SPellIng eRror Parallel Corpus for Arabic Language 248
  Shaimaa Ben Aichaoui, Nawel Hiri, and Mohamd Amine Cheragui

Machine and Deep Learning

VMs Migration Mechanism for Underloaded Machines in Green Cloud
Computing 263
Nassima Bouchareb and Nacer Eddine Zarour

TunBERT: Pretrained Contextualized Text Representation for Tunisian
Dialect 278
Abir Messaoudi, Ahmed Cheikhrouhou, Hatem Haddad,
Nourchene Ferchichi, Moez BenHajhmida, Abir Korched,
Malek Naski, Faten Ghriss, and Amine Kerkeni

Road Recognition for Autonomous Vehicles Based on Intelligent Tire
and SE-CNN 291
Runwu Shi, Shichun Yang, Yuyi Chen, Rui Wang, Jiayi Lu,
Zhaowen Pang, and Yaoguang Cao

Malicious Packet Classification Based on Neural Network Using Kitsune
Features 306
Kohei Miyamoto, Hiroki Goto, Ryosuke Ishibashi, Chansu Han,
Tao Ban, Takeshi Takahashi, and Jun'ichi Takeuchi

An Hybrid Deep Learning Approach for Prediction and Binary
Classification of Student's Stress 315
Nesrine Kadri, Sameh Hbaieb Turki, Ameni Ellouze,
and Mohamed Ksantini

A Novel Deep Convolutional Neural Network Architecture for Customer
Counting in the Retail Environment 327
Almustafa Abed, Belhassen Akrout, and Ikram Amous

Transfer Learning for the Classification of Small-Cell and Non-small-Cell
Lung Cancer 341
Mohamed Gasmi, Makhlouf Derdour, and Abdelatif Gahmous

Attentional Conditional Generative Adversarial Network for Ambient
Occlusion Approximation 349
Fayçal Abbas, Mehdi Malah, and Mohamed Chaouki Babahenini

An Improvement of CNN Model for Traffic Sign Recognition
and Classification 362
Tahar Mekhaznia and Imtiez Fares

Social Media Sentiment Classification for Tunisian Dialect: A Deep
Learning Approach 377
Mehdi Belguith, Nesrine Azaiez, Chafik Aloulou, and Bilel Gargouri

Soil Moisture Prediction Based on Satellite Data Using a Novel Deep
Learning Model 394
    Amina Habiboullah and Mohamed Abdellahi Louly

Author Index 409

Computer Vision

3D Dense & Scaled Reconstruction Pipeline with Smartphone Acquisition

Quentin Thisse[1,2]([⊠]), Dominique Houzet[2]([⊠]), and Jérémy Adoux[1]([⊠])

[1] MyFit Solutions, 70 Quai Perrache, 69002 Lyon, France
{quentin.thisse,jeremy.adoux}@myfit-solutions.com
[2] Univ. Grenoble Alpes, CNRS, Grenoble INP, GIPSA-lab,
38402 Saint-Martin d'Hères Cedex, France
dominique.houzet@gipsa-lab.grenoble-inp.fr
https://myfit-solutions.com/

Abstract. Computer vision tackles the hard problems of understanding images and videos. It is a challenge widely discussed in many recent works. Mobile devices such as smartphones or tablets are equipped with sensors more and more precise. They have powerful processing units to collect information about their environment, making them the perfect tool to understand surroundings. Humans understand their world in 3D and have no problems estimating the approximate scale of an object placed in front of them. We tackle this problematic by using a smartphone to acquire visual data and inertial data to reproduce human vision. In that sense, we propose a pipeline for 3D reconstruction that generates dense, scaled and textured 3D model from a series of images acquired with a monocular smartphone. We present a solution of high quality 3D scan within everyone's reach thanks to data acquisition on a smartphone. We propose a new keyframe selection algorithm that includes an augmented reality object during the scan in order to improve both data quality and ease of use during a scan. Finally, we produce a high quality, dense, textured, scaled 3D model without artifacts thanks to our optimized 3D reconstruction pipeline.

Keywords: 3D reconstruction · Automated · Scaled · Dense reconstruction · Smartphone acquisition

1 Introduction

In this paper, we address the problem of producing good quality 3D models for the average user who does not have specific equipment or knowledge related to the field of 3D reconstruction. We present a pipeline for 3D reconstruction using a mobile device for data acquisition. It generates dense, scaled and textured 3D model from a series of images acquired with a monocular smartphone. The acquisition is made easy for the user with an augmented reality dome placed on top of the scanned object. A keyframe selection is provided in order to increase

© Springer Nature Switzerland AG 2022
A. Bennour et al. (Eds.): ISPR 2022, CCIS 1589, pp. 3–18, 2022.
https://doi.org/10.1007/978-3-031-08277-1_1

the quality of the model, by taking the best image quality and reduce the computing time, by sending only a few images on a remote server for reconstruction. Selected images are then automatically processed and registered with an incremental Structure-from-Motion (SfM) algorithm in order to create a 3D model that is meshed and textured. Then the model is scaled using inertial measurements taken during the scan by the mobile device. After that, the shape of the 3D model is analyzed to remove the surface on which it is placed and which has been reconstructed with the object. Finally, the 3D model is uploaded back to the model device for user visualization. We evaluate our 3D reconstruction pipeline by performing experiments on various objects and on known datasets.

The main contributions of the paper can be summarized as:

- An optimized user experience scan that adds an augmented reality object in the scene. This allows both to guide the user during data acquisition and to select the keyframes needed to produce a high quality model.
- An optimized pipeline for 3D reconstruction that generates dense scaled textured 3D model.

This paper is organized as follow: related work is presented in Sect. 2. Then we get to see in detail each step of the 3D reconstruction pipeline in Sect. 3 including the data acquisitionn and post-processing. Finally, experimental results will be discussed in Sect. 4.

2   Related Work

Our work deals with monocular 3D reconstruction that generates a scaled 3D textured model with high quality with smartphone data acquisition. The issue of 3D reconstruction on mobile devices has been addressed by a lot of work. One of the first is [24]. It fuses PTAM algorithm [11] and inertial data to produce a dense 3D model. Depth map are computed in real-time and then fused into a dense 3D point cloud. Another approach is [18]. It is a more advance approach that updates continuously volumetric surface with new depth measurments. In [20], it performs simultaneous visual-inertial shape-based tracking and 3D shape estimation. Finally, in [15], an approach that combines real-time scanning around the object and post-processing has been presented.

All these methods perform tracking and reconstruction on mobile devices with sometimes heavy computationnaly tasks [24]. Thus a compromise on reconstruction quality has to be made if we want to perform in real-time. Another major drawback is the selection of the keyframes. It requires a trained user in order to produce smooth scanning to get sharp images. The quality of images is closely linked with the quality of the final 3D model.

Other approaches use Structure-from-Motion algorithm with no need of real-time performance. In these cases, cloud computing is often used [3,13,19,26]. Nevertheless, there is no guarantee that the data is of high quality before the algorithm generates the 3D model. Moreover a reference object is often needed in the scene to provide scaling.

Our approach confronts these different drawbacks. We provide an easy scanning experience that ensures the quality of the data. Then we propose a structure-from-motion approach close to [14], with cloud computing on specific selected keyframes. We can at the end provide a high 3D model quality and a decent computational time. Moreover our approach scales the 3D model without the need of a reference object in the scene. Finally, we provide an algorithm that removes unwanted parts of the 3D model such as the surface it is placed on, to get only the object of interest.

3   3D Reconstruction Pipeline

A diagram of our approach is shown in Fig. 1. We start from capturing a sequence of images at a rate of 10 frames per second. At this stage, the user is assisted with an augmented reality model to enhance the data capture. During this acquisition, we also save IMU measurements coming from the accelerometer and the gyroscope. We perform feature extraction with the selected keyframes and feature tracking from one image to another then we use triangulation to get a structure estimation. IMU data are kept for scaling. After computing the first 3D point cloud, we perform bundle adjustment to simultaneously refine 3D coordinates, camera poses and the optical characteristics of the camera. Next, we realize depth map estimation with the keyframes, the poses and the sparse scene structure where one depth map is computed for each keyframe. We can then densify the sparse point cloud by performing depth fusion. After that, we conduct mesh reconstruction and refinement. Given the keyframes and the poses, a texture is generated. IMU data are used to compute the scale of the object in order to ensure the best precision we can. Finally, the computed 3D model is cleaned by erasing outliers and remaining residual item as well as the surface on which the object is placed on.

3.1   Data Capture

The first step of the 3D reconstruction pipeline is to capture data. We need a sequence of images composed of variety of viewpoints of the object and IMU measurement. We propose a new way of capturing data that is user friendly and ensure a high quality of the selected keyframes.

Scan: In order to get a high quality of images, we propose a way to guide the user during the scan with an augmented reality dome placed on top of the object as in Fig. 2. Indeed images selected for the 3D reconstruction must be sharp and represent all the viewpoints of the scanned object. At the same time, we collect IMU data and transform them in information needed for the scaling with Arkit [2] (for iOS) and Arcore [8] (for Android). The augmented reality dome is composed of 456 faces and its radius is scalable depending on the user's needs. At the beginning of a scan, the user places an object on a flat surface. Then, the user points the camera at the object and the dome is placed on it

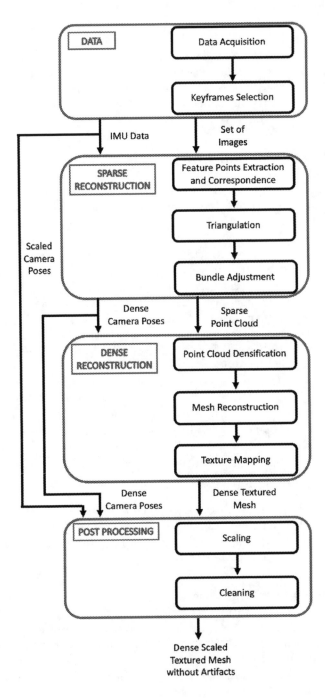

Fig. 1. 3D reconstruction pipeline

using a plane detection algorithm [2,8]. A face of the dome is validated when the ray coming from the object to the camera forms an angle of less than 20° with the normal of the face. When it is the case, an image is taken and IMU data are saved.

Fig. 2. Object with augmented reality dome

Keyframes Selection: At this stage, we have 456 images of an object with all its viewpoints to generate a dense 3D model. We want to select only a few images to ensure a high quality of the model and keep a decent computational time. There are two main contraints for the images: all viewpoints have to be represented and images must be sharp. We decompose the dome into 12 parts. Each of them has 38 images and we keep the 3 sharpest images among them. To compute the sharpness of an image, we attribute a focus score to each image. It is calculated as an alternative definition of the Laplacian [16].

$$\Phi(x, y) = \sum_{(i,j) \in \Omega(x,y)} \Delta_m I(i, j) \tag{1}$$

where $\Delta_m I$ is the modified Laplacian of I computed as $\Delta_m I = |I * \mathcal{L}_x| + |I * \mathcal{L}_y|$, the convolution masks used to compute the modified Laplacian are $\mathcal{L}_x = \begin{bmatrix} -1 & 2 & 1 \end{bmatrix}$ and $\mathcal{L}_y = \mathcal{L}_x^T$.

3.2 Feature Points Extraction and Correspondence

Once the data is selected, we extract and describe the feature points on images to get correspondences between them. We use SIFT [12] method, as its descriptors are accurate, stable and invariant to scale changes and rotations. They are also stable to affine transformations and luminosity. There are several methods to match feature points on a series of images. This includes the brute force algorithm, ANNkD trees [17], or cascade hashing [4]. The cascade hashing method [4] allows us to obtain results 100 times faster than with the brute force method and 10 times faster than with the ANNkD tree method [17], while maintaining a comparable level of accuracy. In the following we will use this method.

3.3   Triangulation

At this point, we know the corresponding pairs of points between two images (x_1, x_2) and we have access to their projection matrix (P_1, P_2). These two points with their respective projection matrix should therefore reconstruct the same 3D point (X, Y, Z). However, the error in estimating the position of the characteristic points or the noise coming from the distortion of the lenses can disturb the coordinates of the 3D points. The latter cannot be calculated with absolute precision because the rays coming from the points on the images do not intersect in 3D space according to Fig. 3.

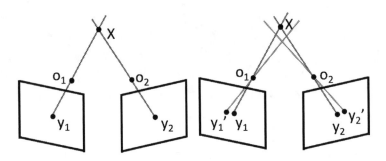

Fig. 3. (left): intersection of two rays in the epipolar geometry case, (right): intersection of two rays in the real case

This error can be minimized in an algebraic way [9], by writing the projection of a point such as:

$$x_1 = P_1 X \Rightarrow \begin{pmatrix} x_1 \\ y_1 \\ 1 \end{pmatrix} \begin{pmatrix} p^{1T} \\ p^{2T} \\ p^{3T} \end{pmatrix} X = 0 \Rightarrow \begin{pmatrix} y_1 \cdot p_1^{3T} - p_1^{2T} \\ x_1 \cdot p_1^{3T} - p_1^{1T} \end{pmatrix} X = 0 \qquad (2)$$

with p^{iT} the ith column of the projection matrix. Combining with the projection equation of the second point gives

$$\begin{pmatrix} y_1 \cdot p_1^{3T} - p_1^{2T} \\ x_1 \cdot p_1^{3T} - p_1^{1T} \\ y_2 \cdot p_2^{3T} - p_2^{2T} \\ x_2 \cdot p_2^{3T} - p_2^{1T} \end{pmatrix} X = 0 \Leftrightarrow AX = 0 \qquad (3)$$

We then obtain a system of linear equations that can be solved with a simple value decomposition. Minimizing the algebraic error is not geometrically significant but can be generalized to the case where the 3D point is observed from more than two viewpoints.

3.4 Pose Estimation

We aim to estimate the pose of the camera from a series of images. The position and relative orientation of two successive images are estimated. Then, a refinement method corrects the errors and rectifies the drift of the visual odometry. In this step, the 3D points that were used for pose estimation in the previous image are projected into the current camera image using the estimated camera pose. This is optimized by minimizing the photometric error of a patch of pixels around the estimated location of the projected point in the current image.

3.5 Bundle Adjustment

We have just presented different methods which, when combined, allow us to estimate the trajectory of a camera and to reconstruct the 3D structure of the observed scene in the form of a point cloud, from a sequence of images. This constitutes the initial estimation of the geometry. Once this initial estimation is available, we refine the parameters of this model (the positions of the points and the camera poses) through an optimization step. An optimal solution can be calculated by beam fitting [25]. The objective is to simultaneously re-estimate the coordinates of the 3D points and the camera poses in order to minimize the sum of squares of the discrepancies between the points detected in the images and the reprojections obtained from the computed model [5, 7]. In order to minimize the reprojection error, we measure the 2D distance between the observation of the 3D point in the image (i.e. the 2D position of the point of interest) and the projection of the reconstructed 3D point in this same image $r = ||x_i - P_i X_i||$. The associated cost function is

$$\epsilon(\{R_j, t_j\}_{j=1}^{N_c}, \{X_i\}_{i=1}^{N_p}) = \sum_{i=1}^{N_p} \sum_{j \in A_i} d^2(x_{i,j}, P_j X_i) \tag{4}$$

with N_p 3D points $\{X_i\}_{i=1}^{N_p}$, N_c the number of camera, $x_{i,k}$ the observation of the 3D point X_i in the kth view, A_i the set of indices of the cameras observing X_i. Finally, R_j, t_j and P_j are respectively the orientation, the optical center and the projection matrix of the jth camera. $d^2(x_1, x_2) = ||x_1 - x_2||^2$ is the point to point distance.

3.6 Point Cloud Densification

This step is crucial for the whole reconstruction process because the mesh estimation and the final result depend closely on the dense point cloud. In a first step, the densification algorithm generates depth maps using the sparse point cloud and the structure from motion data. These maps are refined using PatchMatch [10], then filtered and merged until the desired dense point cloud is obtained. This algorithm can be separated into 4 steps, the stereo pair selection, the depth map computation, the depth map refinement and the depth map fusion.

Stereo Pair Selection: It is crucial to choose the right pair of stereo images within the series to obtain the most accurate dense point cloud. First, we calculate the neighboring views that are most similar and will later be target images. To select the key images, we take those who share a maximum of points in the sparse point cloud and the images that overlap the most. We thus build a duo reference image - target image, forming stereo pairs. We initialize the queue of stereo image pairs.

Depth Map Computation: For each reference image in each pair, its depth map is first initialized using the sparse point cloud and interpolated. The depth map is then computed using spatial propagation and a random assignment approach [10]. The principle is as follows:

– For each pixel in the reference image, a patch (square window) centered around that pixel is selected. For each pixel in this patch, we initialize its depth and a support plane. If no initialization value is found from the sparse point cloud, a random value will be assigned with a predefined interval.
– The found patch is transposed to the target image using a homography. Then, the average normalized cross correlation (NCC) score for the patch is calculated. This is an indicator of the cost of matching pixel p (of coordinates (x, y)).

$$NCC(x,y) = \sum_{x,y \in W} \frac{I^2_{x,y} \cdot I^1_{x,y}}{\sum(\sqrt{I^1_{x,y} - \bar{I}^1_{x,y}}) \cdot \sum(\sqrt{I^2_{x,y} - \bar{I}^2_{x,y}})} \tag{5}$$

with $I^1_{x,y}$ the intensity of the image I^1 at the position (x, y) and W the patch of size $n \times n$.

– We compute the NCC score for all pixels neighboring p. If one of them gets a lower NCC score (smaller matching cost for this pixel), then the previously initialized depth map and the support plane will be propagated to this new pixel. Otherwise, we do not change the initialization values.
– We test random depth map values and support plane parameters and see if they perform better in terms of NCC score.

Depth Map Refinement: For each pixel on each depth map, if the depth values are consistent along the neighboring images, then they are considered as reliable points in the scene. Otherwise, they are removed from the depth map.

Depth Map Fusion: Finally, the depth maps that were refined in the previous step are merged. This process includes a removal of redundant values because different depth maps are likely to have identical points.

3.7   Mesh Reconstruction

We distinguish two steps during mesh reconstruction, first we remove the noise and then we find the best fitting triangles for the points using Delaunay triangulation [21]. A noise filtering is first performed through a statistical study of the 3D point cloud, the algorithm is as follows: let k the number of nearest neighbors of the point P_i. Let α the multiplying coefficient for the standard deviation, this parameter is adjustable according to the data. Then for each 3D point P_i in the point cloud, we first find the position of the k nearest neighbors of P_i. Then we calculate the average distance d_i from the point P_i to its k nearest neighbors. After that, we calculate the average μ_d and the standard deviation σ_d of the lengths d_i. That gives us the threshold defined as $T = \mu_d + \alpha.\sigma_d$. Finally, we eliminate the points of the point cloud for which the average distance to these k nearest neighbors is $d > T$.

Next we generate the meshes. We use the Delaunay triangulation algorithm to create the triangles. Delaunay triangulation maximizes the smallest angle of the set of triangle angles, avoiding elongated triangles. The circumscribed circle of a triangle consisting of three points of the starting set is empty if it contains no other vertices than its own [21]. The other points are thus allowed on the perimeter itself but not strictly inside the circumscribed circle. The Delaunay condition states that a grid of triangles is a Delaunay triangulation if all circumscribed circles of the triangles in the grid are empty. This is the original definition in two dimensions. By replacing the circles by circumscribed spheres, it is possible to extend the definition to three dimensions.

3.8   Texture Mapping

In the case of a perfect reconstruction of the mesh and camera positions, obtaining the texture is a relatively simple step. In reality, the mesh and camera positions contain at best slight variations or errors, and the mesh texturing module must be able to handle them. In this paper, we use a method [27] for texturing models that addresses challenging reconstructions with a large number of input images that can be blurred and occluded.

3.9   Scaling

We now have a dense 3D model without residues but not yet at scale. The objective of this part is therefore to move to a Euclidean reconstruction that respects absolute distances. We retrieve during the scan data from the IMU that are transformed thanks to two augmented reality libraries, the Arkit for iOS [2] or Arcore for Android [8]. These data consist of the points of the scattered point cloud at scale, the intrinsic data and the poses of the cameras in the world coordinate system. Thus, on one hand we have a set of camera poses in the 3D dense model coordinate system and on the other hand we have a set of camera poses in the world coordinate system. We call X_s the set of camera poses retrieved with Arkit or Arcore, and X_d the set of camera poses of the 3D model. We find the greatest distance between two camera poses for both sets, called $Dist_s$ and $Dist_d$. We calculate the scale such as $s = \frac{Dist_s}{Dist_d}$. Finally, we apply this scale to all points in the dense 3D model.

Fig. 4. Examples of reconstructed models

3.10   Model Cleaning

We have a dense 3D model of the scene. This model can contain 3D residues coming from noise or from a parasitic object. If the scanned object has been placed on a horizontal surface, this plane will be reconstructed as well as the object and will be found in the 3D model. We aim to remove any element that does not belong to the object of interest in the 3D model. This algorithm is divided into outliers removal and plane removal.

Outliers Removal: We remove outliers in two ways. First we use the augmented reality dome placed over the object. Since the object is inscribed in the dome, we can remove points according to: $X_{new-model} = \{X \mid d(X - c_{dome}) < r_{dome}\}$, with c_{dome} the center of the dome in the world coordinate system, r_{dome}, the radius of the dome and d the Euclidian distance. Then, we count connected objects. If there are more than one, that means there are still artifacts remaining that need to be deleted. Then we keep the object in the center of the dome.

Plane Removal: The 3D model now consists of the object of interest and a plane that corresponds to the horizontal surface on which it is placed. It is then necessary to find the plane with the largest support, in order not to confuse it with a plane present on the object, its shape not being known. Once this plane is found, it is removed. We choose the RANSAC algorithm [6] with a plane equation model $(a.x + b.y + c.z + d = 0)$ to identify the normal vector of the support plane. Once the plane is known we can remove it.

4   Experimental Results and Limitations

For the evaluation, the data are captured using an iPhone XS, then they are sent to a remote server in order to generate the 3D model. The server used for computation has 8 cores and 16 Go RAM.

We have tested our approach on real data taken in static environment with several objects. The selected objects are a statuette, a ping pong paddle, a case, a cactus. Some of them have asperities while others are specular in nature. Some objects used for the evaluation can be seen in the first column of Fig. 4. The objects were captured indoor under normal illumination conditions. The proposed path is a 360° loop around the objects capturing all viewpoints. Some results of reconstruction on various objects, with different viewpoints, can be seen in Fig. 4.

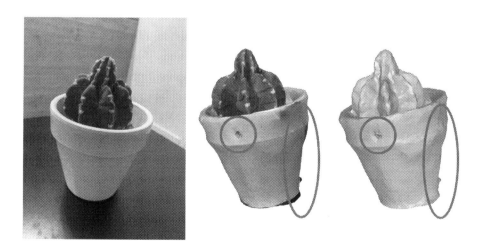

Fig. 5. Example of reconstruction on a reflective surface

4.1   Results

We can see on Fig. 4 that the proposed method can reconstruct different topologies of objects with high precision. Moreover, we notice that the finest parts of the objects are also accurately reconstructed. We can also notice that uniform textured objects are well reconstructed such as the ping pong paddle on Fig. 4. The computation time of our approach depends on the scanned object. If the object has a lot of textures, then many feature points will have to be taken into account and the time will increase. However, the calculation time is around 8 min for most objects. The Table 1 summarizes the results.

Table 1. Calculation time summary table

Object	Running times (s)
Statuette	690
Paddle	544
Case	523
Cactus	459

On Fig. 6, we compare our results with algorithm described in [1] and [22]. The comparison is made on the same input data which is a series of images of different objects with 360° views. We can clearly see that our model is as precise as the one from [1] and less noisy that the one from [22].

4.2   Limitations

We show in Fig. 5 the results of our approach on more challenging datasets. These limitations are well known for monocular reconstruction. They are objects with reflective or shiny surfaces and transparent objects. The Fig. 5 shows that the 3D reconstruction is not faithful to the object, the cause being the reflection of the light on it. Another source of error for this model comes from the fact that there are not enough salient points on the uniform surface. Thus the mapping of the feature points is challenged and inconsistencies such as holes in the model can be found.

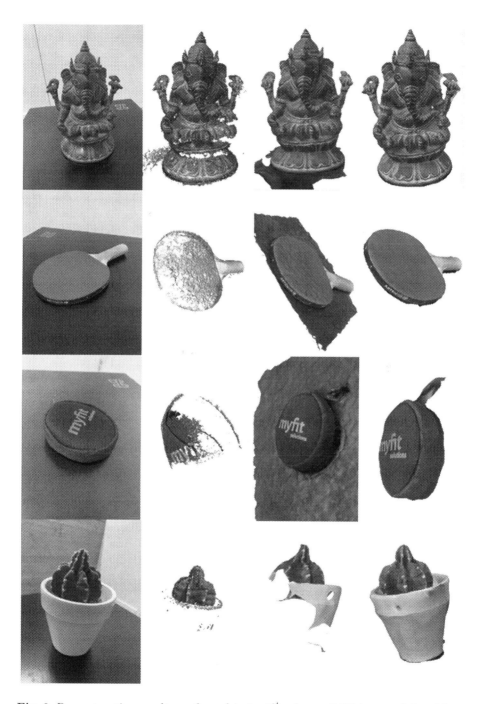

Fig. 6. Reconstruction results on four objects. 1st column: RGB image of the object, 2nd column: MicMac [22], 3rd column: Meshroom [1], 4th column: Ours

5 Conclusion and Future Work

In this paper, we presented a 3D reconstruction pipeline that generates a scaled 3D model of an object as a mesh with a texture by using a mobile device for acquisition. We demonstrated the accuracy of our approach and its ease of use as it does not require a trained user to get high quality models thanks to a new augmented reality approach and an innovative way to select keyframes. We compared our approach to those of the state of the art and demonstrated better quality results on high textured objects and on challenging datasets. Our future work will be devoted to the reduction of the calculation time. Indeed, the most time consuming algorithms in the pipeline (point cloud densification or mesh refinement step) can be replaced by deep learning algorithms such as [23,28]. These techniques can help reduce computation time while ensuring the same quality for the 3D models.

References

1. AliceVision: Meshroom: A 3D reconstruction software (2018). https://github.com/alicevision/meshroom
2. Apple: Arkit (2020). https://developer.apple.com/arkit/
3. Autodesk, INC. https://www.autodesk.com/
4. Cheng, J., Leng, C., Wu, J., Cui, H., Lu, H.: Fast and accurate image matching with cascade hashing for 3D reconstruction. In: Proceedings of the IEEE Conference on Computer Vision and Pattern Recognition (CVPR) (2014)
5. Delaunoy, A., Pollefeys, M.: Photometric Bundle Adjustment for Dense Multi-View 3D Modeling (2014). https://hal.archives-ouvertes.fr/hal-00985811, working paper or preprint
6. Derpanis, K.G.: Overview of the ransac algorithm. Image Rochester NY **4**(1), 2–3 (2010)
7. Furukawa, Y., Ponce, J.: Accurate camera calibration from multi-view stereo and bundle adjustment. Int. J. Comput. Vision **84**, 257–268 (2008). https://doi.org/10.1007/s11263-009-0232-2
8. Google: Arcore (2020). https://developers.google.com/ar/
9. Hartley, R., Sturm, P.: Triangulation. Comput. Vision Image Underst. **68**(2), 146–157 (1997)
10. Hiradate, M., Ito, K., Aoki, T., Watanabe, T., Unten, H.: An extension of patchmatch stereo for 3d reconstruction from multi-view images. In: 2015 3rd IAPR Asian Conference on Pattern Recognition (ACPR), pp. 061–065 (2015). https://doi.org/10.1109/ACPR.2015.7486466
11. Klein, G., Murray, D.: Parallel tracking and mapping for small AR workspaces. In: Proceedings of the 2007 6th IEEE and ACM International Symposium on Mixed and Augmented Reality, ISMAR 2007, pp. 1–10. IEEE Computer Society, Washington (2007). https://doi.org/10.1109/ISMAR.2007.4538852
12. Lowe, D.G.: Distinctive image features from scale-invariant keypoints. Int. J. Comput. Vision **60**(2), 91–110 (2004)

13. Moritani, R., et al.: Streamlining photogrammetry-based 3d modeling of construction sites using a smartphone, cloud service and best-view guidance. In: Osumi, H., F.H.T.K. (ed.) Proceedings of the 37th International Symposium on Automation and Robotics in Construction (ISARC), pp. 1037–1044. International Association for Automation and Robotics in Construction (IAARC), Kitakyushu (2020). https://doi.org/10.22260/ISARC2020/0143

14. Moulon, P., Monasse, P., Perrot, R., Marlet, R.: OpenMVG: open multiple view geometry. In: 1st Workshop on Reproducible Research in Pattern Recognition. LNCS, vol. 10214, pp. 60–74. Springer, Cancun (2016). https://doi.org/10.1007/978-3-319-56414-2_5, https://hal-enpc.archives-ouvertes.fr/hal-01497080

15. Muratov, O., Slynko, Y., Chernov, V., Lyubimtseva, M., Shamsuarov, A., Bucha, V.: 3DCapture: 3D reconstruction for a smartphone. In: 2016 IEEE Conference on Computer Vision and Pattern Recognition Workshops (CVPRW), pp. 893–900 (2016). https://doi.org/10.1109/CVPRW.2016.116

16. Nayar, S., Nakagawa, Y.: Shape from focus. IEEE Trans. Pattern Anal. Mach. Intell. **16**(8), 824–831 (1994). https://doi.org/10.1109/34.308479

17. Olonetsky, I., Avidan, S.: TreeCANN - k-d tree coherence approximate nearest neighbor algorithm. In: Fitzgibbon, A., Lazebnik, S., Perona, P., Sato, Y., Schmid, C. (eds.) ECCV 2012. LNCS, vol. 7575, pp. 602–615. Springer, Heidelberg (2012). https://doi.org/10.1007/978-3-642-33765-9_43

18. Ondruska, P., Kohli, P., Izadi, S.: Mobilefusion: real-time volumetric surface reconstruction and dense tracking on mobile phones. IEEE Trans. Visualization Comput. Graph. **21**(11), 1251–1258 (2015)

19. Poiesi, F., Locher, A., Chippendale, P., Nocerino, E., Remondino, F., Van Gool, L.: Cloud-based collaborative 3D reconstruction using smartphones. In: Proceedings of the 14th European Conference on Visual Media Production (CVMP 2017), CVMP 2017. Association for Computing Machinery, New York (2017). https://doi.org/10.1145/3150165.3150166

20. Prisacariu, V.A., Kähler, O., Murray, D.W., Reid, I.D.: Real-time 3D tracking and reconstruction on mobile phones. IEEE Trans. Visual Comput. Graphics **21**(5), 557–570 (2015). https://doi.org/10.1109/TVCG.2014.2355207

21. Romanoni, A., Delaunoy, A., Pollefeys, M., Matteucci, M.: Automatic 3D reconstruction of manifold meshes via delaunay triangulation and mesh sweeping (2016). https://doi.org/10.1109/WACV.2016.7477650

22. Rupnik, E., Daakir, M., Pierrot Deseilligny, M.: Micmac - a free, open-source solution for photogrammetry. Open Geospat. Data Softw. Stand. **2**(1), 14 (2017)

23. Sun, J., Xie, Y., Chen, L., Zhou, X., Bao, H.: Neuralrecon: Real-time coherent 3D reconstruction from monocular video. CoRR abs/2104.00681 (2021). https://arxiv.org/abs/2104.00681

24. Tanskanen, P., Kolev, K., Meier, L., Camposeco, F., Saurer, O., Pollefeys, M.: Live metric 3D reconstruction on mobile phones. In: Proceedings of the IEEE International Conference on Computer Vision (ICCV) (2013)

25. Triggs, B., Mclauchlan, P., Hartley, R., Fitzgibbon, A.: Bundle adjustment - a modern synthesis. In: Triggs, B., Zisserman, A., Szeliski, R. (eds.) International Workshop on Vision Algorithms. Lecture Notes in Computer Science, vol. 1883, pp. 298–372. Springer-Verlag, Corfu (2000). https://doi.org/10.1007/3-540-44480-7_21, https://hal.inria.fr/inria-00548290, this work was supported in part by the European Commission Esprit LTR project CUMULI (B. Triggs), the UK EPSRC project GR/L34099 (P.McLauchlan), and the Royal Society (A. Fitzgibbon)

26. TRNIO. https://www.trnio.com/

27. Waechter, M., Moehrle, N., Goesele, M.: Let there be color! large-scale texturing of 3D reconstructions. In: Fleet, D., Pajdla, T., Schiele, B., Tuytelaars, T. (eds.) ECCV 2014. LNCS, vol. 8693, pp. 836–850. Springer, Cham (2014). https://doi.org/10.1007/978-3-319-10602-1_54

28. Wang, F., Galliani, S., Vogel, C., Speciale, P., Pollefeys, M.: Patchmatchnet: Learned multi-view patchmatch stereo. CoRR abs/2012.01411 (2020). https://arxiv.org/abs/2012.01411

A Genetic Model for Medical Images Reproduction

Karima Benhamza[1]([⊠]), Ines Guerziz[2], Amel Bentagine[3], and Hamid Seridi[1]

[1] LabSTIC, University of 08 Mai 45 of Guelma, Guelma, Algeria
{Benhamza.Karima,Seridi.hamid}@univ-guelma.dz
[2] ESI, 8 Mai 1945, Sidi Bel Abbas, Algeria
[3] University of 8 Mai 1945, Guelma, Algeria

Abstract. Reproducing images arise in many applications such as image compression, Image optimization, graphic art, and medical image processing. For medical images, image quality is crucial for proper diagnosis from an imaging study. The challenges in medical image processing occur due to poor image contrast and artifacts that outcome from missing organ boundaries. In this paper, a new variant of the Genetic Algorithm (GA) is proposed to provide an optimal solution to the medical image reproduction problem. The genetic operators have been adapted and the fitness function has been adjusted to produce good solutions. The implemented method, tested with different medical images, offers good results and agrees well with the complex medical images and even with low-quality images.

Keywords: Medical image · Genetic algorithm · Reproducing image · Similarity · Fitness function

1 Introduction

One of the most useful tools in modern medicine is medical imaging. Its role is not to produce a perfect image, but an image clear enough to allow the diagnosis of the suspected health problem accurately and quickly and thus improve the effectiveness of treatments. However, the quality of the obtained medical images may not be sufficient for processing and thus allow diagnosis. To improve their quality, it is necessary to increase the radiation dose sent to the patient, which increases the radiation risk.

Reproducing images is a known problem in digital image processing. This axis of research is well-used in medical image compression and encryption. In healthcare, reproducing images can be very useful in regenerative medicine. This recent technology may offer novel therapies for patients with injuries, organ failure, or other clinical problems.

Many imaging techniques have emerged in different fields. Some of these techniques are now well used, most are still under development and others are the subject of mainly academic research [1]. Mathematical methods have been used in image reconstruction in field of radiology using Back-projection, iterative and analytical procedures (Two-dimensional Fourier, Filtered Back-projection) [2, 3]. These techniques are used in several imaging modalities (PET, CT and others see Fig. 1).

© Springer Nature Switzerland AG 2022
A. Bennour et al. (Eds.): ISPR 2022, CCIS 1589, pp. 19–28, 2022.
https://doi.org/10.1007/978-3-031-08277-1_2

However, mathematical methods have drawbacks such as increasing time processing with iterative method. Besides, the back-projection method produces many artifacts if the medical image has a high density in the center.

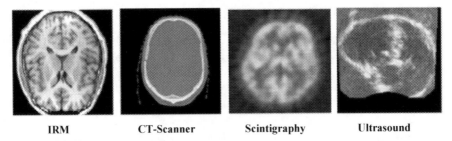

IRM   CT-Scanner   Scintigraphy   Ultrasound

Fig. 1. Main imaging modalities

In addition, reproducing images has been performed with artificial intelligence techniques [4]. Thus, supervised learning with Convolution Neural Networks (CNN) has been applied in medical imaging applications [5, 6]. In the other hand, this problem has been considered as an optimization problem where metaheuristic methods has been applied such as Harmony search algorithm [7] and also Ant Colony Optimization algorithm (ACO) [8].

In this paper, the Genetic Algorithm (GA) [9] is applied to reproduce medical images. GA is heuristic search approach inspired from the biological evolution and has proven to be an enormously powerful problem solving strategy in many complex problems [10]. This algorithm is based on a population of candidate individuals that represent a set of solutions. The representation of individual (solution) plays an important role. It is usually list of values called values strings [9, 10].

Genetic algorithms involve three fundamental genetic operations: selection, crossover, and mutation. In the selection operation, some individuals are selected from the population as parents. in the crossover, parents are crossed to produce offspring, while in mutation manipulation, offspring can be changed according to the rules of mutation.

The parameters of the GA are summarized as follows: Population size is the number of individuals (solutions) in the population. The crossover rate and mutation rate are, respectively, the probability that parents will cross and the offspring will mutate. The fitness function is used to evaluate the objective function of the problem. Algorithm execution stops when the maximum number of generations is reached or the value of the fitness function has not changed over the past few generations [10–12].

The structure of this paper is as follows: Sect. 2 presents the proposed steps of GA to reproduce medical images. In Sect. 3, the implemented model and experimental results are exposed. Finally, Sect. 4 presents the conclusions and future work.

2   Proposed Method

2.1   Principle

The image reconstruction is performed using a superposition of squares forms of a divided image area. At the first step, all image pixels are evaluated and the average values of red, green, blue channels of selected area are determined. In the second step, the image is divided in four areas.

For each section, parallel genetic algorithms are applied to retrieve the set of optimal red, green, and blue channels values. This process is repeated until the resulting image is similar to the original image. This similarity is evaluated in each zone by an appropriate fitness formula. The achieved set of red, green, and blue values are the result optimization values.

2.2   Modeling Steps

In this work, reproducing high-quality medical images using a genetic algorithm is considered. The aim is to provide an output image as similar as possible to the input image.

After the encoding step, the proposed model is following the main steps of the genetic algorithm: Initializing a population of chromosomes; evaluation of each string (fitness function); selection/reproduction procedure and genetic operations: crossover and mutation (see Fig. 2).

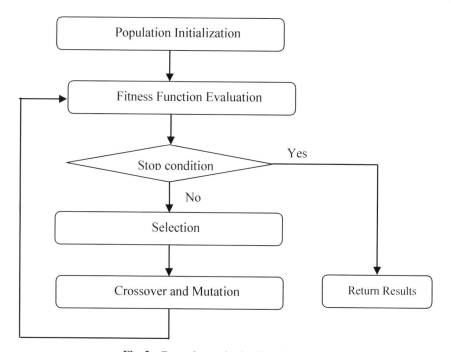

Fig. 2. General genetic algorithm flowchart

We detail each step of the proposed variant of GA below:

Encoding Individuals. A digital image is a 2D array of pixels. Genetic algorithm accepts a chromosome (i.e. solution) as a 1D row vector. Thus, Image 2D matrix is converted in 1D.

In the other hand, each pixel is represented with RGB color (Interval of possible values [0.255]). Thus, it will be encoded with three values representing red, green and blue channel (Table 1).

Table 1. Table of encoding individuals (from (a) to (b))

(200,5,140)	(100,5,14)	(1,15,210)	(0,47,6)
(233,44,3)	(1,37,100)	(87,43,41)	(0,0,6)
(4,55,69)	(250,88,3)	(73,66,0)	(5,100,87)
(120,154,189)	(1,37,100)	(2,22,6)	(4,44,25)

(a) 2D Pixels Matrix

(200,5,140)	(100,5,14)	(1,15,210)	(0,47,6)	(233,44,3)	(1,37,100)	(87,43,41)	....

(b) 1D Pixels Matrix

Initial Population. The first step is to generate a set of possible solutions randomly as an initial population. This initialization is recommended to randomly cover the whole solution space or to model and incorporate expert knowledge [9–11].

Selection. The selection operator aims to exploit the best characteristics of good candidate solutions in order to improve these solutions throughout generations. There are several selection methods: Roulette Wheel Selection, Stochastic Universal Sampling, Ranking selection, tournament selection and others [12–14]. In this work, Ranking selection method is adopted. First, individuals are sorted according to their fitness value in descending order and then the ranks are assigned to them.

Crossover. The result of the selection determines which parent is used at this stage. In effect, the crossover operator will produce new offspring based on the selected exchange points with parts of the parents. There are three types of crossovers: one-point crossover, two-point crossover, and multipoint crossover [9, 10]. In this work, a random crossover point is chosen and the parts of both parents are exchanged to obtain a new offspring (Fig. 3).

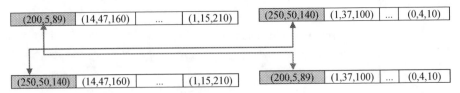

Fig. 3. Crossover step

Mutation. Mutation operation is a random tweak in the chromosome to produce a new solution. It is related to the exploration parameter of the search space essential to the convergence of the genetic algorithm and is used with a low probability [15]. In this work, uniform mutation is applied according to a probability. Each individual of population is modified by a random value drawn according to a uniform distribution over the interval of possible solutions [0.255] (Fig. 4).

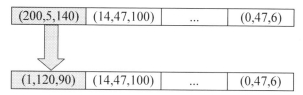

Fig. 4. Uniform mutation

Fitness. For each generation, algorithm genetic selects the best solutions from the current population and evolves them to make them better. First, the population is sorted based on the individual fitness. The fitness function used in this work accepts two parameters: the Input image and the output image (current solution). The fitness formula returns a number which measures the similarity between the two images. It is based on a Manhattan's distance measure [11] and according the Eq. (1):

$$\text{fitness} = \Delta \text{red} + \Delta \text{green} + \Delta \text{blue} \tag{1}$$

3   Results and Discussion

Determining the initial parameters used by the GA directly affects the solution quality and execution time [16]. There are four basic and important parameters:

1. **Population size**: This parameter represents the total number of individuals.
2. **Number of generations**: corresponds to the number of cycles. Depending on the problem model, this parameter can be omitted, notably, when the algorithm convergence depends on certain criteria (fitness function).
3. **Crossover rate (probability)**: The number of times a crossover occurs for chromosomes in one generation, i.e., the probability that two chromosomes swapping some of their parts.
4. **Mutation rate (probability)**: The final operator used to model the evolution of species is mutation. This parameter specifies how many chromosomes must be mutated in one generation. Like biology, mutation is a phenomenon that involves the alteration of one or more genes in an individual. This is a peculiar phenomenon because some genes cannot exhibit favorable values without the mutation.

The proposed method is evaluated on a sample of images from MedPix: Medical Image Database [17]. MedPix is a free and open-access medical image database containing nearly 59,000 images and textual metadata. The initialization values of the GA parameters, based on the quality of the solution (generated image) and time processing; are presented below:

Population $= 50$,
Maximum generation $= 10$,
Selection factor $= 0.95$,
Crossover rate Pc $= 0.8$
Mutation rate Pm $= 0.001$.

Table (2) shows the iterative results for four medical images. The results are good and similar to the input images (results for iterations 9 and 10 are not shown because the visual difference is not visible). The implemented model adapts well to different images.

The execution time depends on the size and complexity (variation) of the image. It is considered acceptable for low contrast medical images such as radiological images (Table 3). On the other hand, small population sizes could quickly reach the maximum number of generations, whereas the large population sizes executed more slowly.

In this study, we aim to generate medical images with maximum similarity to the originals. The choice of fitness function contributed effectively to achieving this goal. Figure 5 shows the evolution of the fitness curve by iteration for image 4. The fitness values (errors between the two images) decrease rapidly during the iterations, which shows the high efficiency of the algorithm and its convergence.

The experimental results show that the GA based reproducing method is simple and efficient. It has proven to be fairly robust for reproducing medical images. Indeed, it usually find near optimal solutions even with low images quality (Table 2).

Table 2. Reproducing medical images using genetic algorithm

(*continued*)

Table 2. (*continued*)

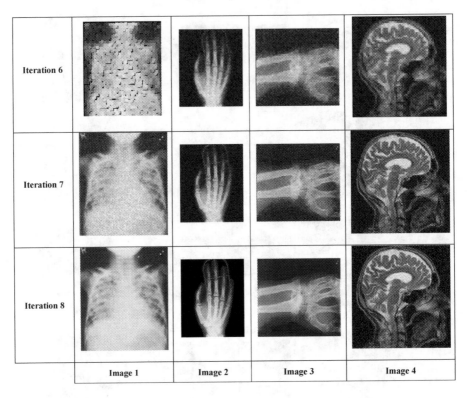

	Image 1	Image 2	Image 3	Image 4
Iteration 6				
Iteration 7				
Iteration 8				

Table 3. Execution time for producing the four medical images using GA

Images	Time_Unit
Image 1	23,104
Image 2	11,054
Image 3	12,415
Image 4	31,306

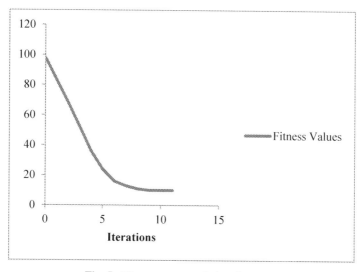

Fig. 5. Fitness curve evolution (image 4)

4   Conclusion

In this paper, a variant of GA for image reconstruction is presented. The proposed method uses a simple chromosome representation with novel genetic operators adapted to the problem. To validate this model, medical images with different resolutions were tested. The results showed the performance of the proposed model to reproduce good solutions even with low-quality images.

This research can be used in medical image compression and it can be applied also for image encryption in various fields such as radiology, biology, geophysics, and any type of optical image processing. It can be very useful in regenerative medicine to offer novel therapies for patients.

This model can be improved in the future by realizing parallel execution of the code and thus minimizing the execution time for complex and panoramic images. On the other hand, the efficiency of the GA is based on the appropriate choice of the genetic parameters such as the population number, the maximum iteration and fitness function. Strategy parameters such as selection, crossover, and mutation rates also affect the speed of GA convergence. Thus, this work can be extended by the study of GA strategies to optimize reproducing medical images.

References

1. Natterer, F., Wubbeling, F.: Mathematical methods in image reconstruction. Society for Industrial and Applied Mathematics (2001)
2. Brooks, R.A., Di Chiro, G.: Theory of image reconstruction in computed tomography. Radiology **117**(3), 561–572 (1975)
3. Bankman, I. (ed.): Handbook of Medical Image Processing and Analysis. Elsevier, Amsterdam (2008)

4. Hosny, A., Parmar, C., Quackenbush, J., Schwartz, L.H., Aerts, H.J.: Artificial intelligence in radiology. Nat. Rev. Cancer **18**(8), 500–510 (2018)
5. Sun, J., Li, H., Deep, X.Z.: AD MM-net for compressive sensing MRI. Adv. Neural Inf. Process. Syst., 10–18 (2016)
6. Eo, T., Jun, Y., Kim, T., Jang, J., Lee, H.J., Hwang, D.: KIKI-net: crossdomain convolutional neural networks for reconstructing undersampled magnetic resonance images. Magn. Reson. Med. **80**(5), 2188–2201 (2018)
7. Ouaddah, A., Boughaci, D.: Harmony search algorithm for image reconstruction from projections. Appl. Soft Comput. **46**, 924–935 (2016)
8. Pintea, C.-M., Ticala, C.: Medical image processing: a brief survey and a new theoretical hybrid ACO model. In: Hatzilygeroudis, I., Palade, V., Prentzas, J. (eds.) Combinations of Intelligent Methods and Applications. Smart Innovation, Systems and Technologies, vol. 46, pp. 117–134. Springer, Cham (2016). https://doi.org/10.1007/978-3-319-26860-6_7
9. Hynek, J.: Genetic algorithms and genetic programming, Grada, Prague (2008)
10. Bekhet, S., Ahmed, A.: Evaluation of similarity measures for video retrieval. Multimedia Tools Appl. **79**(9–10), 6265–6278 (2019). https://doi.org/10.1007/s11042-019-08539-4
11. Kramer, O.: Genetic Algorithm Essentials, vol. 679. Springer, Heidelberg (2017). https://doi.org/10.1007/978-3-319-52156-5_2
12. Mirjalili, S., Song Dong, J., Sadiq, A., Faris, H.: Genetic algorithm: theory, literature review, and application in image reconstruction. In: Mirjalili, S., Song Dong, J., Lewis, A. (eds.) Nature-Inspired Optimizers. SCI, vol. 811, pp. 69–85. Springer, Cham (2020). https://doi.org/10.1007/978-3-030-12127-3_5
13. Sivaraj, R., Ravichandran, T.: A review of selection methods in genetic algorithm. Int. J. Eng. Sci. Technol. **3**(5), 3792–3797 (2011)
14. Shukla, A., Pandey, H.M., Mehrotra, D.: Comparative review of selection techniques in genetic algorithm. In : 2015 International Conference on Futuristic Trends on Computational Analysis and Knowledge Management (ABLAZE), pp. 515–519. IEEE (2015)
15. De Falco, I., Della Cioppa, A., Tarantino, E.: Mutation-based genetic algorithm: performance evaluation. Appl. Soft Comput. **1**(4), 285–299 (2002)
16. Hassanat, A., Almohammadi, K., Alkafaween, E., Abunawas, E., Hammouri, A., Prasath, V.B.: Choosing mutation and crossover ratios for genetic algorithmsl a review with a new dynamic approach. Information **10**(12), 390 (2019)
17. MedPix, Medical image database. https://medpix.nlm.nih.gov/home

A New Study of Needs and Motivations Generated by Virtual Reality Games and Factor Products for Generation Z in Bangkok

Kawin Meksumphun and Chutisant Kerdvibulvech[✉]

Graduate School of Communication Arts and Management Innovation, National Institute of Development Administration, 148 SeriThai Rd., Klong-chan, Bangkapi, Bangkok 10240, Thailand
chutisant.ker@nida.ac.th

Abstract. Metaverse has recently been an emerging field in computer science, especially virtual reality games. Therefore, this paper aims to find the need and motivation for virtual reality games and the factor products via correlational research. The target group is framed from the demographic data in Bangkok in 2019 by the National Statistical Office of Thailand. 40 people around 18–24 years old are selected. We then develop new virtual reality games from free assets on Unity for testing and gathering information. Findings from the study showed that the product motives affecting Generation Z in Bangkok differ according to demographic characteristics. The results found that the highest average of need and motivation of Generation Z is convenience (4.25%), product appearance (4.20%), game effects (4.18%), pictures and graphics (4.05%), sound effects (3.93%), and game challenge (3.93%). However, the most negligible impact shows that the needs and motivations of Generation Z are branding (3.93%).

Keywords: Virtual world · Metaverse · Augmented reality · Games · Motivation · Correlational research · Generation Z

1 Introduction

Nowadays, many companies have begun to adopt metaverse, particularly virtual reality technology, to increase brand appeal and engagement. To attract and motivate people to interact with the industry's marketing such as a vehicle, accommodation, fast-moving consumer goods (FMCG), and online games. According to the Steps Academy article in 2018, the number of virtual reality (VR) users reached 171 million people, 62% of the users said they feel engaged with a brand experiencing virtual reality, and 71% of consumers believe the brands using virtual reality are forward-thinking in e-commerce. However, people prefer to shop online rather than buy by themselves. However, people still want to see the product for themselves. That is why many brands have started using augmented reality (AR) and virtual reality technology to make the online shopping experience more convenient and drive faster purchase decisions.

© Springer Nature Switzerland AG 2022
A. Bennour et al. (Eds.): ISPR 2022, CCIS 1589, pp. 29–42, 2022.
https://doi.org/10.1007/978-3-031-08277-1_3

The Facebook IQ report found that 63% of respondents from 11 markets said they would be interested in using virtual reality to view products without entering or going to a store. They were attracted to the companies; travel (71%), entertainment (59%), retail (58%), automotive (49%), and game (48%); that they can test before buying. This means virtual environment simulation hugely affects the market in this era. According to [1], the recent uprising in artificial intelligence also helps contribute to smarter, more realistic, more responsive, and smoother experiences, bringing the virtual and real worlds closer together. From projected investment value in technology based on IDC's estimated global investment in augmented reality and virtual reality in 2019 [2], it is estimated to be worth approximately $20.4 billion or about 652.8 billion baht, a 68.8% growth from 2018. And for its predictions for 2022, IDC pointed out that year-over-year growth will average 69.6% and that expansion of the augmented reality/virtual reality market will continue for another decade. Consumers will have more options for using augmented reality/virtual reality devices and software, and the service sector will benefit from market growth in the business sector. IDC also predicts that the industry will invest 64.5% in augmented reality/virtual reality in 2019 and grow to more than 80% in augmented reality/virtual reality. By 2022, the industries that will invest the most in 2019 are personal use (51.2 billion baht), retail (49,920 million baht), and factory and manufacturing businesses (49,280 million baht). The industries that are likely to be used in the future more than 100% each year are government and resource industries. With this growing speed, we will see many organizations focusing on building a virtual reality and the ways of using it. Therefore, it became a question in research which platform users prefer, or what product factors will motivate users to use virtual reality?

1.1 Desire and Motivations for Playing Virtual Reality Games

Cuthbert et al. [3] give an overview of the main effects of customization on the motivation of players in a game of virtual reality. Three key product factors affecting online gaming motivation are game content, game system, and graphics. The game's content will determine the direction of play and the mood and experience that the player will receive. Motivation for playing content games is related to the need for existence, such as relieving stress, winning, and being accepted and praised in playing skills. Therefore, researchers started to study virtual reality games and game products in demand and motivate Thai people to use them.

1.2 Generation Z in Bangkok

Framing the research down to Thai people, the researcher surveyed more information on the part of Thai gamers based on the Association of Radio and Media for Children. Youth report during 2019 found that a group of students in grades 6–12, vocational certificates, and Diploma, totaling 3,056 people across the country from September to October 2019. In most of the sample, 89% or 2,730 people used to play online games, of which percentage of the sample group 64% have an average rate of playing a game is 3–5 h per day, and 8% play games continuously for more than 8 h per day. Including the latest Twitter survey results, more than half of Twitter users in Thailand play games to "kill time," with many gamers being Generation Z (58%) and Generation Y (56%) playing games to create a routine.

In this way, the game has become a way of reducing stress and giving players happiness. These reflect the growing gamer population in Generation Z. The exciting thing in a Twitter poll in April 2020 found that more than a third of Generation Z (34%) gamers view gaming as a hobby and share the content of playing games. The impressive moments from watching favorite streaming games are also shared, making the game market more valuable, and seem to have purchasing power in the future. Generation Z is a target group because of a point. The starting point for the research question came from NZ, a website analyzing and exploring consumer behavior in the video game market, which has revealed the results of an in-depth survey on behavior motivation to play games of men and women playing games. What are your hobbies? The result shows the achievement of goals (55% male, female 49%/to challenge themselves and practice planning) (51% male, 39% female/to see the growth and development of the playing character) (50% male, 38% female/indulge in survey and story in the game) (50% male, 37% female/choose an easy-to-play game, finish faster).

Indicating a consumer motivation towards games is diverse. It can vary with state, context, or geographic factors. Virtual environments will be a matter of physical aspects, and some may play without any abnormality while others may play for a short time. Playing for a long time causes motion sickness because the water in the ear is not related to the direction of the view, which is a common symptom among virtual environment simulation game players. Another important factor from the research of Chanchuea [4], the researchers concluded that convenience and being able to do it at any time and place would cause satisfaction. Customer satisfaction due to various factors mentioned above, the researcher was interested in a study on the needs and motivations generated by virtual reality games and the production factors of Generation Z in Bangkok. So that the educators or those who have read this research will be able to further develop into marketing or game development and meet consumers' needs more in the future and hope this study's results will help understand the motivation and benefit the government and private sectors in the future.

2 Theoretical Framework and Bases for Study Measures

2.1 Uses and Gratifications

Uses and gratifications were improved and developed by Katz et al. [5]. They conclude that audiences are responsible for choosing media based on their preferences, using media by the audience, and fulfilling their needs. The definition of the theory is consistent with the research of [6] concluded through research that uses and gratification theory. Humans choose the communication channel to meet their needs and behavior. Moreover, as explained in [7], humans exhibit different exposure behaviors according to different experiences, needs, attitudes, feelings, and physical. According to the above research, the Uses and Gratifications theory is a theory that focuses on explaining behavior and causes of behavior. In choosing an audience, the media focuses on different experiences, needs, attitudes, feelings, demographic factors, and the core theory. People will select the media and the type of media for themselves.

Therefore, media production based on theory must design for the audience's need and interest and study the needs and motivations of Generation Z playing virtual reality games in Bangkok. They test with in-built tools and an evaluation form based on the theory of uses and gratifications.

2.2 Concepts of Game Types Affecting Gaming Motivation

Hussain et al. [8] explained the game types that motivate people to play in seven categories; exotic games (game novelty), games played together as a group (Social and Discovery-Oriented Game), games with rather violent content (Aggressive, Anti-Social, Non-Curious Game), games with highly competitive within society (Highly Social and Competitive Game), games that will connect the community around the players (Social Game), games that focus on a fun mood (Low-Intensity Enjoyment Game), and games which are divided into social classes (Social Classes Game). The preferences of each game type determine demographic factors, especially age and gender. When a game motivates and attracts more players, it creates behavior in choosing the game [9]. The top three product-driven factors influencing motivation to play online games at a high level are game content, game system, and game graphics. The emotions and experiences players receive are included. Research and investigation of games in virtual reality platforms based on data from the Oculus store (game download service platform) have 12 virtual reality games categories; Enter the Fast Lane, Explore New Worlds, Amazing Hand-Tracking Apps, Essential Quest Games, Create a Masterpiece, Mind-Bending Puzzles, Feel the Music, Break a Sweat, Heart-Pounding Action, Adventure Awaits, New Premium Content, and Play with Friends. Virtual reality games have dimensions of players' actions and natural game communication that differentiate them from other games. Combining virtual reality with physiological signals like heart rates as proposed in [10] allows more personalized gaming experiences to be produced in real-time for each player at an exact emotional state, opening the whole new gaming experience that immerses players deep into the virtual world.

Resulting in a combination of many types of games. For example, it is an action game mixed with a strategy game or a casual game combined with role-playing. Referring to the previous points, we found that the product component of each genre has its game content and system integration which affects consumer motivation.

2.3 Demographic Concepts that Affecting the Gaming Motivation

Lee [11] found that the relationship between like-minded individuals and social expressions was similar to groups of people with different personality types and different social terms. People with similar personalities and social faces who coexisted together were more likely to be friends than those with other characters. Apart from the mentioned research before, Wei and Lu [12] described the influence of peers in gaming as the external effect of the network, and the critical factor is the benefit of other users in the network. As a result, the web grows as the number of users increases, concluding people will use a service or product more frequently when they see people around them or people in society buying or choosing them. The provision of commercial game service components affects demographics. Therefore, consumer experience, perceived value, and social relationships among customers are essential factors in purchasing products. Furthermore, Jairak et al. [13] analyzed the people of each age group. They described age variables in their study and found that age variables are consistent with categorizing people by generation. They classified people into four age groups. Generation Z had the highest percentage of active users and the largest share of social network adoption. Age increases as the proportion of acceptance and use of social networks decrease.

Among social network adoption users are Generation Y (aged 24 to 35), followed by Generation X (aged 36 to 50), and the last group is Baby Boomers or Generation B (They are 51 years old or older). We focus on Generation Z, 13–23 years old, the population in Bangkok, 2020. According to data from the Thai Bureau of Statistics, this generation has a total of 735,756 people, divided into 376,393 men and 359,363 women. The main reason for choosing this demographic is that Generation Z is the group with the most acceptance on social networks.

H1. The effect of the product on the gaming motivation among Thai Generation Z groups in Bangkok was different according to demographic characteristics.

3   Research Questions

In this research, we identified player motivation and product factors for researching and developing a suitable prototype for testing.

The Question Was: Only two levels of headings should be enumerated. Lower level headings can still be unnumbered; they are formatted as run-in headings.

RQ1: RQ1: What needs and motivations for products affect the Thai Generation Z in Bangkok differently based on demographic characteristics?

RQ2: Does the product affect the gaming motivation of Thai Generation Z in Bangkok differently based on demographic characteristics and how?

4   Methods

This research is experimental research that developed an application for augmented reality glasses from Free Asset in Unity. And test with the target audience to determine their needs and motivations for playing virtual reality games. Initially, we started letting users play with the game prototypes; two modes for the same purpose: to escape from the room; a low graphics method that is easy to play, and a high graphics method. However, the high graphic way is more challenging to play because the increased graphics and decorations obscure the vision.

Experimental Group. "X" Is action management (Treatment) by experimenting with users to experiment with prototypes through virtual reality technology and "O" Is the posttest observation with a questionnaire (Table 1).

Table 1. Experimental group.

X	O
Tester	Result

4.1 Prototype

In collecting information, we developed a prototype for testing as a game in a virtual application using free assets on Unity and created in a high graphics mode and a low graphics mode, as shown in Fig. 1. The free assets in Unity support the prototype development process. The assets include models, textures, sound, lighting, and code. The free purchase can upload models, textures, sound, lighting, and code within Unity for use as textures in the virtual reality world, images, and models for particle effects, or as part of GUIs for menus and interactive objects. The prototype is a role-playing game. The player is a mage trapped in a laboratory, so they are responsible for mixing the potion according to the manual and melting the door to exit the room.

Fig. 1. During our game development, we pictured the modeling with Unity.

Next, we developed a prototype from the model of a free asset and enameled it with the texture and effects, then downloaded code to combine everything into Unity. After that, we created a file in ".apk" format to install on virtual reality devices (Oculus Quest 2). To play, the players play the role of a wizard trapped in a house and find a way out. There are clues and riddles, such as finding a wand or raw materials to make a potion or finding a secret recipe. At the end of the game, the player will use the potion to open a door. After prototype testing, the players complete a questionnaire for evaluation. Figure 2 illustrates examples of our game after rendering (Table 2).

Table 2. Oculus Quest 2 capabilities

Topic	Detail
Product dimensions	191.5 mm × 102 mm × 142.5 mm (strap folded in), 191.5 mm × 102 mm × 295.5 mm
Product weight	503 g
Tracking	Supports 6 degrees of freedom head and hand tracking through integrated Oculus Insight technology
Storage	256 GB
Display panel	Fast-switch LCD
Display resolution	1832 × 1920 per eye
Display refresh	72 Hz at launch; 90 Hz support to come
SoC	Qualcomm® Snapdragon™ XR2 Platform
Audio	Integrated speakers and microphone; also compatible with 3.5 mm headphones
RAM	6 GB
Battery life	You can expect several hours according to the type of content you are streaming on Quest 2; nearly two hours if you are using it for games and approximately three hours if you are using streaming media. At any moment in time, you are able to inspect the battery charge level of the headset device in the Oculus application settings or virtual reality via Oculus Home
Charge time	With the given USB-C power adapter for Quest 2, the battery can be fully charged in nearly 2.5 h
Interpupillary Distance (IPD)	Adjustable interpupillary distance with three settings for 68 mm, 63 mm, and 58 mm, respectively
Playspace	Supported stationary and/or roomscale. Roomscale needs at least 6.5 ft × 6.5 ft of obstruction-free floor space

4.2 Survey Design

After experimenting with the prototype, we decide to use a questionnaire to collect data. The questionnaire format was a closed-ended question consisting of 2 parts of 14 items as below.

Part 1. Basic information.
Part 2. Questionnaire about motivation affecting the Generation Z virtual reality game in Bangkok.

The questions and scoring criteria in the questionnaire are a research tool. The closed-ended questions are similar to the ones in the Prototype test, and there are details as follows.

Fig. 2. Some example images after rendering on our virtual reality game developed by us.

Part 1. Questionnaire about the basic information.

1. Sex (Nominal Scale)
2. Age (Ordinal Scale)
3. Levels of Education (Ordinal Scale)
4. Occupation (Nominal Scale).

Sex or gender for respondents. The questions and scoring criteria in the questionnaire used as a tool in this research are closed-ended questions that are similar to those in the prototype test. There are details as follows (Table 3).

Part 2 is a questionnaire on the motivations that affect Generation Z virtual reality games in Bangkok, divided into 2 dimensions such as

1. Reasoning Motivation
2. Emotional Motivation.

The question format is the Likert Scale. The Interval Scale has 5 levels which define the score as follows.

Level 5 means respondents have the highest level of motivation.
Level 4 means the respondents have a high level of motivation.
Level 3 means the respondents have a moderate level of motivation.
Level 2 means the respondents have a low level of motivation.

Table 3. Level of measurement for respondents

Variables	Level of measure	Categorization criteria
Gender	Nominal Scale	1 = Male
Age	Ordinal Scale	1 = 12 years old 2 = 13 years old 3 = 14 years old 4 = 15 years old 5 = 16 years old 6 = 17 years old 7 = 18 years old 8 = 19 years old 9 = 20 years old 10 = 21 years old 11 = 22 years old 12 = 23 years old 13 = 24 years old
Education level	Ordinal Scale	1 = Elementary Education 2 = junior high school 3 = High school or equivalent 4 = Bachelor's degree or equivalent 5 = Master's degree or equivalent 6 = Ph.D. or equivalent
Occupation	Nominal Scale	1 = student/student 2 = government service/state enterprise 3 = Employee/private company employee 4 = business owner 5 = other (specify)

Level 1 means respondents have the lowest level of motivation.

The five-level motivation-level assessment criteria were based on the mean criteria for interpretation using the formula for calculating the width of the class ratio. Therefore, the width will be 0.8.

The Mean Scores. The mean scores of the motivation levels in effect for Generation Z virtual reality game in Bangkok are as follows:

Average score 4.21–5.00 means the highest level of motivation.
Average score 3.41–4.20 means a high level of motivation.
Average score 2.61–3.40 means moderate motivation level.
Average score 1.81–2.60 means a low motivation level.
Average score 1.00–1.80 means the lowest level of motivation.

Reason Motivation. Measuring the level of reason motivation in a questionnaire that affects the Generation Z virtual reality game in Bangkok (Table 4).

Table 4. Reason motivation

Variables	Level of measure	Categorization criteria
1. The hints and manuals can tell you a lot of details about the game's content 2. If someone you know plays the same game as you, it makes you want to play more 3. If you can create a character like you in the game, you will be more motivated to play the game 4. Does the beautiful appearance of the product make you more interested? 5. Does a comfortable product make you feel more interested? 6. Does the brand make you feel more interested?	Interval	1 = Least motivation level 2 = Low motivation level 3 = Moderate motivation level 4 = Extreme motivation level 5 = Highest level of motivation
Education level		

Emotional Motivation. Measuring the level of reason motivation in a questionnaire that affects the Generation Z virtual reality game in Bangkok (Table 5).

Table 5. Emotional motivation

Variables	Level of measure	Categorization criteria
1. The pictures and graphics in the game make you feel more wanting to play the game 2. The lighting and effects in the game make you feel that the game is more playful 3. Sound effects in the game make you feel that the game is more fun to play 4. The challenge of the game makes you feel that the game is more fun to play	Interval	1 = Least motivation level 2 = Low motivation level 3 = Moderate motivation level 4 = Extreme motivation level 5 = Highest level of motivation

4.3 Sampling Frame

The selecting method is from the purposive sampling of 40 age groups in Generation Z (18–24 years old). According to the survey, Generation Z has the highest percentage of adoption of innovation and gaming.

4.4 Sampling Techniques

After data collecting, we conducted a validation check and analyzed the data in the statistical calculation to present and summarize the results as below.

1. Descriptive statistics analysis depends on the percentage, mean, standard deviation for describing personal data.
2. The result compared the Post-test analysis of the experimental groups in different prototypes and testing variables with the hypothesis that set the statistical significance level at 0.05 or the confidence level at 95.

Operational Definitions

1. Start to contact the tester and his parents for permission. We select qualified people according to their needs and schedule an appointment at the right place.
2. Before the trial, we will overview the games before testing.
3. Advise how the testers use the device and start playing the game. The tester will not be interfered with until the end of the test. The Institute's ethics department certified me in the research process after taking a research ethics test.
4. Before the measurement, get feedback on the experience and motivation.
5. Finally, say thank you after receiving the completed evaluation form, and then give a souvenir to all who participated in the experiment to express their gratitude for taking this time and completing the steps in the section of conducting research.

4.5 Variables

There were two variables in this research, independent and dependent. The researcher has defined the details of each variable as follows;

Independent Variables. Groups precede and cause different outcomes for each feature. The behavior of the age group of users in Generation Z.

The Dependent Variable. Is the test result of a function in the program. Which divided into two parts;

Wizard Trapped (Low Graphics Mode). The player can assume the role of a wizard trapped in a house and find a way out. There are clues and riddles, such as finding a wand or raw materials to make a potion or finding a secret recipe. The players have to use the Potion to open the door and consider it by the end of the game.

Wizard Trapped (High Graphics Mode). The graphics are high resolution but harder to play because the clarity and texture make it hard to find objects.

This mode aims to find a way out of the same room, where different game elements are presented for the same purpose, allowing product motivation to be collected.

5   Results

Forty participants passed the prototype test and completed the questionnaire after the test. The age range of the participants was in the field of 18–24. Specifically, they were 14 females (35%) and 26 males (65%). The participants of 24 - year old were 18 (45%), 18 - year old were 12 (30%), 19 - year old were 3 (7.5%), 22 - year old were 3 (7.5%), 23 - year old were 2 (5%), 20 - year old were 1 (2.5%), and 21 - year old were 1 (2.5%).

Most of them have education at the graduate level, or equivalent 15 people accounted for 37.50%, followed by 12 people in high school, accounting for 30.00%, followed by a group of 4 second-year students accounting for 10.00%. They are studying students in Year 1 and Year 4–6, which have the same number of 3 students, representing 7.50%, followed by two people who have completed a master's degree accounting for 5.0%. And the group with the least number of respondents was the group studying for 3rd-year students, which consisted of 1 person, representing 2.50%. There were no respondents in the group who were looking in junior high school and in the group who graduated at the doctoral level. Most of the occupations are students and university students who were 24 people (60.50%), employees or private employees were 12 people (30.50%), business owners were five people (12.50%), programmers were two people (5.00%), a government/state enterprises' officer (2.50%), and an engineer (2.50%).

6   Discussion

The first purpose of virtual reality games and the product study is the needs and motivations of Generation Z in Bangkok. The results showed that Thai Generation Z in Bangkok with different demographic characteristics had various product incentives to play the game. Through the survey and analysis, separating the results of data collection by gender; the male group has rational impulse in product appearance and convenience at the highest level. Thus, the ease of comprehension affects the motivation to use it. In addition, research has indicated that the application itself is well-formed and easy to understand in use will affect the satisfaction of using the application. The female group matters how easy it is to use at the highest level in terms of motivational reasons. And the level of motivation, among other factors, was only moderately different from that of males.

In terms of emotional motivation, it will be possible to see the difference when the answers divide according to gender. From the data collection results, the males had the highest level of motivation among all factors, which showed the effect of the elements in the game that affect the motivation level related to the game object. Male players focus on the game elements, regardless of the graphics, lighting effects, sound effects, and challenge levels. Compared to female players, the level of emotional motivation was relatively low. All the emotional motivation factors that the researcher collected in the female group were moderate. Although, the brand perspective had a relatively small impact on males' and females' motivation. Other motivations that showed significant differences between the two genders are the hypothesis that the product affects the gaming motivation among Thai Generation Z groups in Bangkok differently based on demographic characteristics.

7 Conclusion and Future Work

According to the research results, the product motives affecting Generation Z in Bangkok differ according to demographic characteristics.

Rational Motivation. Rational motivation consists of product appearance (4.20% of motivation level), product usability (4.25% of motivation level), brand (3.60% of motivation level).

Emotional Motivation. Emotional motivation includes images and graphics in the game (4.05% of motivation level), lighting and effects (4.18% of motivation level), game sound effects (3.93% of motivation level), game challenges (3.93% of motivation level).

The gender-segregated analysis found that rational and emotional motivation were significantly different for males than female players, who are influenced by logic rather than emotion. Another point is that males and females also have moderate brand influences. Note that, compared to other factors, brands have little effect on the motivation of genders. Apart from this research on virtual reality games, our future work is to also focus on geo-based mixed reality games [14, 15] in different aspects.

References

1. Siriborvornratanakul, T.: Through the realities of augmented reality. In: Stephanidis, C. (ed.) HCII 2019. LNCS, vol. 11786, pp. 253–264. Springer, Cham (2019). https://doi.org/10.1007/978-3-030-30033-3_20
2. IDC's Estimated Global. https://www.idc.com/getdoc.jsp?containerId=prUS44511118. Accessed 13 Nov 2022
3. Cuthbert, R., Türkay, S., Brown, R.: The effects of customisation on player experiences and motivation in a virtual reality game. In: Proceedings of the 31st Australian Conference on Human-Computer-Interaction, December 2019, pp. 221–232 (2019)
4. Chanchuea, T.: Empirical study of customer satisfaction and loyalty in internet commerce, Independent Study. Master's Degree. Thammasat University (2010). (in Thai)
5. Katz, E., Blumler, J.G., Gurevitch, M.: Uses and gratifications research. Public Opinion Q. 37(4), 509–524 (1974)
6. McQuail, D.: McQuail's Mass Communication Theory. Sage, London (2010)
7. Chirasopone, P.: News selection and finding. In: Communication Theory, pp. 636–640. STOU, Nonthaburi (1986)
8. Hussain, Z., Williams, G.A, Griffiths, M.D.: An exploratory study of the association between online gaming addiction and enjoyment motivations for playing massively multiplayer online roleplaying games. Comput. Hum. Behav. 50, 221–230 (2015). ISSN 0747-5632
9. Roongsathaporn, T., Satawedin, P.: The consumer behavior and online shopping in the amidst of Covid-9 in Bangkok, Metropolitan and Phitsanulok. J. Commun. Arts 39(2) (2021)
10. Siriborvornratanakul, T.: A study of virtual reality headsets and physiological extension possibilities. In: Gervasi, O., et al. (eds.) ICCSA 2016. LNCS, vol. 9787, pp. 497–508. Springer, Cham (2016). https://doi.org/10.1007/978-3-319-42108-7_38
11. Lee, S.Y.: Homophily and social influence among online casual game players. Telematics Inform. 32(4), 656–666 (2015)

12. Wei, P.-S., Lu, H.-P.: Why do people play mobile social games? An examination of network externalities and of uses and gratifications. Internet Res. **24**(3), 313–331 (2014)

13. Jairak, R., Sahakhunchai, N., Jairak, K., Praneetpolgrang, P.: Factors affecting intention to use in social networking sites: an empirical study on Thai society. In: Papasratorn, B., Lavangnananda, K., Chutimaskul, W., Vanijja, V. (eds.) IAIT 2010. CCIS, vol. 114, pp. 43–52. Springer, Heidelberg (2010). https://doi.org/10.1007/978-3-642-16699-0_6

14. Kerdvibulvech, C.: Geo-based mixed reality gaming market analysis. Hum. Behav. Emerg. Technol. **2022**, 9 (2022). Article ID 1139475

15. Bhattacharya, A., et al.: The pandemic as a catalyst for reimagining the foundations of location-based games. In: Proceedings of ACM Human-Computer Interaction (CHI), vol. 5, pp. 1–25 (2021)

A Hybrid Method for Window Detection on High Resolution Facade Images

Kujtim Rahmani$^{(\boxtimes)}$ and Helmut Mayer$^{(\boxtimes)}$

Institute for Applied Computer Science, Bundeswehr University Munich,
Neubiberg, Germany
`kujtim.rahmani@gmail.com`, `helmut.mayer@unibw.de`

Abstract. In this paper we present a hybrid method for detecting windows on high-resolution rectified images of building facades combining deep learning with traditional geometric processing. As initial step we use a deep learning object detection method. As we observed that in most cases the detector outputs a larger object than the ground truth. We employ geometric processing based on image gradients to precisely delineate the window edges. For the evaluation of the algorithm we have created a high resolution dataset with more than 2000 annotated windows. The obtained results show that the detector's bounding box differs from ground truth mostly by less than six pixels. The Intersection over Union IoU of the objects is 96.9%. Geometric processing improves IoU by 1.7% leading to an IoU score of 98.6%.

Keywords: Facade interpretation · Window detection · Object detection · Optimization

1 Introduction

3D models of buildings are becoming more and more important in several industries including city modelling, gaming industry, and culture heritage. To create high quality 3D building models, one needs to understand each facade object's location. Facade objects consists of window, door, roof, balcony and shops. Of those, window is the most common and the most important. Thus, correct detection of windows is a very important subproblem of understanding building facade.

Window detection has been investigated in images and 3D point clouds [5, 15], identifying several challenges. The most common are: different architectural styles of the facade, obstacles on the facades like flower pots, occlusion by trees or cars, as well as images taken under different lighting conditions with shadows and unusual camera perspectives.

Lately, machine learning methods [14] and sliding windows have been used for window detection [1]. With the emergence of convolutional neural networks (CNN), researchers started to employ them for window detection.

© Springer Nature Switzerland AG 2022
A. Bennour et al. (Eds.): ISPR 2022, CCIS 1589, pp. 43–50, 2022.
https://doi.org/10.1007/978-3-031-08277-1_4

In this paper, we combine the traditional geometric processing and deep learning to build a system for high precision window detection. Current deep learning methods basically localize the objects correctly, but the location is found with low precision. In our case, the window detector outputs in most of the cases larger bounding boxes than given by ground truth. Thus, we have created a method to improve the bounding box location. To evaluate our method, we have created a high resolution dataset consisting of rectified facade images.

The first contribution of this paper is that we show that the state-of-the-art YOLOv5 object detector achieves good results for window detection, but in most cases it returns too large bounding boxes. The second contribution consists in that we improve the detection quality of windows with very low running time effort using domain knowledge. Finally, we present a very high quality dataset for evaluating window detection approach based on rectified facade images.

2 Related Work

At the beginning window detection was mostly based on image processing techniques producing regions for windows. A prominent work is [5]. The employed detector is based on the assumption of a grid structure for windows. Their hypothesis was that windows are located on facade regions with a larger number of lines in comparison to regions without windows.

In recent years, deep learning is improving all computer vision tasks [2,3,7,9]. The authors of [9] have introduced a street view dataset containing non-rectified facade images. The Faster R-CNN architecture [14] is used as detector. The authors have modified the anchors so that they correspond to aspect ratios as well as the sizes of the windows on the facade. Since some windows are omitted or their confidence is rather low, they use the grid structure assumption to re-evaluate the objects with low confidence.

[2,3] first use a CNN-based object detector and then an optimization method to improve the detections. [2] employ Faster R-CNN [14] as detector and [3] YOLOv3 [13]. Another difference between the two approaches is the employed post-processing. [2] uses mixed integer linear programming optimization technique which clusters windows and corrects their dimensions based on windows of the same clusters. The other approach uses binary integer programming as an optimization approach. Both employ the assumption of a grid of windows.

[7] utilizes a completely different approach for window detection on facades. Window detection is approached similarly to pose estimation. The four corners (top–left, top–right, bottom–left, bottom–right) of the window are detected, and considered as key points by training a Deep Neural Network. After obtaining the heatmap of the key points, an optimization method is employed to connect the key points. Our method is most similar to this method, but we use edges instead of corners to refine the windows.

Furthermore, there are several approaches for facade segmentation that are based on traditional machine learning [10–12] and deep learning [8,19] for which window is one of their classes. These approaches perform pixel wise segmentation approach which is different from object detection. Thus, we do not compare our method with these approaches.

Finally, several datasets for facades [16,17,20] and window detection [7,9] exists. Current facade datasets have a very low resolution and some of them are not properly rectified since they have (barrel) distortion. The window datasets [7, 9] contain a large number of images of different facades, but they are not rectified and the resolution is low. Because of this, we have devised a new high quality dataset consisting of rectified images together with manually annotated ground truth.

3   Dataset

For our research we have created a dataset consisting of 50 images that contain more than 2150 windows (Fig. 1). To rectify the images, several photos of the building have been taken, a 3D reconstruction of the building is created using [6], and from it the rectified images without (barrel) distortion are generated. Each image has a height or width (the longer side) of 2048 pixels and the shorter side is wider than 1400 pixels. For data annotation, ground truth generation, we have used the tool LabelMe [18].

Fig. 1. Two images from dataset

4   Window Detection Network

As detection network, we use YOLOv5 [4]. It is shown that this network currently outperforms all other one step end-to-end detection networks. Since it has a very good learning and representation capability, we first train the network with facade patches where there is just one window, perform augmentation only for it and use small input image. After training just with one object per image for some epochs, we train the network with the complete facade image. The latter step leads to that the network can distinguish windows from other parts of the facade.

5   Refinement of the Windows by Finding the Edges

Current detectors have a high accuracy but still do not delineate precisely the objects: The bounding box of the object might have a few pixels deviation from that of the ground truth. This issue is also perceived for the window detectors. To refine the bounding boxes, we use the rectangular structure of windows by locating the horizontal and vertical edges of the windows employing the image gradients (Eq. 1, $p(x_i, y_j)$ – greyscale pixel value at the pixel position (x_i, y_j)).

$$g_{i,j}(x) = \begin{cases} p(x_i, y_j) - p(x_i, y_{j-1}), & \text{for horizontal gradient and} \\ p(x_i, y_i) - p(x_{i-1}, y_j), & \text{for vertical gradient} \end{cases} \quad (1)$$

Fig. 2. Region (orange) around the border of the bounding box where the horizontal or vertical gradient is computed. (Color figure online)

For each detection (bounding box) we compute the gradient around the border. Particularly, the gradient is computed in a region of $2n + 1$ pixels, with n pixel inside and n outside the bounding box (Fig. 2). For our application, we have empirically determined the value of $n = 5$. From the $2n + 1$ candidates, the line with the highest gradient score is selected as the new edge of the object bounding box. From this, we differentiate between positive and negative gradient values by considering for each candidate two values, the sum of the negative s^- (Eq. 2, h, w-bounding box height and width, respectively) and the sum of positive s^+ (Eq. 3) gradients. The gradient score of a candidate is the highest absolute value of the negative or positive gradient value c_i (Eq. 4). Finally, the box is chosen with the maximal gradient score (Eq. 5).

$$s^-(i) = \begin{cases} \sum_{k=0}^{k \leq w} min(0, g(x_i, y_k)), & \text{if horizontal gradient} \\ \sum_{k=0}^{k \leq h} min(0, g(x_k, y_i)), & \text{if vertical gradient} \end{cases} \quad (2)$$

$$s^+(i) = \begin{cases} \sum_{k=0}^{k \leq w} max(0, g(x_i, y_k)), & \text{if horizontal gradient} \\ \sum_{k=0}^{k \leq h} max(0, g(x_k, y_i)), & \text{if vertical gradient} \end{cases} \quad (3)$$

$$c_i = max(|s^-(i)|, |s^+(i)|) \quad (4)$$

$$edge = \max_i(c_i) \quad (5)$$

6   Evaluation

For evaluation we use our own dataset of German buildings. For training, we use images from Munich, Muehldorf and Berlin while for testing, we have selected four facade images from a street in Berlin containing 165 windows. The algorithm was evaluated in two stages: Detection based on YOLOv5 and refinement. We have computed the difference of the bounding box and of detector ground truth in each direction (top, bottom, right and left). From the histograms (Fig. 3), one can see that the difference between ground truth and detector is for most of the windows smaller than 6 pixels. There are also several larger differences between ground truth and the detector's output, resulting from the presence of obstacles and vegetation on the facades (Fig. 4).

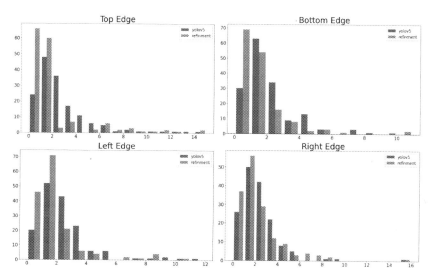

Fig. 3. The deviation of the detector bounding box and ground truth on each bounding box side for the detection with YOLOv5 (blue) and after refinement (orange) (Color figure online)

The histograms in Fig. 3 also show that in some cases the refinement can increase the deviation from the ground truth (Fig. 5 first and second window of the first row and Fig. 4). In most cases this happens due to an occlusion or a very high contrast of glass and frame. Furthermore, from Fig. 3 one can also observe that the refinement improves the top and the bottom edge of the bounding box more than the left and the right edge. Around 70 from 165 windows get the top or the bottom edge correct, but less than 45 the left or the right edge. The opposite is true for one pixel difference. The large improvement for top and bottom might stem from the fact that the images have been taken from ground, and, thus, the appearance of the bottom and top edge changes due to occlusion and change of the perspective. After refinement, 80% of the edges differ from

Fig. 4. Results of the windows that are covered by occlusion or vegetation. The red bounding box is the YOLOv5 output, the blue box represents the refinement of the YOLOv5 output and the green box represent the ground truth. (Color figure online)

the ground truth at most one pixel. Overall, refinement improves Intersection over Union IoU by 1.7 % (Table 1). From the results in Fig. 6 one can see that the YOLOv5 detector detects all the windows, but their bounding box deviate for a few pixels from the ground truth, which the refinement corrects them.

Fig. 5. Sample results from the test set. The red bounding box is the YOLOv5 output, the blue box represents the refinement of the YOLOv5 output and the green box represent the ground truth. (Color figure online)

Table 1. Results of window detection as % IoU.

Class	YOLOv5	Refinement
Windows	96.9	98.6

Fig. 6. Results for parts of facades. The red bounding box is the YOLOv5 output, the blue box represents the refinement and the green box the ground truth. (Color figure online)

7 Conclusion and Future Work

We have presented a hybrid method that uses YOLOv5 to detect windows and image gradients to improve the localization accuracy. The latter step helps to precisely delineate the bounding boxes of the windows using gradients, choosing the lines with the highest gradient scores as the bounding box edges.

For future work, we plan to experiment more in depth with YOLOv5 and use different object proposal configurations. Additionally, we want experiment with a learned method for the refinement step to select the best candidate while at the same time making use of the grid structure of the windows. We also plan to extend the dataset with more annotated images and add arc shaped windows to the dataset.

References

1. Ali, H., Seifert, C., Jindal, N., Paletta, L., Paar, G.: Window detection in facades. In: International Conference on Image Analysis and Processing, pp. 837–842 (2007)
2. Hensel, S., Goebbels, S., Kada, M.: Facade reconstruction for textured LoD2 CityGML models based on deep learning and mixed integer linear programming. ISPRS Ann. Photogrammetry Remote Sens. Spat. Inf. Sci. **4** (2019)
3. Hu, H., Wang, L., Zhang, M., Ding, Y., Zhu, Q.: Fast and regularized reconstruction of building facades from street-view images using binary integer programming. arXiv preprint arXiv:2002.08549 (2020)
4. Lazebnik, S.: Ultralytics. YOLOv5. https://github.com/ultralytics/yolov5
5. Lee, S.C., Nevatia, R.: Extraction and integration of window in a 3D building model from ground view images. In: Computer Vision and Pattern Recognition, vol. 2, p. II (2004)

6. Ley, A., Hellwich, O.: Depth map based facade abstraction from noisy multi-view stereo point clouds. In: Rosenhahn, B., Andres, B. (eds.) GCPR 2016. LNCS, vol. 9796, pp. 155–165. Springer, Cham (2016). https://doi.org/10.1007/978-3-319-45886-1_13

7. Li, C.K., Zhang, H.X., Liu, J.X., Zhang, Y.Q., Zou, S.C., Fang, Y.T.: Window detection in facades using heatmap fusion. J. Comput. Sci. Technol. **35**(4), 900–912 (2020)

8. Liu, H., Zhang, J., Zhu, J., Hoi, S.C.H.: DeepFacade: a deep learning approach to facade parsing. In: International Joint Conference on Artificial Intelligence, pp. 2301–2307 (2017)

9. Ma, W., Ma, W.: Deep window detection in street scenes. KSII Trans. Internet Inf. Syst. (TIIS) **14**(2), 855–870 (2020)

10. Martinovic, A., Van Gool, L.: Bayesian grammar learning for inverse procedural modeling. In: Computer Vision and Pattern Recognition, pp. 201–208 (2013)

11. Rahmani, K., Huang, H., Mayer, H.: Facade segmentation with a structured random forest. ISPRS Ann. Photogrammetry Remote Sens. Spat. Inf. Sci. **4**, 175–181 (2017)

12. Rahmani, K., Mayer, H.: High quality facade segmentation based on structured random forest, region proposal network and rectangular fitting. ISPRS Ann. Photogrammetry Remote Sens. Spat. Inf. Sci. **4**(2) (2018)

13. Redmon, J., Farhadi, A.: YOLOv3: an incremental improvement. arXiv preprint arXiv:1804.02767 (2018)

14. Ren, S., He, K., Girshick, R., Sun, J.: Faster R-CNN: towards real-time object detection with region proposal networks. In: Advances in Neural Information Processing Systems, pp. 91–99 (2015)

15. Reznik, S., Mayer, H.: Implicit shape models, self-diagnosis, and model selection for 3D façade interpretation. Photogrammetrie Fernerkundung Geoinformation, pp. 187–196 (2008)

16. Riemenschneider, H., Bódis-Szomorú, A., Weissenberg, J., Van Gool, L.: Learning where to classify in multi-view semantic segmentation. In: Fleet, D., Pajdla, T., Schiele, B., Tuytelaars, T. (eds.) ECCV 2014. LNCS, vol. 8693, pp. 516–532. Springer, Cham (2014). https://doi.org/10.1007/978-3-319-10602-1_34

17. Riemenschneider, H., et al.: Irregular lattices for complex shape grammar facade parsing. In: Computer Vision and Pattern Recognition, pp. 1640–1647 (2012)

18. Russell, B.C., Torralba, A., Murphy, K.P., Freeman, W.T.: LabelMe: a database and web-based tool for image annotation. Int. J. Comput. Vis. **77**(1–3), 157–173 (2008)

19. Schmitz, M., Mayer, H.: A convolutional network for semantic facade segmentation and interpretation. Int. Arch. Photogrammetry Remote Sens. Spat. Inf. Sci. **XLI**(133), 709–715 (2016)

20. Teboul, O., Kokkinos, I., Simon, L., Koutsourakis, P., Paragios, N.: Shape grammar parsing via reinforcement learning. In: Computer Vision and Pattern Recognition, pp. 2273–2280 (2011)

Neuro-Fuzzy Predictive Approach for Visual Analytics Evaluation of Medical Data

Saber Amri[1,2](✉) and Med Lassaad Kaddachi[1,2]

[1] The REsearch Group on Intelligent Machines, University of Sfax, Sfax, Tunisia
saberamri089@gmail.com, mkaddachi@tvtc.gov.sa
[2] Technical and Vocational Training Corporation, 5000 Monastir, Tunisia

Abstract. In Visual analytics evaluation field we still do not know what would look like an efficient application. We then aim to develop guidelines (design then development), in order to obtain a coherent information base. This paper introduces a new intelligent approach based on neural network and fuzzy logic techniques allowing an automated visual analytics evaluation. This novel approach executes a Self-Organizing Feature Map (SOFM) neural network model that communicates with human environment using natural language, interacts with users, understands the context of conversations, and detects each sentence meaning. Then, we use fuzzy logic to process participant responses. By this way, an intelligent evaluation procedure is generated. After executing a learning algorithm, our application becomes capable to automatically capture new knowledge and reorganize it in visualization evaluation procedures. This enables an efficient visualizations evaluations taking into account different criteria and measures of visualization characteristics. This feature cancels required limitations imposed on users using other evaluations methods. It allows them to freely evaluate visualizations and discovering each time new criteria evaluations. Moreover this method allows an automatic learning of evaluation procedure following sentence given by users.

Keywords: Evaluation · Visualization · Artificial neural networks (ANNs) · Self-Organizing Feature Map (SOFM) · Fuzzy logic

1 Introduction

Recently, abstract data visualization techniques were developed. Prototypes include business, demographic, social and scientific information. The used data are standard types (numeric, textual) or graphic, sound and video type data or sophisticated data used in the context of the Semantic Web [23, 24].

New visualization techniques are implemented, e.g. parallel coordinates, visual data representations based on glyphs and pixels, and several techniques to reduce the clutter of information on the screen. Mention may also be made of techniques for visualizing structured data, for example those used to represent networks in the form of graphs, and those for the geo-visualization of spatiotemporal dimensions [23, 25].

Since visual tools incorporate multiples techniques classified based on their functionalities, their tasks and data types. This taxonomy can be used to evaluate tools based

© Springer Nature Switzerland AG 2022
A. Bennour et al. (Eds.): ISPR 2022, CCIS 1589, pp. 51–64, 2022.
https://doi.org/10.1007/978-3-031-08277-1_5

on the software applicability domain, tasks and activities [8]. The growing amount of information captured and produced in modern life covers knowledge to be integrated into the process of decision making [7]. The visualization of information seems insufficient in the face of a large volume of complex data. For this, a new area of research in visualization has emerged: it is the visual analytics [9].

To improve the usability of information visualization tools (VT), evaluation metrics must affects the objectives of such evaluation. Selection of appropriate VT tool is taking into account of taxonomies of tools using a standard set of criteria, allowing the end user free evaluation that allows discovering of new criteria evaluations [1, 5].

In this context our novel approach execute a Self-Organizing Feature Map (SOFM) neural network model that communicates with human environment using natural language to evaluate visualizations generated by visual tools. Using this new method, this system interacts with users, understands the context of conversations, and detects each sentence meaning. After executing a learning algorithm, our application becomes capable to detect new knowledge and rang existing terms in visualization evaluation procedures.

This paper is structured as follows. Section 2 introduces the visual analytics evaluation field. Section 3 presented a new intelligent evaluation approach. Section 4 introduces the experimentation and the results. Conclusion is described in Sect. 5.

2 Visual Analytics Evaluation

The evaluation of users is a priority of research on Human-Computer Interaction and their fields of application of usability [6]. First, researchers are well aware of these limited abilities to predict participants' evaluations of complex interactive systems. It is essential to carry out the evaluation process, in the presence of the real users, involving a tight cycle of evaluation [2].

With the development of modern technologies, visual analytics systems become increasingly complex. In designing such systems, the evaluation task seems paramount. This is a very complex task. It is therefore crucial to establish a systematic, scientific, comprehensive and reasonable for the evaluation of visual analytics and visualization systems [5, 10].

In fact, the visual analytics systems incorporating many subsystems are often large scale, So that the metric of the overall evaluation of these complex systems are multivaried. Indeed, the relationship between these metrics is very complex; Moreover, these metrics involve many types, costs, and measurement standards. In addition, the descriptive terms of each indicator are different [4]. Some indicators measure the accuracy of a quantitative manner, others provide a semi-quantitative and qualitative evaluation, and others combine the qualitative analysis and quantitative analysis [3].

These evaluation methods improved that are important for visualizations. Yet, they ignore the judgments of users as well as the imprecision in the declarations during the questionnaires during the evaluation phase, and determines the precise weights specifying the impact of the visualization evaluation criteria [11–14]. An intelligent analysis of user evaluations can be effective thanks to its capacity of uncertainty modeling of visualization tools and subjectivity in user responses. Many methods for evaluating DSS/VA are introduced in many research works (usability evaluation, controlled experiments, heuristic testing, focus groups, case studies, etc.). However, they seem insufficient and missing due to several limitations.

There are also approaches based on insight, inspection such as communication, reflection and eye tracking. These methods do not reach participants per interview, no longer detect imprecision in ordinal judgments and neglect the importance of the evaluation criteria describing the visual aspect in the decision-making process.

The described evaluation approach helps inexperienced users ensure the visualization evaluation generated by VTs. It offered fuzzy modeling of judgments and statements during the evaluation process.

3 Learning Phase

3.1 Vague Nature of User's Language

Users use multiple formulations to answer evaluation questions. Generally, these declarations are with vagueness and imprecision, for example "very easy" or "absolutely hard". These affirmations do not signify any accepted representative values. To deal with this uncertainty, we can express them in fuzzy values form. After obtaining a set of users' natural language expression, we pass to convert each expression to a fuzzy description of evaluation criterion (intensifier + linguistic variable).

Evaluation data expressed by users are collected by evaluator controlling the neural network based application. This data is then converted in universal counterpart's expression with the help of other linguistic convertor module including several databases containing various expressions. Such expression is converted to one of normalized evaluations that represent the same value of variable.

First, an admission of words to be learned qualifying evaluation procedure is an essential for executing the learning algorithm (LA). Then it communicates with the user until a satisfactory qualification of new term is realized. Learning processes is accomplished basing on user response and past experience. It is building to update the intern illustration of known terms until its user interaction. The interaction supports the LA via feedback regarding the system's actions. After acquisition of unknown word to be learned as inputs, the LA request to user to specify types of inputted terms. Then the knowledge base is analyzed for checking the description of this word. If a description (explicated later) of the term exists, a connection of every node with same term's type in the intermediate layer is established with its corresponding output layer node. If this description of type word is not found, we create an input node as new input word and we save the word's characteristics in local memory of this node. In the next step, we demand to participant to deal an inputted word description. Then, the node belonging to input word layer and the corresponding intermediate layer node are connected. Finally, a weight W is saved in the output node, and updated since the intermediate layer to the input layer.

3.2 Fuzzy Intensifier Learning Process

For fuzzy intensifier learning process, the user is introduced with three description choices: a "LESS THEN" judgment, an "EQUAL TO" judgment, and a "BETTER

THEN" judgment. These judgments have the form: "LESS THEN" intensifier, "EQUAL TO" intensifier, and "BETTER THEN" intensifier.

Concerning the "EQUAL TO" description, we create a node Xi with type intensifier of the "EQUAL TO" sentence. Then, a connection weight Wij between Xi and Zj output layer is joined after an establishment of a connection between the input layer node Xi and the intermediate layer node Zj and the LA sets the connection weight Wij by using a backward link.

We do the same for treatment for the "LESS THEN" descriptive learning sentence and the "BETTER THEN" descriptive learning sentence.

To describe the learning process of fuzzy intensifier "very" using a "BETTER THAN" and "LESS THEN" sentence, we propose that the knowledge base includes the fuzzy intensifiers "medium" and "very-high".

Firstly, learning algorithm required a selection of entity types. Then, user must select the type of inputted term as fuzzy intensifier type. The Learning Algorithm (LA), creates a new input node, conserves "very" as unknown term in local memory node, finds description syntax choices (LESS THEN, EQUAL TO, BETTER THEN), asks a description of the term "very". Then, the user gives a descriptive judgment "very is LESS THEN medium and BETTER THEN very-high". In this step, the LA creates an output node for fuzzy intensifier Zj, creates input node X1 for "LESS THEN" sentence operand "medium", creates input node X2 for "BETTER THEN" sentence operand "very-high", matches Xi to Zj and sets a weight Wij.

3.3 Known Terms Learning Process

To adapt the representation of known terms following the fuzzy intensifiers previously mentioned (the term "easy" proceeded by the term "very"), the solution was to represent each word by the context in the sentences. The input representation consisted of two parts: one that presents description of inputted words and another (hidden layer) that represented context in which the word appears. For each input layer node Xi and hidden layer (context layer) Zj, if a connection Wij from Xj to Zj, it's OK. Else we find intermediate layer node Zj as a corresponding meaning context of inputted term and connection weights Wij and Wjk is joined (Fig. 1).

3.4 SOM Creation

SOM represent a neural network with unsupervised learning. The organization of neurons is with unidirectional architecture. The first layer represents the inputs; it includes m neurons working as buffers and distributes the information detected by the input space with stochastic samples. The next layer included rectangular grid "nx.ny" neurons. Each neuron is described by m weights called synapsis. Each neurons belonging in the output layer is connected to the neurons belonging in the input layer (See Fig. 1). The SOM contains 2 phases, learning and execution phases [6].

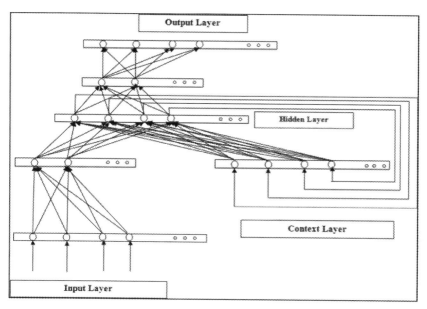

Fig. 1. Neural network architecture

3.5 Learning Phase

During this phase, the neurons belonging to the second layer calculate for the learning privilege between them. In this case the correct judgments are not yet known and only one vector is activated for a certain given input vector. This activation is determined as a function of the input vector relative to the synaptic weight vectors. The winning neuron always has the closest values to the input vector. Consequently, the neighborhood function updates the dominant neuron weights and its neighboring neurons.

A sample is necessary for the organization of the two-dimensional map neurons. This is a set of SOM input variables. The learning process is done by minimization of Euclidian distance calculated by neighborhood function between input samples and the prototypes weighted (See Fig. 2).

The similarity function is based on a similarity predefined criterion. Next, it is considered a winning neuron having the closest synaptic weight vector to the input. The neurons are shown by blue dots between their weights (See Fig. 3). At the beginning, each neuron is modeled by a single point since all neurons have the same weight. After a time, the new weights are redrawn and the neurons have started self-organizing in a way where each neuron locates in an input space zone, then adjacent neurons belong to adjacent zones. The distance between inputs and weight vectors are calculated. The dominant neuron is the one having the minimum distance with input sample.

The network is configured to match the dimensions of the inputs. This step is required here because we will plot the initial weights. Normally configuration is performed automatically when training. The learning phase repeats since no more change of weight values. The neural network toolbox MATLAB [20] is used for SOM implementation. The result is a set of values given by participants, where every variable evaluation is a

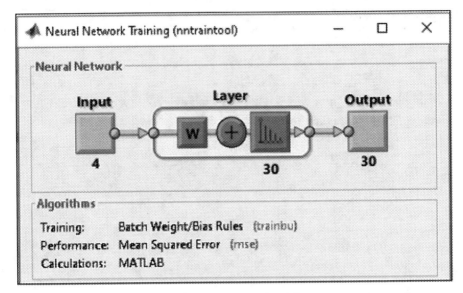

Fig. 2. Neural network training

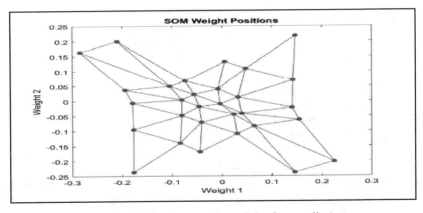

Fig. 3. SOM weight positions (Color figure online)

specific value assigned to an output layer neuron. Finally, a synaptic weight matrix is obtained to identify each input and output layer connection between (See Fig. 4).

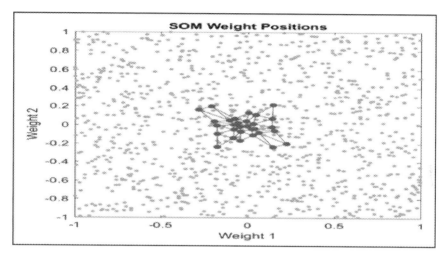

Fig. 4. New SOM weight positions

During the competition phase, SOM update the weight values of the winner neuron and its neighbors in the neighborhood radius (See Fig. 5).

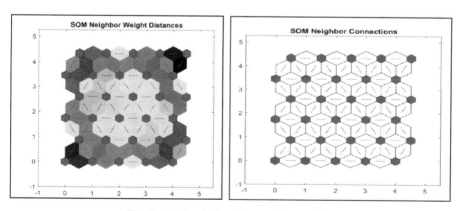

Fig. 5. SOM neighbor distances/connections

Finally, a single neuron is named the winner: it is the neuron with the weight vector the most similar to the input vector. This process is determined by direct calculation of the Euclidean distance between the two vectors (input and weight).

3.6 Execution Phase

During the execution phase, we declare the weights as fixed values. Then, each neuron must calculate the similarity rate between the input vector and its own synaptic weight vector (See Fig. 6).

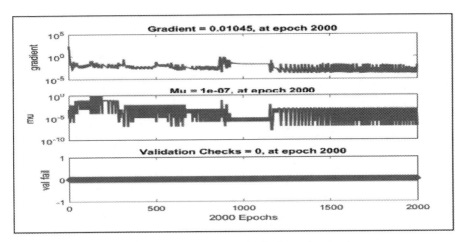

Fig. 6. Gradient, mu and val fail of neural network

The gradient value represents the slope of the tangent of the function and which alerts about the direction for which the rate of increase is high for the function in consideration. The value 'mu' corresponds to the control parameter of the back propagation network affecting the convergence of the error. This value is used to complete the learning by arriving at the number of iterations (See Fig. 7).

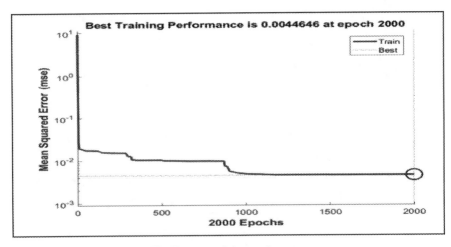

Fig. 7. Best training performance

After 2000 epochs, the values of Mean Squared Error (generated by calculating the difference between the actual values and the desired values) prove that the best training performances is 0.004. This value is near the value 0, so the learning process is efficient.

4 Experimentation and Results

The introduced evaluation method was used for evaluation of visualization produced by a medical visual system [11] installed in the Teaching Habib Bourguiba Hospital of Sfax, Tunisia. This system was implemented to interpret clinical parameters and compute the daily probability of nosocomial infections occurrence in the intensive care unit. It includes a visualization techniques set among them the perspective wall, the star representations and the lifelines technique.

To calculate the visual representation usability such as the time series Bubble Chart visualization technique, our learning algorithm is used in a real context to evaluate our approach. User's judgment is rich with abstract terms (single or compound evaluation term).

The proposed process occurs in two steps: (1) An evaluation questionnaire; (2) An application of the fuzzy logic for participant's responses analyze.

4.1 Step 1: Evaluation Questionnaire

Twenty seven (27) participants in 9 groups (9 physicians (PH1,., PH9), 9 health informatics professional (HIP1, …, HIP9) and 9 research assistants (RA1, …, RA9)) participated in our evaluation study: each group integrates a resident physician, a health informatics professional and a research assistant.

Each participant present an:

– Expert in the field: resident doctors specializing in surveillance of nosocomial infections.
– Novice in the field: health informatics professional with some experience in the analysis of medical data.
– Research assistants: researchers with a master's degree in computer science.

Firstly, a questionnaire procedure is used to collect evaluation data from users. A detailed questionnaire can be an effective approach to describe the evaluation [21, 22, 26, 27]. The participants should answer a set of questions related to: (1) users skills and experience, and (2) visualization tools use after a training session.

We assess how visualization tool's simulate visual analytics [14] by considering a set of evaluation criteria cited in usability studies and by experts' recommendations for visualization aspects and features [15–20]. The participants reply to the questionnaire related to the following criteria (Table 1) and describe each criterion using their natural language. In this second case, we use our intelligent linguistic converter having capabilities of learning to extract a set of linguistic variables qualifying each evaluation criterion from natural language of users.

Table 1. Evaluation criteria

Criterion	Evaluation question
Comprehensibility	To what percent do you think that the information is comprehensible?
Speed of working (SW)	Evaluate the speed of working and the information retrieval
Speed of use (SU)	Qualify the speed of information's loading
Visual prediction (VP)	To what percent do you think that the visualization tool is preferment in the prediction task?

The layer containing the words as inputs captures the words that form the sentences cited by the user. The middle (fuzzy) layer uses two types of terms for the evaluation procedure: simple (qualifier only) or compound (intensifier + qualifier). We initialize the base application with knowledge specified by the participants. This set of initial knowledge data is essential during the first phases of execution, and then it loses its relevance as new knowledge is automatically learned in the context of the application. For example, we assume that initial knowledge is some evaluation criteria (Comprehensibility, Speed of use, Data comparison) and some fuzzy intensifier (very, medium, and low).

(1)   **Scenario (1):**

     With initial knowledge evaluation criteria; Comprehensibility, Speed of use, Data comparison and fuzzy intensifiers; very, medium, and low, user evaluates a generated visualization by the sentence "Speed of use is absolutely slowly" were "absolutely" and "slowly" are new unknown words. The interaction between user and interface of our application is described below:

(2)   User gives the sentence "Speed of use is absolutely slowly".

(3)   After checking the existence of connection between input layer and hidden layer (context layer), LA classified this term as known terms.

(4)   LA proceeds to learning of new term "absolutely", and required from the user a word type specification.

(5)   User selects the type "intensifier".

(6)   After checking the knowledge base, LA detects that this type is not found and request description of terms "absolutely" using three operands: EQUAL TO, LESS THEN and BETTER THEN.

(7)   User describes the term "absolutely" with "absolutely is" EQUAL TO "very".

(8)   LA proceeds to learning of new term "slowly", and required from the user a word type specification.

(9)   La request description of terms "slowly" using three operands: EQUAL TO, LESS THEN and BETTER THEN.

(10)   User describes "slowly" term as LESS THEN "high".

(11)   LA shows "slowly" is EQUAL TO "medium".

(12)   Unsatisfying with the result, user provides again a description of term "slowly" with LESS THEN "medium".

(13)   LA shows "slowly" is EQUAL TO "low".

(14)   Satisfying with this description, user responds with "OK".
(15)   LA shows as output "Speed of use is very low", once both terms are now known and saves this procedure.

Table 2 summarizes the conversion procedure of data sentence given by the user and their conversion result following the procedure of learning. This conversion is the result of several sentences given by users in form of natural language for evaluating different visualizations generated by visualizations tools. It is a set of evaluation criteria such as the "speed of use" which his learning processes is described in scenario 1 (previous section). The result is a description of each criterion by a linguistic variable that will be introduced later in a fuzzy inference system which will produce an accurate evaluation score of the different types of visualization.

Table 2. Conversion procedure of natural language sentence to fuzzy linguistic variable

Criterion	Expression	Natural intensifier	Universal intensifier	Natural qualifier	Universal qualifier	Converted evaluation
Comprehensibility (COM)	Very well	Very	Very	Well	High	Very high
Speed of use (SU)	Good			High	High	High
Speed of use (SU)	Absolutely slowly	Absolutely	Very	Slowly	Low	Very low
Speed of Working (SW)	Above average	Above	Above	Average	Medium	Above medium
Speed of Working (SW)	Extremely good	Extremely	Very	Good	Clear	Very clear
Comprehensibility (COM)	Fully unquiet	Fully	Very	Unquiet	Unclear	Very unclear
Comprehensibility (COM)	Great		Very	Great	High	Very high
Visual prediction (VP)	Doubtful			Doubtful	Low	Low
Visual prediction (VP)	Enough			Enough	Medium	Medium

Once linguistic values are obtained from user's natural language thanks to neural network training, we apply the fuzzy logic technique to interpret the participant opinion and deal with uncertainty in order to obtain evaluation result.

4.2   Step 2: *Fuzzy Logic Application*

A group of physicians, and research assistants noted each evaluation criterion (Usability Category, Data manipulation Category and Patterns discovery Category) using her natural language. Our intelligent system interacts with participants, understands the conversation's context, detects the sentence meaning and interprets corresponding linguistic values. For example, for the first physician ("high" to Comprehensibility criterion (COM), "medium" to Speed of use criterion (SU), "above-medium" to Speed of working (SW) and "below-medium" to Visual prediction criterion (VP)). After application of fuzzy logic, an overall evaluation score is calculated. This process is shown by Table 3.

Table 3. Fuzzy logic application

Participant	Results
Physician 1	COM = high, SU = medium, SW = above-medium, and VP = below-medium Evaluation = 5.48
Physician 2	COM = high, SU = medium, SW = above-medium, and VP = above-medium Evaluation = 5.24
Physician 3	COM = above-medium, SU = below-medium, SW = above-medium, and VP = above-medium Evaluation = 4.93
Assistant 1	COM = medium, SU = below-medium, SW = high, and VP = medium Evaluation = 6.1
Assistant 2	COM = above-medium, SU = medium, SW = above-medium, and VP = High Evaluation = 6.9
Assistant 3	COM = medium, SU = high, SW = above-medium, and VP = High Evaluation = 5.5

Each endpoint specified by a linguistic value corresponds to an input to the inference controller. Then, the active rules are used to calculate the output which corresponds to the final evaluation score. This intelligent calculation takes into account, for each evaluation, the influence of each criterion in the overall evaluation process.

5 Conclusion

This work we have introduced a new intelligent approach based on neural network technique allowing an automated visual analytics. This novel approach executes a Self-Organizing Feature Map (SOFM) neural network model that communicates with human environment using natural language to evaluate visualization generated by tools. Using this new method, this system interacts with users, understands the conversation's context, and detects each sentence meaning. Then, we use fuzzy logic to interpret responses given by participants. By this way, an intelligent evaluation procedure of visualizations generated by the visual tool is realized. After executing a learning algorithm, our application becomes capable to detect new abstract terms and arrange existing ones in visualization evaluation procedures. This enables an efficient visualizations evaluations taking into account different criteria and measures of visualization characteristics.

References

1. Brahmi, A., Ltifi, H., Ben Ayed, M.: Approach for the evaluation of a KDD based DSS visual representations. In: 2014 Middle East Conference on Biomedical Engineering (MECBME), 17–20 February, Hilton Hotel, Doha, Qatar (2014)
2. Brehmer, M., Sedlmair, M., Ingram, S., Munzner, T.: Visualizing dimensionally-reduced data: Interviews with analysts and a characterization of task sequences. In: Proceedings of the Fifth Workshop on Beyond Time and Errors: Novel Evaluation Methods for Visualization, pp. 1–8. ACM (2014)
3. Brooke, J.: SUS: a quick and dirty usability scale. In: Usability Evaluation in Industry, pp. 189–194. Taylor & Francis, London (1996)
4. Chrimes, D., Kushniruk, A., Kitos, N.R., Mann, D.M.: Usability testing of Avoiding Diabetes Thru Action Plan Targeting (ADAPT) decision support for integrating care- based counseling of pre-diabetes in an electronic health record. Int. J. Med. Inform. **83**(9), 636–647 (2014)
5. Flavián, C., Guinalíu, M., Gurrea, R.: The role played by perceived usability, satisfaction and consumer trust on website loyalty. Inf. Manag. **43**(1), 1–14 (2006)
6. Ho, H.Y., Yeh, I., Lai, Y.C., Lin, W.C., Cherng, F.Y.: Evaluating 2D flow visualization using eye tracking. Comput. Graph. Forum **34**(3), 501–510 (2015)
7. Isenberg, T., Isenberg, P., Chen, J., Sedlmair, M., Möller, T.: A systematic review on the practice of evaluating visualization. IEEE Trans. Vis. Comput. Graph. **19**(12), 2818–2827 (2013)
8. Kurzhals, K., Bopp, C.F., Bässler, J., Ebinger, F., Weiskopf, D.: Benchmark data for evaluating visualization and analysis techniques for eye tracking for video stimuli. In: Proceedings of the Fifth Workshop on Beyond Time and Errors: Novel Evaluation Methods for Visualization, pp. 54–60. ACM (2014)
9. Lam, H., Bertini, E., Isenberg, P., Plaisant, C., Carpendale, S.: Empirical studies in information visualization: seven scenarios. IEEE Trans. Vis. Comput. Graph. **18**(9), 1520–1536 (2012)
10. Lewis, J.R., Sauro, J.: The factor structure of the system usability scale. In: Kurosu, M. (ed.) HCD 2009. LNCS, vol. 5619, pp. 94–103. Springer, Heidelberg (2009). https://doi.org/10.1007/978-3-642-02806-9_12
11. Ltifi, H., Ben Mohamed, E., Ben Ayed, M.: Interactive visual KDD based temporal Decision Support System. Inf. Vis. **14**(1), 1–20 (2015)
12. North, C.: Toward measuring visualization insight. IEEE Comput. Graph. Appl. **11**(4), 443–456 (2005)
13. Pike, W., et al.: Scalable visual reasoning: collaboration through distributed analysis. In: International Symposium on Collaborative Technologies and Systems, pp. 24–32 (2007)
14. Can, G.F., Demirok, S.: Universal usability evaluation by using an integrated fuzzy multi criteria decision making approach. Int. J. Intell. Comput. Cybern. **12**, 194–223 (2019)
15. Shneiderman, B., Plaisant, C.: Strategies for evaluating information visualization tools: multi-dimensional in-depth long-term case studies. In: Proceedings of BELIV, pp. 81–87. ACM, New York (2006)
16. Siang, C.V., Mohamed, F.B., Salleh, F.M., Isham, M.I.B.M., Basori, A.H., Selamat, A.B.: An overview of immersive data visualization methods using type by task taxonomy. In: 2021 IEEE International Conference on Computing (ICOCO), pp. 347–352. IEEE (2021)
17. Cuadrado-Gallego, J.J., Demchenko, Y., Losada, M.A., Ormandjieva, O.: Classification and analysis of techniques and tools for data visualization teaching. In: 2021 IEEE Global Engineering Education Conference (EDUCON), pp. 1593–1599. IEEE (2021)
18. Yahya, N., Zainuddin, N.M.M., Sjarif, N.N.A., Azmi, N.F.M.: Predictive visual analytics for machine learning model in house price prediction: a case study. Open Int. J. Inform. **9**(1), 1–29 (2021)

19. Kumar, D.I., Kounte, M.R.: Comparative study of self-organizing map and deep self-organizing map using MATLAB. In: 2016 International Conference on Communication and Signal Processing (ICCSP), pp. 1020–1023. IEEE (2016)
20. Yukish, M.A., Miller, S.W., Martin, J.D., Bennett, L.A., Hoskins, M.E.: Set-based design, model-based systems engineering, and sequential decision processes. Naval Eng. J. **130**(4), 93–104 (2018)
21. Ricca, F.: Practical decision aid for complex decision processes: why strategic analysis with STAN is not a black box. Ital. J. Plan. Pract. **8**(1), 86–102 (2018)
22. Hrabovskyi, Y., Brynza, N., Vilkhivska, O.: Development of information visualization methods for use in multimedia applications. Phys. Eng. **1**, 3–17 (2020)
23. Tamara, M.: Visualization Analysis and Design. AK Peters/CRC Press, Natick (2014)
24. Chang, Y.C., Ku, C.H., Chen, C.H.: Using deep learning and visual analytics to explore hotel reviews and responses. Tour. Manag. **80**, 104129 (2020)
25. Mei, H., Ma, Y., Wei, Y., Chen, W.: The design space of construction tools for information visualization: a survey. J. Vis. Lang. Comput. **44**, 120–132 (2018)
26. Yuan, J., Chen, C., Yang, W., Liu, M., Xia, J., Liu, S.: A survey of visual analytics techniques for machine learning. Comput. Vis. Med. **7**(1), 3–36 (2020)
27. Unrau, R., Kray, C.: Enhancing usability evaluation of web-based geographic information systems (Web GIS) with visual analytics. In: 11th International Conference on Geographic Information Science (GIScience 2021)-Part I. Schloss Dagstuhl-Leibniz-Zentrum für Informatik (2020)

Improved Cerebral Images Semantic Segmentation Using Advanced Approaches of Deep Learning

Abderraouf Zoghbi[1,4], Maroua Benleulmi[1,2], Soraya Cheriguene[1,3], Nabiha Azizi[1,2(✉)] ⓘ, Samira Lagrini[1,2], and S. Nadine Layeb[1,4]

[1] Labged Laboratory, Badji Mokhtar University, Annaba, Algeria
abderraouf.zoghbi@etu.u-paris.fr, azizi@labged.net
[2] Department of Computer Science, Badji Mokhtar University, Annaba, Algeria
[3] Saad Dahlab University, Blida, Algeria
[4] University of Paris, Paris, France

Abstract. Reliable detection of brain tumors is a challenging task, even with the proper acquisition of Magnetic resonance imaging (MRI) images. Computer-aided detection (CADe) systems can reduce the workload of physicians and minimize the time required for accurate segmentation of illnesses. CADe systems for brain tumors comprises two principles stages: pre-processing of MRI images, and segmentation to define the region of interest (ROI). This paper describes the application of deep learning to detect tumors on brain MRI images where the number of defective samples available is small, which is fairly common in many real practical applications and can negatively affect the model performance. In the presented study, the Generative Adversarial Networks (GANs) learned how to synthesize realistic images to improve the training of DL models. We also explored CyclaGAN architecture via hyperparameter tuning and performed image segmentation for brain tumor. The proposed CADe system was validated on Figshare dataset of brain MRI images. Experimental results show that, the data augmentation method can increase the segmentation performance efficiently and effectively.

Keywords: Brain tumor · Medical image · MRI · Computer-Aided Detection · Deep learning · Imbalanced data · Generative Adversarial Networks · Synthesis image · Data augmentation · Segmentation

1 Introduction

Nowadays, brain tumors are classified as one of the most common major causes of mortality in the world. A brain tumor consists of a group of cells that grows abnormally by multiplying rapidly with each other inside of the brain, or around the brain. Besides the pressure in the brain, tumors also cause abnormal neurological symptoms, which can lead to the death of a patient. Early diagnosis of brain tumors is imperative to prevent permanent damage to the brain or death of

© Springer Nature Switzerland AG 2022
A. Bennour et al. (Eds.): ISPR 2022, CCIS 1589, pp. 65–77, 2022.
https://doi.org/10.1007/978-3-031-08277-1_6

the individual [1,2]. Brain tumor detection is a complicated job because of their varied behavior both in terms of structure and intensity. Advanced paradigms in imaging systems have greatly enhanced the interpretation of medical images [3,4]. Magnetic resonance imaging (MRI) is preferred over other imaging modalities for brain tumor analysis, monitoring [5]. To detect an abnormality, these images are visually scanned by physicians to assure a reliable result. In some detection cases, complex anatomy and the varying abilities of the physicians may result in an interpretation errors [6]. In this regard, Computer-Aided Detection (CADe) systems have taken a major place in routine clinical work to assist medical experts in decision-making. Those systems aim to enhance the diagnostic capabilities of physicians and reduce the time required for accurate diagnosis by providing a computer output as a second opinion that can supply a fast and precise diagnosis [7]. The goal of CADe system in brain images is to help radiologists avoid missing a tumor by detecting and marking suspicious areas in an image [8]. Different CADe systems may apply different steps. A CADe system typically comprises two principles stages, namely: (1) Pre-processing (2) Segmentation. The objective of image pre-processing is to enhance the quality of data by eliminating noise and other useless information from the raw images. Segmentation is an important step in CADe process, because the effectiveness of subsequent tasks, including feature extraction and classification, depends highly on the quality of the Region of interest (ROI). The main purpose of segmentation stage in brain tumor detection is to accurately separate the tumor parenchyma from other tissues [9]. Recently, Deep Learning (DL) [10,11] technologies have played a crucial roles in CADe as well as they have demonstrated remarkable abilities in detecting a variety of tumors, such as skin cancers [12], breast [13] andd Glaucoma [14]. Using a large dataset for training helps the learned model to achieve an accuracy comparable to human experts [15].

Unfortunately, many application fields, such as medical imaging diagnosis systems, do not have access to big data. Moreover, the majority of medical data are unbalanced and usually the data with abnormalities are less which leads to unsatisfying results. Most deep learning methods assume an equal occurrence of classes and do not consider the misclassification cost in a general classification process. This imbalance distribution makes these models tend to be biased toward the majority class, while the ability of positive cases detection is fair weak. Therefore, traditional data augmentation techniques have been introduced to generate new synthetic data and overcome this shortage of data. Synthetic data can be obtained in several ways, making simple adjustments to the visual data is common [16]. Generative Adversarial Networks (GAN) [17] is one of the very powerful data augmentation approaches, that aim to enhance the size and quality of training datasets and build more accurate detection models. This type of generative networks has proven its ability to generate very convincing samples of a particular class as a result of the game between a discriminator and a generator unit.

Another challenge about AI and medical data is detecting the object such as tumors from an MRI image. With advancement in machine learning techniques, different types of DL models were proposed to detect abnormalities in brain images [18–21]. An exhaustive review of these techniques and their application in medical domain, can be found in Liu et al. [22]. Advanced deep learning techniques such as UNet and SegNet are used for Computer Aided Detection systems (CADe) to detect the region of interest (ROI) in other words the region that has an abnormality in order to classify it, meanwhile a new architecture based on adversarial networks named CycleGAN proved satisfying results in object detection.

The objective of this paper is the investigation of different variants of Generative Adversarial Networks to solve these two problems; use GAN to synthesis images of the minority class since it is one of most performant techniques for data augmentation, and investigate CycleGAN in a new domain: Brain tumor detection.

The remainder of this paper is organized as follows: Sect. 2 reviews some related works on GANs architectures for data augmentation and synthesis. Section 3 presents an ensemble of used concepts followed by Sect. 4 describing the proposed approach and its main parts. Experimental results are presented in Sect. 5. Finally, a conclusion and future works are outlined in Sect. 6.

2   Related Work

This field has been treated from different points of view, for instance, there existed some work that focalized on data augmentation or data segmentation to improve the classification model using GAN. In this section, we review some of the major studies about brain reported in the literature. Most of the Brain are working with Magnetic Resonance Imaging (MRI). Important studies have been published about cancer, epilepsy, Alzheimer's disease. These studies used different models for either data augmentation or data segmentation. For instance, Moeskops et al. [23] used adversarial training and dilated convolutions for Brain MRI Segmentation to improve its performance (Their average DC for 7 classes is 0.85 ± 0.01 using the dilated network). On the other hand, Borne et al. [24] used 3D U-Net on a heterogeneous training dataset proving a good results of 85%. Rezaei et al. [25] used cGAN for a semantic segmentation convolutional neural network. This latter had better performance for brain tumor segmentation. Several researches about segmentation and image synthesis are presented in Table 1.

3   Used Concepts

- Generative Adversarial Networks (GAN) were be a solution for generating images based on perceptron neural networks [21].
  GANs consist of two models: the generator (G) and the discriminator (D). These neural networks can be likened to an artist who paints and another one who criticizes and advises him to improve his work. The generator is the artist. It generates the data based on noise vector randomly z a sample of

Table 1. Segmentation and image synthesis publications.

Reference	Method	Object	Dataset
Moeskops et al. [23]	GAN	Brain	MRBrainS13
Borne et al. [24]	3D U-Net	Brain	62 healthy brain images
Rezaei et al. [25]	cGAN	Brain	BRATS 2017
Bermudez et al. [27]	DCGAN	Brain	BLSA
Han et al. [28]	DCGAN, WGAN	Brain	BRATS2016
Olut et al. [29]	Baseline GAN, sGAN	Brain	IXI

Fig. 1. GAN model components.

the distributed $p(z)$ that has a Gaussian or a uniform distribution; and the discriminator is the person who criticizes the artist. It checks how realistic is the generated data and gives feedback to the generator. So the input of D is the generated fake data $G(z)$ and real data X used for the training. Figure 1 presents the structure of a basic GAN model.

The objective is to minimize the generator's loss L_G and maximize the discriminator's loss L_D.

- U-Net architecture is proposed for image segmentation [12] and improved to serve better the medical images. This symmetric architecture has a "U" shape as its name. It consists of two paths: the down sampling "encoder" (for contraction) and the up sampling "decoder" (for expansion). The neck of the bottle is where the two paths meet.

- Many variants are made from the GAN, as the CycleGAN [13]. This latter is made for image-to-image translation. As a basic GAN, CycleGAN also has a discriminator and a generator, but with the image-to-image translation CycleGan uses two generators and two discriminators in order to have two image domains. Using this architecture makes the data flow more complex. Transformations will have place from domain A to domain B by G_B and from domain B to domain A by G_A, which is similar to two reciprocal mappings.

Images X_{fA} are generated from images X_B of domain B by G_A using domain A characteristics. On the other hand, images X_{fB} are generated from images X_A of domain A by G_B using domain B characteristics. Images of domain A are identified by discriminator D_A and images of domain B are identified by discriminator D_B (Figs. 2 and 3).

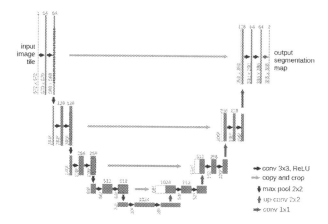

Fig. 2. UNET architecture (ZHANG et al. 2008 [26]).

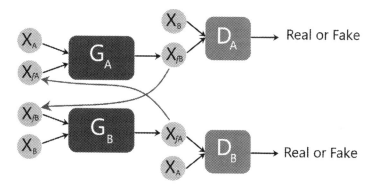

Fig. 3. Segmentation using CycleGAN.

4   Proposed Approach

Figure 4 presents the architecture of the proposed system. At first, a preprocessing of the data is necessary in order to improve the segmentation results. This is followed by the following stages:

In this work, GAN is applied on the minority data class to generate synthetic images. Once the used dataset is balanced, CycleGAN is applied on it to detect the tumors also U-Net (as a referential model).

The training stage: during this stage the data was augmented using GAN, and the generated brain tumor MRI images were then set as an input to the next step, that is, the segmentation. The dataset was segmented using CycleGAN and U-Net. As a result, two models were generated.

The decision stage: during this stage, we used the CycleGAN based model and U-Net based model to classify the input images. Each model generates a contour of the detected object.

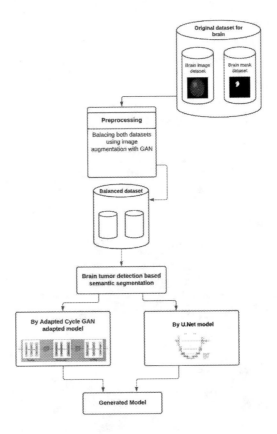

Fig. 4. Architecture of the proposed approach.

4.1 GAN for Generating Synthesis Images of the Minority Data Class

As mentioned in the previous section, the GAN has two models: the generator and the discriminator.

Discriminator:

This model is a classifier which is trained twice, one time for the real images and another for the generated ones from the generator model. When we start, it is easy for the discriminator to classify the results since the generator outputs noise. We compare the discriminator's output to the real images to calculate the loss for this cycle. This loss is used to adjust the hyper-parameter of the discriminator, so it classifies more precisely the next cycle. This network consists of three linear layers. The activation function of the output layer is sigmoid (in order to have a probability that ranges between one and zero when the image is real).

Generator:

This network is made of three linear layers. The activation function of the output layer is tanh. It generates a batch of fake images that are transmitted to the discriminator. If this latter classifies them as "fake", which will be the case at the beginning since the generator starts with random noise, we use the loss to update the hyper-parameter of this network, in other words $D(X)$ is close to 1 since X are real samples. In order to reach this optimization $D(G(z))$ decreases among the process and at the end we will have a high-dimensional real data space out from a low-dimensional noise space.

4.2 CycleGAN and UNet for Data Segmentation

The cycleGAN's generator performs the segmentation. It generates segmented cartographic images of brain tumors from MRI images. The discriminator compares the generated images to the real images that are segmented by health experts. This process continues until the generator generates segmented images that are close to the real ones, and the discriminator is no more able to distinguish whether the images are real or fake. This is the CycleGAN's objective function:

$$L(G_A, G_B, D_A, D_B) = L_{GAN}(G_A, G_B, X_A, X_B) + L_{GAN}(G_B, G_A, X_B, X_A) \quad (1)$$

$$+ L_{cyc}(G_A, G_B, X_A, X_B) \quad (2)$$

Our objective is :

$$\arg \min_{G_A, G_B} \max_{D_A, D_B} L(G_A, G_B, D_A, D_B) \quad (3)$$

In the U-Net architecture, the encoder (down sampling path) is used to capture the context of the image. This path is a stack of convolutions and max pooling [15]. The decoder (up sampling path) is used for a precise localization via transposed convolutions.

5 Experiments and Results

5.1 Dataset

The used dataset from Figshare is a referential for tumor diagnostic [18]. It has 3064 contrasted images that are improved at T1 of 233 patients, and present three types of tumors: Glioma, Meningioma, and pituitary gland tumor. These data are collected in China from Nanfang hospital and the medical university of Tranjing during five years (2005 till 2010) (Figs. 5 and 6).

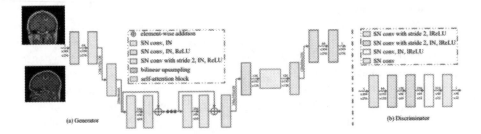

Fig. 5. Architecture of the used cycleGAN.

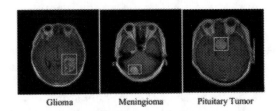

Fig. 6. Brain tumor images.

5.2 Augmentation of the Minority Data Class Using GAN

The minority data class concerns brain MRIs with abnormalities. After using different parameters, a precis brain MRI image was generated from a random noise, showing a frontal lobe tumor. The shown result in Fig. 7 is after one hour only of GAN training for 3000 epochs.

Figure 8 presents the GAN's loss, the generator's loss decreases and almost be stable over 5000 iterations, while the discriminator's loss increases over the iterations, as mentioned in Sect. 2 the optimal result is to minimize the generator's loss and maximize the discriminator's loss.

5.3 Data Segmentation Using CycleGAN and U-Net

In order to detect brain tumors in MRI images CycleGAN is used on the balanced dataset. Figure 9 represents the CycleGAN segmentation results.

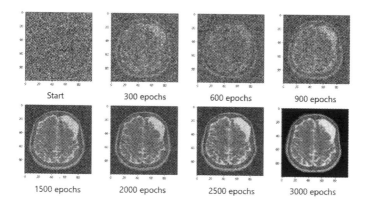

| Start | 300 epochs | 600 epochs | 900 epochs |
| 1500 epochs | 2000 epochs | 2500 epochs | 3000 epochs |

Fig. 7. GAN generated image after 3000 epochs (one hour).

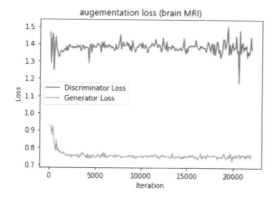

Fig. 8. GAN's loss.

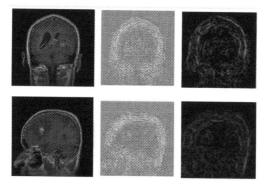

Fig. 9. MRI Brain image, CycleGAN segmented result, Prediction of the corresponding segmented MRI.

5.4   Evaluation

To evaluate the segmentation performance we used ROC, DICE and precision measures. The following table shows that CycleGAN outperformed U-Net. Cycle-GAN's performance is 0.9, 0.76, 0.74 and U-Net's performance is 0.79, 0.75, 0.7 respectively ROC, PR and DICE.

Table 2. Quantitate comparison of the models, using ROC, PR and DICE (brain tumor).

Brain tumor			
Model	ROC	PR	DICE
U-Net	0.792442	0.759346	0.701426
CycleGAN	**0.909608**	**0.765179**	**0.743937**

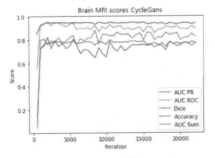

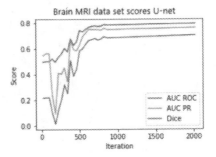

(a) Brain tumor MRI dataset scores with CycleGAN.

(b) Brain tumor MRI dataset scores with U-Net.

Fig. 10. Data segmentation model's performance.

The CycleGAN performances directly reach the top over the first 1000 iterations but never stabilize (even after 20000), while U-Net performances decrease over the first 200 iterations then increases to reach the top at 1000 iterations ans stabilize.

5.5   Discussion

After comparing the performance of the two models, it is clear that U-net has good but lower performance than CycleGAN. Both models were trained using the Adam optimizer. U-Net was run for 2000 iterations, while CycleGAN was run for 50000 iterations. The results of the proposed CycleGAN are presented in Table 2 and Fig. 10(a).

Although CycleGAN adds a certain quality, it ignores important diagnostic information during the translation process. Thus, it was hard to extract the characteristics from this type of results such as in Fig. 9.

Qualitatively, we observe good representation using CycleGAN, we see in Fig. 9 distribution of images from input of MRI images is indistinguishable from the distribution of segmented results using an adversarial loss.

6   Conclusion

In this study, the imbalanced learning problem in brain tumor MRI images was tackled and a CADe system based adversarial networks approach for tumor detection was proposed. At first, GAN was used to synthesize the data, which has proven good results with brain tumor MRI images. Then, to segment the brain tumor images, two models were trained: CycleGAN and U-Net as a referential model. As a conclusion, the use of GAN-generated images significantly has influenced the performance of the model network trained for tumor segmentation. GAN permits to generate realistic MRI images that are useful to solve the problem of limited data or imbalanced datasets a, d we can see it as an efficient approach for augmentation, and improves the predictive power of the segmentation step by applying the particular CycleGAN consistency loss.

Qualitative results shows generative adversarial networks gave significant results, and can be used in handling medical data, and in particularly for brain tumor detection.

In future work, we plan to explore other types of medical datasets through the transfer of the knowledge gained while learning using CycleGAN for MRI segmentation. We also aim to optimise the model complexity for a better interprabilty.

References

1. Darko, O., et al.: Glycemia and venous thromboembolism in patients with primary brain tumors - a speculative review. Med. Hypotheses **157**, 110719 (2021)
2. Benzebouchi, N.E., Azizi, N., Ayadi, K.: A computer-aided diagnosis system for breast cancer using deep convolutional neural networks. In: Behera, H.S., Nayak, J., Naik, B., Abraham, A. (eds.) Computational Intelligence in Data Mining. AISC, vol. 711, pp. 583–593. Springer, Singapore (2019). https://doi.org/10.1007/978-981-10-8055-5_52
3. Wang, S., et al.: Annotation-efficient deep learning for automatic medical image segmentation. Nat. Commun. **12**, 5915 (2021)
4. Azizi, N., Farah, N.: From static to dynamic ensemble of classifiers selection: application to Arabic handwritten recognition. Int. J. Knowl.-Based Intell. Eng. Syst. **12**(4), 279–288 (2012)
5. Lu, S.-L., Liao, H.-C., Hsu, F.-M., Liao, C.-C., Lai, F., Xiao, F.: The intracranial tumor segmentation challenge: contour tumors on brain MRI for radiosurgery. Neuroimage **244**, 118585 (2021)

6. Young, G.S.: Advanced MRI of adult brain tumors. Neurol. Clin. **25**(4), 947–973 (2007)
7. Castellino, R.A.: Computer aided detection (CAD): an overview. Cancer Imaging **5**(1), 17 (2005)
8. Cheriguene, S., Azizi, N., Dey, N., Ashour, A.S., Ziani, A.: A new hybrid classifier selection model based on mRMR method and diversity measures. Int. J. Mach. Learn. Cybern. **10**(5), 1189–1204 (2016)
9. Fenton, J.J., et al.: Influence of computer-aided detection on performance of screening mammography. New Engl. J. Med. **356**(14), 1399–1409 (2007)
10. Zeiler, M.D., Fergus, R.: Visualizing and understanding convolutional networks. In: Fleet, D., Pajdla, T., Schiele, B., Tuytelaars, T. (eds.) ECCV 2014. LNCS, vol. 8689, pp. 818–833. Springer, Cham (2014). https://doi.org/10.1007/978-3-319-10590-1_53
11. Gu, J., et al.: Recent advances in convolutional neural networks. Pattern Recogn. **77**, 354–377 (2018)
12. Pacheco, A.G., Krohling, R.A.: Recent advances in deep learning applied to skin cancer detection. arXiv preprint arXiv:1912.03280 (2019)
13. Yari, Y., Nguyen, T.V., Nguyen, H.T.: Deep learning applied for histological diagnosis of breast cancer. IEEE Access **8**, 162 432–162 448 (2020)
14. Touahri, R., Azizi, N., Hammami, N.E., Aldwairi, M., Benzebouchi, N.E., Moumene, O.: Multi source retinal fundus image classification using convolution neural networks fusion and Gabor-based texture representation. Int. J. Comput. Vis. Robot. **11**(4), 401–428 (2021)
15. Zhu, X.J.: Semi-Supervised Learning Literature Survey. University of Winsconsin, Madison (2005)
16. Antoniou, A., Storkey, A., Edwards, H.: Data augmentation generative adversarial networks. arXiv preprint arXiv:1711.04340 (2017)
17. Creswell, A., White, T., Dumoulin, V., Arulkumaran, K., Sengupta, B., Bharath, A.A.: Generative adversarial networks: an overview. IEEE Signal Process. Mag. **35**(1), 53–65 (2018)
18. Badrinarayanan, V., Kendall, A., Cipolla, R.: SegNet: a deep convolutional encoder-decoder architecture for image segmentation. IEEE Trans. Pattern Anal. Mach. Intell. **39**, 2481–2495 (2017)
19. Ronneberger, O., Fischer, P., Brox, T.: U-Net: convolutional networks for biomedical image segmentation. In: Navab, N., Hornegger, J., Wells, W.M., Frangi, A.F. (eds.) MICCAI 2015. LNCS, vol. 9351, pp. 234–241. Springer, Cham (2015). https://doi.org/10.1007/978-3-319-24574-4_28
20. Milletari, F., Navab, N., Ahmadi, S.-A.: V-Net: fully convolutional neural networks for volumetric medical image segmentation. In: Proceedings of the 2016 Fourth International Conference on 3D Vision (3DV), Stanford, CA, USA, 25–28 October 2016, pp. 565–571 (2016)
21. Goodfellow, I., et al.: Generative adversarial nets. In: Advances in Neural Information Processing Systems, vol. 27, pp. 2672–2680 (2014)
22. Liu, X., Song, L., Liu, S., Zhang, Y.: A review of deep-learning- based medical image segmentation methods. Sustainability **13**(3), 1224 (2021)
23. Moeskops, P., Veta, M., Lafarge, M.W., Eppenhof, K.A.J., Pluim, J.P.W.: Adversarial training and dilated convolutions for brain MRI segmentation. In: Cardoso, M.J., et al. (eds.) DLMIA/ML-CDS -2017. LNCS, vol. 10553, pp. 56–64. Springer, Cham (2017). https://doi.org/10.1007/978-3-319-67558-9_7

24. Borne, L., Rivière, D., Mangin, J.F.: Combining 3D U-Net and bottom- up geo-metric constraints for automatic cortical sulci recognition. In: Proceedings of the International Conference on Medical Imaging with Deep Learning, London, UK, 8–10 July 2019 (2019)

25. Rezaei, M., et al.: A conditional adversarial network for semantic segmentation of brain tumor. In: Crimi, A., Bakas, S., Kuijf, H., Menze, B., Reyes, M. (eds.) BrainLes 2017. LNCS, vol. 10670, pp. 241–252. Springer, Cham (2018). https://doi.org/10.1007/978-3-319-75238-9_21

26. Zhang, H., Fritts, J.E., Goldman, S.A.: Image segmentation evaluation: a survey of unsupervised methods. Comput. Vis. Image Underst. **110**(2), 260–280 (2008)

27. Bermudez, C., Plassard, A.J., Davis, L.T., et al.: Learning implicit brain MRI manifolds with deep learning, vol. 10574, p. 105741L. International Society for Optics and Photonics (2018)

28. Han, C., Hayashi, H., Rundo, L., et al.: GAN-based synthetic brain MR image gen-eration. In: International Symposium on Biomedical Imaging, pp. 734–738 (2018)

29. Olut, S., Sahin, Y.H., Demir, U., Unal, G.: Generative adversarial training for MRA image synthesis using multi-contrast MRI. In: Rekik, I., Unal, G., Adeli, E., Park, S.H. (eds.) PRIME 2018. LNCS, vol. 11121, pp. 147–154. Springer, Cham (2018). https://doi.org/10.1007/978-3-030-00320-3_18

Self-supervised Learning for COVID-19 Detection from Chest X-ray Images

Ines Feki[1], Sourour Ammar[1,2(✉)] ⓘ, and Yousri Kessentini[1,2] ⓘ

[1] Digital Research Center of Sfax, B.P. 275, Sakiet Ezzit, 3021 Sfax, Tunisia
`ines.feki.doc@enetcom.usf.tn`
[2] SM@RTS: Laboratory of Signals, systeMs, aRtificial Intelligence and neTworkS,
Sfax, Tunisia
{`sourour.ammar,yousri.kessentini`}`@crns.rnrt.tn`

Abstract. Most of existing computer vision applications rely on models trained on supervised corpora, this is contradictory to what the world is seeing with the explosion of massive sets of unlabeled data. In the field of medical imaging for example, creating labels is extremely time-consuming because professionals should spend countless hours looking at images to manually annotate, segment, etc. Recently, several works are looking for solutions to the challenge of learning effective visual representations with no human supervision. In this work, we investigate the potential of using a self-supervised learning as a pretraining phase in improving the classification of radiographic images when the amount of available annotated data is small. To do that, we propose to use a self-supervised framework by pretraining a deep encoder with contrastive learning on a chest X-ray dataset using no labels at all, and then fine-tuning it using only few labeled data samples.

We experimentally demonstrate that an unsupervised pretraining on unlabeled data is able to learn useful representation from Chest X-ray images, and only few labeled data samples are sufficient to reach the same accuracy of a supervised model learnt on the whole annotated dataset.

Keywords: Deep learning · Self-supervised learning · X-ray images · COVID-19 detection

1 Introduction

Currently, the world is looking to make use of less expensive efforts of creating a huge amount of labeled dataset and limit the need for manually annotated data. That's why, there has been an increasing research oriented to the exploitation of large amount of unlabeled data.

Generally, methods based on unsupervised learning, and especially on self-supervised learning (referred as SSL), have shown great performance in this issue with respect to their supervised counterparts. We note that we do not require explicit labels to train a model following a self-supervised fashion. This means

A. Bennour et al. (Eds.): ISPR 2022, CCIS 1589, pp. 78–89, 2022.
https://doi.org/10.1007/978-3-031-08277-1_7

that only the unlabeled dataset is used to learn features from different visual representations for a later fine-tuning using a small fraction of labeled data.

Among recent and famous methods in self-supervised setting, SimCLR [1] and SimCLRv2 [2] showed that good quality representations can be learned without any explicit supervision. They are based on the principle of considering the model as a brain that can learn the high-level features of objects in our world in order to recognize similarities and differences between them.

Recently, self-supervised models are receiving more and more attention due to the use of unlabeled images in an agnostic manner meaning that the representations are not directly adapted to a specific classification task [7,21]. Especially, in the context of medical image classification using SSL remains helpful and useful because the amount of labeled data is relatively limited and requires a lot of effort and time while the unlabeled data is comparatively large. Therefore, the effectiveness of the SSL approach have been demonstrated by several works throughout various medical image analysis [11,14].

However, methods that are based on SSL are operating as an hybrid learning approach by learning in two steps and therefore combining the benefit of both supervised and unsupervised learning. First, they perform feature learning from the pool of unlabeled data, then, they use self-supervision to fine-tune the model and improve it from a smaller labeled dataset [4].

Motivated by the latest advances of the SSL, we investigate in this paper the potential of using a SSL as a pre-training phase in improving the classification of radiographic images when the amount of available annotated data is small, and we conduct a fair comparison between self-supervised and supervised training. To do that, we conducted extensive experiments and comparisons while varying the fraction of used labeled data. We showed that an unsupervised pre-training on unlabeled data is able of learning useful features from radiographic images, and only few labeled data samples are sufficient in fine-tuning to reach the same accuracy of a supervised model learnt on the whole annotated dataset. We experimentally showed that our framework surpasses the supervised model trained on the entire annotated dataset when it is fine-tuned on only a fraction of 50 % of the labeled data.

2   Related Work

We review in this section related works about the SSL approaches and the COVID-19 detection methods from medical images.

Self-supervised Learning (SSL)

SSL can be considered a kind of unsupervised learning methods that exploit unlabeled data to yield labels. It aims at learning to do tasks without humans annotated data [20]. Methods based on SSL have shown great performance [15,19] regarding to their fully unsupervised counterparts e.g. predicting image rotations [10], order sequences of the same video [18], etc. Indeed, Self-Supervised contrastive learning is one of several related approaches that used SSL and it has shown recently promising results in computer vision like the work in [1] that proposed to use contrastive SSL following 3 steps: first, data augmentation is performed on input images, secondly, representation learning, and finally few-shot classification is made. The authors in [30] also used contrastive SSL on multiple views to understand the importance of view selection. In the same direction, the authors in [6] have explored contrastive SSL to classify agricultural images. In view of the advantages of the self-supervised contrastive representation learning, this work is an exploration of the use of self-supervised representation for chest X-ray images classification.

COVID-19 Detection Methods

Following the outbreak of Coronavirus pandemic disease, several deep neural networks based works have been proposed to automatically screening this disease from chest X-ray images. We cite the work in [23] where authors proposed using a dense convolutional neural network (CNN) to detect pneumonia disease from radiographic images beyond the level of radiologists.

In addition, many chest X-ray image databases are collected and made available online, but the number of samples remains limited. Because deep learning based methods require large datasets to achieve higher performance [29], many works have been introduced in the literature to address the lack of labeled data [22,28]. The authors in [28] proposed a patch-based neural network model. This model is suitable for training with a limited dataset for COVID-19 patients. To deal with the problem of lack of labeled data, unsupervised learning techniques have been proposed to learn efficiently deep networks on unlabeled data. Indeed, unsupervised techniques have been previously applied in clustering [9], visualization [17], anomaly detection [16], etc. In the medical field, the authors in [13] proposed an unsupervised network to classify X-ray images of COVID-19 affected patients, using clustering algorithm. They showed that using unsupervised learning allows to build models that are able to extract useful features from medical images.

We are interested in this work on existing literature in both self-supervised and supervised representation learning. When we talk about self-supervised learning, we mean that it is possible to train the model to learn a lot about our data without any annotations or labels. We have built on recent success on sub-field of SSL: the contrastive learning of visual representations [3,5,7,8]. We have exploited this technique because it allows us to learn the global features of a dataset without using any annotations or labels. This is done by precising to the model which data samples are similar (positive samples) and which are different (negative pairs). That is, the model learns higher-level features about the data.

3 Method

We illustrate in Fig. 1 an overview of our proposed framework consisting of two phases: 1) self-supervised pre-training phase: pre-training the feature encoder with unlabeled data using contrastive learning. 2) supervised fine-tuning phase: fine-tuning the pretrained feature encoder with a sample of labeled data.

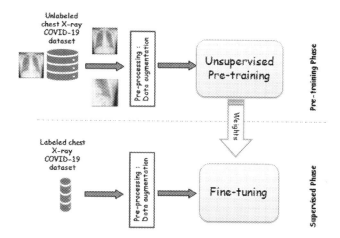

Fig. 1. Illustration of the proposed framework consisting of two phases: a pre-training phase to learn representations from unlabeled Chest X-ray data in a self-supervised fashion; and a supervised fine-tuning phase for performing COVID-19 detection.

3.1 Self-supervised Pre-training Based on Contrastive Learning

For the unsupervised pre-training phase, we adopt SimCLR [1] algorithm. Sim-CLR learns representations to distinguish between similar and dissimilar images by encouraging two views $\tilde{x}_i$ and $\tilde{x}_j$ from the same image x to be similar, and two views $\tilde{x}_i$ and $\tilde{x}_k$ ($k \neq i$) from different images to be dissimilar.

Following the SimCLR protocol, the unsupervised learning consists of four components as described in Fig. 2: A stochastic data augmentation module (referred as $\mathcal{T}(.)$), a neural network base encoder (referred as $f(.)$), a projection head (referred as $g(.)$), and a contrastive loss function $\mathcal{L}_c(.)$. In this work, the base encoder is a Resnet-50 and the projection head is a 2-layer MLP.

Given an input image x, by applying data augmentation twice ($\mathcal{T}(x)$), we get two copies $\tilde{x}_i$ and $\tilde{x}_j$ of the image. Both copies are given as input for the base encoder to get a normalized embedding vector. The obtained vector is then propagated through the projection head to obtain a 224-dimensional feature vector during the training phase. After that, we compute the supervised contrastive loss on the output of the projection head as follows:

$$\mathcal{L}_c = -\log \frac{exp(sim(z_i, z_j))/\tau)}{\sum_{k=1}^{2N} \mathbb{1}_{[k \neq i]} exp(sim(z_i, z_k))/\tau)} \tag{1}$$

where z_i, and z_j denote the output of the projection head for $\tilde{x}_i$ and $\tilde{x}_j$, respectively, $\mathbb{1}_{[k \neq i]}$ is an indicator function (equal to 1 if $k \neq i$), N is the size of the batch, τ is a temperature parameter, and $sim(.)$ is a similarity measure.

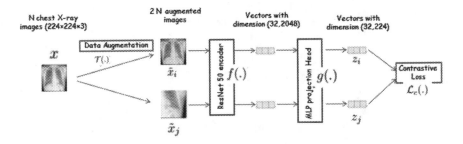

Fig. 2. Illustration of the first phase: Self-supervised pre-training

3.2   Supervised Fine-Tuning

The fine-tuning phase is a usual way to adapt the pre-trained network for our COVID-19 classification task. During this phase, the projection head $g(.)$ is totally discarded from the network and only the base encoder $f(.)$ is conserved with its weights learnt during the pre-training phase. The network is then composed of the base encoder $f(.)$ and 2 fully connected layers. The last layer is composed of three neurons with softmax as activation function. During the supervised fine-tuning phase, we use the standard SGD optimizer to minimize the loss function and then update the network parameters. Finally, the categorical cross-entropy loss function is used. Figure 3 shows an illustration of this second phase. The network takes as input a labeled subset and uses the weights of the pre-trained network as initialization.

4   Experiments and Results

We first introduce in this section the used dataset as well as the implementation details of our simulations. Then we provide and discuss the obtained results.

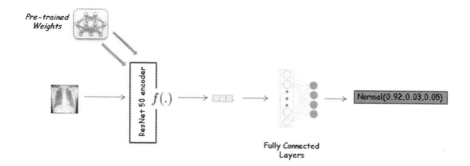

Fig. 3. Illustration of the second phase: Supervised fine-tuning

4.1   Dataset

For this study, we take images from COVID-19 Radiography Database[1]. Because the number of images in this database is expected to increase over time with more available data, we notice that our taken dataset consists of 15,153 chest X-ray images belonging to three classes: Normal, COVID-19, and Viral Pneumonia. It contains 10,192 chest X-ray images diagnosed as Normal (not affected patients), 3,616 chest X-ray images diagnosed as COVID-19, and 1,345 chest X-ray images for Viral Pneumonia. We split the dataset at random into 12,121 training images (we refer to this set as the D_{train}) and 3,032 test images (we refer to this set as the D_{test}). Table 1 provides a description of the distribution of each class images into training and test sets. Figure 4 shows sample examples from the used COVID-19 Radiography Database.

Table 1. Distribution of the dataset among different classes.

Class label	Training set	Test set
COVID-19	2892	724
Normal	8153	2039
Viral Pneumonia	1076	269
Total	12121	3032

---

[1] https://www.kaggle.com/tawsifurrahman/covid19-radiography-database.

For the unsupervised pre-training using the SimCLR algorithm, we consider the whole dataset discarding the labels and images are merged to consider them as unlabeled dataset. Labels are left for the supervised fine-tuning. As a result, we obtain 15,153 unlabeled chest X-ray images for the pre-training phase.

For the fine-tuning phase, we consider each time a fraction of D_{train} set for training the model. D_{test} is used to evaluate and compare the top-1 accuracy of all our simulations.

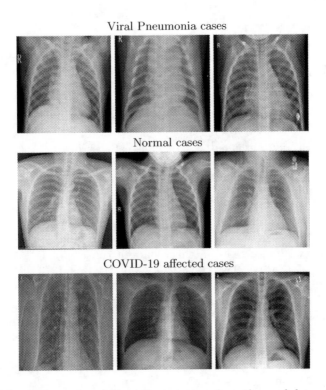

Fig. 4. Examples of Chest X-ray images from the used dataset

4.2   Implementation Details and Evaluation Metric

In this work, we adopt the SimCLR algorithm for self-supervised pre-training. For the feature embedding network, ResNet-50 is used as encoder network. For the pretraining protocol, we do not know how many categories the images belong to. In our approach, the images are ordered in a batch of 128 samples and we train SimCLR for 500 epochs with learning rate = 0.1. We use a 2-layer MLP projection head on the output of a ResNet-50 encoder to a 224-dimensional embedding, which is used for contrastive learning and the contrastive loss (NT-Xent) with temperature = 0.1. Three simple augmentations are used (those used by SimCLR): random crop, Gaussian blur, and color distortion (strength = 0.5).

During fine-tuning, we train the network using the SGD optimizer with a smaller learning rate 0.001 and a batch size of 32. The categorical cross Entropy loss is used, and the training is controlled according to a fraction of data as validation set.

Since the published images that we have taken are of variable sizes, all images are resized to the same dimension: $224 \times 224 \times 3$. We carry out simulations for different label fractions during the fine-tuning phase, from 10% up to 100%. We provide the results of all our simulations in terms of top-1 accuracy as test metric on the test set D^{test}.

4.3   Experimental Results

We evaluate in this section the potential of the proposed framework and then we compare its achievements to those of the supervised learning method, considered as baseline.

Supervised Baseline: We first evaluate the performance of a supervised ResNet-50 model. The training is performed on different label fractions (from 10% up to 100%) of COVID-19 training dataset (D_{train}) and evaluated on D_{test}. The supervised model is trained separately on each subset using the same procedure and settings as for fine-tuning. Our supervised baseline model is trained from scratch using random initialisation. The performance of the supervised baseline is showed in Table 2. The obtained results show that the supervised baseline model provides better results when it is trained on more data samples. In fact, the higher accuracy is obtained when the model is trained on the entire D_{train}. This accuracy is about 95.87%, with an improvement of 14,89% compared to the result obtained with a fraction of only 10%.

Table 2. Test accuracy of the supervised baseline when it is trained on different fraction of the training dataset D_{train}.

Label fraction	10%	20%	30%	40%	50%	60%	70%	80%	90%	100%
Supervised baseline	80.98	84.77	88.26	93.03	93.82	94.41	94.15	94.61	95.71	95.87

The Proposed Method Based on SSL: To investigate the potential of using a self-supervised learning as a pretraining phase in improving the classification accuracy on X-ray images, we fine-tune the pretrained model on different label fractions of the training data ranging from 10% to 100% and report the final test accuracy (top-1 accuracy) performances for these experiments in Table 3.

Table 3 shows the performance variation according to using different label fractions of annotated data. We observe that for all fractions, self-supervised based model outperforms the supervised one. This table shows also that unsupervised pretraining without using any annotated data followed by fine-tuning using only 50% of labeled data can achieve same performance (around 95%) as

Table 3. Test Accuracy of our self-supervised ResNet50 finetuned on different label fractions of D_{train}.

Label fraction	10%	20%	30%	40%	50%	60%	70%	80%	90%	100%
Proposed method	85.61	88.16	92.25	94.51	95.01	96.24	96.21	96.51	96.88	97.07

the supervised training on the entire training dataset (label fraction = 100%) and it can surpass it with only 60% of label fraction.

Figure 5 illustrates the curves of test accuracy plotted against the used label fractions for the supervised baseline (red curve) and our self-supervised framework (blue curve).

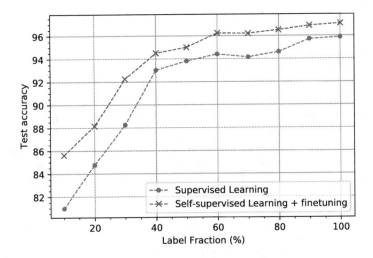

Fig. 5. Variation of test accuracy for the proposed method based on self-supervised learning (blue curve), and supervised baseline (red curve) according to different label fractions. (Color figure online)

Our self-supervised framework not only reaches better test accuracy values then supervised baseline, but it also produces proportionally larger gains when fine-tuned with less labeled examples and less learning epochs as shown in Fig. 5. Indeed, to reach the 95% accuracy, our self-supervised framework needs to run for only 117 epochs and using 50% of labeled samples. The same performance is achieved by the supervised baseline but after 125 epochs and requires a larger fraction ($\approx$90%) of labeled data. We notice also that with a label fraction 60%, the self-supervised framework surpasses the higher accuracy reached by the supervised baseline, when trained on the entire dataset (label fraction = 100%).

We can conclude that for the self-supervised learning on COVID-19 chest X-ray dataset, using more labeled data for fine-tuning the pretrained ResNet-50 encoder improves the accuracy of the model. In addition, the learning process needs fewer training epochs to converge. Unlike the supervised baseline, accuracy does not increase in the same manner even if we use the totality of the labeled dataset.

5   Conclusion

Supervised learning is well used for classification of medical images and provides good accuracy results when there are big training datasets, but such approaches may suffer from the lack of annotated data. Annotated medical images datasets are always of small size. In this paper, we investigated the impact of using a self-supervised learning as pretraining phase for a neural network encoder in improving the classification of chest X-ray images when the amount of available annotated data is small. The self-supervised pretraining is proposed to learn specific visual representations from unlabeled data. To do that, we presented a simple framework based on two phases: a self-supervised pretraining on unlabeled Chest X-ray images of COVID-19 dataset, and a supervised fine-tuning phase on few data samples. We demonstrated that the self-supervised framework, using only 50% of labeled data, surpasses the higher accuracy reached by the supervised baseline, when trained on the entire dataset. This result highlights the power of the self-supervised pretraining in learning meaningful visual representations from X-ray images.

We aim in the future to provide experiments with bigger and deeper architectures of the encoder network like ResNet-152 to validate our results (as demonstrated in [2]). We aim also to explore larger dataset in the pretraining phase such as CheXpert [31]. In addition, Transfer knowledge learnt from the first chest X-ray unlabeled dataset to the second chest X-ray labeled dataset can be tested with changing the second dataset by adding other labels to judge the suitability of the self-supervised learning even if in the fine-tuning level, the network has not seen the labels of the pretraining level.

References

1. Chen, T., Kornblith, S., Norouzi, M., Hinton, G.: A simple framework for contrastive learning of visual representations. In: International Conference on Machine Learning (2020)
2. Chen, T., Kornblith, S., Swersky, K., Norouzi, M., Hinton, G.: Big self-supervised models are strong semi-supervised learners. In: 34th Conference on Neural Information Processing Systems (NeurIPS 2020) (2020)
3. Dosovitskiy, A., Springenberg, J.T., Riedmiller, M., Brox, T.: Discriminative unsupervised feature learning with convolutional neural networks. In: Advances in Neural Information Processing Systems, pp. 766–774 (2014)
4. Xie, Y., Xu, Z., Zhang, J., Wang, Z., Ji, S.: Self-supervised learning of graph neural networks: a unified review. arXiv preprint arXiv:2102.10757 (2021)
5. Hénaff, O.J., Razavi, A., Doersch, C., Eslami, S.M., van den Oord, A.: Data-efficient image recognition with contrastive predictive coding. arXiv preprint arXiv:1905.09272 (2019)

6. Güldenring, R., Nalpantidis, L.: Self-supervised contrastive learning on agricultural images. In: Computers and Electronics in Agriculture (2021). https://doi.org/10.1016/j.compag.2021.106510

7. He, K., Fan, H., Wu, Y., Xie, S., Girshick, R.: Momentum contrast for unsupervised visual representation learning. arXiv preprint arXiv:1911.05722 (2019)

8. Wu, Z., Xiong, Y., Yu, S.X., Lin, D.: Unsupervised feature learning via non parametric instance discrimination. In: Proceedings of the IEEE Conference on Computer Vision and Pattern Recognition, pp. 3733–3742 (2018)

9. Lakoju, M., Ajienka, N., Ahmadieh Khanesar, M., Burnap, P., Branson, D.T.: unsupervised learning for product use activity recognition an exploratory study of a "chatty device". In: MDPI (2021). https://doi.org/10.3390/s21154991

10. Gidaris, S., Singh, P., Komodakis, N.: Unsupervised representation learning by predicting image rotations. In: ICLR 2018 (2018)

11. Sriram, A., et al.: Covid-19 prognosis via self-supervised representation learning and multi-image prediction. arXiv preprint arXiv:2101.04909 (2021)

12. Bradski, G.: The OpenCV library. Dr. Dobb's J. Softw. Tools **25**, 120–123 (2000)

13. King, B., Barve, S., Ford, A., Jha, R.: Unsupervised clustering of COVID-19 chest X-ray images with a self-organizing feature map. IEEE (2020)

14. Lu, M.Y., Chen, R.J., Mahmood, F.: Semi-supervised breast cancer histology classification using deep multiple instance learning and contrast predictive coding (conference presentation). In: Medical Imaging 2020: Digital Pathology, vol. 11320 (2020). https://doi.org/10.1117/12.2549627

15. Feng, Z., Xu, C., Tao, D.: Self-supervised representation learning by rotation feature decoupling. In: 2019 IEEE/CVF Conference on Computer Vision and Pattern Recognition (CVPR) (2019). https://doi.org/10.1109/CVPR.2019.01061

16. Li, T., Wang, Z., Liu, S., Lin, W.-Y.: Deep unsupervised anomaly detection. In: CVF, pp. 3636–3645 (2021)

17. Inyang, U.G., Umoh, U.A., Nnaemeka, I.C., Robinson, S.A.: Unsupervised characterization and visualization of students' academic performance features. Comput. Inf. Sci. **12**(2), 103–116 (2019)

18. Lee, H.-Y., Huang, J.-B., Singh, M., Yang, M.-H.: Unsupervised Representation Learning by Sorting Sequences (2017)

19. Fernando, B., Bilen, H., Gavves, E., Gould, S.: Self-supervised video representation learning with odd-one-out networks. In: CVPR (2017)

20. Wang, Y., Zhang, J., Kan, M., Shan, S., Chen, X.: Self-supervised equivariant attention mechanism for weakly supervised semantic segmentation. In: Proceedings of the IEEE Conference on Computer Vision and Pattern Recognition (CVPR), pp. 12272–12281 (2020)

21. van den Oord, A., Li, Y., Vinyals, O.: Representation learning with contrastive predictive coding. arXiv preprint arXiv:1807.03748 (2018)

22. Ma, J., et al.: Toward data-efficient learning: a benchmark for COVID-19 CT lung and infection segmentation. Med. Phys. **48**, 1197–1210 (2021)

23. Rajpurkar, P., et al.: CheXNet: radiologist-level pneumonia detection on chest X-rays with deep learning. arXiv preprint arXiv:1711.05225v3 (2017)

24. Xu, S., Wu, H., Bie, R.: CXNet-m1: anomaly detection on chest X-rays with image-based deep learning. IEEE Access **7**, 4466–4477 (2019)

25. Doersch, C., Gupta, A., Efros, A.A.: Unsupervised visual representation learning by context prediction. In: Proceedings of the IEEE International Conference on Computer Vision, pp. 1422–1430 (2015)

26. Bachman, P., Hjelm, R.D., Buchwalter, W.: Learning representations by maximizing mutual information across views. In: Advances in Neural Information Processing Systems, pp. 15509–15519 (2019)

27. Asano, Y.M., Rupprecht, C., Vedaldi, A.: A critical analysis of self-supervision, or what we can learn from a single image. arXiv preprint arXiv:1904.13132 (2019)

28. Oh, Y., Park, S., Ye, J.C.: Deep learning COVID-19 features on CXR using limited training data sets. IEEE (2020)

29. Shahinfar, S., Meek, P., Falzon, G.: "How many images do I need?" Understanding how sample size per class affects deep learning model performance metrics for balanced designs in autonomous wildlife monitoring. EcolInform. **57**, 101085 (2020)

30. Tian, Y., Sun, C., Poole, B., Krishnan, D., Schmid, C., Isola, P.: What makes for good views for contrastive learning. arXiv preprint arXiv:2005.10243 (2020)

31. Irvin, J., et al.: CheXpert: a large chest radiograph dataset with uncertainty labels and expert comparison. In: Proceedings of the AAAI Conference on Artificial Intelligence, vol. 33, pp. 590–597 (2019)

32. Azizi, S., et al.: Big self-supervised models advance medical image classification. arXiv preprint arXiv:2101.05224 (2021)

33. Sowrirajan, H., Yang, J., Ng, A.Y., Rajpurkar, P.: MoCo-CXR: MoCo pretraining improves representation and transferability of chest X-ray models. arXiv preprint arXiv:2010.05352 (2020)

Data Mining

Deep Learning-Based Segmentation of Connected Components in Arabic Handwritten Documents

Takwa Ben Aïcha Gader$^{(\boxtimes)}$ and Afef Kacem Echi

ENSIT-LaTICE, University of Tunis, Tunis, Tunisia
`takwa.ben.aichaa@gmail.com` , `afef.kacem@ensit.u-tunis.tn`

Abstract. This work proposes a practical and powerful segmentation approach that allows touching or overlapping characters in adjacent text lines or words within Arabic manuscripts to be segmented correctly. It is the first deep learning-based method proposed to solve this problem. It is based on a modified U-Net named AR2U-net: an Attention-based Recurrent Residual U-net model trained to separate touching characters. It is trained on the LTP (Local Touching Patches) database to segment touching characters in a pixel-wise classification. The network labels pixels of the touching characters' images in four classes: pixels of background, pixels of the first character, pixels of the second character, and those where characters touch. Once the segmentation is done, the separation of touching text lines or words can be done efficiently and speedily. We also propose a post-treatment to segment successive touching text lines in this work. Experimental results on the LTP database show that our proposed method is practical in copes with touching and overlapped characters separation. It achieves higher accuracy of 94.6% than those reported in the state-of-the-art.

Keywords: Handwritten characters · Touching characters · Deep learning · Segmentation · Attention mechanism

1 Introduction

Text line/word segmentation has been a crucial and challenging step in many document analysis and recognition tasks such as skew detection, layout analysis, and word recognition. In the printed text, text line segmentation can be considered easier than handwriting due to the writing's uniformity, the nonexistence of touching characters, font size, etc.). Still, it is quite tricky in the handwritten text due to character size variations, the non-uniform spacing between words and text lines, the overlapping and touching of characters, and the different writing styles. Poor text line/word segmentation leads to wrong results in the recognition step. Although to date, there have been made several attempts of achieving correct text segmentation results, there are still many difficulties. Methods previously proposed for machine-printed text lines segmentation do not adapt well to handwritten texts.

© Springer Nature Switzerland AG 2022
A. Bennour et al. (Eds.): ISPR 2022, CCIS 1589, pp. 93–106, 2022.
https://doi.org/10.1007/978-3-031-08277-1_8

Touching Characters (TCs) are connection zones between adjacent text lines, words of the same text line, or even between letters of the same word. These connection zones are a real problem that makes unconstrained handwritten text segmentation exceptionally challenging. They frequently appear in Arabic manuscripts (see Fig. 1) where 21 characters from 28 are ascendant or descendant and include special dots and marks, and the calligraphy is of big jambs. Note also that these TCs generally happens when inter-lines spacing is narrow.

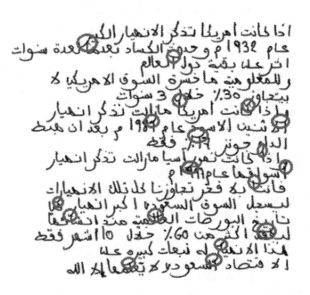

Fig. 1. Example of Arabic handwriting with overlapped and touching characters.

TCs can be due to the simple touching of just two characters, as shown in Fig. 2(a), (e)). They can be multi-touching if more than two characters touch each other (see Fig. 2(b)). Characters can also be found overlapped depending on writing style and organization; close characters or characters with long strokes may also overlap with their neighbors (see Fig. 2(c), (d)).

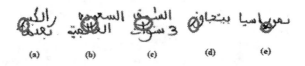

(a) (b) (c) (d) (e)

Fig. 2. (a) Simple touching, (b) Multi-touching, (c) Overlapping, (d) Connection between a word characters, (e) Connection between characters of different words.

The separation of touching components is critical as a wrong separation leads to incorrect segmentation and bad recognition. Many proposed approaches for separating connected components are based on component features analysis and structural information. Other methods are recognition-based ones. These methods are robust against the non-uniformity of connected components, but they succeed only if the correct segmentation exists in the dictionary or the candidate set. We propose a robust and unsupervised deep learning-based TC segmentation approach in this work. It is writer-independent, script-independent, and can cope with skew and warping disturb. It is based on a modified U-Net named AR2U-net: an Attention-based Recurrent Residual U-net model trained to separate touching characters. The model was first used in [15] to perform handwritten Arabic text lines segmentation and achieved a remarkable result. It is trained to perform a pixel-wise classification to separate touching and overlapped characters' pixels in our work. We tested the model on the LTP database: the only public database used for the touching Arabic handwritten letter segmentation task. Most state-of-the-art works were tested on private datasets where images of touching characters are extracted from public datasets such as Khatt, INF/ENIT, AHDB, IBN SINA, etc. We also propose here a post-treatment for adjacent touching text lines separation.

The rest of the paper is structured as follows. Some related works review is presented in Sect. 2. The proposed AR2U-net model for touching and overlapping handwritten Arabic characters separation is described in Sect. 3. Afterward, some experimental results are discussed. In Sect. 4, some conclusions and prospects are finally given.

2   Related Works

TC segmentation approaches are either Recognition-free or recognition-based ones. The first approach uses projection profile analysis, skeletons, contours, and the TCs structural information. Therefore, a TC can be split into fragments by rules without recognition. Although this approach can strongly solve some problems, it may not be sufficiently robust to deal with multiple variations or uncertainties. The recognition-based approach provides numerous possible segmentation hypotheses and chooses the best based on recognition or alternative evaluation functions. Nevertheless, this approach succeeds just if the optimal segmentation already exists in the provided candidates. Table 1 summarizes some state-of-the-art methods divided into recognition-free and recognition-based ones.

3   Proposed Use of AR2U-Net

To segment TCs, we used a deep-learning-based architecture: an AR2U-net trained to perform pixel-wise labeling to differentiate between TCs pixels and the background ones.

Table 1. Some of the state of the Art methods of TCs segmentation.

	Ref	Year	Used concept	Script	Results
Recognition free approaches	[16]	2019	Overlapping set theory	Arabic	97.27%
	[6]	2012	Contour based shape decomposition	Arabic	28%
	[9]	2011	Convex hull	Arabic	–
	[1]	2011	Contour tracing	–	28%
	[8]	2010	Classification using affinity propagation	Arabic	71.4%
	[12]	2009	Angular variation	Arabic	Avg. 94%
	[17]	2009	Block Covering	Arabic	96.6%
	[12]	2009	Morphology analysis	Arabic	96.88%
Recognition based approaches	[5]	2011	Dictionary, Shape context and TPS transformation	Arabic	70%
	[13]	1994	Dictionary and decision tree	–	90%

3.1   AR2U-Net Architecture

AR2U-net is a modified U-net. This latter is built upon the Fully Connected Network (FCN) and adjusted to yield better results in the image segmentation task. The U-net architecture is symmetric, and the skip connections between the down-sampling path and the up-sampling path apply the concatenation operator. While up-sampling, these skip connections deliver local information to the global ones. The U-net symmetry offers the model the possibility of having many feature maps in the up-sampling path, which permits information transferring. The U-net's spatial dimensions in each hierarchy space are the same for a schematic presentation of a U-net. Therefore, the U-net output is a feature map (Z features) having the same spatial dimension as the input. It is an Attention-based R2U-net. It is set up to improve the training and the testing steps using a Residual unit (R), which aids when training deep architecture and Recurrent (R) convolutional layers for features collection, allowing improved feature representation for segmentation problems. R2U-net was used for the first time in [2] to segment medical images. Here, we added an Attention mechanism to enhance the model's performance allowing searching in particular images areas as a human does; when looking for a precise pattern, it orients itself to specific regions of an image. Following are the fundamental concepts of the AR2U-net model.

1. **Recurrent Convolutional Unit**
   Basic U-net is typically a feed-forward architecture (see Fig. 4(a) in [2]). At first, a U-net extension is proposed by incorporating Recurrent connections into each convolutional layer to have an RU-net. The added layers allow

feature accumulation inside the model and, therefore, a better features representation (see Fig. 4(b) in [2]). Though the input is static, recurrent convolutional units' activities evolve so that their neighboring units' activities modulate each unit's activity. This property performs very low-level features extraction and context information integrity which is required for segmentation tasks. As shown in Fig. 3, the recurrent convolutional operation includes one convolution layer in the used AR2U-net model.

2. **Residual Convolutional Unit**

   Deep residual networks (Res-net) use residual blocs for two main reasons: to avoid vanishing gradients or decrease the degradation (accuracy saturation) problem. They do this by using skip connections or shortcuts to jump over some layers (see Fig. 4(c) in [2]). Residual connections are added to a model to perform practical training. The model is split into slighter and simpler ones joined by shortcuts, allowing simple identity propagation and error back-propagation. Figure 4(b) in [2] shows the Recurrent Residual convolutional units.

3. **Attention Mechanism**

   To cope with the variety of writing styles, we used a pixel-wise spatial Attention mechanism. It permits selective visual information, concentrating on the image content at various positions and scales. Recall that the initial U-net employs de-convolution to up-sample the feature maps. In AR2U-net, a bilinear up-sampling technique is applied as done by [14]. This technique helps in extracting crucial information from high-level and low-level features maps. After each convolution layer, high-level features are up-sampled and concatenated with the low-level features. More precisely, the encoder convolves and down-samples the input to create various scales feature maps. Each of these features maps will be concatenated with the features maps of its respective layers in the decoder. The relevant features are extracted from the concatenated result. Such a mechanism quickly improves the model's sensitivity and accuracy for labeling problems by neglecting feature activations in unessential regions.

As displayed in Fig. 3, AR2U-net, like the initial U-net, consists of convolutional encoding and decoding units. Nevertheless, the RCLs, with residual blocs, are operated rather than traditional forward convolutional layers. The residual unit with RCLs holds the benefit of getting an effective deep model. Note that the basic U-net allows a better convergence during the training step. However, the AR2U-net is efficient in both train and test phases. This effectiveness is due to the helpful feature accumulation in the RCL units of the model. Thus, AR2U-net became capable of selecting very low-level features crucial for TC segmentation. Unlike the U-net model, the AR2U-net has an asymmetrical architecture. The basic U-net operates a de-convolution for features maps' up-sampling in the decoder part, whereas the AR2U-net operates a bi-linear up-sampling. Furthermore, we changed the cropping and copying unit in the U-net model by a concatenation function, which enhanced the model's performance. The model

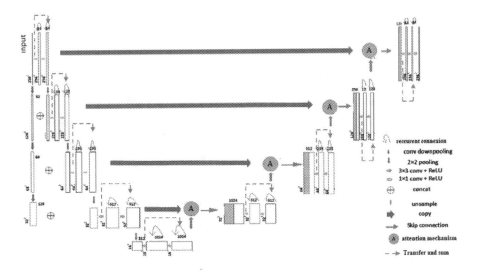

Fig. 3. The used AR2U-net's architecture [15].

takes as input an image of a Local Touching Patch (LTP) and returns the corresponding labeled image (with a different color for each component). An LTP is the localized bitmap including the touching strokes and usually covers part of connected components shared by two characters [5] (see Fig. 4 for an example).

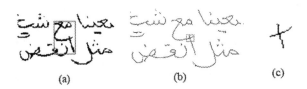

Fig. 4. (a) presents an example of detected touching letters and (b) and (c) present its corresponding LTP.

3.2 Post-processing

To well exploit the result of the model's inference, we propose post-processing. It is a simple method to segment successive touching text lines, which consists of three steps:

1. Text lines' baselines detection.
2. Using algorithm 1 for text line border detection.
3. Applying algorithm 2 for text line extraction and touching characters segmentation.

In Fig. 5, we display the result of a handwritten Arabic text image post-processing where (a) is the Arabic handwritten text image, (b) is the detected TC, its labeled image generated by the AR2U-net model, and its correct segmentation, and from (c) to (f) are the segmented text lines. Hereafter are the definition of the abbreviations in the first and the second algorithms.

- lb, lb_c, lb_1 and lb_n be respectively the baselines positions vector composed of baselines pixels represented by an (x, y) form, the current baseline, the first baseline and the last baseline of the text image.
- I_m: is the text image result of AR2U-net (touching characters segmented with colors).
- w_{I_m} and h_{I_m} are, respectively, the width and height of image I_m.
- I_{mask}: the mask image, which has the same shape as the input image. It is a black image with touching characters pixels represented by white color.

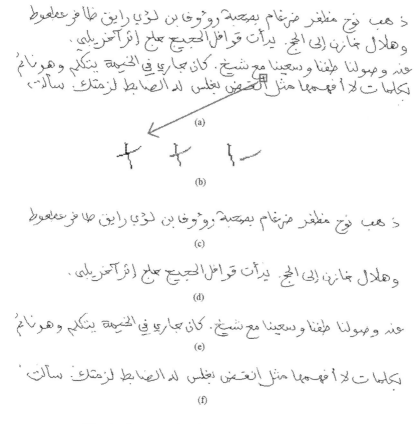

Fig. 5. An example of the post-processing result.

Algorithm 1. Text-line Borders

Require: $I_m, lb, w_{I_m}, h_{I_m}$
Ensure: Pos: the text-lines cut positions in the input image.
```
1:  Pos ← φ
2:  for each lb_c ∈ lb do
3:      cut ← φ                    the positions of interline cuts
4:      for each i ∈ [1..w_{I_m}] do
5:          Add(cut,1)             Initialization for the first text line
6:      end for
7:      if lb_c ≠ lb_n then
8:          P ← 1
9:          y_s ← min(lb_c[1][2], lb_{c+1}[1][2])          start of baseline
10:         y_e ← max(lb_c[length(lb_c)][2], lb_{c+1}[length(lb_{c+1})][2])      end of baseline
11:         for each y ∈ [y_s..y_e] do
12:             x_1 ← lb_c[1]
13:             x_2 ← lb_{c+1}[1]
14:             p_1 ← x_1
15:             p_2 ← x_2
16:             get the last black pixels of l_c and the first black pixels of l_{c+1} in column y
17:             while x_1 < x_2 do
18:                 if x_1 is a black pixel
19:                     if x_1 = 0 then
20:                         p_1 ← x_1
21:                     end if
22:                     if x_2 = 0 then
23:                         p_2 ← x_2
24:                     end if
25:                 x_1 ← x_1 + 1
26:                 x_2 ← x_2 − 1
27:             end while
28:             If the current baseline does not start from the first column, we add cut positions
                to the cut vector
29:             if p=1 then
30:                 for j ∈ [1..lb_c[1][2]] do
31:                     Add(cut, (int)(p_2 + p_1)/2)
32:                 end for
33:             end if
34:         end for
35:         If the current baseline ends before the last column, we add cut positions to the cut
            vector
36:         if p < w_i then
37:             for j ∈ [pos..w_{I_m}] do
38:                 Add(cut, (int)((p_2 + p_1)/2))
39:             end for
40:         end if
41:         Add(Pos , p)
42:         p ← p + 1
43:     else
44:         for j ∈ [1..w_{I_m}] do
45:             Add(cut, h_{I_m})
46:         end for
47:     end if
48:     Add(Pos, p);
49: end for
```

Algorithm 2. Text-line Segmentation

Require: $I_m, I_{mask}, lb, Pos, w_{I_m}, h_{I_m}$
Ensure: NULL
1: **for** $i \in [2..length(Pos)]$ **do**
2:     there are no touching characters in the current text line
3:     $w_I \leftarrow w_{I_m}$
4:     $h_I \leftarrow \max_{j \in [1..length(Pos(i))]}(Pos(i)[j] - Pos(i-1)[j])$
5:     $I_c \leftarrow \mathbf{Zeros}(h_I, w_I) + 255$ current text-line image
6:     **if** $\forall I_{mask} : pixel \in [Pos(i)..Pos(i-1)], \exists! pixel = 1$ **then**
7:         The midpoint (x: position) of the image part to copy to I_c
8:         $abs \leftarrow Position_x(\max_{j \in [1..length(Pos(i))]}(Pos(i)[j] - Pos(i-1)[j]))$
9:         **for** $l \in [1..h_{I_m}]$ **do**
10:             **for** $k \in [Pos(i)[l]..abs]$ **do**
11:                 $I_c(k,l) \leftarrow I_m(k,l)$
12:             **end for**
13:             **for** $k \in [abs..Pos(i+1)[l]]$ **do**
14:                 $I_c(k,l) \leftarrow I_m(k,l)$
15:             **end for**
16:             **imshow**(I_c)
17:         **end for**
18:     **else**
19:         there are touching characters in the current text line
20:         $h_{I+1} \leftarrow \max_{j \in [1..length(Pos(i))]}(Pos(i+1)[j] - Pos(i)[j])$
21:         $I_c \leftarrow \mathbf{Zeros}(h_{I+1}, w_I) + 255$ next text line image
22:         $i \leftarrow i + 1$
23:         $abs \leftarrow Position_x(\max_{j \in [1..length(Pos(i))]}(Pos(i)[j] - Pos(i-1)[j]))$
24:         $abs_{+1} \leftarrow Position_x(\max_{j \in [1..length(Pos(i))]}(Pos(i+1)[j] - Pos(i)[j]))$
25:         **for** $k \in [1..h_I]$ **do**
26:             **for** $m \in [Pos(i)[k]..abs]$ **do**
27:                 green or blue pixels
28:                 **if** $I_m(m,k) = [0, 255, 0]$ OR $I_m(m,k) = [0, 0, 255]$ **then**
29:                     $I_c(m,k) \leftarrow I_m(m,k)$
30:                 **end if**
31:             **end for**
32:         **end for**
33:         **for** $k \in [1..h_{I+1}]$ **do**
34:             **for** $m \in [Pos(i+1)[k]..abs_{+1}]$ **do**
35:                 green or red pixels
36:                 **if** $I_m(m,k) = [0, 255, 0]$ OR $I_m(m,k) = [255, 0, 0]$ **then**
37:                     $I_{c+1}(m,k) \leftarrow I_m(m,k)$
38:                 **end if**
39:             **end for**
40:         **end for**
41:         **imshow**(I_c)
42:         **imshow**(I_{c+1})
43:     **end if**
44: **end for**

---

4   Experimental Results and Discussion

4.1   The Used Database

To test the AR2U-net model for TCs segmentation, we used the LTP database [5]. It is a public database of touching and overlapped handwritten Arabic letters and their ground truth. On 250 pages of handwritten Arabic documents, authors reduced the spacing between text lines to create a touching and obtained LTPs with ground truths (isolated components forming the given LTP). The touching letters images are binary, white pixels belong to the touching characters, and the black ones present the background. The images of ground truth comprise four classes: 1) white for the background, 2) blue for the first character, 3) red for the second character, and 4) green for touching zone. The database contains 1488 images: 744 for training (where 20% were dedicated for validation) and 744 for testing. These images are either inter-word or inter-lines TCs. Figure 6 shows an example of an LTP and its ground truth from the LTP database.

(a)   (b)   (c)

Fig. 6. (a), (b) an image and its ground truth extracted from the LTP database and (c) its correct segmentation.

4.2   AR2U-Net Training

Experiments are done on a Hp Z-440 workstation. The model was trained for 100 epochs, using a learning rate of 10^{-6} and the Adam Optimizer [7]. We operated the classification loss and accuracy metrics for the model training evaluation. All parameters settings are illustrated in Table 2. While training, the best model was saved based on an evaluation process done on a resistant validation dataset independent of the training data set. The training and validation curves are shown in Fig. 7. And Fig. 8 illustrates a model inference example.

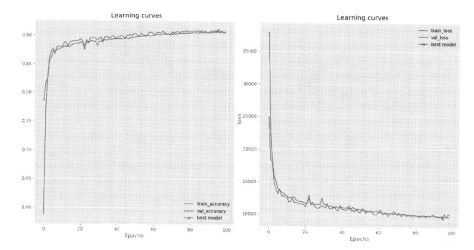

Fig. 7. Accuracy and Loss validation curves.

Table 2. Parameter settings.

Pre-processing	1488 touching characters: 744 for training (20% for validation) and 744 for testing. Images of 120 × 120 pixels. No additional treatment
Training setting	Initial weights: 0.01 for the 4 classes. Initial learning rate: 10^{-6}, Optimizer: Adam, epochs: 100, Batch-size per epoch: 128, Evaluation metrics: Accuracy and Loss

4.3 Analysis

Define Accuracy as the ratio of correctly segmented LTPs among all testing LTPs. We tested the proposed segmentation method on the test dataset composed of 744 images with a shape of 120 × 120 and used Accuracy as an evaluation metric. This section presents the results of the experiments conducted to prove the performance of the proposed deep learning-based approach with an accuracy of 94.6%. Table 3 offers a comparison of the proposed system with state-of-the-art methods.

In Fig. 8, examples of the trained AR2U-net model inference are given where (a) present the TCs images fed to the model, (b) are labeled images resulting from the model, (c) presents ground truths, and (d) are correct segmentation of input TCs (Fig. 9).

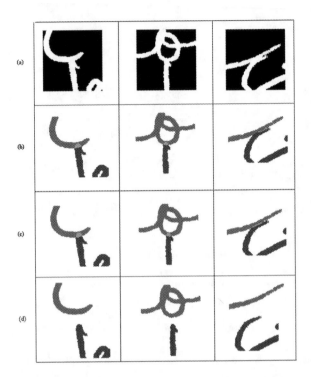

Fig. 8. Examples of segmentation: green areas are shared by both blue and red components where: (a) Images from the test database, (b) Segmentation results, (c) Ground truths and (d) separated TCs. (Color figure online)

Fig. 9. Samples of our results.

Table 3. Analysis.

Method		Database	Total used images	Accuracy	
[3]		TCs images extracted from INF/ENIT	620 for inter lignes and 220 for inter words	Inter-lines	Inter-words
				0.94	0.95
[12]		TCs images extracted from 100 private documents	640	0.968	
[16]		TCs images extracted from AHDB and other datasets	220	0.972	
[11]		TCs images extracted from Tunisian National Archives and from LTP dataset	–	0.867	
Full-dictionary [5]	SC+TPS [4]	LTP dataset	744 for training and 744 for testing	0.696	
	IDSS+DP [10]	LTP dataset	744 for training and 744 for testing	0.563	
Exemplar-only dictionary [5]	SC+TPS [4]	LTP dataset	744 for training and 744 for testing	0.714	
	IDSS+DP [10]	LTP dataset	744 for training and 744 for testing	0.555	
Our method		**LTP dataset**	**744 for training and 744 for testing**	0.946	

5   Conclusion and Prospects

In this work, we proposed a novel deep learning segmentation method for touching connected components separation in unconstrained Arabic handwritten text. This approach is applicable for connections between successive text lines and between text line words. The used deep architecture model is an AR2U-net trained on the LTP dataset and achieved an accuracy of 0.946%. The proposed method is robust and efficient since it is based neither on morphological analysis nor on previously constructed dictionaries. It takes an image of a TC as input, and it returns an image where each pixel is classified into one of the four classes: background, the first character, the second character, and the parts where the characters touch. Results are encouraging. To improve them, we intend to strengthen the training dataset so that the model can segment the multi-touching characters.

References

1. Alaei, A., Pal, U., Nagabhushan, P.N.: A new scheme for unconstrained handwritten text-line segmentation. Pattern Recogn. **44**(04), 917–928 (2011)
2. Alom, M.Z., Hasan, M., Yakopcic, C., Taha, T., Asari, V.: Recurrent residual convolutional neural network based on U-net (R2U-net) for medical image segmentation (2018)

3. Aouadi, N., Kacem, A.: A proposal for touching component segmentation in Arabic manuscripts. Pattern Anal. Appl. **20**, 1–23 (2017)
4. Belongie, S.J., Malik, J., Puzicha, J.: Shape matching and object recognition using shape contexts. TPAMI **24**(04), 509–522 (2002)
5. Kang, L., Doermann, D.: Template based segmentation of touching components in handwritten text lines, pp. 569–573 (2011)
6. Kang, L., Doermann, D.S., Cao, H., Prasad, R., Natarajan, P.: Local segmentation of touching characters using contour based shape decomposition. In: 2012 10th IAPR International Workshop on Document Analysis Systems, pp. 460–464 (2012)
7. Kingma, D.P., Ba, J.: Adam: a method for stochastic optimization. In: Bengio, Y., LeCun, Y. (eds.) 3rd International Conference on Learning Representations, ICLR 2015, San Diego, CA, USA, 7–9 May 2015, Conference Track Proceedings (2015)
8. Kumar, J., Abd-Almageed, W., Kang, L., Doermann, D.S.: Handwritten Arabic text line segmentation using affinity propagation. In: DAS 2010, pp. 135–142 (2010)
9. Kumar, J., Kang, L., Doermann, D., Abd-Almageed, W.: Segmentation of handwritten textlines in presence of touching components. In: 2011 International Conference on Document Analysis and Recognition, pp. 109–113 (2011)
10. Ling, H., Jacobs, D.W.: Shape classification using the inner-distance. IEEE Trans. Pattern Anal. Mach. Intell. **29**(02), 286–299 (2007)
11. Amiri, S., Aouadi, N., Echi, A.K.: Segmentation of connected components in Arabic handwritten document. In: International Conference on Computational Intelligence: Modeling Techniques and Applications (CIMTA), vol. 10, pp. 738–746 (2013)
12. Ouwayed, N., Belaïd, A.: Separation of overlapping and touching lines within handwritten Arabic documents. In: Jiang, X., Petkov, N. (eds.) CAIP 2009. LNCS, vol. 5702, pp. 237–244. Springer, Heidelberg (2009). https://doi.org/10.1007/978-3-642-03767-2_29
13. Piquin, P., Viard-Gaudin, C., Barba, D.: Coopration des outils de segmentation et de binarisation de documents. Olloque National sur l'Ecrit et le Document, pp. 283–292 (1994)
14. Sun, H., et al.: AUnet: attention-guided dense-upsampling networks for breast mass segmentation in whole mammograms. Phys. Med. Biol. **65**, 055005 (2019)
15. Aïcha, B., Takwa, G., Echi, A.K.: Unconstrained handwritten Arabic text-lines segmentation based on AR2U-net. In: 2020 17th International Conference on Frontiers in Handwriting Recognition (ICFHR), pp. 349–354 (2020)
16. Ullah, I., Azmi, M.S., Desa, M.I., Alomari, Y.M.: Segmentation of touching Arabic characters in handwritten documents by overlapping set theory and contour tracing. Int. J. Adv. Comput. Sci. Appl. **10**(5), 155–160 (2019)
17. Zahour, A., Taconet, B., Likforman-Sulem, L., Boussellaa, W.: Overlapping and multi-touching text-line segmentation by block covering analysis. Pattern Anal. Appl. **12**, 335–351 (2008)

Classifying the Human Activities of Sensor Data Using Deep Neural Network

Hussein A. A. Al-Khamees[✉][ID], Nabeel Al-A'araji[ID],
and Eman S. Al-Shamery[ID]

Babylon University, Babylon - Hilla, Iraq
Hussein.alkhamees7@gmail.com,
{nhkaghed,emanalshamery}@itnet.uobabylon.edu.iq

Abstract. Today sensors represent one of the most important applications for generating data stream. This data has a number of unique characteristics, including fast data access, huge volume, as well as the most prominent feature, the concept drift. Machine learning in general and deep learning technique in particular is among the predominant and successful selections to classify the human activities. This is due to several reasons such as results quality and processing time. The recognition of human activities that produced from sensors considers is an effective and vital task in the healthcare field, meanwhile, it is an attractive to researchers. This paper presents a DNN model to classify the human activities of the HuGaDB sensor dataset by implementing multilayer perceptron (MLP) structure. The current model achieved results, 91.7% of accuracy, 92.5% precision, 92.0% recall, and 92.0% of F1-score, using a tiny time. The model results were compared with the previous models and it has proven its efficiency by outperforming those models.

Keywords: Deep neural network · MultiLayer Perceptron (MLP) · Human activities classification · Sensor data stream · HuGaDB dataset

1 Introduction

Many real-world applications in different domains can generate a massive amount of data; It is known as a data stream which has various unique properties that traditional data do not have. Some of these characteristics are unlimited data size, fast-access data from the source, limited memory, processing time and the evolving in its nature this causes the concept drift [1]. Most traditional data algorithms fail when dealing with a data stream, this is due to newly characteristics of the data stream [2].

Machine learning is a sub-field of Artificial Intelligence (AI). In reality, machine learning consists of many techniques that can be used on data stream

Supported by Babylon University.

such as classification, clustering, regression, ..., etc. [3]. Despite these techniques, neural networks (NN) are just as important as those techniques and that can be also implemented on the data stream. Neural networks have two types, shallow or deep. Recently, deep learning techniques that use deep neural networks (DNN) are a major area of interest and increasingly being applied [4]. Therefore, DNN is applied in various fields such as healthcare [5].

Deep learning depends mainly on Artificial Neural Networks (ANN), which are originally inspired by neurons in the human brain [6]. However, the DNNs structure involves three layers (input, hidden and output), where every layer has several neurons and the neuron numbers differ from a layer to another [4]. Multilayer Perceptron (MLP) is an important and widely used architectural type of deep learning [7].

The recognition task of human activities that produced from sensors considers is an effective and vital task in the healthcare field. Indeed, the recognition models are either wearable or external sensor-based models [8].

This paper presents a deep learning model based on MLP and the backpropagation algorithm to train MLP for classifying the human activities. This model consists of four hidden layers that able to implement the classification task in a short period of time. For evaluating the proposed model, the HuGaBD sensor dataset was used. More specifically, five sub-datasets of the main HuGaDB dataset were selected for the current model.

The proposed model achieved results as follow, 91.7% of accuracy, 92.5% precision, 92.0% recall, and 92.0 % of F1-score, using a tiny time. Accordingly, this model outperforms many previous models that used the same dataset (HuGaDB dataset) to classify the human activities. Furthermore, our evaluation demonstrates how this DNN model proved the enhancing of results by implementing it into different numbers of both hidden layers and also neurons for every hidden layer.

The current paper organizes as follows. Section 2 discusses related works which related to deep neural network that implemented on HuGaDB dataset. Section 3 explains the DNN structure. The methodology of the proposed model is presented in Sect. 4. While dataset description is introduces in Sect. 5. Section 6 illustrates the evaluation metrics and Sect. 7 dedicates to the results of the model and finally, the conclusion of the current paper summarizes.

2   Related Work

This section covers the studies based on NNs as a machine learning technique that applied to the HuGaDB dataset to classify the human activities.

In [9], the authors presented model aims to classify different activities of the human. The model depended on ANN to estimate many parameters such as IMUs displacements, velocity, and angle. The study focuses on three body area that are shin, thigh and waist that resulted in accurate results of the lower limbs of the human body. Moreover, the proposed model aims to solve an important issue, which is the contradictions that occur (while capturing the motion signal) to the movements of body parts such as the hand and the leg. In general, the model consists of two phases that are training and application. In the first phase, the ANN is trained to estimate the received signals while in the second phase, the ANN that was trained is implemented to estimate the signals related to the lower extremities (during real time). This model achieved an accuracy of 88.0%.

According to [10], the authors applied feature vector length reduction and how it affects deep learning networks besides other techniques of machine learning. The key idea behind the model is to apply Long Short-term Memory (LSTM) as a deep learning classifier to extract different high dimensional features. The model has several phases which are data pre-processing, feature extraction, feature selection, training and finally the testing phase. The proposed model attained an accuracy of 91.1%.

B. Fang et al. [11] suggested a gait neural network (GNN) model which depended on a temporal convolutional neural network. The model aims to predict a human activity in the lower limbs. In general, the structure of the proposed model consists of gait prediction and gait recognition where it focuses on the gait data that received from the right leg. The accuracy achieved by the model based on GNN is 79.24%, which is considered the highest accuracy among the techniques used in the same study.

3   DNN Structure

The DNN structure consists of three layer types that are, input layer, hidden layers and output layer. The data are received from the external source through the input layer, therefore there isn't any processing (computations). Most of the processing steps that implemented in the hidden layers are nonlinear computations, whereas the processing in the output layer either linear or nonlinear [12]. The nonlinear transforming which starts from the input to the hidden layers till the output layer, is called as the forward propagation.

The number of hidden layers and the number of neurons in each layer has an effective effect on the final results of the deep neural network model. Therefore, it must be carefully selected (after testing) [13].

Each layer contains several neurons, take into consideration that the neuron number are differs from a layer to another. In a specific layer, every neuron is connected to their counterparts in adjacent layers. This connection can be indicated by weights which reflecting both strength and direction. Every neuron can transform data through computation of weighted sum (of the output neurons in past layer) and then passes it by a nonlinear function (activation functions) for deriving the neuron outputs [14].

3.1   Multilayer Perceptron (MLP)

It's a feed-forward neural network with multi hidden layers. MLP doesn't require any prior assumptions about the distribution of data. In MLP, the neurons are connected by weights and also the signals of output that represented as a function of the sum of the inputs to the neuron modified by an activation function [15].

3.2   MLP Training

Usually, the training of the deep neural network is more difficult and complex than the classic neural network [16].

The training of DNN contains many sequential steps for adjusting the weights between the neurons in the network, in a similar way to the learning of the human brain. But before the adjustment step, the model must initialize these weights. This initialization is done randomly [17], where the resulting weights have the ability to [18]:

- Maximize the relationship strength between network input and its output.
- Minimize a difference of the neural networks (such as an error) between a specific task and its real target (i.e. between the network prediction and its associated target). Usually, a neural network technique aims to minimize this error value.

More specifically, the back propagation (BP) is the most successful and widely used algorithm for MLP training [15]. BP repeatedly can analyze the errors and optimize every value of weight depending on the errors that generated by the next layer [18]. Accordingly, this algorithm was used in the current model.

To simplify the weight computation, suppose a neural network contains (m) neuron, this neuron is driven by input vector X_n, where n indicates to the time step of the iterative process contains the adjusting step of the input weights $w_{(mi)}$. Therefore, each sample of data passes through the training step of a DNN containing $X_{(n)}$ and its output denoting by $d_{(n)}$.

Then the processing step to $X_{(n)}$, of a neuron (m) is generating an output which is referred by $y_{m(n)}$, and computed by:

$$y_{m(n)} = f \sum_{i=1}^{j} x.w_{(mi)} \tag{1}$$

where f indicates to activation function. This output is compared with the target output $d_{m(n)}$ which normally is given in a sample. The error $e_{m(n)}$ can compute by:

$$e_{m(n)} = (d_{m(n)} - y_{m(n)}) \tag{2}$$

Because its capacity of the back propagation, it is a very appropriate method to problems that don't have any relation between the input and output [19].

4   Methodology

The proposed DNN model consists of:

1. Prepare the dataset that will be used in DNN model. In this model, HuGaDB is used.

2. Apply the data pre-processing step by implementing an appropriate technique. Normalization is a major step in most problems. The normalization technique has several methods, including the Min-max that applied to this model. Mathematically, if there is a set of matching scores (Ms) where, s = 1, 2, ..., n, the normalized scores (Ms') calculate as:

$$Ms' = (Ms - min)/(max - min) \qquad (3)$$

3. Divide the dataset into training and testing data by applying a suitable technique. In this model, the cross validation is used, 80% as a training data and 20% as a testing data.
4. Determine the number of hidden layers that required to build the MLP model. For further analysis, two and four hidden layers were applied.
5. Determine the number of neurons in each hidden layer. In the case of two hidden layers, the number of neuron is set to (10, 10, 12) while in the case of four hidden layers, the number of neuron is set to (10, 12, 14, 26, 30).
6. Determine the training algorithm. In this model, the back propagation (BP) is used for training MLP. In addition to the number of hidden layers and neurons for every layer, setting another parameters such as, (a) the weights that can be computed according to equation (1); (b)the error based on equation (2); and (c) the learning rate that set to 0.001.
7. Start the training phase using the training data (step 3) and parameters (steps 4 and 5) by the back-propagation (BP) training method (step 6).
8. Start the testing phase by using the test data (step 3). However, in this phase, the ability of the proposed model is tested if it has been trained to accurately classify data samples.
9. After completing the training and testing phases, the evaluation step is implemented, as it is the last step in this model. The model uses four different measures, namely, accuracy, precision, recall and F1-score to evaluate the current model.

Figure 1 shows the model methodology.

5   Data Set Description

Human Gait Database (HuGaDB) to activity recognition from six inertial sensor networks was presented in 2017 [20], these sensors can be shown in Fig. 2(a). HuGaDB dataset contains 12 behaviors actions which are: walking, sitting, sitting down, sitting in a car, going up, going down, standing, standing up, up by elevator, down by elevator, bicycling, and running. However, some of these actions are displayed in Fig. 2(b).

According to these behaviors actions, the dataset contains static and dynamic activities. These several activities are implemented and recorded at various times like recording the running behavior over about 20 min. Additionally, all the behaviors actions are gathered by 18 participants.

Furthermore, the main HuGaDB dataset consists of 637 data files and all of them has the same number of features that are 39 features. Also, all these files

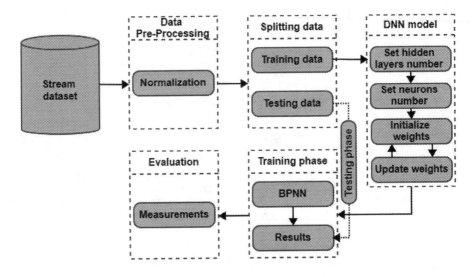

Fig. 1. Methodology of proposed DNN model.

contain the sentence (various) in their titles to indicate the various activities it contains. This dataset is a publicly available[1].

In the current model, five sub-datasets from the main HuGaDB dataset are used therefore, it 10 of the 12 activities have been covered through this study. The activities covered are all activities above except sitting in a car and bicycling. These sub-datasets are:

1. HuGaDB-v2-various-01-01: consists of 2435 records and it has four classes that are, 'sitting', 'sitting-down', 'standing', and 'standing-up'. This dataset denotes by DS1.
2. HuGaDB-v2-various-05-12: it has 4393 records and it has three classes that are, 'going-down', 'standing', and 'walking'. DS2 is the symbol of this dataset.
3. HuGaDB-v2-various-13-10: it contains 4850 records and it has three classes that are, 'down-by-elevator', 'standing', and 'up-by-elevator'. HuGaDB-v2-various-13-10 has the symbol DS3.
4. HuGaDB-v2-various-14-05: this dataset has 2392 records. Two classes for this dataset which are 'running' and 'walking' and denotes by DS4.
5. HuGaDB-v2-various-17-07: it consists of 2930 records and it has three classes that are, 'going-up', 'standing', and 'walking'. DS5 is the symbol for this dataset.

6   Evaluation Metrics

The performance of the proposed model is evaluated by four different measurements that are [10]:

---

[1] https://www.kaggle.com/romanchereshnev/hugadb-human-gait-database.

1. Accuracy (refers to the ratio of all true cases divided by the overall dataset cases).
   Accuracy = TP + TN/(TP + TN + FP + FN)
2. Precision (determine the number of true cases predictions which really belong to the true cases).
   Precision = TP/(TP + FP)
3. Recall (determines the number of true cases predictions that implemented over all true cases).
   Recall = TP/(TP + FN)
4. F1-score (indicates the harmonic mean measure to both the precision and recall).
   F1-score = $2 \times (Precision \times Recall)/(Precision + Recall)$

7   Results

The model implements with two hidden layers, four hidden layers respectively.
   Figure 2 shows the comparison of accuracy between the two implementations.

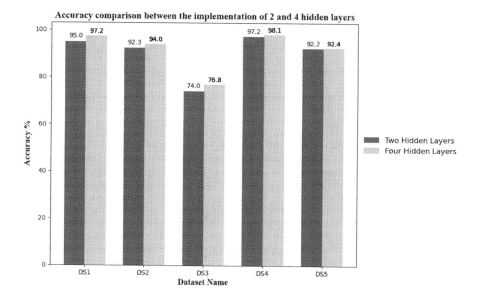

Fig. 2. The accuracy for all sub-datasets of HuGaDB dataset with two and four hidden layers.

Furthermore, Table 1 describes the measurements with two hidden layers, while these measurements with four hidden layers, detail in Table 2, and the best results are highlighted in bold font. While Figs. 3 and 4 visualize these measurement values.

Table 1. The measurements of the model (two hidden layers).

Dataset name	Accuracy	Precision	Recall	F1-score
DS1	95.0	96.3	92.5	94.4
DS2	92.3	61.5	63.2	62.3
DS3	74.0	75.9	74.0	74.9
DS4	97.2	97.7	96.4	97.0
DS5	92.4	93.8	93.9	93.8
AVE	90.1	85.0	84.0	84.4

Table 2. The measurements of the model (four hidden layers).

Dataset name	Accuracy	Precision	Recall	F1-score
DS1	97.2	97.3	96.4	96.9
DS2	94.0	95.8	96.0	95.9
DS3	76.8	78.7	77.1	77.9
DS4	98.1	98.1	97.8	97.5
DS5	92.4	92.6	92.9	91.9
AVE	**91.7**	**92.5**	**92.0**	**92.0**

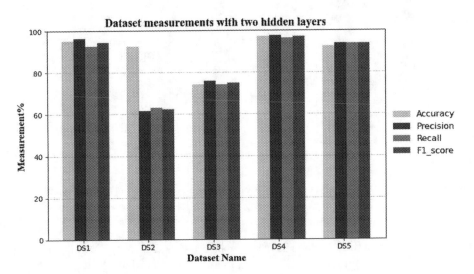

Fig. 3. The measurements of implementation with two hidden layers for every dataset.

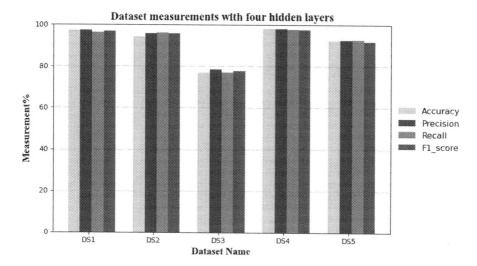

Fig. 4. The measurements of implementation with four hidden layers for every dataset.

After all these implementations, we notice that the proposed model with four hidden layers achieves higher accuracy (in all five sub-datasets) than its counterpart when implementing with two hidden layers.

In the same context, it achieves the highest results in terms of other measurements (precision, recall, and also F1-score) as shown in Table 2 and Fig. 4.

In fact, the overall accuracy of the proposed model is 91.7%, which is superior to many other methods that implemented on the same dataset (HuGaDB dataset). Table 3 and Fig. 5 indicate the comparison between the previous models and our model that implemented for HuGaDB dataset.

Additionally, in term of processing time, the proposed DNN model needs 1.71 s to classify the first sub-dataset (DS1) and 1.66 s to the second sub-dataset (DS2). While it needs 1.84 s to implement (DS3) and 1.93 s for (DS4). Finally, it requires 1.85 s to do the classification of the last sub-datasets (DS5). Figure 6 indicates these time details.

Table 3. The accuracy comparisons between previous models and our model.

No	Study, publication year	Accuracy %
1	[9], 2018	88.0
2	[10], 2020	91.1
3	[11], 2020	79.2
4	**Our model**	**91.7**

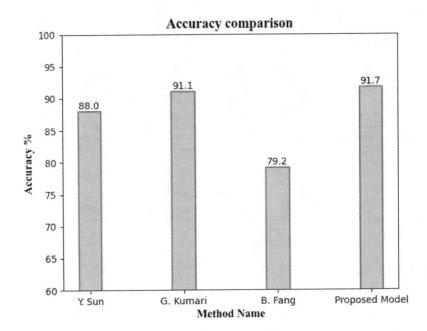

Fig. 5. The accuracy comparisons between previous models and our model.

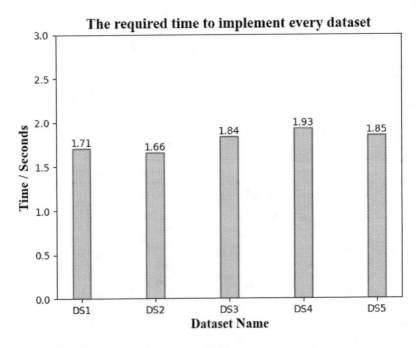

Fig. 6. The time needed to implement every dataset.

8   Conclusion

The past decade witnessed a prominent development in sensors to generate the data stream in various fields includes the health field. In this field, the classification of the patient's activities has become the focus of many researchers because it provides knowledge of the current state of a patient.

Deep Neural Networks (DNNs) are the latest and most preferred machine learning techniques, especially when processing the data stream. DNN includes many architectures, the Multi-Layer Perceptron (MLP) is a significant architecture.

This paper presents a deep neural network model based MLP architecture to classify the human activity during a tiny time. The proposed model was tested by HuGaDB dataset and evaluated its performance by four measurements which are accuracy, precision, recall and F1-score. The results proved the superiority of the proposed model over the previous works, as it achieved an accuracy of 91.7%, precision of 92.5%, recall of 92.0% recall, and F1-score as 92.0%.

References

1. Al-Khamees, H.A.A., Al-A'araji, N., Al-Shamery, E.S.: Survey: clustering techniques of data stream. In: 1st Babylon International Conference on Information Technology and Science (BICITS), pp. 113–119. IEEE, Babil (2021). https://doi.org/10.1109/BICITS51482.2021.9509923

2. Bahri, M., Bifet, A.: Incremental k-nearest neighbors using reservoir sampling for data streams. In: Soares, C., Torgo, L. (eds.) DS 2021. LNCS (LNAI), vol. 12986, pp. 122–137. Springer, Cham (2021). https://doi.org/10.1007/978-3-030-88942-5_10

3. Al-Khamees, H.A.A., Al-A'araji, N., Al-Shamery, E.S.: Data stream clustering using fuzzy-based evolving Cauchy algorithm. Int. J. Intell. Eng. Syst. **14**(5), 348–358 (2021). https://doi.org/10.22266/ijies2021.1031.31

4. Saikiaa, P., Baruaha, R.D., Singhb, S.K., Chaudhurib, P.K.: Artificial neural networks in the domain of reservoir characterization: a review from shallow to deep models. Comput. Geosci. **135**, 104357 (2020). https://doi.org/10.1016/j.cageo.2019.104357

5. Al-Khamees, H.A.A., Al-Jwaid, W.R.H., Al-Shamery, E.S.: The impact of using convolutional neural networks in COVID-19 tasks: a survey. Int. J. Comput. Digit. Syst. **11**(1), 189–197 (2022). https://doi.org/10.12785/ijcds/110194

6. Lee, J., Chang, C., Kao, T., Wang, J.: Age estimation using correlation-refined features of convolutional neural network. J. Inf. Sci. Eng. **37**(6), 1435–1448 (2021). https://doi.org/10.6688/JISE.202111-37(6).0014

7. Zhang, S., Yao, L., Sun, A., Tay, Y.: Deep learning based recommender system: a survey and new perspectives. ACM Comput. Surv. (CSUR) **52**(1), 1–38 (2019). https://doi.org/10.1145/3285029

8. Jansi, R., Amutha, R.: A novel chaotic map based compressive classification scheme for human activity recognition using a tri-axial accelerometer. Multimed. Tools Appl. **77**(23), 31261–31280 (2018). https://doi.org/10.1007/s11042-018-6117-z

9. Sun, Y., Yang, G., Lo, B.: An artificial neural network framework for lower limb motion signal estimation with foot-mounted inertial sensors. In: 15th International Conference on Wearable and Implantable Body Sensor Networks (BSN), pp. 132–135. IEEE, Las Vegas (2018). https://doi.org/10.1109/BSN.2018.8329676

10. Kumari, G., Chakraborty, J., Nandy, A.: Effect of reduced dimensionality on deep learning for human activity recognition. In: 11th International Conference on Computing. Communication and Networking Technologies (ICCCNT), pp. 1–7. IEEE, Kharagpur (2020). https://doi.org/10.1109/ICCCNT49239.2020.9225419

11. Fang, B., et al.: Gait neural network for human-exoskeleton interaction. Front. Neurorobot. **14**, 1–9 (2020). https://doi.org/10.3389/fnbot.2020.00058

12. Sarker, I.H.: Deep learning: a comprehensive overview on techniques, taxonomy, applications and research directions. SN Comput. Sci. **2**(6), 1–20 (2021). https://doi.org/10.1007/s42979-021-00815-1

13. Madhiarasan, M., Deepa, S.N.: Comparative analysis on hidden neurons estimation in multi layer perceptron neural networks for wind speed forecasting. Artif. Intell. Rev. **23**, 1–23 (2016). https://doi.org/10.1007/s10462-016-9506-6

14. Goli, P.: A new perceptually weighted cost function in deep neural network based speech enhancement systems. Hear. Balance Commun. **17**(3), 191–196 (2019). https://doi.org/10.1080/21695717.2019.1603948

15. Gardner, M.W., Dorling, S.R.: Artificial neural networks (the multilayer perceptron) a review of applications in the atmospheric sciences. Atmos. Environ. **32**(14–15), 2627–2636 (1998). https://doi.org/10.1016/S1352-2310(97)00447-0

16. Xu, Z.-Q.J., Zhang, Y., Xiao, Y.: Training behavior of deep neural network in frequency domain. In: Gedeon, T., Wong, K.W., Lee, M. (eds.) ICONIP 2019. LNCS, vol. 11953, pp. 264–274. Springer, Cham (2019). https://doi.org/10.1007/978-3-030-36708-4_22

17. Larochelle, H., Bengio, Y., Louradour, J., Lamblin, P.: Exploring strategies for training deep neural networks. J. Mach. Learn. Res. **10**(1), 1–40 (2009)

18. Vieira, S., Pinaya, W.H.L., Garcia-Dias, R., Mechelli, A.: Machine Learning Methods and Applications to Brain Disorders, 1st edn. Academic Press, San Diego (2019)

19. Nawi, N.M., Khan, A., Rehman, M.Z.: A new back-propagation neural network optimized with Cuckoo search algorithm. In: Murgante, B., et al. (eds.) ICCSA 2013. LNCS, vol. 7971, pp. 413–426. Springer, Heidelberg (2013). https://doi.org/10.1007/978-3-642-39637-3_33

20. Chereshnev, R., Kertész-Farkas, A.: HuGaDB: human gait database for activity recognition from wearable inertial sensor networks. In: van der Aalst, W.M.P., et al. (eds.) AIST 2017. LNCS, vol. 10716, pp. 131–141. Springer, Cham (2018). https://doi.org/10.1007/978-3-319-73013-4_12

Exploratory Analysis of Driver and Vehicle Factors Associated with Traffic Accidents in Morocco

Hamza Khyara[✉], Aouatif Amine, and Bouchra Nassih

Ibn Tofail University, B.P 242, Kenitra, Morocco
{hamza.khyara,aouatif.amine}@uit.ac.ma,
nassih.bouchra@univ-ibntofail.ac.ma

Abstract. In Morocco, road safety corresponds to a major public health and personal protection issue. According to statistics from the Ministry of Equipment, Transport, Logistics, and Water (METLW), the number of personal injuries reached 89,375 with an average of 10 deaths and 361 injured per day in 2017. This study tends to analyze Moroccan road traffic accidents and reveal the most influencing driver and vehicle factors on them. We implement a statistical analysis based on descriptive and exploratory analysis on the Moroccan accident database between 2013 and 2017. The database is provided by METLW and includes information about the driver and motor vehicle characteristics. Drivers between the ages of 18 and 53 are the most vulnerable to road accidents, accounting for 76% of all drivers. Male drivers represent a high percentage, around 95.2%. Most of the victims drivers were uninjured or slightly injured, which means that accidents are more likely to occur at intersections. Vehicle type and usage do not have a significant effect on Moroccan accident casualties and fatalities.

Keywords: Road safety · Road traffic accident · Exploratory data analysis · Statistical analysis · Descriptive analysis

1 Introduction

Road accidents continue to claim many lives in many countries around the world. Morocco is ranked among the countries with a very high number of traffic accidents, which result in a large number of deaths and injuries each year. In Morocco, the number of personal injury accidents reached 89,375 every day an average of 10 people die and 361 are injured as a result of traffic accidents. It is true that statistics allow us to appreciate the level of road insecurity at the global and national levels, but the figures, with all their coldness, never reveal the pain of the families, the broken destinies and lives. In addition to the human tragedy, these accidents weigh heavily on health and economic services[1]. Road

---

[1] http://www.equipement.gov.ma/Transport-routier/Securite-routiere/Pages/
Strategie-Nationale-de-la-securite-routiere-2017-20261009-7462.aspx.

© Springer Nature Switzerland AG 2022
A. Bennour et al. (Eds.): ISPR 2022, CCIS 1589, pp. 119–131, 2022.
https://doi.org/10.1007/978-3-031-08277-1_10

safety is a very complicated field because it is affected by many factors such as road users factors, environmental factors, road conditions, and economic factors, so forth. Statistical analysis is the science of collecting, exploring and presenting large amounts of data to discover underlying patterns and trends. We implement a statistical analysis based on descriptive and exploratory analysis on the Moroccan accident database between 2013 and 2017. The use of exploratory analysis of road traffic accidents is incontestable due to its ability to discover patterns and disclose the hidden information that can give insights to road stakeholders and law enforcement in order to take some preventive action against accidents. Several research have been done in this field to analyze road users behavior [12], some focusing on road conditions and infrastructure [1], others on environmental factors [9]. Gameh et al. explored and analyzed the evolution of Moroccan accidents and revealed the factors that most affect them, namely the human factor, population growth and the number of vehicles [4]. Janani et al. Implemented K-means to group the accident locations into three clusters, and used the Association Rule Mining to characterize them. Apriori algorithm is used to generate the rules in order to find the strong association rules minimum support of 5% is set [6]. Association rules provide the correlation between the different attributes when an accident happens, its benefit when it applies to a various clusters is displaying the factors behind the accident and they reveal the correlation between different attributes [6]. Men and young people are the most vulnerable in low-income and lower-middle-income countries, as the burden of traffic injuries mostly affected men (about 80%) as well as young people (15–34 years). The introduction of the seat belt law was also affected them, where the mortality decreased in all countries: 4% in Nigeria, 18% in Sri Lanka, 20% in Morocco [8]. Ennajih et al. focused on road accidents in urban area in their study, they used the Principal Component Analysis PCA for analyzing different factors and geographical distribution [5]. Timmermans et al. investigated the relationship between the occurrence rate of different types of Road Traffic Casualties (RTC) and seasonal weather variation using a Multivariate Analysis of Variance (MANOVA), The MANOVA analysis measures 6 different RTC types (either severe injury RTC or fatal RTC with three victim types being driver, passenger or pedestrian) as dependent variables and the four seasons with different weather conditions as independent variables, it was performed using SPSS with a significance level of $\alpha = 0.05$ [10]. Touzani et al. addressed the impact of road and environmental factors on road traffic accidents using data mining [3]. Makaba et al. proposed an exploratory framework for analyzing a road traffic accidents real-life dataset using graphical representations, their findings revealed that the Naïve Bayes classifier performed marginally better across all the experiments when Linear Discriminant Analysis (LDA) dimensional reduction was applied to the k-NN imputation method dataset [7]. Wenzhao et al. used geographical location, multi-component, and exploratory data analyses to analyze the relationships of variables such as collision date, road surface and weather conditions, and vehicle condition, the results revealed that the high alcohol content and improper vehicle speed often cause vehicle collisions [14]. Driver behavior and vehicle factors were shown significant influence on road traffic accidents in many studies. We addressed this aspect, due to the lack of any Moroccan accident analysis that explains its impact. First, we prepared our data by involving processes such as cleaning and transformation, then implemented descriptive analysis to show a summary of our data to get the most useful information to understand the evolution of our data, and finally, an exploratory analysis based on graphical visualization was adopted. The outline of this paper is as follows: Sect. 2 provides the study methodology. The findings and discussion are presented in Sect. 3. Finally, we finished by conclusion.

2 Study Methodology

This section describes the Exploratory Data Analysis (EDA) and the first work based on the experiment methodology used in this work based on Moroccan accidents data records.

2.1 Exploratory Data Analysis

EDA refers to the critical process of performing primary investigations on the data so as to discover patterns, spot anomalies, test hypotheses, and check assumptions with the help of summary statistics and graphical representations. Despite the emergence of data mining techniques and their robust analytical results, the EDA is still broadly used due to its good performance.

Road Traffic Accident Dataset: The accident data used in this investigation was provided by the Ministry of Equipment, Transport, Logistics, and Water (METLW) in Morocco. The dataset consists of 1691 driver and vehicle records during the period from 2013 to 2017 with 30 variables which represent the table columns. Since our dataset contained 29.44% missing values spread over 22 variables, in addition to outliers and unnecessary variables, we had to clean it before the exploratory analysis to have better results.

Experiment Methodology: In order to analyze road traffic accident, we followed the methodology illustrated in Fig. 1. First, we prepared our data by involving processes such as cleaning and transformation, then we implemented descriptive analysis to summarize the characteristics of our data and describe the useful features. Finally, an exploratory analysis based on graphical visualization was adopted. More details about each steps are presented in Sects. 2.2, 2.3, and 2.4.

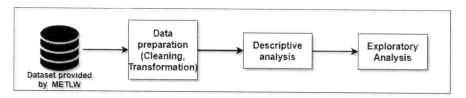

Fig. 1. Experiment methodology

2.2   Data Preparation

The concept of missing values is important to understand in order to successfully manage data. If the missing values are not handled properly, it may end up drawing an inaccurate inference about the data[2]. There are many approaches to deal with missing values[3] namely:

- A simple option: remove columns or rows with missing values, it is useful when most of the values in a column are missing.
- Imputation fills in the missing value with a number such as the mean value, the most frequent value or to be predicted by machine learning algorithms.

First, we took a look at a sample of the data and extract some helpful information to figure out if everything is being read correctly. We found that missing values represent 29.44% of drivers-vehicles data spread over 22 variables. So we removed unnecessary variables and variables with a large number of missing values, for variables with fewer missing values, we only removed their rows with missing values. After the cleaning step, 1563 records and 8 variables had left for analysis include information about the driver and motor vehicle characteristics (accident year, age, sex, occupation, injuries, deaths, vehicle type, vehicle usage).

2.3   Descriptive Analysis

In most practical data science use cases, descriptive analysis helps to get high-level insights from the data and understand the dataset. We implemented a descriptive analysis to get a summary value of the numeric and categorical variables.

Table 1. Descriptive analysis of categorical variables

	Accident year	Driver sex	Driver occupation	Injuries	Deaths	Vehicle type	Vehicle usage
Count	1563	1563	1563	1563	1563	1563	1563
Unique	5	2	9	3	5	12	7
Top	2017	Male	Non-farm worker or laborer	Not injured	Not killed	Passenger car	Driver's property
Freq	332	1488	726	801	1548	818	1004

Table 2. Descriptive analysis of numerical variable

	Count	Mean	Standard deviation	Median	Min	Max
Driver age	1563	36.85	13.63	35	10	92

---

[2] https://www.statisticssolutions.com/dissertation-resources/missing-values-in-data/.

[3] https://www.kaggle.com/rtatman/data-cleaning-challenge-handling-missing-values.

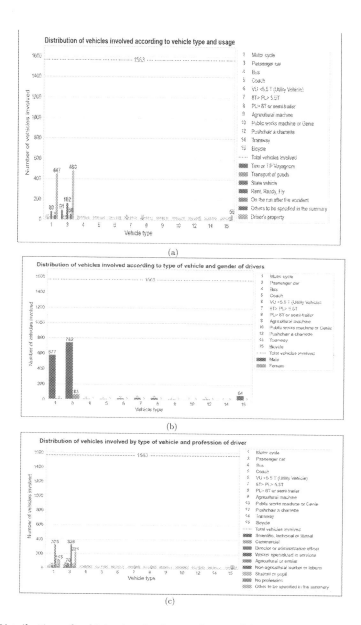

Fig. 2. Distribution of vehicles involved according to (a) vehicle type and usage, (b) vehicle type and gender of drivers, (c) vehicle type and profession of driver. (d) vehicle type and fatalities, (e) vehicle type and injuries.

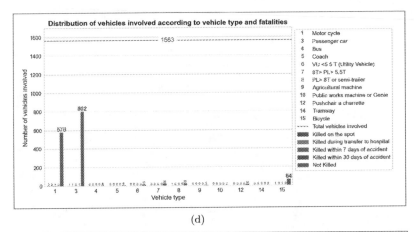

(d)

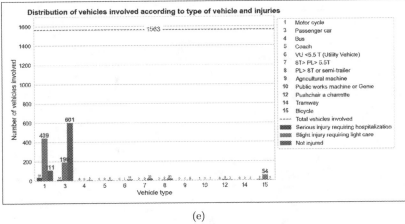

(e)

Fig. 2. (*continued*)

Tables 1 and 2 present the descriptive analysis of categorical and numerical variables, we note that male drivers, non-farm worker or laborer, and children and young drivers are the most vulnerable to accidents, but most of them are not injured or killed. We observe that vehicles of the type of passenger cars and vehicles of the driver's property are the most vulnerable groups to road accidents.

2.4 Exploratory Analysis

The exploratory analysis is the visual means of data analysis. We performed two types of exploratory analysis, univariate analysis, and bivariate analysis. The univariate analysis helped us to detect outliers which we also removed in data preparation. While the bivariate analysis is detailed in the following figures.

Analysis of Fig. 2(a, b, c, d, e) revealed that passenger cars are the most vehicle type affected by road accidents in such a way that contribute to 51.4% of the total vehicles involved in accidents. The vehicle usage category "Driver's property" presents 59.7% of passenger cars affected. Male drivers affected by crashes represent 92.1% of total passenger car drivers involved in crashes and 98.2% of total motorcycle drivers affected by crashes. The "Non-agricultural workers or laborer" and the "Other to be specified in the summary" classes are far ahead of the other profession categories such that they represent respectively 41% and 27.4% of the total drivers of passenger cars victims of accidents. Vehicle type had little effect on mortality, with only 4% of deaths recorded. With the exception of the vehicle types "Motor cycle", "Pushchair a charrete" and "Bicycle", the "Not injured" drivers predominate in other cases relating to driver casualties.

Figure 3(a, b, c) shows that the number of male drivers involved in accidents varies with vehicle usage. For the vehicle usage class "Driver's property", the male drivers represented the affected majority with 64.2% of the total male drivers involved in the accidents. Followed by "Rent, Ready, Fly" class where male drivers represent 15.7% of the total male drivers who are victims of accidents. Vehicle usage does not have a significant impact on accident casualties and fatalities, where the vehicle usage category "Driver's property" the highest record with 12 deaths. With the exception of the vehicle usage class "Driver's property", the "Not injured" drivers predominate in the other classes.

Examination of the Fig. 4 (a, b, c, d) revealed that male crashed drivers exceeds female drivers in all occupation classes. The profession category "Non-agricultural workers or laborer" predominates over other classes for both sexes, as this category alone accounts 46% of the total drivers involved in accidents, and almost all of them are not injured or have minor injuries. It showes that whatever the drivers' occupation is, there are almost no fatalities, which is 99% of the total of drivers affected by road accidents. The vehicle usage category "Driver's property" includes 64% of the total vehicles involved in the accidents. 49% of the vehicles involved in the accidents attributed to the driver's ownership fall on the level of the "Non-agricultural workers or laborer" class, 21% relate to the "Other" class, and 6.7% go to the "students or pupils" class.

Examination of Fig. 5(a, b) showed that driver deaths represented only 1% of all drivers involved in road accidents and they were all male, that is, no female deaths were recorded. Male drivers affected by crashes represent 94.1% of total uninjured drivers, 96% of all slightly injured drivers in road crashes, and all seriously injured drivers.

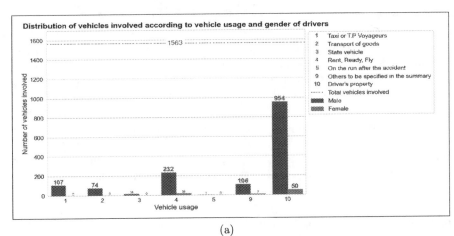

(a)

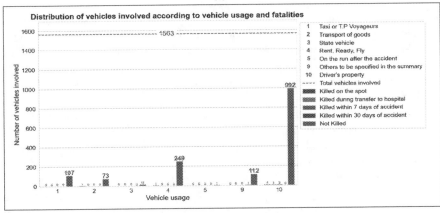

(b)

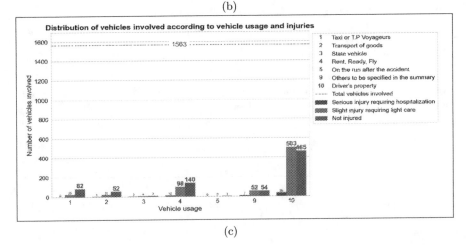

(c)

Fig. 3. Distribution of vehicles involved according to (a) vehicle usage and gender of drivers, (b) vehicle usage and fatalities, (c) vehicle usage and injuries.

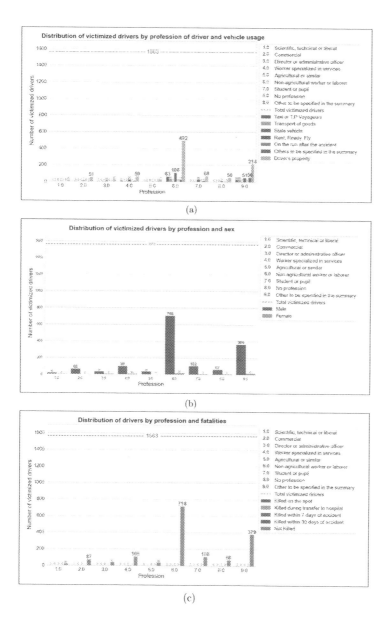

Fig. 4. Distribution of victimized drivers by (a) profession of driver and vehicle usage, (b) profession of driver and gender of drivers, (c) profession of driver and fatalities, (d) profession of driver and injuries.

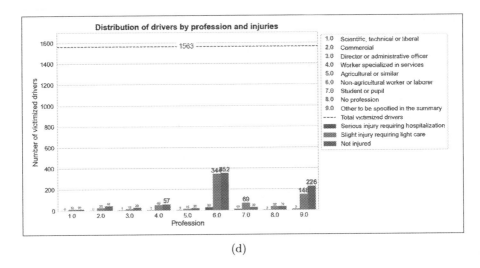

(d)

Fig. 4. (*continued*)

3   Results and Discussion

Following the various results obtained from the analysis of the database of road accidents in Morocco, the following was revealed:

Male drivers represent a high percentage, around 95.2%. Globally, we note a fluctuation in the number of drivers involved in accidents over the 5 years for all categories of occupation, "non-agricultural workers or laborers" and "others" are the drivers most vulnerable to accidents, males represent 95% of the total drivers affected by road accidents, surpassing those of females for all occupation classes. The high percentage of male exposure to accidents can be explained by the high percentage of male driver's license holders. Given the increasing demand of females in the labor market and the participation of banks in car loans, it may have a strong reflection on the number of accidents in the coming years. Increasing the number of vehicles without planning increases traffic accidents [2],[4]. We note that the number of deaths remains low and almost stable during the 5 years and the uninjured drivers slightly outperforms the slightly injured drivers, 1% of the drivers killed as a result of road accidents concerns only the male sex, that is to say, that no deaths were recorded for the female sex. It was found that male drivers account for 96% of all slightly injured drivers in road crashes, which means that male drivers are more aggressive than female drivers on the road. This analysis reveals the influence of different types of transport. It is noted that motor cycles can be more dangerous because they are less safe, showing 60% of the total drivers fatalities in road accidents and 62.8% of the total drivers seriously injured in road accidents. Vehicle owners make up 80% of fatalities and 61% of total seriously injured drivers during road crashes, indicating that drivers lack vigilance and responsibility on the road on their vehicles, especially cyclists who ride. Also allow you to burn the

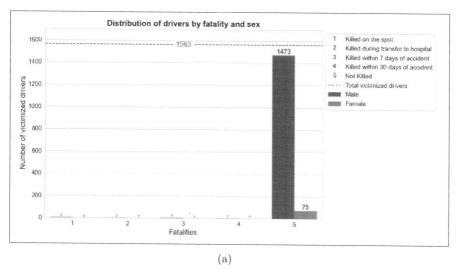

(a)

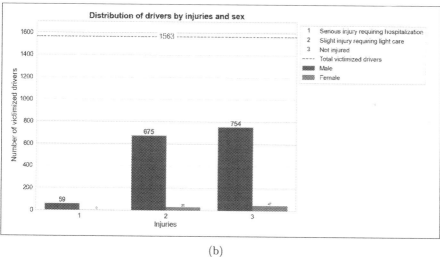

(b)

Fig. 5. Distribution of victimized drivers by (a) fatality and sex, (b) injuries and sex.

red light while crossing the intersection, without even slowing down, resulting in serious injury or death. The factors that contribute most to crashes and deaths are alcohol which impairs motor coordination, lowers the reaction rate, and limits the visual field causing an incorrect assessment of distance and speed. Speed, preoccupation while driving, and aggressive driving are major factors that increase the risk of accidents, especially for males [1, 12]. Density, visibility, and time also influence driver behaviors and lead to more serious situations [1]. Drivers are more prone to traffic accidents in developing countries because of fatigue driving for economic/financial reasons and adherence to work schedules, especially commercial vehicle drivers [13]. The risk of cyclists collision increases when cyclists do not wear their helmets and designated vests [11]. Most of the vehicles don't respect the international norms and standards in terms of safety and approval [4]. The main factor of the road accidents is the irresponsible behavior of drivers: driver inadvertence, failure to respect priority, speeding, failure to respect the safety distance, change of direction unauthorized, loss of control, change of direction without the use of a signal, failure to respect the stop sign, traffic in the left lane, failure to comply with traffic lights, traffic in the prohibited direction, driving while intoxicated (indicated by the General direction of the national security). EDA using graphical representations provided satisfactory results corroborated by previous work, but this may not be the case when dealing with a large and diverse amount of data, data mining is a more efficient alternative to traditional statistical methods [3,6].

4   Conclusion and Perspective

In Morocco, road safety corresponds to a major public health and personal protection issue. In this study, we have conducted an analysis of a Moroccan database provided by the METLW to reveal the impact of driver and vehicle factors on traffic accidents. Findings revealed that Drivers between the ages of 18 and 53 are the most vulnerable to road accidents, accounting for 76% of all drivers. Male drivers represent a high percentage, around 95.2%. Most of the victims drivers were uninjured or slightly injured, which means that accidents are more likely to occur at intersections. Due to the limited scope of variables involved in this dataset and the large number of missing values and outliers that we can't fill, it was not possible to examine deeply some other potential risk factors on the risk of Moroccan accidents. This is due to the data collection issue where accident details may not be scrutinized or the unreliability of driver information.

Our future work will address a large accident dataset and explore other factors using data mining techniques.

Acknowledgement. This work is part of the project "SafeRoad Meta-platform Road Safety (MSR)" which is supported by the METLW and the National Center of the Scientific and Technical Research (CNRST) under contract No: 24/2017.

References

1. Chen, H., Cao, L., Logan, D.B.: Analysis of risk factors affecting the severity of intersection crashes by logistic regression. Traffic Inj. Prev. **13**(3), 300–307 (2012)
2. Doğan, A.A.E., Ngüngör, A.P.: Estimating road accidents of turkey based on regression analysis and artificial neural network approach. Adv. Transp. Stud. **16**, 11–22 (2008)
3. DrissiTouzani, H., Faquir, S., Yahyaouy, A.: Data mining techniques to analyze traffic accidents data: case application in morocco. In: 2020 Fourth International Conference On Intelligent Computing in Data Sciences (ICDS), pp. 1–4. IEEE (2020)

4. El Gameh, M., et al.: Quantitative analysis and study on the evolution of road safety in morocco. Int. J. Res. Stud. Sci. Eng. Technol. **1**(9), 210–215 (2014)
5. Ennajih, D., Laaraifi, A., Elgameh, M., Sallik, A., Chaouch, A., Echchelh, A.: The quality management system on road safety in morocco. Int. J. Res. Stud. Sci. Eng. Technol. **5**(9), 1–6 (2018)
6. Janani, G., Devi, N.R.: Road traffic accidents analysis using data mining techniques. JITA-J. Inf. Technol. Appl. **14**(2), 617–625 (2016)
7. Makaba, T., Doorsamy, W., Paul, B.S.: Exploratory framework for analysing road traffic accident data with validation on Gauteng province data. Cogent Eng. **7**(1), 1834659 (2020)
8. Martin, A., Lagarde, E., Salmi, L.R.: Burden of road traffic injuries related to delays in implementing safety belt laws in low-and lower-middle-income countries. Traffic Inj. Prev. **19**(sup1), S1–S6 (2018)
9. Sapri, F.E., Nordin, N.S., Hasan, S.M., Yaacob, W.F.W., Nasir, S.A.M.: Decision tree model for non-fatal road accident injury. Int. J. Adv. Sci. Eng. Inf. Technol. **7**(1), 63–70 (2017)
10. Timmermans, C., et al.: Analysis of road traffic crashes in the state of Qatar. Int. J. Inj. Contr. Saf. Promot. **26**(3), 242–250 (2019)
11. Tiwari, G.: Sustainable development goals and road traffic injuries: the new research challenge (2017)
12. Wachnicka, J., Jamroz, K.: Speed, alcohol and safety belts as important factors influencing the number of fatalities in road accidents in the voivodships. J. KON-BiN **13**(1), 235–246 (2010)
13. Zhang, G., Yau, K.K., Zhang, X., Li, Y.: Traffic accidents involving fatigue driving and their extent of casualties. Accid. Anal. Prevent. **87**, 34–42 (2016)
14. Zhang, W., Zhang, S.: Chicago traffic collision data analysis based on multi-component analysis and exploratory data analysis. In: CICTP 2020, pp. 4684–4696 (2020)

Building a Multilingual Corpus of Tweets Relating to Algerian Higher Education

Asma Siagh[1(✉)], Fatima Zohra Laallam[1], and Okba Kazar[2,3]

[1] Laboratoire d'INtelligence Artificielle et des Technologies de l'Information (LINATI), Department of Computer Science and Information Technologies, Kasdi Merbah University Ouargla, Ouargla, Algeria
siagh.asma@univ-ouargla.dz

[2] Smart Computer Science Laboratory (LINFI), Computer Science Department, University of Biskra, Biskra, Algeria
o.kazar@univ-biskra.dz

[3] Department of Information Systems and Security, College of Information Technology, United Arab Emirate University, Al Ain, United Arab Emirates
o.kazar@uaeu.ac.ae

Abstract. Nowadays, sentiment analysis on user-generated content on social media platforms has shown outstanding benefits in various fields such as marketing, politics, and medicine. Likewise, higher education institutions can draw advantages from the knowledge gained by sentiment analysis of student-generated content on social media to improve their policies and services. However, there has been no available social media corpus concerning Algerian higher education. In light of this, we provide Algerian higher education institutions with the first multilingual tweets corpus. This paper describes the undertaken steps for the corpus-building involving data collection, data preprocessing, and data annotation.

Keywords: Corpus annotation · Higher education · Sentiment analysis · Social media

1 Introduction

The rise of user-generated content, resulting from the exponential use of social media, requires automatic analysis of this big data to better understand the opinions, emotions, and sentiments users have about any subject in any field. Data mining techniques play a significant role in managing the large amount of data by enabling efficient filtering, extraction, and analysis. The application of data mining techniques in social media, also referred to as social media analytics (SMA), yields valuable hidden insights that can address many issues. SMA includes other techniques such as sentiment analysis, text classification, topic modeling, and network analysis [1–3].

Besides machine efficient performance compared to humans performance, the main benefits of SMA based on research studies purposes can be categorized

© Springer Nature Switzerland AG 2022
A. Bennour et al. (Eds.): ISPR 2022, CCIS 1589, pp. 132–138, 2022.
https://doi.org/10.1007/978-3-031-08277-1_11

into business, and non-business [1]. The business benefits pertain to business decision-making that would increase profits and improve products' and services' quality based on customer feedback. For example, the study of [4] applied SMA for analyzing restaurant customers' opinions to assist marketers in interpreting customers' behavior and improving their sales strategies. The authors in [5] also used SMA, especially sentiment analysis, to help Taiwan telecommunication companies maintaining and attracting new customers as well as improving their marketing strategies. On the other hand, SMA can provide non-business benefits such as detecting problems, understanding situations and audience, staying informed and identifying trends. For example, the work in [6] used SMA to track the performance of political candidates during a presidential campaign, the study of [7] explored what Facebook users talk about COVID-19. Moreover, the investigation study in [8] has been conducted to understand the sorts of communication Lebanon universities employ and its effects on Lebanon citizens during the 2019 protests.

Sentiment analysis, also known as opinion mining, is now the focus of SMA in social media research. Sentiment analysis is a study field that seeks to detect the polarity (positive, negative, and neutral) of peoples' opinions towards specifics entities such as organizations, services, products, events, topics, etc. within a large amount of textual data by which it offers outstanding benefits for different applications [9]. To perform efficient sentiment analysis, the data has to pass through three primary phases: corpus annotation phase, preprocessing phase, and analysis phase. The annotation process is the most important step, as the more accurate it is, the more accurate sentiment classification polarities we get. Corpus annotation can be done manually by skilled individuals or automatically using pre-existing annotated corpus along with machine learning algorithms.

The present paper aims to provide the first knowledge base for sentiment analysis concerns higher education in Algeria. Based on the same principle of using sentiment analysis in a business context, conducting sentiment analysis on student-generated content on social media can reveal the students' opinions regarding the teaching and learning process, the university curriculum, the university services such as transport, restaurant, and residence. So that knowledge can assist in enhancing education quality and improving higher education services by taking into account students' opinions. The rest of the paper describes data collection, data preprocessing, and manual annotation phases to prepare the data for further sentiment analysis.

2   Data Source

Traditionally, collecting peoples' opinions of any subject was hard, time-consuming, and scale-limited [10]. However, with the rising use of social media platforms such as Facebook and Twitter, this task is no longer difficult.

Twitter is regarded as one of the leading social media platforms with 192 million active users [11]. Its popularity comes from providing users the ability to exchange and share short information known as "tweets" with a 280 characters limit. In spite of Twitter's low rank compared to Facebook and other social media platforms, it still gains the interest of most social media researchers, especially in which concerns sentiment analysis research. Since users post tweets to express their opinions, sentiments, and emotions about topics and events related to their daily lives, Twitter became a valuable information source for organizations to extract and analyze customers' opinions about their products and services.

Higher education institutions could draw benefits from social media in the same manner as marketing organizations. As such, extracting and analyzing the tweets students post about their learning experiences, their criticism, and their dissatisfaction will serve these institutions to meet students' needs, solve their issues, and eventually improve education quality.

3   Data Collection

At first, we would have liked to use Twitter's API to collect the tweets data. However, since Twitter's API does not allow collecting tweets older than seven days, we have chosen web-based scraper solutions to bypass this limitation. Using a Python script[1], we have defined several search queries such as "higher education in Algeria", "Algerian university", and "Algerian college". Each query has been searched in three languages: Arabic, English, and French. As a result, 21887 public tweets generated by 9477 unique users during the last nine years from January 2011 to March 2020 have been retrieved. The following attributes categorize each collected tweet:

- ID: the tweet's identifier.
- Text: the content of the tweet.
- Username: the tweet's creator.
- Date: the date of the publication, including the year, the month, the day, and the time.
- Retweets: includes how many times the tweet has been retweeted.
- Favorites: the number of times the tweet has been liked.
- Mentions: the mentioned users within the tweet.
- To: the tweet receiver's username.
- Replies: the number of the tweet's replies.
- Hashtags: the list of hashtags within the tweet.
- Permalink: the tweet's link.

The tweets and their corresponding attributes have been stored in a csv format (.csv), where each attribute is separating by a comma as illustrated below:

date, username, to, replies, retweets, favorites, text, mentions, hashtags, id, permalink

The Fig. 1 below shows how many generated tweets relating to Algerian higher education matched our defined search queries before March 2020. Overall,

---

[1] https://github.com/Mottl/GetOldTweets3.

we can partition the graph into three periods. The first period ranges from 2011 to 2013, the second from 2014 to 2018, and the last period from 2019 to March 2020. In the first period, the number of these tweets was steadily declined, such that the maximum generated tweets were 15. We can explain this downturn with the small number of Algerian Twitter users, especially since Twitter was recently launched (in 2006). The second period shows stability in the number of tweets, where it ranges between 2792 and 3278. While the last period, which covered the two recent years, 2019 and the beginning of 2020, has known a rise in the tweets' number reaches 4766 tweets in 2019 and 1245 at the beginning of 2020. This rise returns to the events of Algerian protests, also called Hirak, that involved all the Algerians, including students.

It is important to note that the tweets are publicly available in the open research data repository Mendeley Data[2].

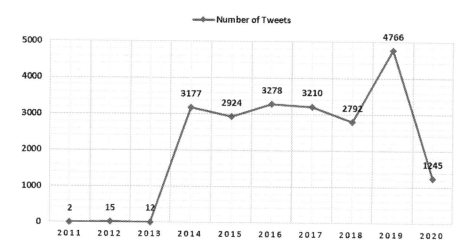

Fig. 1. The number of collected tweets by year.

4   Data Preprocessing

The data preprocessing has been conducted using the Python programming language. Firstly, we have deleted 445 duplicate tweets. Afterward, since the tweet content is our main interest, we have eliminated all the tweets with empty content. On the other hand, because of the diversity of dialects Algerians speak and their way of writing, analyzing all the retrieved tweets is challenging. Thus, we have handled just the tweets written in the three standard languages: Arabic, French, and English. To do so, we have used LangDetect.py[3] library to detect

---

[2] https://data.mendeley.com/datasets/6ndwt6s5ry/1.
[3] https://github.com/Mimino666/langdetect.

the tweets' predominant language and kept those written in the languages stated earlier (Arabic, French, and English). Furthermore, to respect the user's privacy, the tweet's creator, the username of the recipient, the mentions, and the tweet's Permalink have been removed from the dataset.

Consequently, the data size has been reduced from 21887 to 18018 tweets, where 50% are Arabic, 39% are French, and 11% are English tweets. Figure 2 shows these proportions.

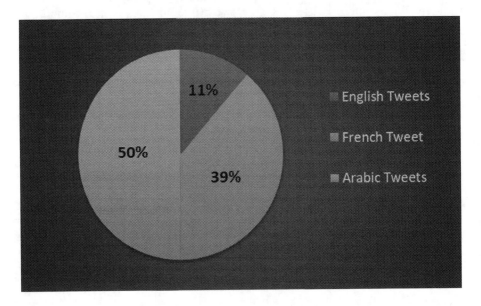

Fig. 2. Tweets' language proportions.

5   Sentiment Polarity Annotation

Once the data has been preprocessed, we aim through this section to provide machine learning algorithms that will implement sentiment analysis with the knowledge they will use during the training phase. As stated, our purpose is using social media data, more precisely tweets, to improve Algerian higher education services. To do so, we would like to conduct sentiment analysis on the multilingual tweets mentioning Algerian higher education. The first phase in achieving our research goal is annotating tweets regarding the sentiment's polarity they express.

Annotating or labeling is the process of adding information depending on the annotators' purpose to documents, sentences, or words [12]. Corpus annotation can be conducted manually by experts or automatically using machine learning algorithms that rely on a previously annotated corpus to assign tags to the new corpus [13].

In our case, we have chosen to perform manual annotation because of the unavailability of pre-existing data related to our interest. The tweets got labeled by binary labels, "1" and "0". Since our main interest is to assist higher education institutions in revealing students' dissatisfaction and issues, we were more interested in the tweets that express negative sentiments. Therefore, each tweet has been tagged by "1" if it indicates negative sentiment, while the label "0" has been assigned if it is not the case (i.e., if the tweet expresses positive or neutral sentiment). As a result, we have ended up with 2924 relevant tweets labeled "1" and 15094 irrelevant tweets labeled "0". This disparity of tweets distribution over the two classes is known as an imbalanced data problem.

6   Conclusion and Future Work

Like other fields that drew advantages from implementing sentiment analysis on social media, higher education can derive interesting insights that benefit both students and educational institutions. In order to conduct sentiment analysis, a corpus related to the domain of higher education is required. However, Algerian higher education lacks this corpus resource. In this paper, we provide the first multilingual tweets corpus concerning Algerian higher education that will serve the educational institutions to improve services by considering students' opinions.

This study has presented some limitations that need future improvements. We have chosen Twitter as a data source due to its widespread use in sentiment analysis research. However, because of the imbalanced small-scale data we got, we will widen our exploration of other social media platforms, especially Facebook, the leading platform in Algeria. Furthermore, we will also deal with Algerian dialect as being the most used language among the Algerian public. On the other hand, the manual annotation of the tweets has been time-consuming, so that it would be more practical to perform an automatic annotation.

References

1. Kordzadeh, N., Young, D.K.: How social media analytics can inform content strategies. J. Comput. Inf. Syst. **62**(1), 128–140 (2022)
2. Holsapple, C.W., Hsiao, S.H., Pakath, R.: Business social media analytics: characterization and conceptual framework. Decis. Support Syst. **110**, 32–45 (2018)
3. Stieglitz, S., Dang-Xuan, L.: Social media and political communication: a social media analytics framework. Soc. Netw. Anal. Min. **3**(4), 1277–1291 (2012). https://doi.org/10.1007/s13278-012-0079-3
4. Micu, A., Micu, A.E., Geru, M., Lixandroiu, R.C.: Analyzing user sentiment in social media: implications for online marketing strategy. Psychol. Mark. **34**(12), 1094–1100 (2017)
5. Wu, S.-J., Chiang, R.-D., Chang, H.-C.: Applying sentiment analysis in social web for smart decision support marketing. J. Ambient Intell. Human. Comput. 1–10 (2018). https://doi.org/10.1007/s12652-018-0683-9

6. Franch, F.: Political preferences nowcasting with factor analysis and internet data: the 2012 and 2016 US presidential elections. Technol. Forecast. Soc. Chang. **166**, 120667 (2021)

7. Amara, A., Hadj Taieb, M.A., Ben Aouicha, M.: Multilingual topic modeling for tracking COVID-19 trends based on Facebook data analysis. Appl. Intell. **51**(5), 3052–3073 (2021). https://doi.org/10.1007/s10489-020-02033-3

8. Katia, R., D'almeida, N., Chamoun, M.: Social big data: a Twitter text mining approach to the communication of universities during the Lebanese protests. In: 2020 International Conference on Cyber Security and Protection of Digital Services (Cyber Security), pp. 1–8. IEEE (2020)

9. Stieglitz, S., Dang-Xuan, L., Bruns, A., Neuberger, C.: Social media analytics. Wirtschaftsinformatik **56**(2), 101–109 (2014)

10. Chen, X., Vorvoreanu, M., Madhavan, K.P.: Mining social media data for understanding students' learning experiences. IEEE Trans. Learn. Technol. **7**(3), 246–259 (2014). https://doi.org/10.1109/TLT.2013.2296520

11. Tankovska, H.: Twitter-statistics & facts. https://www.statista.com/topics/737/twitter/

12. Wissler, L., Almashraee, M., Díaz, D.M., Paschke, A.: The Gold Standard in Corpus Annotation. In: IEEE GSC (2014)

13. de Carvalho, V.D.H., Nepomuceno, T.C.C., Costa, A.P.C.S.: An automated corpus annotation experiment in Brazilian Portuguese for sentiment analysis in public security. In: Moreno-Jiménez, J.M., Linden, I., Dargam, F., Jayawickrama, U. (eds.) ICDSST 2020. LNBIP, vol. 384, pp. 99–111. Springer, Cham (2020). https://doi.org/10.1007/978-3-030-46224-6_8

Recursive Feature Elimination Technique for Technical Indicators Selection

Naik Nagaraj[1(✉)], B. M. Vikranth[2], and N. Yogesh[2]

[1] Vellore Institute of Technology, Vellore, India
nagaraj.naik@vit.ac.in, nagaraj21.naik@gmail.com
[2] B.M.S. College of Engineering, Bangalore, India
{vikranth.cse,yogeshn.ise}@bmsce.ac.in

Abstract. Stock price movements are determined by several factors such as demand and supply, political stability, company earnings, and foreign portfolio investments. These factors are reflected in stock price, and the market becomes volatile. Most of the studies related to stock price classification are considered limited technical indicators. However, there are more than 100 technical indicators are available. Therefore in this paper, we explored 35 technical indicators. We have considered the recursive feature elimination (RFE) feature selection method to find relevant technical indicators. Final selected feature by the RFE method are given input to a random forest classifier to classify the stock price movements. We have considered Infosys and Reliance stock for the experiments. We found the 0.90 Area Under Curve (AUC) for Infosys stock and the 0.93 AUC for Reliance stock. The experimental results using random forest outperformed compared to Artificial Neural Network (ANN) method.

Keywords: Random forest classification · Recursive feature elimination (RFE) · Technical indicators

1 Introduction

Stock prices are frequently volatile due to speculation in the stock market. Technical analysis is considered to estimates the stock price. It is a statistical method and forecasts the stock price based on historical data. There are two approaches to stock data analysis. First is the stock price classification, and the second is the stock price prediction. In stock price classification considered the stock price movements to classify up or down of stock price. Where as stock price prediction is forecasting the future value of stock price. Timely prediction helps the investors to gain best returns from the market. This is the primary motivation of this study.

In this work, we considered the stock price classification method. However, there are more than 100 technical indicators are available [11], and most of the work considered limited technical indicators and considered the constant value

© Springer Nature Switzerland AG 2022
A. Bennour et al. (Eds.): ISPR 2022, CCIS 1589, pp. 139–145, 2022.
https://doi.org/10.1007/978-3-031-08277-1_12

for calculating the number of days in technical analysis. Therefore, in this work, it is essential to explore the number of days in technical indicators and identify the relevant feature of technical indicators. We considered 35 different sets of technical indicators, and the task is to identify the relevant technical indicator using the RFE method. This is the first approach stock price classification using RFE method. Later random forest method is considered to classify the stock up and down movements.

2   Related Work

Hsu et al. [8] considered genetic programming method to select a technical indicator feature for stock price prediction. Technical analysis using moving average and Bollinger-band was used to predict stock prices. Different trading rules were computed using technical indicator and minimize the risk in trading the stock [6]. Zhong et al. [23] considered Principal Component Analysis (PCA) to reduce the dimensionality in data. PCA has been considered to identify high correlation features from the macro-economic and technical indicator data [2]. However, PCA performs fits well in linear datasets.

Cao et al. [4] proposed the Kernel PCA technique to deal with the nonlinear data and tune the kernel parameters to get the best results. Nahil et al. [14] considered Kernel PCA to reduce the dimensions of the technical indicators and used SVM for stock price classification, i.e., up and down movements. KPCA has been proposed to identify the essential technical indicators and multilayer perceptron and support vector regression was used to predict the stock prices [10]. Krist et al. [12] proposed a hybrid neural network autoregressive conditional heteroskedasticity method to predict bitcoin prices. The Zahedi et al. [22] studied 20 accounting variables to predict the stock prices and considered PCA to reduce the dimension of feature. However, PCA method improves the prediction accuracy is significantly less.

Data mining methods have been considered to predict the stock price and returns [3]. Elman backpropagation ANN and different types of SVM was used to predict stock prices every week [9]. In sentiment analysis, retrieved related topics from the texts and predict the stock price movements [15]. Kara et al. [11] studied ten technical indicators and classification of the stock price is carried out by using SVM and ANN. Patel et al. [17] proposed deterministic trend data based on ten technical indicators. These deterministic trend data are considered to predict stock price movements based on different classification algorithms, namely ANN, SVM, random forest, and naive Bayes. The summary of related work are described in Table 1. Wu et al. [21] discussed face recognition using machine learning method. Patel et al. [17] considered limited technical indicators and it is described in Fig. 1.

3   Proposed Method

The overall work is depicted in Fig. 2. These technical indicators are CCI, EMA, MOM, R, RSI, SMA, and WM [11]. The technical indicators are calculated

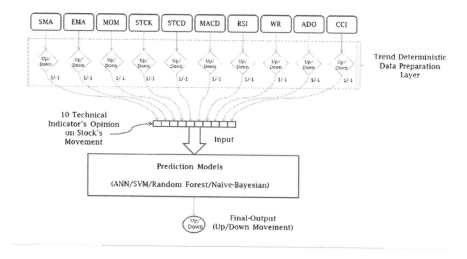

Fig. 1. Patel et al. [17] without feature selection.

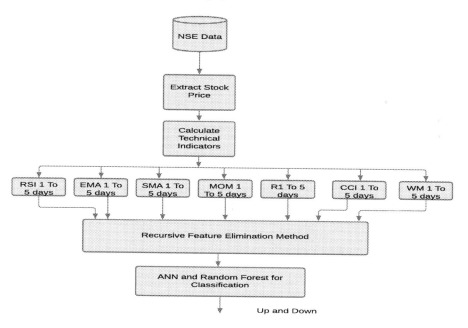

Fig. 2. Overall work

based on several days (n value). Here n represents the number of days. For each technical indicators, we have explored n values from 1 to 20 d, 20 × 7, i.e., a total of 35 technical indicators features are considered in this study. Technical

Table 1. Related work on stock price classification

Author	No. of technical indicator	Feature selection	Method
Enke et al. [7]	20 (S&P 500 index)	No	NN
Niaki et al. [16]	21 (S&P 500)	No	ANN
Cervello et al. [5]	10 (US Dow Jones)	No	Template matching
Kara et al. [11]	10 (Istanbull Stock Exchange)	No	ANN, SVM
Patel et al. [17]	10 (India CNX and BSE index)	No	ANN, RF, SVM
Patel et al. [18]	10 (India CNX and BSE index)	No	SVR + ANN, RF, SVR
Qiu et al. [19]	21 (Japan Nikkei 225 index)	No	ANN

indicators are calculated based on the statistics method [11]. The study is carried out in two stages. The first is feature selection using the RFE [1] method.

The step-by-step RFE feature selection algorithms are described in Algorithm 1. In stage 2, stock price movements classification using a random forest classifier.

Algorithm 1. RFE algorithm

1: Input technical indicators.
2: Select best feature using RFE feature selection method.
3: RFE Algorithm as follows:
4: Train the model for all technical indicator feature.
5: Calculate model performance and technical indicator feature importance
6: For each technical indicator feature T_i, $i = 1..T$ do
7: Keep important technical indicator feature T_i
8: Train the model T_i technical indicator feature and calculate performance
9: end

The feature selection method is **RFE**, The RFE is a backward-compatible way of features selection technique. Initially, it considered all the technical indicators and built the model. It checks the accuracy score to evaluate the features, and the next step is to remove one feature, build the model again and see how many variations are caused in the accuracy score. If changes the significant enough, keep the technical indicators; otherwise, remove the technical indicators.

The final selected features using the RFE method are described in Table 2. The selected feature is given as input to the random forest method [13] for classification. Random forest is the most popular ensemble-based classification method. The aim of the work is to classify the up and down movement of stock price. Using random forest, we created multiple decision trees. Here classification prediction decision is based on the majority class.

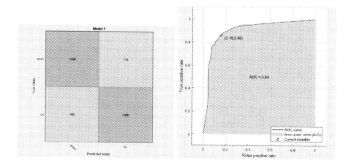

Fig. 3. Confussion matrix and ROC curve of infosys stock

Table 2. Number of features selected using RFE method.

Stock	Technical indicator	RFE
Infosys	CCI	6
Infosys	EMA	5
Infosys	MOM	5
Infosys	R	7
Infosys	RSI	5
Infosys	SMA	12
Infosys	WM	2
Reliance	CCI	6
Reliance	EMA	6
Reliance	MOM	5
Reliance	R	3
Reliance	RSI	6
Reliance	SMA	10
Reliance	WM	3

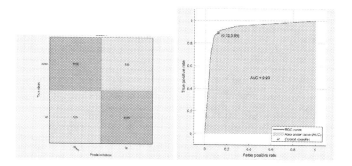

Fig. 4. Confussion matrix and ROC curve of reliance stock

4   Experimental Results

To carry out the experiments, we have considered the National Stock Exchange (NSE) data https://www.nseindia.com. We considered nifty top stock, namely reliance and Infosys, from 2008 to 2021. The performance of the model is evaluated using the confusion matrix, and ROC curve [20], and it is depicted in Fig. 3 and Fig. 4. The random forest method performed better than the ANN method, and it is depicted in Table 3.

Table 3. Results comparison

Stock	ANN	Random forest
Infosys	79.13 %	85.13%
Reliance	82.67 %	88.70%

5   Conclusion

Classification of the stock price is a difficult task due to volatility in the stock market. In this work, we have considered technical indicators to classify the stock. We considered the RFE method to identify the important features of technical indicators. The Random forest classifier is considered to classify the up and down movements of stock. National Stock Exchange, India datasets were considered for the experiments. We conclude that the RFE feature selection-based random forest method performed better than ANN method.

References

1. Albashish, D., Hammouri, A.I., Braik, M., Atwan, J., Sahran, S.: Binary biogeography-based optimization based SVM-RFE for feature selection. Appl. Soft Comput. **101**, 107026 (2021)
2. Badge, J., et al.: Forecasting of Indian stock market by effective macro-economic factors and stochastic model. J. Stat. Econom. Methods 1(2), 39–51 (2012)
3. Barak, S., Modarres, M.: Developing an approach to evaluate stocks by forecasting effective features with data mining methods. Expert Syst. Appl. **42**(3), 1325–1339 (2015)
4. Cao, L.J., Chua, K.S., Chong, W.K., Lee, H.P., Gu, Q.M.: A comparison of PCA, KPCA and ICA for dimensionality reduction in support vector machine. Neurocomputing **55**(1–2), 321–336 (2003)
5. Cervelló-Royo, R., Guijarro, F., Michniuk, K.: Stock market trading rule based on pattern recognition and technical analysis: forecasting the DJIA index with intraday data. Expert Syst. Appl. **42**(14), 5963–5975 (2015)
6. Chen, J.C., Zhou, Y., Wang, X.: Profitability of simple stationary technical trading rules with high-frequency data of Chinese index futures. Phys. A: Stat. Mech. Appl. **492**, 1664–1678 (2018)

7. Enke, D., Mehdiyev, N.: Stock market prediction using a combination of step-wise regression analysis, differential evolution-based fuzzy clustering, and a fuzzy inference neural network. Intell. Autom. Soft Comput. **19**(4), 636–648 (2013)
8. Hsu, C.-M.: A hybrid procedure with feature selection for resolving stock/futures price forecasting problems. Neural Comput. Appl. **22**(3–4), 651–671 (2013)
9. Huang, W., Nakamori, Y., Wang, S.-Y.: Forecasting stock market movement direction with support vector machine. Comput. Oper. Res. **32**(10), 2513–2522 (2005)
10. Ince, H., Trafalis, T.B.: Kernel principal component analysis and support vector machines for stock price prediction. IIE Trans. **39**(6), 629–637 (2007)
11. Kara, Y., Boyacioglu, M.A., Baykan, Ö.K.: Predicting direction of stock price index movement using artificial neural networks and support vector machines: the sample of the Istanbul stock exchange. Expert Syst. Appl. **38**(5), 5311–5319 (2011)
12. Kristjanpoller, W., Minutolo, M.C.: A hybrid volatility forecasting framework integrating GARCH, artificial neural network, technical analysis and principal components analysis. Expert Syst. Appl. **109**, 1–11 (2018)
13. Liu, K., Hu, X., Zhou, H., Tong, L., Widanage, W.D., Marco, J.: Feature analyses and modelling of lithium-ion batteries manufacturing based on random forest classification. IEEE/ASME Trans. Mech. **26**(6), 2944–2955 (2021)
14. Nahil, A., Lyhyaoui, A.: Short-term stock price forecasting using kernel principal component analysis and support vector machines: the case of Casablanca stock exchange. Procedia Comput. Sci. **127**, 161–169 (2018)
15. Nguyen, T.H., Shirai, K., Velcin, J.: Sentiment analysis on social media for stock movement prediction. Expert Syst. Appl. **42**(24), 9603–9611 (2015)
16. Niaki, S.T.A., Hoseinzade, S.: Forecasting S&P 500 index using artificial neural networks and design of experiments. J. Ind. Eng. Int **9**(1), 1–9 (2013)
17. Patel, J., Shah, S., Thakkar, P., Kotecha, K.: Predicting stock and stock price index movement using trend deterministic data preparation and machine learning techniques. Expert Syst. Appl. **42**(1), 259–268 (2015)
18. Patel, J., Shah, S., Thakkar, P., Kotecha, K.: Predicting stock market index using fusion of machine learning techniques. Expert Syst. Appl. **42**(4), 2162–2172 (2015)
19. Qiu, M., Song, Y., Akagi, F.: Application of artificial neural network for the prediction of stock market returns: the case of the Japanese stock market. Chaos, Solitons Fractals **85**, 1–7 (2016)
20. Rachakonda, A.R., Bhatnagar, A.: ARatio: extending area under the ROC curve for probabilistic labels. Pattern Recogn. Lett. **150**, 265–271 (2021)
21. Lin, W., Shen, C., Van Den Hengel, A.: Deep linear discriminant analysis on fisher networks: a hybrid architecture for person re-identification. Pattern Recogn. **65**, 238–250 (2017)
22. Zahedi, J., Rounaghi, M.M.: Application of artificial neural network models and principal component analysis method in predicting stock prices on Tehran stock exchange. Phys. A: Stat. Mech. Appl. **438**, 178–187 (2015)
23. Zhong, X., Enke, D.: A comprehensive cluster and classification mining procedure for daily stock market return forecasting. Neurocomputing **267**, 152–168 (2017)

Document-Based Knowledge Discovery
with Microservices Architecture

Habtom Kahsay Gidey$^{(\boxtimes)}$, Mario Kesseler, Patrick Stangl, Peter Hillmann,
and Andreas Karcher

Department of Computer Science, Universität der Bundeswehr München,
Werner-Heisenberg-Weg 39, 85577 Neubiberg, Germany
{habtom.gidey,mario.kesseler,patrick.stangl,peter.hillmann,
andreas.karcher}@unibw.de

Abstract. The first step towards digitalization within organizations lies
in digitization - the conversion of analog data into digitally stored data.
This basic step is the prerequisite for all following activities like the digitalization of processes or the servitization of products or offerings. However, digitization itself often leads to "data-rich" but "knowledge-poor"
material. Knowledge discovery and knowledge extraction as approaches
try to increase the usefulness of digitized data.

In this paper, we point out the key challenges in the context of knowledge discovery and present an approach to addressing these using a
microservices architecture. Our solution led to a conceptual design focusing on keyword extraction, similarity calculation of documents, database
queries in natural language, and programming language independent provision of the extracted information. In addition, the conceptual design
provides referential design guidelines for integrating processes and applications for semi-automatic learning, editing, and visualization of ontologies. The concept also uses a microservices architecture to address non-
functional requirements, such as scalability and resilience. The evaluation of the specified requirements is performed using a demonstrator that
implements the concept. Furthermore, this modern approach is used in
the German patent office in an extended version.

Keywords: Knowledge discovery · Ontology · Microservices ·
Servitization

1 Introduction

Digitization coupled with fast-paced advances in various areas of computing has
resulted in an unprecedented volume of data. Every application produces volumes of data for which usable information must be searched and analyzed. This
data growth, in return, challenges existing knowledge systems in knowledge-
based organizations. Taking the intellectual property (IP) institutions as an
example, the European Patent Office has experienced a boom in technical patent
applications since 2009. Patent applications have increased by more than 34% [1].

© Springer Nature Switzerland AG 2022
A. Bennour et al. (Eds.): ISPR 2022, CCIS 1589, pp. 146–161, 2022.
https://doi.org/10.1007/978-3-031-08277-1_13

Success in digitization has also intensified the increase in the patent examination workload by changing how IP applications are submitted and processed. While almost 100% of all patent applications were filed in writing in 2004, nearly 90% of submissions are now made digitally [2]. Processing within the office is fully digital. The figures are likely similar for many other property rights. The growing number of applications also increases the workload for patent offices worldwide. In particular, the search, retrieval, and examination workload, which takes up the largest share of time in granting a patent, increases with each patent application. For example, some patent offices completed more than 40,000 examination procedures in 2019, which is a significant increase in workload in patent examinations [2]. However, this processing capacity is small compared to the 67,000 new applications in the same year. The examination time expenditure also signifies the high level of knowledge that patent examiners must maintain to carry out their daily work. It starts with classifying patent applications according to the international classification scheme, particularly the search for similar patents. Then, a patent examiner must complete searches and examinations not to grant the IP right erroneously, requiring corresponding domain knowledge for the examiner. Consequently, the training period of a patent examiner is five years before he can perform patent examinations entirely independently. Previous attempts to raise the number of examinations processed have been to increase the number of patent examiners.

However, the goal must be to use knowledge systems to support the knowledge worker and change the "data-rich", but "knowledge-poor" scenario by reducing the processing times for classification, search, and examination, and the training time for new patent examiners. Intellectual property institutions process digitized unstructured documents instead of structured information.

As a result, this paper presents a contribution, a conceptual model for KD, that addresses the knowledge systems challenges in document-based knowledge discovery (KD) with a highly flexible microservices architecture (MSA). The work also sets the background and related work to the contribution and evaluates the model with an implementation.

2   Research Context

KD is a topic of broad scientific interest in information systems research. Automated processing of unstructured data classification, retrieval, and testing is of particular interest for this work. In this context, the knowledge system for KD is set around the processes of classification, search, and examination of patent applications. The classification of a patent application serves the correct assignment of a patent submitted to the responsible examining office. For this purpose, the International Patent Classification (IPC) scheme is applied, which provides uniform hierarchical classes and specific sub-classes [3].

First, patent applications are classified roughly into the relevant classes during the classification process. Next, the applications are submitted in a round-robin procedure to the presumably competent preliminary examiner based on the classification. Then, the latter either confirms the classification carried out, refines it according to sub-classes, or determines that the assigned class is incorrect. In case of an error, the final classification is determined by other possibly competent auditing bodies of auditors.

The classification of the applications is based on the intellectual registration of the contents of the respective patent specification. In particular, the claims, descriptions, or attachments are of specific interest. The focus of the intellectual content to be examined varies from one examination area to another. For example, in the case of applications in chemistry, the representations of chemical compounds are decisive, whereas, in electrical engineering, the claims for classification are more important.

A search process always precedes the patent examination process, which looks for similarities among applications. In general, this process follows a sequence characterized by the intellectual acquisition of the contents of the patent application and the search for already filed applications with similar contents. These are intelligent comprehension of the contents of the new patent application, compilation keywords of the technical concepts that characterize the described patent, search of referenced documents or documents that in turn reference this application, and then search for the assigned keywords in the documents of the corresponding IPC class.

Similar to the classification, the contents essential for the search differ depending on the examination field. When searching in the respective IPC classes, up to 2000 documents may have to be searched for similar contents and concepts. The concepts can be realized by technical drawings or defined descriptively by terms and relations to other terms. The search for similar concepts also explains the high time expenditure of a patent examination.

2.1   Example Scenario

The following scenario describes the vision of the new examination process of a patent application as it appears after a potential deployment of an exemplary KD system: *Julia is one of 700 examiners and 2000 other employees at a hypothetical patent office. She works at different office locations, including from home. Currently, she is a trainee investigator and has to process the new applications assigned independently as part of her training. She has just received a patent application from a company working on cognitive systems. Since all new applications are automatically classified and assigned keywords when they arrive, the system notifies her immediately after a submitted application. Opening the patent specification document, she gets live support with various keywords that capture the core of the application. Julia then reads the relevant passages of the patent specification and determines the classification recommendations are valid. She now has two different ways to start searching for similar patent applications. In the first case, she receives a list of all other applications sorted by relevance to which comparable keywords have been assigned. In the second approach, she actively searches for comparable content. To minimize the training effort, she can ask the question in a natural language. Julia thus writes into the search field:*

'Show me all applications with the keyword cognitive systems.' She receives a list of all applications containing the keywords, sorted by relevance. In both cases, she has an up-to-date and limited list of documents based on which she can make an intellectual comparison of the keywords without having to click through several hundred applications. Since Julia is still a trainee, she needs to understand the interrelationships of patents in cognitive systems before comparing individual patent applications. For this purpose, she looks at an ontology provided by the system, which represents the concepts and relationships between cognitive systems and other related topics - such as cognitive models and cognitive architectures. After comparing submitted applications, Julia decides on the novelty of the patent application.

2.2 Research Questions

We posed the following research questions (RQs) to conceptualize and evaluate the document-based KD solution. **RQ1**:*What are the workload challenges for knowledge workers in existing workflows of a patent application and examination?* **RQ2**: *What are the main aspects of knowledge systems that address practical KD requirements in processing and examining patent applications?* **RQ3**: *What are the ways to realize architecturally significant requirements of a future-proof document-based KD system in patent classification and examination?*

3 Background and Related Works

Architectural approaches and design decisions make significant contributions toward making software systems scalable, resilient, and future-proof [4–6]. The MSA is, for instance, an architectural pattern that has demonstrated value in addressing the challenges caused by the increased need for rapid digitalization and servitization in data-rich domains [7,8]. The MSA separates application services based on business capabilities or a domain's functional requirements [9]. Services are then restricted on domain context and size [10]. They are also deployed, managed, and scaled independently of each other. Similarly, services communicate with each other independently with messaging protocols such as HTTP/REST. [9,11]. Due to the strongly decoupled micro-sized services, MSA's software components are easy to maintain or even replace. As a result, MSA has also been a preferred path for architecture-driven software modernization [12]. MSA further addresses the architectural challenges of KD by componentizing the extensive functional domains such as natural language processing, keyword extraction for text mining, and ontology management into services [10]. As a process of useful knowledge extraction from unstructured documents, document-based KD has distinct technical requirements that differ from other types of KD. [13]. The key differences lie in the requirements for which the need is 'information retrieval' vs. 'text mining.' According to Ben-Dov et al., this topic corresponds to the sub-area 'information retrieval,' which is concerned with finding new information across individual data records [14]. Hotho et al. [15] also show the lack of clarity in the definition of the term itself, which ranges from information extraction to an all-encompassing 'knowledge discovery' process.

Besides, MSA has grown as an architecture of choice for diverse applications in software development practices [16]. Although literature presents several MSA implementations for a growing number of software solutions, very few select exist that address architectural challenges in KD services. Singh et al. [17], for example, have implemented a reference application based on a microservice-based model, which they proposed for Big Data KD. Vekaria et al. [18] also have presented a chatbot-based recommender system for Science gateways to support KD with augmentable modules as microservices. However, those few examples have no focus on the challenges of document-based KD and significantly differ from our solution of document-based KD with an MSA.

4   Conceptual Approach

In the following, we conceptualize the essential aspects of KD application with MSA to address knowledge-intensive document processing challenges. The conceptual design determines the individual microservices' specification, the necessary data model, and each service's data persistence. Furthermore, we briefly describe individual microservice size, functionality, and communication between the respective services. We also describe the design decisions made throughout the conceptualization, alternative design rationales considered, advantages and disadvantages of each possible design choice, and the selected design justifications.

4.1   The Microservices Specification

We specify the necessary microservices into two parts. The first part specifies the microservices related to the domain, KD requirements. The second part specifies the services significant for the infrastructure of the MSA.

Domain Related Microservices: In Fig. 1, following Domain-Driven Design [19], we identify domain-related microservices from the four subdomains. The document processing subdomain contains the functionalities for determining keywords and calculating the similarity of documents. The Querying domain provides all query mechanisms for standard queries for keywords and queries via

Fig. 1. Subdomain structure   **Fig. 2.** Document processing structure

Natural Language Interfaces. The domain Ontology-Learning contains the missing layers for automatically extracting ontologies from unstructured text. Since term extraction has already been done in the Document Processing domain, all tasks are built on top of it after the Ontology Learning Layer Cake. The last domain to note is Ontology Management, which allows the editing and visualization of automatically generated ontologies. The subdomains form self-contained units, which have the following advantages:

1. Self-contained, independent data models,
2. Independent scalability of each subdomain,
3. Internal subdomain changes do not affect the entire system.

Independence of the individual domains at runtime, for example, queries via querying, can be performed without functioning document processing. However, independence does not mean that the system can work in a meaningful way without processed documents. A filling with documents from which keywords and ontologies are extracted is a prerequisite for the system's usability. Following the top-down approach, these coarse sub-domains can now be precisely subdivided into 'sub-sub domains.' Thus, a structure can be determined for the processing of the documents, as shown in Fig. 2. Here, the service 'Preprocessing' takes over converting the specified file formats into pure, machine-readable text. The service 'Termextraction' extracts the keywords from the text, and the service 'SimComputation' computes the similarities between the newly added documents and the documents already existing in the system. Based on the controller and reporter pattern, the parent service Document-Processing handles the processing control and maintains the documents' status.

An alternative approach for the similarity analyses would be to determine the similar documents only at the time of a potential request to the system - i.e., only when similar documents are to be output for a given document. However, this has a disadvantage: the user expects a prompt, timely response to a request. Similarity computations are performed only at a point in time, resulting in higher requirements on the performance of the service, which has to process several requests simultaneously and perform the computations. An improvement of the situation at the user request time would occur if the service to which the request goes does not compute the analysis at the request time but at the integration time of a new document. However, the approach chosen here has the advantage over the approach in the service in which the queries are processed that only database operations are running, and no additional computations have to be performed. This ensures the highest possible performance for queries by users.

For the subdomain 'Querying,' a microservices structure results as shown in Fig. 3. Here, the individual subordinate services provide different possibilities for searching. The service 'Searching' provides web services for standard

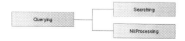

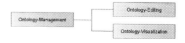

Fig. 3. Querying subdomain   **Fig. 4.** Ontology management

queries for similar documents or keywords. The service NliProcessing, on the other hand, processes queries formulated in natural language. The parent service 'Querying' bundles the queries, can be used to provide caching for searches and search results and is furthermore available for aggregating search results from the different search possibilities. Caching within the parent service allows very fast response times. At the same time, the splitting into individual subordinate services ensures that in case of a failure of a sub-service not all queries come to nothing. Figure 5 shows the exemplary service structure for the ontology learning subdomain taken from the ontology learning layer cake as a basis for defining the subordinate microservices according to the presented layers. After determining the synonyms for the extracted keywords in the service 'Synonym-Recognition,' the concepts are determined in the service 'Concept-Generating,' and the relations between the individual concepts are extracted in the following service 'Relations-Extraction.' The rules or axioms, which can be derived automatically from the previous information, are created in the service 'Rules-Generating.' As can be seen, the keywords extraction service is omitted here since this has already been performed in the document processing context. Since the existing and outdated solutions of ontology learning perform the whole task of ontology learning as a black box in an application, the problem arises that an ideal-type separation into the layers of the ontology learning layer cake seems impractical.

The structuring into a superordinate and a subordinate service allows the integration of a single ontology learning framework into the learning service or an ideal-typical implementation where the ontology learning service takes over the control of the workflow. For the last subdomain, ontology management, a microservices structure results as shown in Fig. 4. The automatically generated ontologies additionally require monitoring and editing capabilities. Editing capabilities are provided by the service 'Ontology-Editing,' whereas the service 'Ontology-Visualisation' provides visualization possibilities for the presentation of the ontologies. The higher-level service 'Ontology-Managment' is primarily used for forwarding the queries and the learned ontologies.

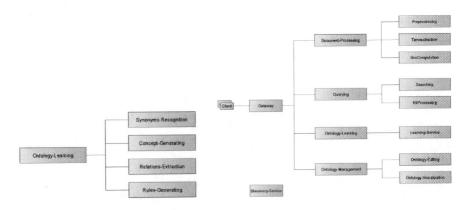

Fig. 5. Ontology-Learning subdomain   **Fig. 6.** System structure with components

Infrastructure Related Microservices: Loose coupling between the individual microservices is a fundamental advantage of the MSA. At the same time, it leads to the need to integrate services for localizing the individual microservices. For the localization of all microservices instances, a registration and discovery service is necessary, which is continuously informed about available instances of services and returns an instance of the desired service to the caller upon request. A gateway service must also be integrated to hide non-public interfaces from external clients. Additionally, other infrastructure services can be integrated, such as authentication. After the integration of the newly added infrastructure components, the overall system corresponds to Fig. 6. In addition to the functional and infrastructural services listed here, further services for persistence and asynchronous communication are necessary. These will be integrated successively in the following chapters.

4.2   Data Model

The conceptual approach divides the data model into internal and external elements. The internal data model serves data processing within the individual microservices and data transfer between them. The external data model is used for communication with the clients who access the rest of the web services provided.

Internal Data Model: The services data model results altogether from the required input of the service and its output, which can represent the input of another service or the information requested by the user. For this task, a distinction must be made between the subdomains of document processing or querying and the subdomains focusing on learning and managing ontologies. For the subdomains Document-Processing and Querying, an overall data model is composed of the data models of the subordinate services.

In addition, it requires the ability to uniquely identify a file and the information derived from it across the individual microservices. For this purpose, an ID must be assigned while uploading a document, which is available in the data model of all further microservices. The algorithm used must also be provided to the services' output to meet different keyword extraction and similarity analysis methods requirements. For the data model of the ontology-related services, it should be noted that the data input for ontology management and ontology learning services is different. The data model of the Ontology-Management service is the ontology itself. Since this service provides methods or applications for manual editing of ontologies, the data model of the input also corresponds to the data model of the output. In both cases, editing and visualization ontologies are involved.

This restriction does not apply to the ontology learning service. Here, two factors have to be taken into account: first, the data model of a newly processed document from which further information for new or existing ontologies shall be extracted by processing in the ontology learning process, which corresponds to the data model of the term extraction service and second, the data model of the ontology that is either already exists due to automatic ontology extraction of previous runs or is provided to the ontology learning microservice after a manual modification via the ontology editing microservice.

Thus, the picture for the ontology-learning microservice is that both a data model for reproducing a new document and a data model for reproducing ontologies are necessary. For this purpose, the Web Ontology Language is chosen. This decision is equally viable if a microservices structure is envisaged, following the Ontology Learning Layer Cake layers. OWL is also used as a data model for the ontology management subdomain since existing applications support this data model either directly or via plugins.

External Data Model: A different approach has to be chosen for the data model used to communicate with the clients. Decisive here is the web services that are made available to the client. In this concept instance, a distinction has to be made between document processing, querying, and ontology management domains. The domain Ontology-Learning only processes data internally and has no external interfaces. The domain Ontology-Management allows the processing and visualization of ontologies. Since only existing applications like WebProtege or WebVOWL are linked here, reference shall be made to their possibilities to download data. In querying, a distinction has to be made between Searching and NliProcessing. While the Searching Microservice only allows predefined queries defined in requirements, the NliProcessing Microservice allows free text input. Since no exact data structure of the response is known under these conditions, a generic data model must be implemented.

Persistence: To conclude the chapter on data models, the persistence of the data in the individual microservices shall be considered. Here, a basic decision between relational and NoSQL databases has to be made for each microservice. The question of the type of database used depends primarily on the structure of the data to be stored. The simpler the data structure, the better the data can be mapped into an SQL database without complex joins. The more complex or flexible the data structures are, the easier it is to store data in NoSQL databases. This is also true for large amounts of text or when the data structure to be stored changes. NoSQL databases have supported both aspects since their creation. The full support of reactive programming by NoSQL databases is another advantage, especially in areas where performance plays an important role. The databases shown in Fig. 7 are chosen for the persistence layer for this concept considering the reasons above. The schemas of the individual databases are based on the classes of the internal data model. Persistence in caching in the Querying Microservice relies on a NoSQL database since different results with different structures have to be kept. In the NliProcessing microservice, on the other hand, the use of an SQL database is necessary. Here, however, it is additionally important to adapt the database schema to the possibilities of the service to convert text into SQL commands since not all SQL constructs are

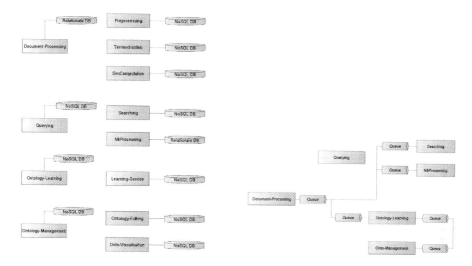

Fig. 7. Databases for the microservices   **Fig. 8.** Cross-domain communication

supported. In all microservices of the ontology management sub-domain, the ontologies in OWL format are also kept in a no-SQL database.

4.3   Communication

After conceptualizing the data models, we defined and specified the communication between the individual services on three levels. These are the communication between client and public interfaces, the communication within the cross-subdomain microservices, and data transfer within the domain-specific microservices. The specification is limited to functional communication. Moreover, communication to the infrastructure services is exclusively synchronous and will not be considered.

External Communication: A client accesses the public interfaces via the web services provided by the system. The services mentioned are offered in the form of URLs and accept data synchronously or deliver information synchronously. These are transmitted according to REST-compliant standards, i.e., marshaling to or unmarshalling from JSON takes place. Only standard HTTP methods such as POST and GET are used for communication. This applies to all public interfaces, except for the interfaces provided in the ontology management domain, since there are no web service-compatible applications that could be integrated. The interfaces provided have to be used to integrate an existing ontology management software like WebProtégé. This also applies to the visualization component to be integrated. The decision in favor of synchronous communication between client and system is based on the expectation of a timely and high-performance response, even though asynchronous communication is preferable in MSAs.

Cross-domain Technical Communication: Communication within the system across the individual subdomains is asynchronous since this type of data transfer creates additional decoupling. This requires an additional messaging service in the system that provides the necessary queues. The standard JSON is again used as the data transfer format, and the FIFO principle is used to process the messages in the queues. The entire cross-domain communication then corresponds to Fig. 8. Since the further processing or provision of the data within the subdomains Querying and Ontology Learning depends on the preprocessing within Document Processing, the data is forwarded asynchronously from Document Processing to the services mentioned earlier. However, data querying is not forwarded through the higher-level Querying microservice to lower-level Searching and NliProcessing services but directly to the latter two. This is done with regard to the performance and error resilience of the querying services. This approach ensures that the querying service is only burdened by the requests from the outside and does not have to process the forwarding of the newly processed documents additionally. Second, this means only two instead of three queues are needed in the messaging service, and the network load is reduced by a third. Third, it allows new documents to be integrated into the two lower-level microservices even if the querying service is down or overloaded.

This approach is not target-oriented when providing data for the Ontology-Learning service. Since this microservice does not provide any public interfaces, allowing for future changes regarding the pragmatic approach described above or a split along with the layers of the Ontology Learning Layer Cake, the asynchronous delivery of the data to the parent Ontology-Learning Microservice is to be preferred. Furthermore, for the cases considered so far, the response of successful processing to document processing is also asynchronous. The last thing to specify is the communication between the ontology-learning and ontology-management microservices. The ontology management applications do not need direct input from the document-processing microservice but only the ontologies elaborated in the ontology-learning subdomain. At the same time, ontology management, in turn, has to provide the ontologies revised manually to the ontology learning microservice. Thus, data exchange has to take place in both directions, whereby asynchronous communication is also preferred in each case.

Communication in Document Processing: In the Document-Processing subdomain, internal communication with the subordinate microservices occurs in both asynchronous and synchronous forms. The document processing microservice accepts documents uploaded by the client synchronously and forwards the entire processed result to querying and ontology learning subdomains asynchronously. The processing of the documents takes place in individual steps, which are broken down into subordinate microservices. The communication can be differentiated into the normal processing flow and the data retrieval in the event of an error. The document processing service provides the individual subordinate microservices with the required input data asynchronously and receives the result asynchronously at the end of the respective processing step. In the event of an error, the subordinate microservices provide synchronous interfaces to return the analyzed result of a document that has already been processed. This allows the document processing service to fall back on the result of the previous processing step if errors occur and feed it back into the normal workflow.

Communication in Querying: The communication in the Querying subdomain is a purely synchronous data transfer. The querying microservice mediates with the respective subordinate microservices. In addition to the publicly provided interfaces, the services in this domain do not include any other interfaces.

Communication in Ontology-Learning: Communication in the ontology-learning subdomain is structured asynchronously. This is due to the potentially long runtime of the generation of ontologies and the individual steps involved. It should also be noted that an asynchronous workflow can also be set up in parallel to the procedure in document processing when using individual microservices per task of the Ontology Learning Layer Cake.

Communication in Ontology Management: Data transfer in ontology management is also asynchronous. The ontologies generated in the Ontology Learning domain and edited via the Ontology Editing service are provided asynchronously to other services.

Ontologies provided by the Ontology-Learning service are forwarded asynchronously to both subordinate microservices via the Ontology Management microservice. Ontologies that the Ontology-Editing service has edited are, in turn, provided asynchronously to Ontology-Learning and the Onto-Visualization service via the Ontology Management service. In addition to this asynchronous communication, synchronous public interfaces forward the user to the web applications for editing or visualization.

After integrating communication and persistence into the system, the structure shown in Fig. 9 results for the entire system. Solid lines with queues between the individual microservices correspond to asynchronous communication and dotted lines to synchronous communication. The synchronous communication of all microservices to the discovery service is hidden in the diagram.

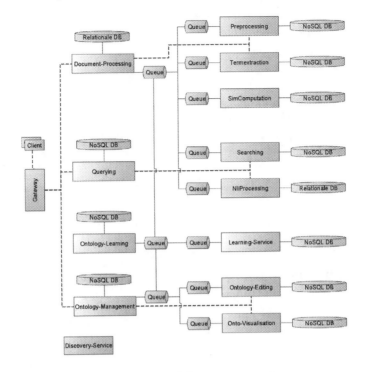

Fig. 9. Overview of the system structure

5 Evaluation and Assessment

5.1 Implementation

The conceptual model discussed in the previous section is implemented in separate domain-relevant components where microservices are also divided into technical and infrastructure-related services. Besides, all the microservices described are implemented in Java using the Spring Boot Framework and Docker. Some parts are fully implemented, such as Document-Processing and Querying microservices. However, the Ontology-Management service is partially implemented using existing ontologies. The implementation is set up as a multi-project build containing a separate Gradle project for each required microservice.

5.2 Evaluation

We evaluate our concept according to our scenario in Section II, based on typical processes at a patent office. It includes using an MSA, RESTful APIs, existing libraries, frameworks, and services already in use, with an example scenario of a patent office.

For the testing, we used the Postman tool and cURL, which allows for sending whole collections of requests. For instance, the requirement, which entails the application to process PDF format documents, is assessed as the first step in the success of uploading documents via the provided REST API. In this case, forty document packages related to patents and science were uploaded, and the processing was monitored. The success of the upload was traced in the database successfully.

A second requirement, which entails automatic text extraction from the available documents, evaluates the preprocessing microservice. Proof of successful processing can also be observed on the content of the microservice's database. Figure 10 shows a section of the 'Extractions' collection after successful text extraction. Other requirements, such as the automatic extraction of keywords from documents and presenting a requested list of keywords for each document, can be evaluated together.

Fig. 10. Extract from collection 'Extractions' with extracted text.

Furthermore, the evaluation of the requirement that the application must support integrating tools for visualizing ontologies is conducted assuming the ontology in OWL format exists. The visualization component WebVowl is called with an existing ontology in OWL format. Figure 11 shows this component after calling the web service 'ontomanagement/getVisualisation'.

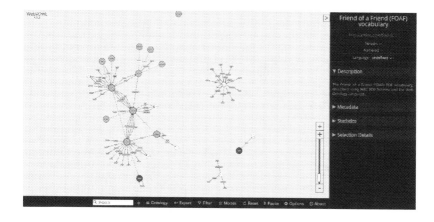

Fig. 11. Redirection to WebVowl

6   Conclusion

KD is an integral part of knowledge-intensive organizations and their processes servitization. To this end, in this paper, we have presented a conceptual model and an evaluation of document-based KD with an example scenario at an intellectual property institution. The conceptual approach mainly focused on using MSA to model and implement four main domain-relevant microservices: document processing, querying, ontology learning, and ontology management services. Due to its extensibility, MSA is an ideal basis for creating knowledge-based applications. Workflows for processing documents can be easily implemented and almost completely separated from the provision of the resulting information. As a result, keyword extraction, similarity determination, and provision of information based on a RESTful API were successfully implemented for the document-based KD. Then, examples of key requirements were demonstrated on how implemented services were assessed and examined. The benefits of the KD implemented are identifying keywords from knowledge-intensive documents, supporting the recognition of similarities among them, and generating and retaining essential knowledge of the documents.

As an outlook, future work can extend this concept from several points of view. An apparent investigation is the creation of a microservice-based concept of the 'Ontology Learning Layer Cake.' Furthermore, the general consideration of NLP-based problems is interesting. The question to be answered here is how small-scale NLP tasks can be decomposed into individual microservices to act as part of different problem-specific NLP tasks. Further research based on this work could, in turn, aim to develop MSA-based NLP analysis frameworks.

References

1. EPO. European Patent Office - statistics and trends (2020). https://www.epo.org/about-us/annual-reports-statistics/statistics.html. Accessed 21 Nov 2021
2. DPMA. Deutsches patent- und markenamt: Deutsches patent- und markenamt produktiv wie nie zuvor (2020). https://bit.ly/3yk8NBJ. Accessed 18 Nov 2020
3. IPC. World intellectual property organization: international patent classification (IPC) (1971). https://www.wipo.int/classifications/ipc. Accessed 18 Nov 2020
4. Furrer, F.J.: Future-Proof Software-Systems. Springer, Wiesbaden (2019). https://doi.org/10.1007/978-3-658-19938-8
5. Jansen, A., Bosch, J.: Software Architecture as a Set of Architectural Design Decisions. IEEE Computer Society. WICSA 2005, Washington, DC (2005)
6. Gidey, H.K., Marmsoler, D., Eckhardt, J.: Grounded architectures: using grounded theory for the design of software architectures. In: 2017 ICSAW. IEEE (2017)
7. Kohtamäki, M., Parida, V., Patel, P.C., Gebauer, H.: The relationship between digitalization and servitization: the role of servitization in capturing the financial potential of digitalization. Technol. Forecast. Soc. Change 151, 119804 (2020)
8. Vandermerwe, S., Rada, J.: Servitization of business: adding value by adding services. Eur. Manag. J. 6(4), 314–324 (1988)
9. Richardson, C.: Microservices Patterns. Manning Publications Company, Shelter Island (2018)

10. Dragoni, N., Giallorenzo, S., Lafuente, A.L., Mazzara, M., Montesi, F., Mustafin, R., Safina, L.: Microservices: yesterday, today, and tomorrow. In: Present and Ulterior Software Engineering, pp. 195–216. Springer, Cham (2017). https://doi.org/10.1007/978-3-319-67425-4_12

11. Garriga, M.: Towards a taxonomy of microservices architectures. In: Cerone, A., Roveri, M. (eds.) SEFM 2017. LNCS, vol. 10729, pp. 203–218. Springer, Cham (2018). https://doi.org/10.1007/978-3-319-74781-1_15

12. Knoche, H., Hasselbring, W.: Using microservices for legacy software modernization. IEEE Softw. 35(3), 44–49 (2018)

13. Ahonen, H.: Knowledge discovery in documents by extracting frequent word sequences (1999)

14. Ben-Dov, M., Feldman, R.: Text Mining and Information Extraction. In Data Mining and Knowledge Discovery Handbook, Springer, Boston (2005)

15. Hotho, A., Nürnberger, A., Paaß, G.: A Brief Survey of Text Mining. In Ldv Forum, Citeseer (2005)

16. Di Francesco, P., Malavolta, I., Lago, P.: Research on architecting microservices: trends, focus, and potential for industrial adoption. In: 2017 ICSA. IEEE (2017)

17. Singh, N., Singh, D.P., Pant, B., Tiwari, U.K.: μ BIGMSA-microservice-based model for big data knowledge discovery: thinking beyond the monoliths. Wirel. Pers. Commun. 116(4), 2819–2833 (2020). https://doi.org/10.1007/s11277-020-07822-0

18. Vekaria, K., et al.: Recommender-as-a-service with chatbot guided domain-science knowledge discovery in a science gateway. Concurrency Comput. (2020)

19. Evans, E., Evans, E.J.: Domain-Driven Design: Tackling Complexity in The Heart of Software. Addison-Wesley Professional, Boston (2004)

Pattern Recognition

Feature Selection for Credit Risk Classification

Dalia Atif[1]($\boxtimes$) and Mabrouka Salmi[2]

[1] University Center of Tipaza, Tipaza, Algeria
atif.dalia@cu-tipaza.dz
[2] National School of Statistics and Applied Economics, Tipaza, Algeria
salmi.mabrouka@enssea.net

Abstract. With the advancement of storage methods, feature selection has become increasingly important in many fields of study, including credit risk classification. To improve model robustness, feature screening has predominated, but it suffers from being trapped at the local optimum. Among the various proposed strategies to deal with this issue is integrating feature selection into the training phase. We compare two of the most commonly used methods in the related field, one parametric (logistic regression) with regularization of the L1 norm and the second non-parametric (random forests) with wrapper-based strategy; while integrating feature selection into the training process. We used the German credit dataset and employed preprocessing steps such as class merging, data standardization, and dummy coding. The results formulated on classification based-measures built on a 70:30 split revealed that logistic regression outperformed with Accuracy = 0.75, Sensitivity (Recall) = 0.9825, Precision = 0.742, F1-score = 0.845, AUC = 0.8, and PR-AUC = 0.877.

Keywords: Credit risk classification · Wrapper · Embedded · Random forests · Lasso · Feature selection

1 Introduction

The bank always examines the credit risk issued to an individual based on the five C: credit history, capacity to repay, capital, collateral, and loan's conditions, to cut losses due to faulty refunds [8]. Researchers used the resulting data to predict a borrower as a good or a bad using data mining tools like random forests, logistic regression, or neural networks [22,25,31]. Today, the evolution of storage methods has resulted in high-dimensional data with highly correlated features and an increase in irrelevant features making the feature selection paramount [35], the aim is to reduce dimensionality in order to enhance the classifier's generalization capacity [7] as well as to reduce the computational cost, to define this field, consider the following: Given a set of starting features $A = (X_1, X_2, ..., X_j, ...X_p)$ with $|A| = p$, the goal of FSA (Features Selection Algorithm) is to select a subset J among 2^p possibilities using an assessment criteria $C(J)$ that must

© Springer Nature Switzerland AG 2022
A. Bennour et al. (Eds.): ISPR 2022, CCIS 1589, pp. 165–179, 2022.
https://doi.org/10.1007/978-3-031-08277-1_14

be optimized, each subset J receives a score of $C : J \subseteq A \to \mathbb{R}$ [28] and when the optimal subset is chosen, the training process improves. In this sense, the link between feature selection and the training process can be done using various strategies: filter, embedded, and wrapper [28], since the performance of feature selection can only be evaluated during the test phase [2], the filter feature selection can be discarded because it employs an independent criterion and has the drawback of being trapped at a local optimum [7], it is therefore recommended to incorporate feature selection during the training phase implementing two strategies (wrapper and embedded) with various machine learning tools (Naive Bayes, RF, SVM, logistic regression) [21], the two most commonly used in credit risk classification being logistic regression and RF [2,23,41], the goal of this study is to compare these two well-known classification methods for which feature selection has been incorporated into the training process using the German credit dataset.

The rest of the paper is organized as follows: Part 2 summarizes related pieces of literature, Part 3 covers the methodologies used in wrapper algorithm based on the importance measure by permutation and the embedded algorithm of a shrinkage method class, and it discusses classification-based measures. Part 4 illustrates the used empirical application, and Part 5 outlines the main results from this work.

2   Related Literature

This section provides a summary of previous work on feature selection and related works in credit risk classification.

2.1   Feature Selection

Filter Approach. Tries to identify the most informative features using a significance criterion (correlation-based feature selection, symmetrical uncertainty, chi-square test, etc.) and can be done using wrapper or embedded feature selection as a two-stage classification model [32,33].

Embedded Approach. The best-known way for integrating feature selection into the training process is decision trees. However, this tool is not recommended due to its instability [6]; adding observations can result in an entirely new tree [16]. Another approach in the literature to deal with the bias-variance trade-off is the lasso regression introduced by Tibshirani (1996) [39] which is a class of shrinkage methods that can also be used for logistic regression [27,40] and SVM [30].

Wrapper Approach. Uses a sequential strategy to provide an optimal subset by adding or removing features (forward/backward) to the current subset a, this strategy is straightforward to implement, but its drawback is that it is a greedy algorithm, which uses a dependent criterion $C(J)$ and does not guarantee the optimal solution. There are two wrapper adaptations to SVM and one to random forests in the literature. The latter overcomes the bias-variance tradeoff by employing two principles: bagging [5] and randomization [6], and it exhibits excellent performance in the presence of a large number of features [16]. To stabilize the OOB (Out Of Bag) error Hasan et al. (2016) [18] require forests with a high number of trees, and to stabilize feature selection Genuer et al. (2010) [14] require a repetition of these forests. The main issue that arises in the presence of high dimensional data is the correlation between features [4,10], the work of Gregorutti et al. (2017) [16] points to masking effects that may appear in the selection. However, for the time being, the majority of work in feature selection by random forests is based on wrapper algorithms [1,11,16,33]. There are two existing adaptations: NRFE (Non Recursive Feature Elimination) [14,15] and RFE (Recursive Feature Elimination) [4,26] that differ in the update of feature rank. The first consists of classifying features according to the importance criterion by permutation [6] at the algorithm's inception, then eliminating features using error rate, always according to the initial classification, which will be fixed throughout the algorithm. Svetnik et al. (2004) [38] compare the two procedures and conclude that the first is more efficient, contradicting Gregorutti's findings (2017) [16].

2.2   Feature Selection for Credit Risk Classification

Many researchers have studied feature selection for credit risk classification in the last decade: Ramya and Kumaresan (2015) [34] compare different filter methods (gain ratio, chi square, correlation-based feature selection) and conclude that they produce roughly the same subset, Dahiya et al. (2016) [9] build MLP (multilayer perceptron) and C4.5 classifiers using an ensemble of ranked feature selection and conclude that ensemble filter feature selection leads to better accuracy than classifiers built with a single filter selection. Arutjothi and Senthamarai (2017) [3] use hybrid feature selection (filter + wrapper) and test classification accuracy using several classifiers on a test dataset: SVM, logistic regression, and C4.5. Meanwhile, Arora and Kaur (2020) [2] use Bolasso as a pre-selection method and use the feature subset obtained to build several models: RF, SVM, Naive Bayes, and KNN, concluding that Bolasso-RF encasement leads to the best accuracy, Zhou et al. (2020) [41] use Lasso and MARS (multivariate adaptive regression splines) as filtering feature selection to build a classifier on several tools, including CART, logistic regression, and SVM and conclude that combining Lasso and SVM produces the best accuracy. Lapas et al. (2021) [24] used expert knowledge to investigate various feature selection scenarios using wrapper-based selection GA (Genetic Algorithm) and Naive Bayes or KNN.

The observation being that most research work focuses on a feature pre-selection phase, which can lead to discriminate features being discarded even when using the most sophisticated methods, it is necessary then to treat feature selection and model construction as a single optimization problem. As a result, we propose to investigate two of the most commonly used classifiers in the field, to which feature selection is integrated within the learning phase one by wrapper-based selection and the second employing penalty regularization of the L1 norm. To evaluate the performance of the two models we employ test samples.

3   Methodology

The methods used in the comparison are described in this section, namely the wrapper algorithm based on importance measure by permutation and logistic regression with lasso regularization, as well as the classification-based measures.

3.1   Wrapper Algorithm Based on Importance Measure by Permutation

As previously stated, the basic idea behind this algorithm is to select features sequentially using the importance measure by permutation as a ranked criterion and prediction error as a selection criterion. This strategy has been shown to be effective in the presence of feature correlations [4, 10, 16]. Several strategies exist in the literature, Mariammal et al. (2021) [26] after selecting the most important features, use a ranking process to eliminate weak features, Mustaqeem et al. (2017) [29] add feature replicas to the dataset to generate noise and carry out the selection by comparing feature importance to the maximum replicas importance. The OOB error is used as a selection criterion in the majority of the work on the field.

We chose to use the algorithm proposed by Genuer et al. (2010) [14] in our work because it is entirely automatic and produces feature selection along two axes: the first is description, where the selected features may influence the target feature and thus be correlated, and the second is prediction (classification), for this, a subset of the previous feature selection is chosen to predict the target feature [13]. As we are interested in the prediction task, our goal is to avoid rejecting true predictive features. Previous studies have already shown that the prediction task is altered when rejected discriminant features [36]. This procedure exists on the VSURF package in R [15]. It aims to stabilize OOB error through dense forests (ntrees = 2000) and repetition of the forests to stabilize the feature selection. The algorithm's steps are as follows [13]:

- Decreasing ranking of the h most important features.
- Selection for description: Add features incrementally from 1 to h, then select the model with the lowest OOB error from 1 to h'.
- Selection for prediction: Add features incrementally as long as the OOB error decreases below a threshold determined by the average variation caused by the addition of irrelevant features (from h' to h).

$$\frac{1}{h - h'} \sum_{j=h'}^{h-1} \left| error_{OOB_{j+1}} - error_{OOB_j} \right| \tag{1}$$

3.2 Logistic Regressiom with LASSO Regularization

Stepwise regression is a prevailing method of selecting important features to obtain a simple and easily interpretable model, and it is commonly used in logistic regression. However, Harell's work (2015) [17] demonstrates all of the drawbacks in this procedure including a bias in the selection. Furthermore, using stepwise regression to select features is highly unstable, especially when the number of features is large [37]. The alternative used in this work is logistic regression with lasso regularization; since the lasso performs better than the stepwise selection [19], we summarize in the following its application to the logistic regression:

To estimate the logistic regression coefficients β_j, we must minimize the negative log likelihood. For that consider, we have a sample Ω of size n, the value assigned by Y to an individual ω is denoted by $y(\omega)$. The likelihood and the log likelihood are then (respectively):

$$L = \prod_{\omega} \pi(\omega)^{y(\omega)} \cdot (1 - \pi(\omega))^{1-y(\omega)} \tag{2}$$

$$LL = \sum_{\omega} y(\omega) \ln \pi(\omega) + (1 - y(\omega)) \ln(1 - \pi(\omega)) \tag{3}$$

Consider now that the problem is to minimize the negative log likelihood with penalty regularization of the L1 norm, in other words, we must consider the size of the coefficients, and the problem becomes:

$$\hat{\beta} = \min_{\beta} \left[-LL + \lambda \sum_{j=1}^{p} |\beta_j| \right] \tag{4}$$

λ determines the coefficients' shrinkage, note that if $\lambda = 0$, we are in the classic logistic regression case. In contrast to ridge regression, lasso regression produces sparse solutions, requiring the process to incorporate feature selection into the training process. The implementation in the software is based on the algorithm developed by Freidman et al. (2010) [12] for the estimation of generalized linear models with convex penalties.

3.3 Classification Based Measures

To evaluate a classifier's performance, we prefer the error calculated on a test set [6]. For this, the commonly used metrics must be introduced which are derived from the confusion matrix (see Table 1):

Sensitivity (SN) $= \frac{TP}{TP+FN}$ called also Recall, is calculated by dividing the number of true positives by the sum of true positives and false negatives.

Table 1. Confusion matrix.

		Actual	
		Negative	Positive
Predicted	Negative	TN	FN
	Positive	FP	TP

Precision $= \frac{TP}{TP+FP}$ determines the rate of true positives among those predicted as positive by the algorithm and thus evaluates the classifier's discriminating power. It is calculated by dividing the number of true positives by the sum of true positives and false positives.

Specificity(SP) $= \frac{TN}{TN+FP}$ is calculated by dividing the number of true negatives by the sum of true negatives and false positives.

Accuracy $= \frac{TP+TN}{TP+TN+FP+FN}$ allows to evaluate the classifier's overall performance.

F1-Score. Is calculated through one of these formulas: $\frac{2}{\frac{1}{precision}+\frac{1}{SN}}$, $\frac{2 precision.SN}{precision+SN}$. Because we are dealing with proportions, we use harmonic average between precision and sensitivity. It's especially useful in case of imbalanced classification, such as fraud detection.

The ROC (Receiver Operating Characteristic) Curve. Represents the rate of true positives as a function of the rate of false positives (i.e. SN as a function of 1-SP) by varying the decision threshold between 0 and 1.

The PR (Precision Recall) Curve. Draws precision against recall for varying decision threshold, it is especially important for imbalanced classification.

AUC and PR-AUC. The former indicates the area under the ROC curve, while the latter represents the area under PR curve.

4   Experiments and Results

The German credit dataset, which was created by Hans Hofman of Hambourg University, has 1000 records on people who got credit from a bank, each with 13 categorical and 7 numerical features, and are then classified as good or bad borrowers. The dataset exists in scorecard package in R, Table 2 contains a description of it.

Table 2. Data description.

Features	Type	Min	Max	Levels
Status of existing checking account	Categorical	–	–	4
Duration in months	Numeric	4	72	–
Credit history	Categorical	–	–	5
Purpose	Categorical	–	–	10
Credit amount	Numeric	250	18424	–
Savings account and bonds	Categorical	–	–	5
Present employment duration	Categorical	–	–	5
Installment rate in percentage of disposable income	Numeric	1	4	–
Personal status and sex	Categorical	–	–	5
Other debtors or guarantors	Categorical	–	–	3
Present residence	Numeric	1	4	–
Property	Categorical	–	–	4
Age in years	Numeric	19	75	–
Other installment plans	Categorical	–	–	3
Housing	Categorical	–	–	3
Number of existing credits at this bank	Numeric	1	4	–
Job	Categorical	–	–	4
Number of people being liable to provide maintenance for	Numeric	1	2	–
Telephone	Categorical	–	–	2
Foreign worker	Categorical	–	–	2
Creditability	Categorical	–	–	2

4.1   Data Pre-processing

The dataset has been fine-tuned in the stage that follows:

Merging Classes. The principle of the CHAID algorithm inspired us to merge classes with similar distributions in order to avoid a different number of classes from one feature to another. As a result, we use the chi-square test: If we consider the target feature with K classes, we cross two levels of a feature with these K classes, resulting in a table $(K \times 2)$ as shown in Table 3, and we calculate the test statistic as follows:

$$\chi^2 = \sum_{k=1}^{K} \frac{\left(\frac{n_{k1}}{n_{.1}} - \frac{n_{k2}}{n_{.2}}\right)^2}{\frac{n_{k1}+n_{k2}}{n_{.1}n_{.2}}} \sim \chi^2_{K-1} \qquad (5)$$

If the test is non-significant (we accept the null hypothesis), merge two adjacent classes if the feature is ordinal, or any pair if it is nominal; we can evenly

Table 3. Contingency table for $K = 2$

	Level 1	Level 2	$\sum$
$k = 1$	n_{11}	n_{12}	$n_{1.}$
$k = 2$	n_{21}	n_{22}	$n_{2.}$
$\sum$	$n_{.1}$	$n_{.2}$	n

Table 4. Merging classes

Feature	Initial levels number	Merged levels number	Merged levels
Present employment duration	5	3	$0 \leq \cdots < 1$; $1 \leq \cdots < 4; \geq 4$
Savings account and bonds	5	4	No savings account; $\cdots < 100$; $100 \leq \cdots < 500; \geq 500$
Personal status and sex	5	3	Male: married/divorced; male:single; female
Job	4	2	Skilled; unskilled
Purpose	10	4	Business; car; domestic appliances; others
Credit history	5	4	All credits paid back duly; existing credits paid back duly till now; delay in paying off in the past; critical account

iterate this step with merged classes in a bottom up strategy. We performed the operation on features for which the test was non-significant for at least two classes of the feature, resulting in the merging of the feature classes for: Present employment duration, Savings account and bonds, Personal status and sex, Job, Purpose, Credit history, more information can be found in Table 4.

4.2 Data Transformation

Data Standardization. The operation results in all data belonging to the same domain, the reference method used for this operation is the Z_{score}; with the average μ_j for the location and the standard deviation σ_j for the dispersion parameter.

$$Z_{score} = \frac{X_j - \mu_j}{\sigma_j} \tag{6}$$

Dummy Coding. Considering categorical features, we used dummy coding with a category of reference. Since each one has l categories, we obtained $l-1$ dummy features; with $l-1$ degrees of freedom we don't need one category because we have enough information to determine which observation belongs in which category. This operation allows us to interpret the coefficients of the logistic lasso regression as opposed to the reference category. Because the selection of the reference category is not part of our research problem, we arbitrarily select the most frequent category as the reference category and refer the reader to a comprehensive study on the subject [20].

4.3   Subdivision into "Training-Test" Datasets

Any knowledge discovery requires the model's quality to be evaluated using prediction criteria. The evaluation must be done on data that was not used in the model's development. In addition, we know the membership class of individuals to the feature of interest, which results in data splitting into two separate samples. We used a 70–30% proportionate stratification strategy to split our dataset. We summarized the workflow in the diagram below (see Fig. 1). Where, after preprocessing our dataset, we standardized the features: duration in months, credit amount, and age in years, and then we dummy encoded the categorical features: Status of existing checking account, Credit history, purpose, Savings account and bonds, Present employment duration, Personal status and sex, Other debtors or guarantors, property, Other installment plans, Housing, Job, Telephone, and Foreign worker only for the logistic regression. After that, we used the same seed to split the dataset for the two models.

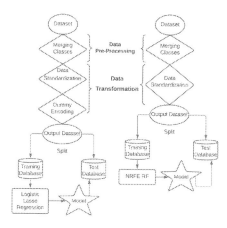

Fig. 1. The workflow diagram.

4.4   Results

Wrapper Algorithm Results. It is worth noting that the algorithm was carried out in four steps:

- Step 1: Training a random forest with ntrees = 2000 trees, all trees in a forest are developed independently on different bootstrap samples, and the importance of all features is obtained by averaging the loss of classification accuracy caused by random permutation of a feature.

$$VI(X_j) = \frac{1}{ntrees} \sum_{t=1}^{ntrees} (error^j_{OOB_t} - error_{OOB_t}) \tag{7}$$

- Step 2: Repeat step one 50 times to calculate the average $\overline{VI}(X_j)$, standard deviation $\sigma_{VI(X_j)}$ of each feature's importance, and rank them in order of importance (top graphs of Fig. 2), then select the h most important features using a threshold based on feature importance standard deviation because an important feature will always have a larger standard deviation [13].
- Step 3: In this step, we select features from the nested models that are relevant to the description task of the feature of interest. We select the model with the lowest OOB error (bottom left graph of Fig. 2), which leads us to choose h' features.
- Step 4: For the prediction feature selection, the algorithm stops until the OOB error decrease is greater than the OOB error variation average resulting from the inclusion of irrelevant features [14] which leads us to consider the fourth model with OOB error of 0.239 (see Table 5) with the four features: Status of existing checking account, Credit history, Other debtors or guarantors, and Savings account and bonds. (bottom right graph of Fig. 2).

Table 5. Feature selection for prediction

Forest (model)	1	2	3	4
OOB error	0.31	0.268	0.257	0.239

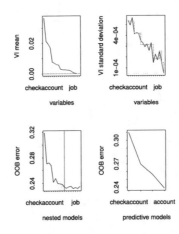

Fig. 2. Wrapper algorithm results (Feature names have been condensed for space reasons).

Logistic Lasso Regression Results. Figure 3 depicts the binomial deviance obtained for various λ values. λ is a parameter that is usually chosen so that the resulting model minimizes the negative binomial log-likelihood loss function, cross-validation (CV) is commonly used to find the optimal value of λ. Because of the parsimony issue we chose the value of $\lambda.1se$ which denotes the value of λ with one standard error of the loss function's minimum, in this case $\lambda.1se = 0.02$. (See Fig. 3) this leads us to consider the features in Table 6. If we consider $\pi(\omega)$ the probability of being a bad borrower then:

$$logit(\omega) = \ln\left(\frac{\pi(\omega)}{1 - \pi(\omega)}\right) = \beta_0 + \beta_1 X_1 + ... + \beta_J X_J \tag{8}$$

The odds ratio (OR) of the status of an existing checking account-$< 0 = 2.85$, It means that being a bad borrower is more common among those who have a checking account <0 than among those who do not have a checking account, making it a risk factor. Additionally, we consider all risk factors with an OR greater than one: Duration in months, Status of existing checking account-$0 \leq ... < 200$, Present employment duration-$0 \leq ... < 1$, and Credit history-critical account, and we consider all protective factors with an OR less than one: Savings account and bonds-≥ 500, Other debtors or guarantors-guarantor, and Credit history-all credits paid back duly. Finally, the features: Credit amount and Housing-for free are thought to have no effect on credit risk classification.

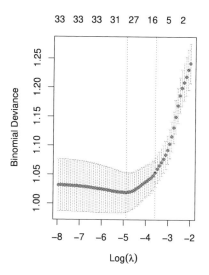

Fig. 3. Binomial deviation as function of lambda. The left dotted line shows the optimal value of log lambda that minimizes the binomial deviance; the right dotted line shows the value of log lambda.1se

Table 6. Estimated model coefficients

Feature	Coefficient	Odds ratio	Reference category
Duration in months	0.166	1.18	–
Credit amount	0.04	1.04	–
Savings account and bonds_ ≥ 500	−0.08	0.92	⋯ < 100
Status of existing checking account_< 0	1.04	2.85	No checking account
Status of existing checking account_ 0 ≤ ⋯ < 200	0.726	2.08	
Other debtors or guarantors_ guarantor	−0.23	0.8	None
Present employment duration_ 0 ≤ ⋯ < 1	0.266	1.31	≥ 4
Housing_for free	0.06	1.06	Own
Credit history_all credits paid back duly	−0.293	0.74	Existing credits paid back duly till now
Credit history_ critical account	0.22	1.25	

4.5 Classification Accuracy

Table 7 shows the results of experiments performed on the test dataset that detail the classification-based measures of feature selection algorithms and Fig. 4 depicts the PR curves for the two models built. We can see from the various metrics that the specificity is very low for both models, which is due to the fact that the negative class has been rebalanced from 5% to 30%, making the study of accuracy uninteresting because it includes the rate of true negatives (TN); the F1-score, which is a harmonic average between precision and sensitivity, is more suitable in this case, and it is superior for logistic lasso regression and even the PR-AUC.

Table 7. Classification measures on test dataset

	NRFE RF	Logistic lasso regression
Accuracy	0.7113	0.7515
Sensitivity (Recall)	0.8182	0.9825
Specificity	0.4390	0.2061
Precision	0.7730	0.7420
F1-score	0.794	0.8454
AUC	0.629	0.800
PR-AUC	0.789	0.877

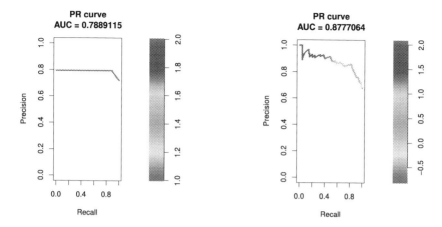

Fig. 4. PR curves for the two models built. The right fig represents the lasso logistic regression PR curve, while the right fig represents the NRFE RF PR curve.

5 Conclusion and Future Work

The credit risk classification is based on the features of the borrower to determine whether he is good or bad. In our study, we used a wrapper approach via random forests and an embedded approach via logistic lasso regression, intending to compare the two models over classification measures; for that, data preprocessing and data transformation via data standardization and dummy coding were required to run the models training, we observed an overall better classification for the logistic lasso regression. Finally, we discovered that the OOB error is optimistic with a value of 0.239, while the empirical estimate of error is 0.289. Another advantage of logistic lasso regression is the ability to individualize the specific effect of each OR. This analysis can be expanded in the future by experimenting with different classifiers and comparison criteria (stability-based measures and run time).

References

1. Acharjee, A., Larkman, J., Xu, Y., Cardoso, V.R., Gkoutos, G.V.: A random forest based biomarker discovery and power analysis framework for diagnostics research. BMC Med. Genomics **13**(1), 1–14 (2020)
2. Arora, N., Kaur, P.D.: A bolasso based consistent feature selection enabled random forest classification algorithm: an application to credit risk assessment. Appl. Soft Comput. **86**, 105936 (2020)
3. Arutjothi, G., Senthamarai, C.: Credit risk evaluation using hybrid feature selection method. Softw. Eng. **9**(2), 23–26 (2017)
4. Bahl, A., et al.: Recursive feature elimination in random forest classification supports nanomaterial grouping. NanoImpact **15**, 100179 (2019)
5. Breiman, L.: Bagging predictors. Mach. Learn. **24**(2), 123–140 (1996). https://doi.org/10.1007/BF00058655

6. Breiman, L.: Random forests. Mach. Learn. **45**(1), 5–32 (2001). https://doi.org/10.1023/a:1010933404324
7. Chen, W., Li, Z., hui Guo, J.: A vns-eda algorithm-based feature selection for credit risk classification. Math. Prob. Eng. **2020**, 1–14 (2020)
8. Chi, G., Uddin, M.S., Habib, T., Zhou, Y., Islam, M.R., Chowdhury, M.A.I.: A hybrid model for credit risk assessment: empirical validation by real-world credit data. J. Risk Model Validation, **14**(4) (2019)
9. Dahiya, S., Handa, S., Singh, N.: A rank aggregation algorithm for ensemble of multiple feature selection techniques in credit risk evaluation. Int. J. Adv. Res. Artif. Intell. **5**(9), 1–8 (2016)
10. Darst, B.F., Malecki, K.C., Engelman, C.D.: Using recursive feature elimination in random forest to account for correlated variables in high dimensional data. BMC Genet. **19**(1), 1–6 (2018)
11. Elavarasan, D., Vincent, P.M.D.R., Srinivasan, K., Chang, C.Y.: A hybrid cfs filter and rf-rfe wrapper-based feature extraction for enhanced agricultural crop yield prediction modeling. Agriculture **10**(9), 400 (2020)
12. Friedman, J., Hastie, T., Tibshirani, R.: Regularization paths for generalized linear models via coordinate descent. J. Stat. Softw. **33**(1), 1 (2010)
13. Genuer, R., Poggi, J.M.: Arbres cart et forêts aléatoires, importance et sélection de variables (2017). arXiv preprint arXiv: 1610.08203
14. Genuer, R., Poggi, J.M., Tuleau-Malot, C.: Variable selection using random forests. Pattern Recogn. Lett. **31**(14), 2225–2236 (2010)
15. Genuer, R., Poggi, J.M., Tuleau-Malot, C.: Vsurf: an r package for variable selection using random forests. R J. **7**(2), 19–33 (2015)
16. Gregorutti, B., Michel, B., Saint-Pierre, P.: Correlation and variable importance in random forests. Stat. Comput. **27**(3), 659–678 (2017). https://doi.org/10.1007/s11222-016-9646-1
17. Harrell, F.E.: Regression Modeling Strategies. SSS, Springer, Cham (2015). https://doi.org/10.1007/978-3-319-19425-7
18. Hasan, M.A.M., Nasser, M., Ahmad, S., Molla, K.I.: Feature selection for intrusion detection using random forest. J. Inf. Secur. **7**(3), 129–140 (2016)
19. Hastie, T., Tibshirani, R., Tibshirani, R.: Best subset, forward stepwise or lasso? analysis and recommendations based on extensive comparisons. Stat. Sci. **35**(4), 579–592 (2020)
20. Huang, Y., Montoya, A.: Lack of robustness of lasso and group lasso with categorical predictors: impact of coding strategy on variable selection and prediction (2020). arXiv preprint arXiv:40b200z6
21. Jović, A., Brkić, K., Bogunović, N.: A review of feature selection methods with applications. In: 2015 38th International Convention on Information and Communication Technology, Electronics and Microelectronics (MIPRO), pp. 1200–1205. IEEE (2015)
22. Kruppa, J., Schwarz, A., Arminger, G., Ziegler, A.: Consumer credit risk: Individual probability estimates using machine learning. Expert Syst. Appl. **40**(13), 5125–5131 (2013)
23. Laborda, J., Ryoo, S.: Feature selection in a credit scoring model. Mathematics **9**(7), 746 (2021)
24. Lappas, P.Z., Yannacopoulos, A.N.: A machine learning approach combining expert knowledge with genetic algorithms in feature selection for credit risk assessment. Appl. Soft Comput. **107**, 107391 (2021)

25. Lessmann, S., Baesens, B., Seow, H.V., Thomas, L.C.: Benchmarking state-of-the-art classification algorithms for credit scoring: an update of research. Eur. J. Oper. Res. **247**(1), 124–136 (2015)

26. Mariammal, G., Suruliandi, A., Raja, S., Poongothai, E.: Prediction of land suitability for crop cultivation based on soil and environmental characteristics using modified recursive feature elimination technique with various classifiers. IEEE Trans. Comput. Soc. Syst. **8**(5), 1132–1142 (2021)

27. McEligot, A.J., Poynor, V., Sharma, R., Panangadan, A.: Logistic lasso regression for dietary intakes and breast cancer. Nutrients **12**(9), 2652 (2020)

28. Molina, L.C., Belanche, L., Nebot, À.: Feature selection algorithms: a survey and experimental evaluation. In: 2002 IEEE International Conference on Data Mining, 2002. Proceedings, pp. 306–313. IEEE (2002)

29. Mustaqeem, A., Anwar, S.M., Majid, M., Khan, A.R.: Wrapper method for feature selection to classify cardiac arrhythmia. In: 2017 39th Annual International Conference of the IEEE Engineering in Medicine and Biology Society (EMBC), pp. 3656–3659. IEEE (2017)

30. Nazih, W., Hifny, Y., Elkilani, W., Abdelkader, T., Faheem, H.: Efficient detection of attacks in sip based voip networks using linear l1-svm classifier. Int. J. Comput. Commun. Control **14**(4), 518–529 (2019)

31. Pandey, T.N., Jagadev, A.K., Mohapatra, S.K., Dehuri, S.: Credit risk analysis using machine learning classifiers. In: 2017 International Conference on Energy, Communication, Data Analytics and Soft Computing (ICECDS), pp. 1850–1854. IEEE (2017)

32. Peng, X., et al.: Random forest based optimal feature selection for partial discharge pattern recognition in hv cables. IEEE Trans. Power Deliv. **34**(4), 1715–1724 (2019)

33. Rahman, M.S., Rahman, M.K., Kaykobad, M., Rahman, M.S.: isGPT: an optimized model to identify sub-golgi protein types using svm and random forest based feature selection. Artif. Intell. Med. **84**, 90–100 (2018)

34. Ramya, R., Kumaresan, S.: Analysis of feature selection techniques in credit risk assessment. In: 2015 International Conference on Advanced Computing and Communication Systems, pp. 1–6. IEEE (2015)

35. Salmi, M., Atif, D.: Using a data mining approach to detect automobile insurance fraud. In: International Conference on Soft Computing and Pattern Recognition, pp. 55–66. Springer (2021). https://doi.org/10.1007/978-3-030-96302-6_5

36. Seijo-Pardo, B., et al.: Biases in feature selection with missing data. Neurocomputing **342**, 97–112 (2019)

37. Smith, G.: Step away from stepwise. J. Big Data **5**(1), 1–12 (2018). https://doi.org/10.1186/s40537-018-0143-6

38. Svetnik, V., Liaw, A., Tong, C., Wang, T.: Application of breiman's random forest to modeling structure-activity relationships of pharmaceutical molecules. In: Roli, F., Kittler, J., Windeatt, T. (eds.) MCS 2004. LNCS, vol. 3077, pp. 334–343. Springer, Heidelberg (2004). https://doi.org/10.1007/978-3-540-25966-4_33

39. Tibshirani, R.: Regression shrinkage and selection via the lasso. J. Roy. Stat. Soc.: B (Methodol) **58**(1), 267–288 (1996)

40. Wang, H., Xu, Q., Zhou, L.: Large unbalanced credit scoring using lasso-logistic regression ensemble. PLOS ONE **10**(2), e0117844 (2015)

41. Zhou, Y., Uddin, M.S., Habib, T., Chi, G., Yuan, K.: Feature selection in credit risk modeling: an international evidence. Economic Research-Ekonomska Istraživanja, pp. 1–31 (2020)

Parameter Identification and Validation of Multi-innovation Least Squares Lithium Battery for Second-Order Battery Model

Jie Wu, Huigang Xu, and Peiyi Zhu[✉]

School of Electric and Automatic Engineering, Changshu Institute of Technology, Suzhou, China
zhupy@cslg.edu.cn

Abstract. Accurate lithium-ion battery models are important for the accurate estimation of battery states as well as the simulation, design, and optimization of new energy electric vehicles. However, the traditional recursive least squares method exhibits disadvantages such as low accuracy and long convergence time when applied to the identification of battery model parameters. In this paper, the second-order RC equivalent circuit model of lithium-ion battery is studied, and the online identification of model parameters by Multi-innovation least squares method is presented, data collected through HPPC cycle conditions and NEDC conditions experiments. The accuracy and convergence speed of the conventional recursive least squares estimation algorithm is described, to compare the absolute error between the estimated battery port voltage and the real value of the battery with different new interest lengths of the new interest least squares algorithm. The experimental results show that the multi-new interest least squares algorithm with longer new interest length has higher accuracy and convergence speed, which verifies the effectiveness and feasibility of the proposed method.

Keywords: Lithium-ion battery · Estimation of battery states · Multi-innovation least squares

1 Introduction

The development of battery management system (BMS) is one of the key technologies for new energy vehicles. Battery charge state estimation is the basic and core function in BMS [1]. Power battery modeling commonly used equivalent circuit models [2], common equivalent circuit models are Rint model, RC network model, Thevenin model and PNGV model, etc.

The accuracy of the lithium battery parameter identification algorithm is directly determined by the accuracy of the identification results. Least Squares (LS) method is a mathematical optimization method that modifies the best data by finding the square of the minimum error [3]. Recursive Least Squares (RLS), as an improved form of least squares, has the characteristics of high recognition accuracy, small data calculation and simplicity and ease of use [4]. However, the RLS has lower recognition accuracy and slower convergence than LS method due to the limitation of information acquisition.

© Springer Nature Switzerland AG 2022
A. Bennour et al. (Eds.): ISPR 2022, CCIS 1589, pp. 180–188, 2022.
https://doi.org/10.1007/978-3-031-08277-1_15

Multi-information least squares (MILS) method expands the single new information scalar used in each recursive operation of the LS method into multiple new information vectors of certain new information length, thus ensuring the recognition accuracy and improving the convergence speed of online parameter recognition [5]. Based on the above factors, this paper proposes the second-order battery equivalent model based on the MILS algorithm for the parameter identification of lithium batteries.

2 Lithium-Ion Battery Model

2.1 Second-Order RC Equivalent Circuit Model

Battery system parameter identification and battery SOC estimation need to establish an accurate battery model, and the more the number of RC links in parallel in the equivalent circuit model, the higher the accuracy of its equivalent circuit model, but the system faces higher computational cost and insignificant improvement in parameter identification accuracy [6]. When a battery is under dynamic conditions such as charging and discharging, its internal electrochemical polarization and differential concentration polarization occur, and the terminal voltage changes dynamically. It is shown that the second-order RC equivalent circuit model can well simulate the internal chemical characteristics of the battery and describe the voltage changes under dynamic conditions [7].

The equivalent circuit model is shown in Fig. 1, in which R_0 is the ohmic internal resistance of the lithium battery, R_{p1} and R_{p2} are the polarized internal resistance, C_{p1} and C_{p2} are the polarized capacitance. I is the battery operating current.

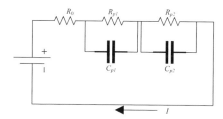

Fig. 1. Second-order RC network cell model

2.2 System Equation of State

Based on the second-order RC equivalent circuit model shown above, the model state equation can be established, and this system is discretized as following:

$$
\begin{cases}
\begin{bmatrix} U_{p1,k+1} \\ U_{p1,k+1} \\ SOC_{k+1} \end{bmatrix} = \begin{bmatrix} 1-\frac{T_s}{R_{p1}R_{p2}} & 0 & 0 \\ 0 & 1-\frac{T_s}{R_{p1}C_{p2}} & 0 \\ 0 & 0 & 1 \end{bmatrix} \cdot \begin{bmatrix} U_{p1,k} \\ U_{p1,k} \\ SOC_k \end{bmatrix} + \begin{bmatrix} \frac{T_s}{C_{p1}} \\ \frac{T_s}{C_{p2}} \\ \frac{\eta T_s}{C_n} \end{bmatrix} I_{b,k} \\
\\
U_{b,k} = [1\ 1\ 0] \begin{bmatrix} U_{p1,k} \\ U_{p2,k} \\ SOC_k \end{bmatrix} + R_0 I_{b,k} + U_{oc,k}
\end{cases}
\tag{1}
$$

where, $x_k = \left[U_{p1,k}, U_{p2,k}, SOC_k \right]^{\mathrm{T}}$

x_k——System state variables;

$U_{p1,k},\ U_{p2,k}$——The voltage across capacitors $C_{p1},\ C_{p2}$ at moment k;

SOC_k——SOC of lithium battery at moment k;

η——Coulomb effect factor;

T_s——System sampling time;

$I_{b,k}$——System input current at moment k.

2.3 Lithium Battery Identifiable Model

Transformation of the second-order RC equivalent circuit state equation into a frequency domain transfer function, make $G(s) = U_b(s) - U_{oc}(s)$. The discrete system transfer function is as follows.

$$
G(s) = \frac{U(s)}{I_b(s)} = R_0 + \frac{R_{p1}}{\tau_1 s+1} + \frac{R_{p2}}{\tau_2 s+1}
\tag{2}
$$

$$
\tau_1 = R_{p1}C_{p1},\ \ \tau_2 = R_{p2}C_{p2}
$$

where, $\tau_1,\ \tau_2$——Lithium battery polarization time constant.

The impulse response invariant method is used to discretize the equation, which is then transformed into the auto regressive exogenous (ARX) model required for lithium battery parameter identification, and the transformation process and related equations are shown in the Table 1 to obtain the lithium battery model parameters [8].

Table 1. Lithium battery parameter identification process

Equivalent circuit model	Second-order RC equivalent circuit model
Continuous system transfer function	$G(s) = R_0 + \frac{R_{p1}}{\tau_1 s + 1} + \frac{R_{p2}}{\tau_2 s + 1}$
Discrete systems transfer function	$G(z) = \frac{a_3 + a_4 z^{-1} + a_5 z^{-2}}{1 - a_1 z^{-1} - a_2 z^{-2}}$
Difference equation	$U_k = a_1 U_{k-1} + a_2 U_{k-2} + a_3 I_{b,k} + a_4 I_{b,k-1} + a_5 I_{b,k-2}$
ARX model	$y_k = h_k^T \theta$
	$h_k = \left[U_{k-1}, U_{k-2}, I_{b,k}, I_{b,k-1}, I_{b,k-2} \right]^T$
	$\theta = \left[a_1, a_2, a_3, a_4, a_5 \right]^T$
Model parameters	$a_1 = e^{-\frac{T_s}{\tau_1}} + e^{-\frac{T_s}{\tau_2}}, \; a_2 = -e^{-\frac{T_s}{\tau_1} - \frac{T_s}{\tau_2}}$
	$a_3 = R_0 + \frac{1}{C_{p1}} + \frac{1}{C_{p2}}$
	$a_4 = -\left(R_0 + \frac{1}{C_{P2}} \right) e^{-\frac{T_s}{\tau_1}} - \left(R_0 + \frac{1}{C_{P1}} \right) e^{-\frac{T_s}{\tau_2}}$
	$a_5 = R_0 e^{-\frac{T_s}{\tau_1} - \frac{T_s}{\tau_2}}$

3 Multi-innovation Least Squares

MILS is a generalization of the single-information correction technique, in which the difference between the output observation and the model estimate corresponding to the parameter identified in the previous moment is corrected for the previous moment's identification using multiple information from an information correction perspective [9]. Compared with the traditional RLS and LS algorithms, MILS algorithm has higher utilization of new interest, faster convergence speed and higher recognition accuracy.

Consider the following scalar system described by a linear regression model:

$$y(t) = 0^T(t)\theta + \upsilon(t) \tag{3}$$

where, $y(t) \in R$ is the system output, $\theta \in R$ is vector of parameters to be identified, $\varphi(t) \in R$ is the regression information vector consisting of the system input $u(t) \in R$ and the output $y(t)$, $\upsilon(t) \in R$ is the random noise with zero mean.

Consider a total of p sets of data from $t - p + 1$ to t. Then let

$$Y(p, t) := \begin{bmatrix} y(t) \\ y(t-1) \\ \vdots \\ y(t-p+1) \end{bmatrix} \in R^p, \; V(p, t) := \begin{bmatrix} v(t) \\ v(t-1) \\ \vdots \\ v(t-p+1) \end{bmatrix} \in R^p, \tag{4}$$

$$\Phi(p, t_s) = (\varphi(t_s), \varphi(t_s - 1), \ldots, \varphi(t_s - p + 1)) \in R^{n \times p}, \tag{5}$$

where p is the message length.

1) The parameter update equation is:

$$\hat{\theta}(t_s) = \hat{\theta}(t_{s-1}) + K(t_s)\left[Y(p,t_s) - \Phi^T(p,t_s)\hat{\theta}(t_s - 1)\right] \tag{6}$$

where $K(t_s)$ is the gain matrix, p ≥ 1 is the new rest length and θ(t) is the estimate of θ at moment t.

2) The gain matrix update equation is:

$$K(t_s) = \frac{P(t_s-1)\Phi(p,t_s)}{I_p + \Phi^T(p,t_s)P(t_s-1)\Phi(p,t_s)} \tag{7}$$

where: I_p is the unit matrix of order p, and $P(t_s - 1)$ is the covariance matrix at time t_s.

3) The updated equation of the covariance matrix is:

$$P(t_s) = \left[1 - K(t_s)\Phi^T(p,t_s)\right]P(t_s - 1) \tag{8}$$

The schematic flow diagram of the identification is shown in Fig. 2 below.

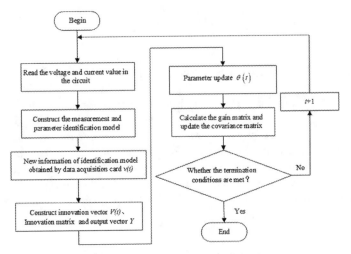

Fig. 2. Flowchart of MILS identification

3.1 .Experimental Validation and Analysis

The effectiveness of the identification is reflected in the accuracy of the identification and the convergence speed. The six parameters in the second-order battery model are identified online using LS and the MILS, respectively. The identification results are transferred to the battery model, and the accuracy of the identification algorithm is analyzed by the absolute error (EA) and the root mean square error (RMSA). The number of steps required to converge the parameters to stable values during the identification process is used to measure the convergence speed.

3.2 Experimental Platform

A special battery test system is used during battery charging and discharging characteristics testing. The voltage detection error of the test system is 2–3 mV, the current detection accuracy is ±0.1%, the temperature detection accuracy is ±1 °C, and the data sampling frequency is 1 Hz. All data of this experiment are conducted at a constant temperature of 25 °C. The experimental platform consists of a lithium battery test system, a constant temperature chamber, and a computer, which is shown in Fig. 3.

3.3 Experimental Procedure

A 25 Ah ternary Li-ion battery monoblock connected by 10 monoblocks in series is selected as the object of study. The battery monoblock has a charge cutoff voltage of 4.2 V and a discharge cutoff voltage of 2.7 V. In order to verify the accuracy and convergence speed of MILS, the experiment was selected to test the lithium battery monomer. Firstly, the series lithium battery was left for 1 h, and the fully charged series lithium battery was discharged at a constant current (12 A) until the SOC of the lithium battery monomer was reduced by 10%, and stopped discharging. Then, after being left for 1 h, it was discharged at constant current for 10 s, and after being left for 40 s, it was charged at constant current for 40 s. So on and so forth, until discharged to the lithium battery monomer cut-off voltage of 2.7 V. Meanwhile, as shown in Fig. 3. To verify the accuracy and convergence of MILS parameter identification under complex operating conditions, the battery current and terminal voltage under European NEDC operating conditions are used as input [10], which consists of two parts, ECE (urban driving cycle) and EUDC (suburban driving cycle), as shown in Fig. 4.

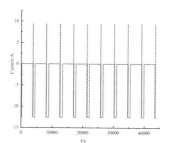 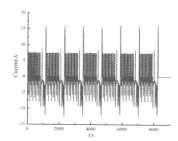

Fig. 3. HPPC working condition experiment   **Fig. 4.** NEDC working condition experiment

3.4 Experimental Results and Analysis

The second-order RC cell model is identified using LS and MILS, respectively. Since the accuracy and convergence of MILS identification results are related to the information length p taken, the results of MILS with information lengths of 5, 10, and 15 are taken for comparison, respectively. The parameter identification is performed by starting RLS with the same initial value and LS with different new interest lengths, respectively, and several error models are used to analyze the parameter identification results of the traditional RLS and MILS with different new interest lengths. The error models are:

$$\begin{cases} E_A = |V_{estimated} - V_{true}| \\ E_{MA} = \frac{1}{N} \sum E_A \\ E_{RMS} = \sqrt{\frac{1}{N} \sum (V_{estimated} - V_{true})^2} \end{cases} \quad (9)$$

where E_A is the absolute error, E_{MA} is the mean error, E_{RMS} is the root mean square error, $V_{estimated}$ is the algorithm estimate, and V_{true} is the measured battery voltage. Error calculations are performed and 2 experimental error comparison tables are obtained according to the error model proposed in Eq. 9 to evaluate RLS, as well as the MILS with different new interest lengths.

Figure 5 shows the absolute error between the true and estimated values of the model voltage for different algorithms under HPPC conditions.

Figure 6 shows the absolute error of the model output values compared with the experimental values for different algorithms under NEDC conditions.

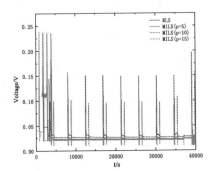 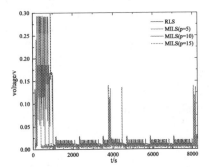

Fig. 5. HPPC working conditions   **Fig. 6.** NEDC working conditions

Table 2 shows the average error between the true value of the voltage output and the estimated value of the voltage identified by the algorithm under HPPC conditions and NEDC condition.

Table 2. Mean errors of different algorithms under HPPC conditions

With different algorithms E_{MA}/V	RLS	$MILS(p = 5)$	$MILS(p = 10)$	$MILS(p = 15)$
HPPC working conditions	0.02892	0.02641	0.02404	0.02197
NEDC working conditions	0.0535	0.0489	0.0412	0.0307

Table 3 represents the root mean square error between the true value of the voltage output and the estimated value of the voltage identified by the discriminated voltage algorithm under HPPC conditions and NEDC condition.

Table 3. Root mean square error of different algorithms under HPPC conditions

With different algorithms E_{RMA}/V	RLS	MILS$(p = 5)$	MILS$(p = 10)$	MILS$(p = 15)$
HPPC working conditions	0.0346	0.0318	0.0279	0.0240
NEDC working conditions	0.0573	0.0456	0.0317	0.0278

From the first 1000 data in Fig. 5 and Fig. 6, it can be found that the MILS with a new interest length p of 15 requires fewer iterations from the start of the algorithm to the convergence of the error to an acceptable range, i.e., the longer the Multi-innovation, the faster the MILS algorithm converges. Compared to RLS and the Multi-innovation lengths p of 5, 10, and 15, the MILS algorithm has higher recognition accuracy.

4 Conclusion

This paper establishes the second-order RC circuit model of lithium battery based on the characteristics of lithium battery, and verifies the traditional RLS and LS with Multi-innovation lengths under the HPPC experimental conditions and NEDC cyclic conditions, and reveals the accuracy and convergence of system parameter identification by changing the new interest lengths for comparison. In summary, the Multi-innovation p is larger, the start-up time of the algorithm is shorter, as well as the convergence speed and the estimation accuracy are improved.

References

1. Ren, Z., et al.: Error analysis of model-based state-of-charge estimation for lithium-ion batteries at different temperatures. Int. J. Electrochem. Sci. **15**(10), 9981–10006 (2020)
2. Wang, Y.J., et al.: A comprehensive review of battery modeling and state estimation approaches for advanced battery management systems. Renew. Sustain. Energy Rev. **131**, 110015 (2020)
3. Li, R., et al. Dynamic parameter identification of mathematical model of lithium-ion battery based on least square method. In: IEEE International Power Electronics and Application Conference and Exposition, Shenzhen, People's Republic of China (2018)
4. Tran, M.K., Fowler, M.: Sensor fault detection and isolation for degrading lithium-ion batteries in electric vehicles using parameter estimation with recursive least squares. Batteries-Basel **6**(1), 1 (2020)
5. Yan, Q.C., et al.: State of charge estimation for lithium-ion battery via MILS algorithm based on ensemble Kalman filter. Int. J. Photoenergy (2021)
6. Ramachandran, R., Subathra, B., Srinivasan, S.: Recursive estimation of battery pack parameters in electric vehicles. In: 9th IEEE International Conference on Computational Intelligence and Computing Research, Thiagarajar College of Engineering, Madurai, India (2018)
7. Xu, Y.D., et al.: State of charge estimation for lithium-ion batteries based on temperature-dependent second-order RC model. Electronics **8**(9), 1012 (2019)

8. Tran, N.T., Khan, A.B., Choi, W.: State of charge and state of health estimation of AGM VRLA batteries by employing a dual extended Kalman filter and an ARX model for online parameter estimation. Energies **10**(1), 137 (2017)
9. Ma, P., Ding, F., Zhu, Q.M.: Decomposition-based recursive least squares identification methods for multivariate pseudo-linear systems using the multi-innovation. Int. J. Syst. Sci. **49**(5), 920–928 (2018)
10. Zhu, G.H., et al.: Experimental study on combustion and emission characteristics of turbocharged gasoline direct injection engine under cold start new European driving cycle. Fuel **215**, 272–284 (2018)

Bat Echolocation Call Detection and Species Recognition by Transformers with Self-attention

Hicham Bellafkir[1]([✉]), Markus Vogelbacher[1], Jannis Gottwald[2],
Markus Mühling[1], Nikolaus Korfhage[1], Patrick Lampe[1], Nicolas Frieß[2],
Thomas Nauss[2], and Bernd Freisleben[1]

[1] Department of Mathematics and Computer Science, University of Marburg,
Marburg, Germany
{bellafkir,vogelbacher,muehling,korfhage,lampep,
freisleb}@informatik.uni-marburg.de
[2] Department of Geography, University of Marburg, Marburg, Germany
{jannis.gottwald,nicolas.friess,nauss}@geo.uni-marburg.de

Abstract. Biodiversity is important for several ecosystem services that provide the existential basis for human life. The current decline in biodiversity requires a transformation from manual, periodic assessment to automatic real-time biodiversity monitoring. Bats as one of the most widespread species among terrestrial mammals serve as important bioindicators for the health of ecosystems. Typically, bats are monitored by recording and analyzing their echolocation calls. In this paper, we present a novel approach for detecting bat echolocation calls and recognizing bat species in audio spectrograms. It is based on a transformer neural network architecture and relies on self-attention. Our experiments show that our approach outperforms state-of-the-art approaches for bat echolocation call detection and species recognition on several publicly available data sets. While our bat echolocation call detection approach achieves a performance of up to 90.2% in terms of average precision, our bat species recognition model obtains up to 88.7% accuracy for 14 bat classes occurring in Germany, some of which are difficult to distinguish even for human experts.

Keywords: Bat echolocation call detection · Bat species recognition · Transformer architectures · Self-attention

1 Introduction

Bats (Chiroptera) belong to the most widespread species group among terrestrial mammals. Except for the Arctic, Antarctic, and a few isolated islands, all regions of the earth are inhabited by bats [14]. With almost 1,400 recognized taxa, they represent almost one fifth to the mammalian diversity [6]. From pest control to seed dispersal, bats contribute to all four ecosystem services defined in the

A. Bennour et al. (Eds.): ISPR 2022, CCIS 1589, pp. 189–203, 2022.
https://doi.org/10.1007/978-3-031-08277-1_16

Millennium Ecosystem Assessment [15]. Thus, they are equally important for the ecosystems they inhabit and for mankind whose well-being depends on the integrity of these ecosystems. Furthermore, bats are important bioindicators for the health of the ecosystems they live in. For example, due to the high trophic level of insectivorous species, fluctuations in bat populations can be indicative of environmental changes affecting their prey of mostly small invertebrates, which are difficult to monitor themselves [10]. Unfortunately, about one third of all bat species are classified as threatened or data deficient by the International Union for Conservation of Nature (IUCN), and about half of all bat species show a declining or unknown population trend [6].

To monitor populations of bat species and thus biodiversity at scale, automatic bat echolocation call detection and bat species recognition approaches are required. With the success of Convolutional Neural Networks (CNNs) in various tasks, audio classification research has evolved over the last decade from models based on hand-crafted features like Mel Frequency Cepstral Coefficients (MFCCs) to CNNs that directly match audio spectrograms to feature representations. Several state-of-the-art bat echolocation call detection and bat species recognition approaches are based on CNN architectures applied to audio spectrograms.

Currently, transformer neural network architectures based on self-attention, such as Vision Transformers (ViT) [5], are successfully applied in computer vision tasks. While CNNs have an inductive bias, such as spatial locality and translation equivariance, vision transformers have a lower bias and can capture global context even in the first layers of a neural network.

In this paper, we present a novel approach for detecting bat echolocation calls and recognizing bat species in audio spectrograms. It is based on a transformer neural network architecture and relies on self-attention. To the best of our knowledge, this is the first work that utilizes fully attentional architectures to solve the problems of bat echolocation call detection and bat species recognition. In particular, our contributions are as follows:

– We present a novel self-attention approach for bat echolocation call detection and bat species recognition in audio spectrograms. It is based on pre-trained data-efficient image transformer models used as components in a workflow that we developed to process audio spectrograms of recorded bat echolocation calls.
– We show that the presented approach outperforms other state-of-the-art approaches for bat echolocation call detection and bat species recognition on several publicly available data sets. Our approach for bat echolocation call detection achieves a performance of up to 90.2% in terms of average precision, and our bat species recognition model obtains up to 88.7% accuracy for 14 bat classes occurring in Germany, some of which are difficult to distinguish even for human experts. Furthermore, we demonstrate that the distribution of the training and test set is an important factor for determining the recognition accuracy.
– We make our transformer models for bat echolocation call detection and bat species recognition publicly available at https://github.com/umr-ds/transformer4bats. In this way, other researchers can use our models to detect and recognize bat calls contained in their audio recordings.

The remainder of the paper is organized as follows. Section 2 discusses related work. The proposed approaches for bat call detection and recognition are presented in Sect. 3. Our experimental results are described in Sect. 4. Finally, Sect. 5 concludes the paper and outlines areas for future work.

2 Related Work

Since manually detecting and recognizing bat echolocation calls is a tedious and time-consuming task, several automated methods have been proposed in the literature. For many years, handcrafted features extracted from the length of the call, the frequencies, and amplitudes were used to train machine learning algorithms. In recent years, several approaches based on CNNs outperformed these methods by learning the features in an end-to-end manner. Usually, the audio recordings are transformed into spectrograms that are then processed by a CNN.

Bat populations are found across all continents except the Arctic, the Antarctic, and a few isolated islands. Nevertheless, each region has an individual set of bat species. Roemer et al. [21] attempted to build a universal model to classify bat calls into species around the world. To do so, they first classified the calls into sonotypes and refined the results by determining the exact species. They used random forests to realize their approach.

Current approaches often use CNNs and mostly consider a specific geographic region. Consequently, models are available for regions in Europe [20,22], North America [24], the Middle East [29], and Asia [2,13].

While most approaches are based on spectrograms generated from standard waveform audio recordings, Tabak et al. [24] trained their CNN on sparse zero-cross data. Using a small ResNet-18 [9] neural network architecture, they achieved good results on out-of-distribution data. The way spectrograms are generated plays an important role for the given task. Zualkernan et al. [29] compared three different kinds of spectrograms, namely Short-Time Fourier Transform (STFT), Mel-Scaled Filterbanks (MSFB), and Mel-Frequency Cerpstral Coefficients (MFCC). For their use case, they found that Mel-Scaled Filterbanks work best. Paumen et al. [20] decided to work with MFCCs for data efficiency reasons. Most approaches make use of the Short-Time Fourier Transform [2,13,22]. Zualkernan et al. [29] and Paumen et al. [20] considered 3 and 1 second snippets, respectively, extracted from spectrograms, whereas the majority of approaches extract single calls [2,13,22] and can thus make use of a higher input resolution per call. Chen et al. [2] showed how manual labeling of bat call events can be improved by a simple peak detection algorithm for detecting potential regions, in order to significantly speed up the labeling process by human experts [13,22].

Nevertheless, the human labeling process is a sophisticated task, infeasible for larger data sets, and the results can differ significantly between different annotators, resulting in a low inter-coder reliability [16].

Furthermore, an extensive publicly available bat call data collection is missing. In particular, certain species are inadequately represented in the existing data sets. To deal with small data sets and the class imbalance problem,

Kobayashi et al. [13] used data augmentation. The authors applied Cutout, Random Erasing, and Salt-and-Pepper noise to the spectrograms.

In terms of the considered bat species, Schwab et al. [22] are closest to our work. The authors first applied a band-pass filter to the audio signal and computed the corresponding spectrogram. Next, they detected peaks in that spectrogram and cut out 10 ms windows around these points. A first CNN was trained to distinguish bat calls from noise and background. Based on the results of this model, a second CNN determined the exact bat species. Optionally, both models can be integrated into a single neural network to make the process more lightweight. The best results were achieved using a modified ResNet-50 [9] architecture. Paumen et al. [20] considered German bat species too, but merged similar bat species into higher classes. While most papers work with species that partly stem from the same kind, Zualkernan et al. [29] took solely groups of bat species into account, which is a much simpler task. In our approach, bat species are only merged if they are not distinguishable by human experts. A list of the bat species we considered is presented in Table 1.

To tackle the problem of hard to classify weak signals, Chen et al. [2] introduced a weak label along with a rechecking strategy that verifies whether the neighboring regions of the weak call belong to the same class. This is a helpful strategy for noisy, passively recorded data. However, this strategy requires additional manual labeling effort. Due to the different species being considered and the lack of publicly available data sets, it is difficult to compare the existing approaches on bat call recognition using deep learning techniques. Furthermore, classes with few samples can often be found in the data sets, which has the risk of overfitting.

To classify bat calls, these calls need to be detected in audio recordings in the first place. This corresponds to localizing audio events in time. Similar to recognition, detection has been performed using handcrafted methods such as amplitude threshold filtering or detection of changes in frequency. However, most available algorithms are closed commercial projects and thus lack transparency. Contrary to that trend, Mac Aodha et al. [16] developed an open-source software based on CNNs. Their software called *BatDetective* is based on a sliding window approach over time-expanded and band-pass filtered FFT spectrograms. Since the used data sets contain rather noisy audio recordings, the mean amplitude of each frequency band is removed [1] as a denoising operation. The resulting image is then fed into a CNN using a sliding window approach, where the window size is 23 ms. The final probabilities of the binary classification problem are obtained by applying non-maximum suppression. BatDetective achieves the best quantifiable results among all available tools by a large margin.

In recent years, CNNs have been the best choice for detecting and recognizing bat calls. Meanwhile, in many computer vision tasks, CNNs have been outperformed by transformer architectures. Transformers are based on self-attention mechanisms and have been applied, e.g., to image classification [5,25], audio event tagging [8], and image captioning tasks [4,28].

3   Methods

Self-attention architectures, in particular transformers, have recently become the model of choice in natural language processing (NLP), where they are often pre-trained on a large corpus of text and fine-tuned for different downstream tasks. Furthermore, transformer architectures, such as Vision Transformers (ViT) [5], have also become state-of-the-art approaches in several computer vision tasks. In an attempt to explain this success, Cordonnier et al. [3] showed that self-attention can express a CNN layer and that convolutional filters are learned in practice by self-attention. Furthermore, Dosovitskiy et al. [5] concluded that transformers do not generalize well when trained on insufficient amounts of data. Contrary to this claim, Touvron et al. [25] showed that it is possible to learn a model that generalizes well using only the ImageNet-1k data set at training time. The authors presented a training process and a distillation procedure based on a distillation token, which plays the same role as the class token used by Dosovitskiy et al. [5], with the exception that it aims to reproduce the distribution of the label vector estimated by the teacher. The authors showed that the trained fully attentional model (i.e., DeiT) can achieve competitive state-of-the-art results on ImageNet. This approach was also successfully used in the Audio Spectrogram Transformer (AST) [8] for audio event tagging using audio set[1] [7].

In the following, we present a novel self-attention approach based on pre-trained DeiT models for the automated analysis of bat calls in audio recordings. In Sect. 3.1, we describe our detection approach for bat echolocation calls, whereas our recognition method is explained in Sect. 3.2.

3.1   Bat Echolocation Call Detection

Our detection approach is based on self-attention and hence free of any convolutional layers. In the following, we describe the steps of our detection workflow, as shown in Fig. 1. First, we generate a spectrogram from the audio recordings to enable the use of pre-trained image transformer architectures. Instead of using traditional MFCCs or PLP (perceptual linear prediction) coefficients, we use log Mel filterbank features that are state-of-the-art for bat call detection and recognition [29]. The input audio waveform of t seconds, time-expanded (TE) by factor 10, is converted into a sequence of 128-dimensional log Mel filterbank features computed by applying a 23 ms TE Hanning window with a large overlap of 84% to better capture short calls.

The resulting spectrogram is then split into multiple views with a sliding window approach, where each view is a 128×64 spectrogram that is equivalent to 230 ms TE. We selected the window size to be sufficiently long to capture the longest search calls in our training data. Each such view is then split into 16×16 patches with a stride of 10 and fed into a linear projection operation before using them as the input sequence to the transformer model to verify the presence of a bat call. The model takes $\lceil (H - 16)/10 \rceil \times \lceil (W - 16)/10 \rceil$ patches,

---

[1] https://research.google.com/audioset.

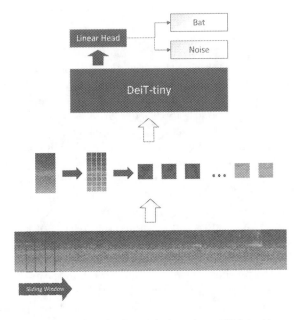

Fig. 1. Workflow for bat echolocation call detection.

which is 60 for an input of 128 × 64. We use overlapping patches that were shown to be beneficial by Gong et al. [8]. Since we split the original spectrogram into overlapping views, a one-dimensional non-maximum suppression operation is required to determine the final predicted time positions.

Our transformer architecture is a pre-trained tiny vision transformer (i.e., DeiT-tiny) [25] with approximately 5 million parameters. This architecture consists of 12 layers, each layer having 3 self-attention heads. The transfer learning approach with respect to processing audio data is applicable since the vision transformer can handle arbitrary sequence lengths. However, the pre-trained position embeddings need to be modified, since DeiT-tiny is pre-trained with a resolution of 224, which results in 14 × 14 position embeddings with patch sizes of 16 × 16. Since using randomly initialized position embeddings leads to poor overall performance in our experiments, we adopted the approach used by Gong et al. [8] and cut the first and second dimension of the 14 × 14 positional embedding to 12 × 5 and use it as the positional embedding in our training phase. Furthermore, we replaced the classification layer of the DeiT-tiny model to adapt the architecture to our audio detection task and initialized it randomly.

3.2   Bat Species Recognition

To build our recognition model, we consider only German bat species of the Tier-stimmenarchiv[2] data set. Some of the bat species have very similar echolocation

---

[2] https://www.tierstimmenarchiv.de/.

calls, e.g., the species of the Myotis kind. Nevertheless, we do not merge any of the classes, but try to distinguish them as annotated except for the Whiskered bat and the Brandt's bat which are not distinguishable by their echolocation calls. All species considered for training our model are presented in Table 1.

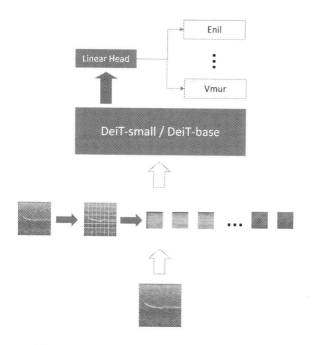

Fig. 2. Workflow for bat species recognition.

Our recognition workflow is shown in Fig. 2. To train our model, we first extracted echolocation calls from the Tierstimmenarchiv data set using our detection approach. For this purpose, the detection model was fine-tuned to the audio recordings of the Tierstimmenarchiv. We selected 90% as the threshold at which a detection is accepted. During training, we generate 128-dimensional log Mel filter bank features computed by applying a 23 ms TE Hanning window with a frame shift of 2.5 ms TE. We place each call in the midst of a 330 ms TE window, which results in an input resolution of 128 × 128. For the recognition task, we selected a deeper architecture to match the complexity of the task. We used two pre-trained data-efficient image base transformers (DeiT-small and DeiT-base) as alternatives. Both architectures consist of 12 layers as in DeiT-tiny, but DeiT-small has 6 self-attention heads per layer and DeiT-base has 12 self-attention heads per layer, whereas DeiT-tiny has only 3 self-attention heads per layer. Each image is then split (as in the detection workflow) into 16 × 16 patches with a stride of 10 in both dimensions, which results in 144 patches in this configuration.

4   Experiments

In this section, our methods are evaluated on different data sets. First, we describe the applied quality metrics as well as the used data sets in Sect. 4.1 and Sect. 4.2, respectively. Afterwards, we present our bat call detection results and the conducted experiments for bat species recognition in Sect. 4.3.

In all experiments, a workstation equipped with an AMD EPYC^{TM} 7702P 64-Core CPU, 256 GB RAM, and four NVIDIA® A100-PCIe-40GB GPUs were used. We implemented our approach using the PyTorch deep learning framework [19], utilizing the Torchaudio library [27] for audio and signal processing. The pre-trained DeiT models are available in the PyTorch Image Models (timm) library [26].

4.1   Quality Metrics

To evaluate the performance of our bat call detection approach, average precision (AP) and recall at 95% precision are used as our quality metrics. The AP score is the most commonly used quality measure for retrieval results and approximates the area under the recall-precision curve. The task of bat call detection can be considered as a retrieval problem where the annotated bat calls represent the relevant documents. Then, the AP score is calculated from the list of ranked documents as follows:

$$AP(\rho) = \frac{1}{|R \cap \rho^N|} \sum_{k=1}^{N} \frac{|R \cap \rho^k|}{k} \psi(i_k), \qquad (1)$$

$$\text{with} \quad \psi(i_k) = \begin{cases} 1 & \text{if } i_k \in R \\ 0 & \text{otherwise} \end{cases}$$

where N is the length of the ranked document list (total number of analyzed audio snippets), $\rho^k = \{i_1, i_2, \ldots, i_k\}$ is the ranked document list up to rank k, R is the set of relevant documents (audio snippets containing a bat call), $|R \cap \rho^k|$ is the number of relevant documents in the top-k of ρ and $\psi(i_k)$ is the relevance function. Generally speaking, AP is the average of the precision values at each relevant document.

To determine whether the model underestimates the number of bat calls in the test set, we further calculate recall at 95% precision, i.e., only 5% of false positives are allowed for this metric.

To evaluate the performance of our bat call recognition approach, we use the accuracy metric as well as the F1-score. These metrics are widely used for evaluating classification models.

4.2   Data

Altogether, three different data sets are used as our test material for the detection task: two data sets provided by the Indicator Bats Program (iBats) [11] and a third data set provided by the Norfolk Bat Survey [17]. They consist of time-

Table 1. Overview of the data set used for bat species recognition, showing the distribution of bat species including the number of recordings, the duration and the number of detected calls per species.

Species	Code	Recordings	Duration (s)(TE)	Detected calls
Eptesicus nilssonii	Enil	26	778	557
Eptesicus serotinus	Eser	75	2,018	1,926
Myotis brandtii/mystacinus	Mbart	24	1,770	2,033
Myotis dasycneme	Mdas	69	1,557	1,613
Myotis daubentonii	Mdau	128	3,370	4,764
Myotis emarginatus	Mema	28	450	597
Myotis myotis	Mmyo	52	1,202	1,598
Myotis nattereri	Mnat	77	1,969	2,714
Nyctalus leisleri	Nlei	78	2,338	1,770
Nyctalus noctula	Nnoc	95	3,236	2,574
Pipistrellus kuhlii	Pkuh	138	3,655	3,493
Pipistrellus nathusii	Pnat	140	3,760	3,279
Pipistrellus pipistrellus	Ppip	267	6,696	6,484
Vespertilio murinus	Vmur	69	1,788	1,654
Σ		1,266	34,587	35,056

Table 2. Number of recordings and bat calls per test set used for bat call detection.

Test set	Number of recordings	Number of calls
iBats R&B	500	1,604
iBats UK	434	842
Norfolk	500	1,345

expanded ultrasonic acoustic data recorded between 2005 and 2011. The number of recordings and bat calls per test set are summarized in Table 2. We used 2,812 recordings containing 4,782 calls for training; these are a subset of the iBats R&B data collection. The described training and test split matches the one used by Mac Aodha et al. [16].

Following Schwab et al. [22], we use a data set provided by the Tierstimmenarchiv for the recognition task. The data was originally recorded by Skiba [23] and later digitized. The mono audio files were provided in the WAV format with a sampling rate of 96 kHz and a bit depth of 24. Table 1 shows the amount of data per class along with the number of detected calls. As mentioned in Sect. 3.2, we first extracted these calls using our detection model. Although the annotations are given only per file, it is viable to assume that all detected calls in a certain recording belong to the corresponding manually annotated class of the file. This procedure is applicable because the data recorded by Skiba consists of high quality active recordings, i.e., the bats were captured for the recording and were close to the microphone.

Table 3. Summary of the training settings for the detection and recognition models.

Hyperparameter	Detection	Recognition
Learning rate	$5e^{-5}$	$1e^{-4}$
Warm up	✓	✓
Optimizer	ADAM [12]	ADAM
Batch size	64	64
Input resolution	128×64	128×128
Time/frequency masking	✓	✓
Patch stride	10	10
Random noise	✓	✓

Table 4. Bat call detection results on three different datasets and comparison to state-of-the-art approaches.

	Average precision			
Testset	Method			
	Random Forest [16]	CNN$_{FAST}$ [16]	CNN$_{FULL}$ [16]	DeiT-tiny
iBats R&B	0.674	0.863	0.895	**0.900**
iBats UK	0.648	0.781	0.866	**0.902**
Norfolk	0.630	0.861	0.882	**0.898**
	Recall at 95% precision			
iBats R&B	0.568	0.777	0.818	**0.821**
iBats UK	0.324	0.570	0.670	**0.681**
Norfolk	0.049	0.781	0.754	**0.801**

4.3 Results

Bat Call Detection. As mentioned above, our bat call detection model is trained using 2,812 recordings containing 4,782 calls. To augment the data, three different time crops were sampled per call, which contain the call or part of the call. For each call, six negative crops were randomly sampled, so that the overall training set contains 14,346 positive samples (bat call) and 28,692 negative samples. Furthermore, data augmentation techniques for spectrograms introduced by Park et al. [18] for speech recognition were used, such as time and frequency masking. The training settings are summarized in Table 3.

We adopted the evaluation protocol used by Mac Aodha et al. [16]. A detection is considered as a true positive if its distance to the ground truth is smaller than a given threshold. We used a threshold of 100 ms TE, similar to Mac Aodha et al. [16]. Table 4 summarizes the results of our approach and compares them to state-of-the-art approaches. The results of the random forest approach, CNN$_{FAST}$ and CNN$_{FULL}$ are reported by Mac Aodha et al. [16]. Our self-attention approach outperforms the other approaches on all three data sets.

Table 5. Comparison of bat call classification results of the DeiT-base model using call-based and recording-based splits of the data set.

Species	F1-score	
	Call-based split	Recording-based split
Enil	0.99	0.75
Eser	0.99	0.82
Mbart	0.99	0.95
Mdas	1.00	0.80
Mdau	0.99	0.92
Mema	1.00	0.98
Mmyo	1.00	0.98
Mnat	1.00	0.93
Nlei	0.99	0.76
Nnoc	1.00	0.91
Pkuh	0.99	0.86
Pnat	0.98	0.78
Ppip	0.99	0.94
Vmur	1.00	0.79
Avg	0.99	0.87

Table 6. Recognition results.

Method	Accuracy
DeiT-base + Log-Mel-Spectrogram	**0.887**
DeiT-small + Log-Mel-Spectrogram	0.882
ResNet-50 + Log-Mel-Spectrogram	0.884
DeiT-base + Log-Spectrogram	0.881
ResNet-50 + Log-Spectrogram	0.879

The model was trained for a maximum of five epochs. While the training took about 146 s per epoch, the average inference runtime is 0.093 s for an audio signal with a length of one second using the hardware/software system described at the beginning of Sect. 4.

Bat Call Recognition. In this section, we evaluate our bat call recognition model. We compare our self-attention approach to the ResNet-50 architecture that was used by Schwab et al. [22]. Additionally, we evaluate the use of Log-Spectrograms vs. Log-Mel-Spectrograms. Furthermore, we show that the way we split the data set into training and test data has a great impact on the result.

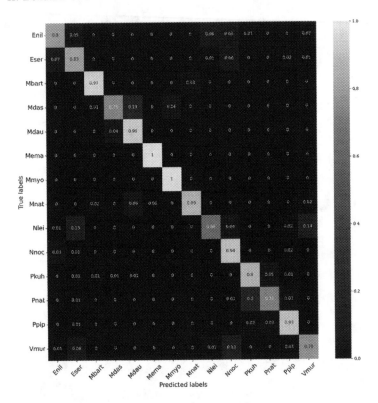

Fig. 3. Normalized confusion matrix of the bat species classification results.

First, we follow the split described by Schwab et al. [22], where 20% of all echolocation calls are used for evaluation, meaning that different calls emitted by the same individual in the same call sequence can be found in both the test and the training set. Since these calls are very similar, this approach is prone to overfitting and leads to high performance values. To better evaluate the generalization capabilities of the model, we split the data set on a recording level. For each class, we use 20% of the files for testing and all remaining files for training to provide a more appropriate evaluation strategy. Table 5 summarizes the results using both splits.

Indeed, the evaluation using a call-based split reaches very high F1-score values (≥ 0.98) for all species, which is consistent with the findings of Schwab et al. [22]. In contrast, these excellent scores cannot be confirmed using a file based split of the data set. However, our model still reaches very good results on this test split, since no class drops below 0.75, as Table 5 confirms. Therefore, we will use the latter, more meaningful data set split in the remainder of this paper.

In the following, we compare two transformer architectures, namely DeiT-base and DeiT-small, with the ResNet-50 CNN architecture. With 6 self-attention heads per layer, DeiT-small is a compromise between DeiT-tiny (3 heads) and DeiT-base (12 heads). As our input, we use both Log-Spectrograms as well as Log-Mel-Spectrograms. Table 6 shows that we achieve better results than the ResNet-50 on both kinds of spectrograms. Furthermore, our best model, i.e., DeiT-base, achieves a 0.6% higher accuracy using Log-Mel-Spectrograms than using simple Log-Spectrograms.

Next, we consider the results of the best model (DeiT-base with Log-Mel-Spectrograms) for individual bat species. For this purpose, the confusion matrix of the classification model is visualized in Fig. 3. The matrix shows a distinct diagonal line, which confirms the good classification results. Furthermore, it reveals that test samples are often mistaken for another species of the same kind. For instance, the model tends to confuse Enil and Eser, Mdas and Mdau or Pkuh and Pnat. Many confusions that span across two different kinds are quite difficult to distinguish as well, e.g., the bats of the Nyctaloid group (Nlei, Nnoc, Eser, Enil, Vmur) [20]. Most of the mistakes made by the model concern species that are hard to distinguish even for human experts, and the model predicted the higher order class correctly.

The recognition model was trained for a maximum of 50 epochs. While the training of the DeiT-base model took about 413 s per epoch, the average inference runtime is 0.02 s per bat call using the hardware/software system described at the beginning of Sect. 4.

5   Conclusion

We presented a novel self-attention approach for detecting bat echolocation calls and recognizing bat species in audio spectrograms. It is based on pre-trained data-efficient image transformer models used as components in a workflow that we developed to process audio spectrograms of recorded bat echolocation calls. We showed that it outperforms state-of-the-art CNN-based approaches for bat call detection as well as for bat species recognition on several publicly available data sets, yielding up to 90.2% average precision for detection and up to 88.7% accuracy for recognition, respectively. Furthermore, we demonstrated that the distribution of the training and test set is important for determining the recognition accuracy. Our neural network models for bat echolocation call detection and bat species recognition is made publicly available to other researchers.

There are several areas of future work. First, the detection performance could be improved by considering different call durations and different types of calls, like social calls and feeding buzzes, and using a special kind of object detection network architecture. Second, the generalization capabilities of the trained neural network models should be further investigated by considering, for example, different hardware devices and recording environments. Finally, the classification of bat behavior and the recognition of individual bats based on different echolocation calls are interesting research directions in the future.

Acknowledgement. This work is funded by the Hessian State Ministry for Higher Education, Research and the Arts (HMWK) (LOEWE Natur 4.0 and hessian.AI Connectom AI4Bats) and the German Academic Exchange Service (DAAD) (Transformation Partnership Program; Project OLIVIA).

References

1. Aide, T.M., Corrada-Bravo, C., Campos-Cerqueira, M., Milan, C., Vega, G., Alvarez, R.: Real-time bioacoustics monitoring and automated species identification. PeerJ **1**, e103 (2013)
2. Chen, X., Zhao, J., Chen, Y., Zhou, W., Hughes, A.C.: Automatic standardized processing and identification of tropical bat calls using deep learning approaches. Biol. Conserv. **241**, 108269 (2020). https://doi.org/10.1016/j.biocon.2019.108269
3. Cordonnier, J., Loukas, A., Jaggi, M.: On the relationship between self-attention and convolutional layers. In: 8th International Conference on Learning Representations, ICLR 2020, Addis Ababa, Ethiopia (2020)
4. Cornia, M., Stefanini, M., Baraldi, L., Cucchiara, R.: Meshed-memory transformer for image captioning. In: 2020 IEEE/CVF Conference on Computer Vision and Pattern Recognition, CVPR 2020, Seattle, WA, USA, June 13–19, 2020, pp. 10575–10584. Computer Vision Foundation/IEEE (2020). https://doi.org/10.1109/CVPR42600.2020.01059
5. Dosovitskiy, A., et al.: An image is worth 16x16 words: transformers for image recognition at scale. In: 9th International Conference on Learning Representations, ICLR 2021, Austria (2021)
6. Frick, W.F., Kingston, T., Flanders, J.: A review of the major threats and challenges to global bat conservation. Ann. N. Y. Acad. Sci. **1469**(1), 5–25 (2020). https://doi.org/10.1111/nyas.14045
7. Gemmeke, J.F., et al.: Audio set: an ontology and human-labeled dataset for audio events. In: 2017 IEEE International Conference on Acoustics, Speech and Signal Processing (ICASSP), pp. 776–780 (2017). https://doi.org/10.1109/ICASSP.2017.7952261
8. Gong, Y., Chung, Y., Glass, J.R.: AST: audio spectrogram transformer. In: Interspeech 2021, pp. 571–575 (2021). https://doi.org/10.21437/Interspeech.2021-698
9. He, K., Zhang, X., Ren, S., Sun, J.: Deep residual learning for image recognition. In: 2016 IEEE Conference on Computer Vision and Pattern Recognition (CVPR) (2016). https://doi.org/10.1109/CVPR.2016.90
10. Jones, G., Jacobs, D.S., Kunz, T.H., Willig, M.R., Racey, P.A.: Carpe noctem: the importance of bats as bioindicators. Endang Species Res. **8**, 93–115 (2009). https://doi.org/10.3354/esr00182
11. Jones, K.E., et al.: Indicator bats program: a system for the global acoustic monitoring of bats. Biodivers. Monit. Conserv. 211–247 (2013). https://doi.org/10.1002/9781118490747.ch10
12. Kingma, D.P., Ba, J.: Adam: a method for stochastic optimization. In: Bengio, Y., LeCun, Y. (eds.) 3rd International Conference on Learning Representations, 2015, San Diego, CA, USA (2015). http://arxiv.org/abs/1412.6980
13. Kobayashi, K., Masuda, K., Haga, C., Matsui, T., Fukui, D., Machimura, T.: Development of a species identification system of japanese bats from echolocation calls using convolutional neural networks. Ecol. Inform. **62** (2021). https://doi.org/10.1016/j.ecoinf.2021.101253
14. Kunz, T.H.: Ecology of Bats. Springer, Boston, MA, 1 edn. (1982). https://doi.org/10.1007/978-1-4613-3421-7

15. Kunz, T.H., Braun de Torrez, E., Bauer, D., Lobova, T., Fleming, T.H.: Ecosystem services provided by bats. Ann. N. Y. Acad. Sci. **1223**(1), 1–38 (2011). https://doi.org/10.1111/j.1749-6632.2011.06004.x

16. Mac Aodha, O., et al.: Bat detective-deep learning tools for bat acoustic signal detection. PLoS Comput. Biol. **14**(3) (2018). https://doi.org/10.1371/journal.pcbi.1005995

17. Newson, S.E., Evans, H.E., Gillings, S.: A novel citizen science approach for large-scale standardised monitoring of bat activity and distribution, evaluated in eastern England. Biol. Conserv. **191**, 38–49 (2015). https://doi.org/10.1016/j.biocon.2015.06.009

18. Park, D.S., et al.: Specaugment: a simple data augmentation method for automatic speech recognition. Interspeech 2019 (2019). https://doi.org/10.21437/interspeech.2019-2680

19. Paszke, A., et al.: Automatic differentiation in pytorch. In: NIPS-W (2017)

20. Paumen, Y., Mälzer, M., Alipek, S., Moll, J., Lüdtke, B., Schauer-Weisshahn, H.: Development and test of a bat calls detection and classification method based on convolutional neural networks. Bioacoustics, 1–12 (2021). https://doi.org/10.1080/09524622.2021.1978863

21. Roemer, C., Julien, J.F., Bas, Y.: An automatic classifier of bat sonotypes around the world. Methods Ecol. Evol. 101526 (2021). https://doi.org/10.1111/2041-210X.13721

22. Schwab, E., Pogrebnoj, S., Freund, M., Flossmann, F., Vogl, S., Frommolt, K.H.: Automated bat call classification using deep convolutional neural networks (2021). https://www.researchgate.net/publication/350978565_Automated_Bat_Call_Classification_using_Deep_Convolutional_Neural_Networks

23. Skiba, R.: Europäische Fledermäuse. Westarp Wissenschaften, Hohenwarsleben (2003)

24. Tabak, M.A., Murray, K.L., Lombardi, J.A., Bay, K.J.: Automated classification of bat echolocation call recordings with artificial intelligence. Ecol. Inform. **68**, 101526 (2022). https://doi.org/10.1016/j.ecoinf.2021.101526

25. Touvron, H., Cord, M., Douze, M., Massa, F., Sablayrolles, A., Jégou, H.: Training data-efficient image transformers & distillation through attention. In: 38th International Conference on Machine Learning, PMLR 139, pp. 10347–10357 (2021)

26. Wightman, R.: Pytorch image models (2019). https://github.com/rwightman/pytorch-image-models. https://doi.org/10.5281/zenodo.4414861

27. Yang, Y.Y., et al.: Torchaudio: building blocks for audio and speech processing. In: IEEE International Conference on Acoustics, Speech, and Signal Processing, Singapore (2022)

28. Yu, J., Li, J., Yu, Z., Huang, Q.: Multimodal transformer with multi-view visual representation for image captioning. IEEE Trans. Circ. Syst. Video Technol. **30**(12), 4467–4480 (2020). https://doi.org/10.1109/TCSVT.2019.2947482

29. Zualkernan, I., Judas, J., Mahbub, T., Bhagwagar, A., Chand, P.: A tiny CNN architecture for identifying bat species from echolocation calls. In: 2020 IEEE / ITU International Conference on Artificial Intelligence for Good (AI4G), pp. 81–86 (2020). https://doi.org/10.1109/AI4G50087.2020.9311084

Scheduling Techniques for Liver Segmentation: ReduceLRonPlateau vs OneCycleLR

Ayman Al-Kababji[1]([⊠]) [ID], Faycal Bensaali[1] [ID], and Sarada Prasad Dakua[2] [ID]

[1] College of Engineering, Qatar University, Doha, Qatar
{aa1405810,f.bensaali}@qu.edu.qa
[2] Department of Surgery, Hamad Medical Corporation, Doha, Qatar
SDakua@hamad.qa

Abstract. Machine learning and computer vision techniques have influenced many fields including the biomedical one. The aim of this paper is to investigate the important concept of schedulers in manipulating the learning rate (LR), for the liver segmentation task, throughout the training process, focusing on the newly devised `OneCycleLR` against the `ReduceLRonPlateau`. A dataset, published in 2018 and produced by the Medical Segmentation Decathlon Challenge organizers, called Task 8 Hepatic Vessel (MSDC-T8) has been used for testing and validation. The reported results that have the same number of maximum epochs (75), and are the average of 5-fold cross-validation, indicate that `ReduceLRonPlateau` converges faster while maintaining a similar or even better loss score on the validation set when compared to `OneCycleLR`. The epoch at which the peak LR occurs perhaps should be made early for the `OneCycleLR` such that the super-convergence feature can be observed. Moreover, the overall results outperform the state-of-the-art results from the researchers who published the liver masks for this dataset. To conclude, both schedulers are suitable for medical segmentation challenges, especially the MSDC-T8 dataset, and can be used confidently in rapidly converging the validation loss with a minimal number of epochs.

Keywords: Liver delineation · Semantic segmentation · Convolutional neural network · Dice score · Schedulers · Learning rate

1 Introduction

Hepatic-related diseases are responsible of two million deaths annually around the world [1]. Half of these diseases are liver cirrhosis and the other half are

This publication was made possible by an Award [GSRA6-2–0521-19034] from Qatar National Research Fund (a member of Qatar Foundation). The contents herein are solely the responsibility of the authors. Moreover, the HPC resources and services used in this work were provided by the Research Computing group in Texas A&M University at Qatar. Research Computing is funded by the Qatar Foundation for Education, Science and Community Development (http://www.qf.org.qa).

A. Bennour et al. (Eds.): ISPR 2022, CCIS 1589, pp. 204–212, 2022.
https://doi.org/10.1007/978-3-031-08277-1_17

hepatitis and hepatocellular carcinoma (HCC) [1]. It is also a destination for metastasis originating from adjacent organs. Nonetheless, the liver and its lesions are usually analyzed in tumor staging [3].

To aid medical personnel in diseases' diagnosis, it is important to create a delineation for the liver from computerized tomography (CT) and magnetic resonance imaging (MRI) scans, especially for its tumors and vessels. It can help surgeons in pre-procedural planning and/or evaluating the successfulness of a procedure by post-procedural segmentation on a follow-up CT scan. However, at the moment, the norm is to manually or semi-automatically segment the liver as it is more accurate. However, these techniques entail radiologists' subjectivity, intra- and inter-radiologist variance, and time-consumption [4].

2   Related Work

In this section, we delve into the most prominent studies that utilized U-Net (or similar) architecture for the liver segmentation task.

In surveying related works, U-Net is found to be an important convolutional neural network (ConvNet) architecture that pushed the biomedical segmentation field [9]. Thus, it was natural for researchers to utilize it extensively. In [2,3], a 2D fully connected network (FCN) following the U-Net scheme is utilized, followed by a 3D conditional random field (CRF). In [15], the U-Net acts as a coarse liver segmenter, but in [5], it is used as the main model. On the other hand, other researchers have become inspired from the U-Net structure given its excellence and popularity in different fields. In [12], the authors use an ensemble of three 2D FCN models having a U-Net-like architecture for the liver segmentation task, and the final mask is their average. In a different direction, [6] create a multi-planar U-Net (MPU-Net) to capture the organ of interest from different angles (generalizing to more views than the three conventional ones), and similarly, fusing the output of all planar segmentation to generate the final output. In [11], both global and local context are used in a U-Net architecture (GLC-UNet), which also is one of the few studies, if not the first, that attempts to automatically delineate the famous Couinaud segmentation of the liver.

Regarding the scheduling techniques, authors in [10] discuss a scheduler called OneCycleLR with the idea of regularization via the manipulation of learning rate (LR) to prevent the model from getting trapped at a local minimum well-suited for the training set [10]. Moreover, super-convergence is achieved as the scheduler allows the model to reach a 'better" minimum for the cost function, for both training and validation set in a shorter time with respect to other scheduling techniques.

The aim of this paper is to compare the ReduceLRonPlateau and OneCycleLR techniques, provided by PyTorch's deep learning library, in training a U-Net ConvNet model for the liver segmentation task. It aims at understanding how different schedulers behave, and the implications a scheduler has on the employed ConvNet. By doing so, we further optimize the performance of the U-Net instead of its structure, showing that it is still a viable ConvNet. The remainder of this paper is organized as follows. Section 3 delves into the methodology highlighting the dataset and pre-processing techniques, training environment and the selected parameters, and the test records with the evaluation metrics. Section 4 portrays and discusses the obtained results, and finally, we conclude the paper in Sect. 5.

3   Methodology

In this section, the followed methodology is explained thoroughly. Firstly, the employed dataset is discussed highlighting its characteristics along with the applied pre-processing techniques. Secondly, the utilized model, the environment, and the training parameters are highlighted (no post-processing techniques are applied). Lastly, the test records and the evaluation criteria that are used to evaluate the models' performance are briefly mentioned. Figure 1 highlights the most important steps of training/testing.

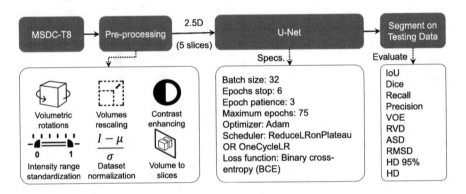

Fig. 1. Training and testing scheme

3.1   Dataset and Pre-processing Techniques

Dataset Summary. Out of the 10 produced datasets in The Medical Segmentation Decathlon Challenge, the Task 8 Hepatic Vessels (MSDC-T8) is the one that is used in this paper. The dataset originally contains 443 contrast-enhanced (CE) CT scan records, out of which 303 are for training, and the remaining 140 are for testing. The intra-slice resolution for the whole dataset varies between 0.56 and 0.98 mm, while the inter-slice distance ranges between 0.80 and 8 mm. The slices have the standard number of pixels for a CT scan, which are (512 × 512), with a varying number of slices between 24 and 251. It is worth noting that the majority, if not all, the records are focused in the abdominal area and contain only the ground-truth labels for both tumors (lesions) and vessels within the livers for the training set. The testing set masks are hidden as part of the challenge. However, the authors in [11] created the liver annotations within the MSDC-T8 dataset for the whole 443 CT records and shared it publicly, along with Couinaud's segmentation for 193 of those records.

Pre-processing. The following pre-processing techniques are applied in the order they are mentioned: 1) volumetric rotations so that all volumes face same direction; 2) volumetric rescaling by a half; 3) clipping voxels' intensity values to be in $[-100, 400]$ where the liver is most situated [14]; 4) intensity range standardization; 5) contrast enhancing via contrast limited adaptive histogram equalization (CLAHE) technique; 6) data normalization; and finally 7) volumes to slices transformation (3D → 2.5D).

3.2   Training Environment and Parameters

The used model in this paper is the famous U-Net. It is used to compare the obtained results with the ones reported in [11]. Moreover, the framework of choice is PyTorch (torch version==1.8.1+cu102) for conducting the comparison, where a 5-fold cross-validation (80% training/20% validation) procedure is applied. The maximum number of epochs per fold is 75, but early stopping is utilized to avoid unnecessary training time (epochs_stop = 6). The 2.5D (5 slices) input shape is utilized with a batch size = 32, and binary cross-entropy (BCE) as the loss function. Adam optimizer is used with two different schedulers that are facilitated by the `torch.optim` library in PyTorch, namely the `OneCycleLR` [7] and the `ReduceLRonPlateau` schedulers [8]. An NVIDIA Tesla V100 GPU with Intel Xeon Skylake CPU are used for the training.

3.3   Test Records and Evaluation Metrics

The 23 testing records were chosen randomly and are mentioned explicitly: [003, 012, 045, 072, 090, 105, 117, 129, 141, 153, 169, 178, 193, 205, 220, 236, 246, 258, 268, 280, 294, 304, 320]. The following metrics are utilized to evaluate the trained models' performance: 1) Dice similarity coefficient (DSC) (per case version) [%]; 2) intersection-over-union (IoU) [%]; 3) relative volumetric difference (RVD); 4) average symmetric surface distance (ASD) [mm]; 5) root-mean squared symmetric surface distance (RMSD) [mm]; 6) maximum symmetric surface distance (MSD)/Hausdorff distance (HD) [mm]; 7) 95% Hausdorff distance (HD95) [mm]; and 8) the number of epochs until early stopping stops the fold run.

4   Results and Discussion

When implementing the 5-fold cross-validation, $-24K$ slices end up in training and $-6K$ slices are in validation. Figure 2 shows how the LR changes using these two schedulers (assuming the absence of early stopping). The `ReduceLRonPlateau` scheduler needs at least four parameters to function: 1) initial LR; 2) validation loss to evaluate the model's generalization; 3) epochs_patience, which is a waiting threshold after which the LR will be changed; and 4) LR_{factor} to reduce the LR by a given factor ($LR_{new} = LR_{initial} \times LR_{factor}$). On the other hand, `OneCycleLR` needs at least two parameters to function: 1) the

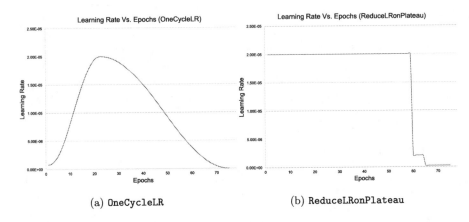

(a) OneCycleLR   (b) ReduceLRonPlateau

Fig. 2. Learning rate change using (a) OneCycleLR and (b) ReduceLRonPlateau

maximum LR it will peak to; and 2) the number of max_epochs that is initially planned.

It can be seen that the OneCycleLR changes the LR irrespective of any metric. On the other hand, ReduceLRonPlateau changes the LR based on saturation or increase in the validation loss. In Fig. 2a, the LR starts small and reaches the LR_{max} that the user specifies

Due to the variance in how these schedulers operate, different LRs are designed for each scheduler, followed by a discussion drawn over the noticed patterns and results. For both schedulers, seven LRs are selected to showcase the performance of the developed U-Net over the segmentation of the liver. Table 1 shows the mean and standard deviation from the 5-fold cross-validation that is implemented per scheduler and LR.

The best results per metrics are bolded in Table 1. Moreover, The aforementioned LRs for the OneCycleLR are the maximum LRs that the scheduler will reach. Firstly, it is worth noting that the achieved results using the original U-Net in 2.5D mode outperforms the ones described in [11]. It achieves better Dice result than the 2D (with and without convolutional long short-term memory (LSTM)), 2.5D, and 3D U-Net counterparts in the liver segmentation task. Moreover, it comes really close to the proposed GLC-Unet $(98.18 \pm 0.85)\%$ in [11], while the best run from ReduceLRonPlateau LR=16×10^{-5} achieves $(98.12 \pm 0.04)\%$ in Dice. This shows that it is possible to extract even higher results from their GLC-Unet if they adopt our pre-processing and scheduling techniques. Additionally, the obtained results per fold are close to each other as the reported standard deviation are relatively small.

Regarding the chosen LR, it must not be too small such that the network does not get stuck in a local minimum and get prolonged training periods. This is evident for both schedulers, by observing that higher LRs tend to generate ConvNets that generalize better (more fine-tuned) with less training time. In comparing both scheduling techniques in the generated results, the best result from

Table 1. Results of both schedulers with different LRs are reported through the mean (standard deviation) of 5-fold cross-validation for each metric. Note: The reported LRs for `OneCycleLR` scheduler are the maximum peaks.

	LR	Dice	IoU	RVD	ASD	RMSD	HD	95% HD	Epochs
OneCycleLR (Max LR)	2×10^{-5}	97.67 (0.12)	95.48 (0.23)	−0.008 (0.004)	1.055 (0.509)	3.81 (1.15)	44.00 (4.43)	5.13 (4.03)	42.6 (2.6)
	4×10^{-5}	97.72 (0.15)	95.58 (0.28)	−0.009 (0.004)	1.002 (0.522)	3.70 (1.58)	41.58 (7.41)	5.09 (4.12)	34.0 (3.1)
	8×10^{-5}	97.93 (0.09)	95.97 (0.17)	−0.009 (0.005)	0.576 (0.089)	2.51 (0.30)	37.78 (1.86)	2.82 (0.70)	29.4 (2.2)
	16×10^{-5}	98.01 (0.06)	96.12 (0.11)	−0.008 (0.005)	0.521 (0.110)	2.05 (0.45)	31.51 (6.71)	2.68 (0.67)	29.0 (2.9)
	24×10^{-5}	98.07 (0.11)	96.24 (0.21)	−0.005 (0.003)	**0.482 (0.076)**	**1.88 (0.29)**	29.25 (5.18)	**2.43 (0.59)**	30.0 (3.8)
	32×10^{-5}	98.03 (0.10)	96.16 (0.19)	**−0.004 (0.005)**	0.606 (0.147)	2.47 (0.71)	34.31 (3.11)	2.61 (0.45)	25.0 (3.7)
	40×10^{-5}	98.04 (0.17)	96.17 (0.32)	−0.007 (0.003)	0.503 (0.131)	1.97 (0.74)	33.17 (8.63)	2.56 (0.82)	25.8 (2.0)
ReduceLRon Plateau	0.4×10^{-5}	97.20 (0.13)	94.60 (0.24)	−0.009 (0.004)	1.541 (0.276)	5.59 (0.63)	59.02 (7.91)	10.63 (3.15)	72.8 (3.9)
	0.8×10^{-5}	97.40 (0.15)	94.96 (0.27)	−0.010 (0.003)	1.097 (0.238)	4.47 (0.86)	59.47 (7.83)	5.56 (3.35)	48.6 (4.0)
	2×10^{-5}	97.69 (0.13)	95.51 (0.24)	−0.011 (0.003)	0.751 (0.130)	3.03 (0.61)	40.43 (1.46)	3.40 (0.76)	30.6 (1.3)
	4×10^{-5}	97.87 (0.06)	95.86 (0.11)	−0.011 (0.003)	0.625 (0.142)	2.57 (0.84)	38.26 (7.34)	2.73 (0.12)	23.0 (2.8)
	8×10^{-5}	98.04 (0.10)	96.18 (0.19)	−0.009 (0.003)	0.528 (0.104)	1.99 (0.52)	**27.03 (6.55)**	2.67 (0.73)	20.8 (3.6)
	16×10^{-5}	**98.12 (0.04)**	**96.33 (0.07)**	−0.008 (0.002)	0.624 (0.443)	2.15 (1.40)	27.16 (4.53)	4.10 (4.37)	22.0 (1.6)
	32×10^{-5}	98.02 (0.10)	96.15 (0.19)	−0.006 (0.004)	0.515 (0.062)	2.09 (0.52)	33.87 (10.39)	2.58 (0.42)	**18.8 (4.2)**

`ReduceLRonPlateau` (LR=16×10^{-5} with Dice = $(98.12 \pm 0.04)\%$) surpasses the best one from `OneCycleLR` (LR=24×10^{-5} with Dice = $(98.07 \pm 0.11)\%$), by not a far margin. Moreover, it converged faster than the `OneCycleLR`. This could be due to the fact that `OneCycleLR` initially starts with a small LR that gradually increases and reaches the peak around epoch 23 (refer to Fig. 2a), while `ReduceLRonPlateau` starts strong with a high LR with respect to `OneCycleLR`. Figure 3 shows a convergence example from the two best runs from `OneCycleLR` and `ReduceLRonPlateau`, respectively, highlighting the aforementioned point on why `ReduceLRonPlateau` converges faster in this context.

After the creation of liver delineations, another script that is developed and built over scikit-image's marching cubes algorithm [13] is used to build the 3D interpolation of the 2D segmented slices. The script is capable of taking multiple delineations and combining them into a single .obj file along with its .mtl file that will build the liver along with its tumors and vessels in the same .obj file. In

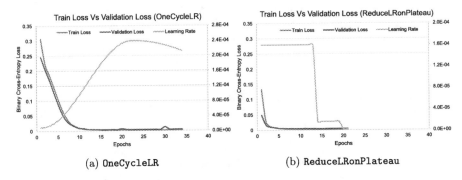

(a) OneCycleLR   (b) ReduceLRonPlateau

Fig. 3. Convergence plots for best fold run (a) OneCycleLR with LR = 24×10^{-5} and (b) ReduceLRonPlateau LR = 16×10^{-5}

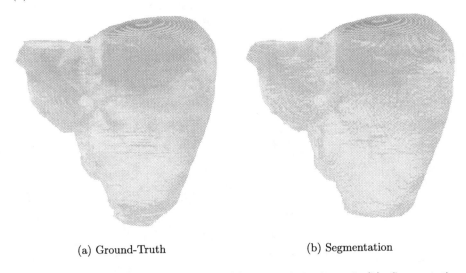

(a) Ground-Truth   (b) Segmentation

Fig. 4. Record 294 from MSDC-T8 (a) Ground-Truth and (b) Segmentation (ReduceLRonPlateau LR=16×10^{-5}) fold 5 with Dice = 98.16%

this paper, the liver delineations are only present and they are shown in Fig. 4 for both the ground-truth and segmented masks for record 294 from the MSDC-T8 dataset.

5   Conclusion and Future Work

To conclude, this paper investigates two different scheduling techniques aimed towards enhancing the convergence of the trained model. Both schedulers vary the LR to further enhance the model generalization (by making the LR higher at the beginning for the OneCycleLR, and by reducing the LR by a factor for the ReduceLRonPlateau). It is observed that the achieved results, using both schedulers, outperformed state-of-the-art results based on U-Net. Moreover, both schedulers performed well on the MSDC-T8 dataset, but `ReduceLRonPlateau` slightly outperformed `OneCycleLR` in this context as it initiates with a large LR which gets minimized when the validation loss plateaus, while the OneCycleLR has a fixed behavior and is independent from the validation loss. For the future work, the aim is to manipulate the number of epochs for the `OneCycleLR` such that the maximum LR occurs much earlier (prior to epoch 23). Moreover, the tumor and vessels segmentation challenges will be tackled and investigated as well.

References

1. Asrani, S.K., Devarbhavi, H., Eaton, J., Kamath, P.S.: Burden of liver diseases in the world. J. Hepatol. **70**(1), 151–171 (2019). https://doi.org/10.1016/j.jhep.2018.09.014
2. Christ, P.F., et al.: Automatic liver and lesion segmentation in CT using cascaded fully convolutional neural networks and 3D conditional random fields. In: Ourselin, S., Joskowicz, L., Sabuncu, M.R., Unal, G., Wells, W. (eds.) MICCAI 2016. LNCS, vol. 9901, pp. 415–423. Springer, Cham (2016). https://doi.org/10.1007/978-3-319-46723-8_48
3. Christ, P.F., et al.: Automatic liver and tumor segmentation of CT and MRI volumes using cascaded fully convolutional neural networks (2017)
4. Hu, P., Wu, F., Peng, J., Liang, P., Kong, D.: Automatic 3D liver segmentation based on deep learning and globally optimized surface evolution. Phys. Med. Biol. **61**(24), 8676–8698 (2016). https://doi.org/10.1088/1361-6560/61/24/8676
5. Ouhmich, F., Agnus, V., Noblet, V., Heitz, F., Pessaux, P.: Liver tissue segmentation in multiphase CT scans using cascaded convolutional neural networks. Int. J. Comput. Assist. Radiol. Surg. **14**(8), 1275–1284 (2019). https://doi.org/10.1007/s11548-019-01989-z
6. Perslev, M., Dam, E.B., Pai, A., Igel, C.: One network to segment them all: a general, lightweight system for accurate 3d medical image segmentation. In: Shen, D. (ed.) MICCAI 2019. LNCS, vol. 11765, pp. 30–38. Springer, Cham (2019). https://doi.org/10.1007/978-3-030-32245-8_4
7. PyTorch: OneCycleLR - PyTorch 1.9.0 documentation. https://pytorch.org/docs/stable/generated/torch.optim.lr_scheduler.OneCycleLR.html#torch.optim.lr_scheduler.OneCycleLR
8. PyTorch: ReduceLROnPlateau - PyTorch 1.9.0 documentation. https://pytorch.org/docs/stable/generated/torch.optim.lr_scheduler.ReduceLROnPlateau.html#torch.optim.lr_scheduler.ReduceLROnPlateau
9. Ronneberger, O., Fischer, P., Brox, T.: U-Net: convolutional networks for biomedical image segmentation. In: Navab, N., Hornegger, J., Wells, W.M., Frangi, A.F. (eds.) MICCAI 2015. LNCS, vol. 9351, pp. 234–241. Springer, Cham (2015). https://doi.org/10.1007/978-3-319-24574-4_28
10. Smith, L.N., Topin, N.: Super-convergence: very fast training of neural networks using large learning rates. In: Artificial Intelligence and Machine Learning for Multi-Domain Operations Applications. vol. 11006. SPIE-Intl Soc Optical Eng (2019)

11. Tian, J., Liu, L., Shi, Z., Xu, F.: Automatic couinaud segmentation from CT volumes on liver using GLC-UNet. In: Suk, H.-I., Liu, M., Yan, P., Lian, C. (eds.) MLMI 2019. LNCS, vol. 11861, pp. 274–282. Springer, Cham (2019). https://doi.org/10.1007/978-3-030-32692-0_32

12. Vorontsov, E., Tang, A., Pal, C., Kadoury, S.: Liver lesion segmentation informed by joint liver segmentation. In: 2018 IEEE 15th International Symposium on Biomedical Imaging (ISBI 2018), pp. 1332–1335. IEEE (2018). https://doi.org/10.1109/ISBI.2018.8363817

13. van der Walt, S., et al.: The scikit-image contributors: scikit-image: image processing in Python. PeerJ 2, p. e453 (2014). https://doi.org/10.7717/peerj.453, https://doi.org/10.7717/peerj.453

14. Yuan, Y.: Hierarchical Convolutional-Deconvolutional Neural Networks for Automatic Liver and Tumor Segmentation (2017)

15. Zhang, Y., et al.: Deep learning initialized and gradient enhanced level-set based segmentation for liver tumor from CT images. IEEE Access 8, 76056–76068 (2020). https://doi.org/10.1109/ACCESS.2020.2988647

An Explainable Predictive Model
for the Geolocation of English Tweets

Sarra Hasni[1,2(✉)] and Sami Faiz[2(✉)]

[1] Department of Information and Communication Technologies, Tunisia Polytechnic School,
La Marsa, Tunisia
hasni.sarra@gmail.com
[2] Laboratory of Remote Sensing and Spatial Information Systems, ENIT, Tunis, Tunisia
sami.faiz@isa2m.rnu.tn

Abstract. With the growing impact of social networks in our daily lives, current trends towards reducing the gap between them and the physical world become more prominent. In this context, some geolocation solutions have recently been developed in order to determine the geographical appurtenance data on those networks. The majority of proposed geolocation strategies is composed of machine learning and neural network-based models. The latter are considered as black boxes, which means the complexity of understanding their structures and their behaviors by humans. This limitation is emphasized by the need to generate interpretable and explainable outputs. In this paper, we demonstrate explainability on the predictions made by an advanced neural-network-based model for tweets geolocation using LIME, a state of the art open source explainability technique. Experiences performed on a set of geotagged tweets showed the aggregation of LIME's explanations with the geolocation model's results by 78% when dealing with two English variants.

Keywords: XAI (Explainable Artificial Intelligence) · LIME (Local Interpretable Model-Agnostic Explanations) · Natural language processing · Neural-network · Geolocation

1 Introduction

Becoming integral parts in our daily lives, social networks are considered as a rich source of information. Shared data on those networks with spatial references allow bridging the gap between the virtual world and the physical one. Twitter as an LBNS (Location Based Social Network) offers the opportunity for data analyzers to better understand users' movements, behaviors and preferences and then, to exploit them for multiple purposes. For example, modeling the propagation of diseases using Twitter is widely studied in several works [1–3]. Other works examine how political parties react and locally impact the public during particular periods like the spread of Coronavirus [4–6]. For other critical situations as disasters, geotagged tweets provide useful information that may be used to intervene quickly and therefore to limit impacts of such natural phenomena [7–9].

© Springer Nature Switzerland AG 2022
A. Bennour et al. (Eds.): ISPR 2022, CCIS 1589, pp. 213–220, 2022.
https://doi.org/10.1007/978-3-031-08277-1_18

Despite the utility of geotagged tweets, their rates are still insufficient compared to non-geotagged ones. In this context, prior studies estimate that less than 1% of tweets are labeled with geographic coordinates [10, 11]. To tackle this limitation, several works are established to propose geolocation solutions for individual tweets. Other works are developed to infer twitterers' locations or simply users' homes. For this aim, a set of tweets is analyzed for each user at a time to determine his most permanent location. Among these works, a recent model denoted by 'DeepGeoloc' is proposed to geolocate both tweets and twitterers [12]. For the first time, this model associates inherent linguistic particularities with location features for tweet classification. Compared with other available algorithms that adopt a purely statistical treatment of tweets, DeepGeoloc achieves better results. It demonstrates its ability to differentiate similar writing styles from English tweets. This neural-network based model also proves its scalability and applicability for the geolocation of new tweets.

Due to the sensitivity of the geolocation problem, ensuring the accuracy of estimated locations is imposed to deploy DeepGeoloc with confidence. For example, though social media, tornadoes that occurred in 2013 in Texas are reported even before they made the news [13]. This allows to determine effected zones and to make accurate decisions. Hence, in such critical situation, DeepGeoloc robustness is important and a better understanding of predicted results is required. This need is emphasized since this model is based on a set of deep neural networks which are in turn considered as black boxes with difficult-to-understand structures and behaviors.

In this paper, we take a step towards reducing the tension between DeepGeoloc's accuracy and explainability. For this aim, a local post-hoc explanation for predicted results is performed using a state of the art open source technique: LIME (Local Interpretable Model-Agnostic Explanation). Note that the choice of this technique among others is to provide a particular explanation for a given tweet which can later be evaluated with a human knowledge. For more details, we are able to rate the relevance of an explanation in relation to the identification of words with high localness indication in English variants.

2   Theoretical Background

2.1   Overview of the DeepGeoloc Model

In order to resolve the geolocation problem of tweets and twitterers, a neural network based model is recently proposed in [12]. This model investigates the relation between linguistic particularities (semantic, orthographic and morphological features) and the spatial evidence. For this aim, a set of advanced sub-models have been used.

In the first layer, two character-based word embedding models are trained to encode linguistic particularities from individual and concatenated tweets. The resulted vector representations of words are fed into the second layer as inputs. The latter is composed of Recurrent Neural Networks (RNNs) which are useful to guarantee a sequential modeling as well as dependencies between words in a given tweet. For more details, Bi-LSTMs (bidirectional Long Short Term Memory) are employed for a word sense disambiguation process. Through this neural architecture, the correct sense is associated to a given word according to its surrounding context. More precisely, senses that may differ from one region to another are distinguished by comparing encoded linguistic features of other words in the same tweet with those in similar tweets. A second Bi-LSTM layer is also defined in order to determine the most important sequences of words in a tweet that may have more spatial indications. Compared to word frequency models, contextual information have shown to be more effective to delimit the use of local words notably in retweets. Then, the average pooling is applied in order to obtain the entire tweet embedding. A softmax layer is finally defined as the output layer in order to predict for each tweet, the probability distribution over all class labels which correspond to regions.

2.2 Overview of Explainable Artificial Intelligence for Natural Language Processing

With the technological advancement, machine learning and deep learning models become more popular and more remarkable in many tasks. For Natural Language Processing applications, advanced models commonly denoted by 'black boxes' have marked their effectiveness. Particularly, neural-network based ones (e.g., LSTMs) are so widely deployed that their potential after-effects can no longer be taken for granted [14]. Due to the increased models' complexity, producing interpretable and explainable predictions is progressively requested [15] which motivates the emergence of a new field denoted by XAI (Explainable Artificial Intelligence). A set of XAI methods are developed to 'explain' complex deep learning models and to bridge the gap between complexity and prediction accuracy.

Recently, Mueller et al., [16] categorizes explanation systems into three generations. The first one includes expert systems from the 70's. The second one contains human-computer systems which aim to generate a cognitive support based on reasoning capacities and human knowledge. As for the third one, it contains systems which goal is to understand the inner workings of the black boxes. In this paper, we are interested in the third category and especially in works that were developed to interpret text data. The latter can be divided into two main classes. The first class relies on saliency-based explanations where a score is assigned to a given word according to its importance to explain a given classification. LIME (Local Interpretable Model-Agnostic Explanations) is a popular example of saliency maps methods [17]. It generates interpretations to a given input and its corresponding prediction scores which are in turn produced by any classifier. Simulated randomly samples around the instance are considered during the interpretation process. An axiomatic attribution method called INTGRAD [18] is also widely exploited for the explanation of text classifiers. Using the gradient of the output, this method provides an explanation for a given prediction with respect to the features of the input. Being a real-time instance-wise feature selection method, L2X [19] is another example of model explainer. Given a training instance and its corresponding prediction, L2X is applied to identify the more informative set of its input features through a variational approximation using a feature selector. The second class for text explanation methods is composed of attention-based ones. For example, the attention matrix explores dependencies between words in order to produce explanations [20]. For a single sequence, it relates all possible words' positions to generate its internal representation. Considering a sequence of N words, an $N \times N$ matrix is constructed where each word in that sequence is represented through a row and a set of columns. Black boxes can be also involved in the process of explainability. Particularly, their attention layers can be used to calculate words' scores in a sentence as detailed in [21].

In addition to these two classes, a variety of methods can be explored in relation to XAI using texts like xspells, Anchors and Doctorxai. For xspells [22] it is represented as an agnostic local explainer for sentiment classification from short texts. Based on a set of extracted rules from a decision tree which is in turn learned in the latent space, this method returns explanations in the form of examples and counterexamples sentences. Anchors [23] is another model-agnostic system that randomly produces rules (anchors) with the highest coverage as explanations. For instances on which the anchor holds, no changes are observed on the prediction outcome. As indicated by its name, Doctorxai [24] operates on healthcare sequential data by exploiting a dedicated ontology for data perturbation and neighbors' generation. But, this explainer can be applied on other types of sequential data with other ontologies.

3   Methodology

Given a particular instance, we aim to explore the degree to which a prediction explanation corresponds to an independent explanation provided by humans. As a local post-hoc technique, LIME is employed to generate explanations for geographical appurtenance individual tweets which locations are already predicted by DeepGeoloc. The flowchart to generate explanations is described in Fig. 1.

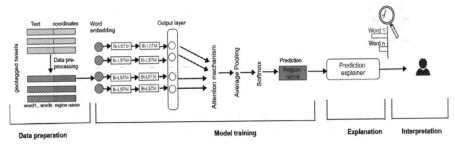

Fig. 1. The process of generating explanations for the tweet geolocation predictions

We refer to Covid-large [12] that consists of a set of geotagged tweets published from the UK and the USA and written in British and American English. These tweets are shared over the last two weeks of March 2021 and each of which contains at least one predefined keyword in relation with Coronavirus. For the text preprocessing phase, authors [12] recommended some treatments that have no impact on the shape of words. Precisely, they proceed to text tokenization and removing URLs, hashtags and @mentions. The resulted texts are then, exported in CSV format. As for longitude/latitude coordinates, they are converted to regions' names in order to make the differentiation of geographical appurtenance of tweets easier. At the third phase, the DeepGeoloc model is ready to be trained and then evaluated on new tweets. For each new tweet, the model predicts a class (region) that contains already geotagged tweets with maximum linguistic similarities.

Generated predictions are finally transferred to the prediction explainer LIME. The latter provides an explanation for each individual instance x as follows [18]:

$$\text{Explanation}(x) = \text{argmin}_{g \in G} L(f, g, \pi_x) + \Delta(g)$$

where g is the explanation model, G denotes the family of all possible explanations, f is the original predictor (which corresponds to DeepGeoloc in our case), π_x is the proximity measure of an instance z from x or simply the neighborhood around x that is considered for the explanation, $\Delta(g)$ represents a measure of model complexity where few features are preferred to keep it low and finally $L(f, g, \pi_x)$ measures unfaithfulness of g when approximating f in the locality defined by $\pi(x)$.

4 Results and Discussion

Our experiments are performed on two subsets of Covid-large. Each subset contains around 650 instances that are selected manually. The first one is composed of geotagged tweets written in both British and American English. Generated Lime explanations for both cases are illustrated in Fig. 2 and Fig. 3. At a country level, the LIME explanations match with our explanations. While the word 'breathalyses' is commonly used in the U.S, it can be replaced by 'breathalyzes' in the U.K due to differences in regional linguistic particularities. According to the prediction explainer, this word is the most discriminant so that the first tweet is supposed to be written in American English which corresponds to DeepGeoloc's prediction. In the second example, two local words of the same country are identified which increases prediction probabilities of the corresponding class. These results match with our explanation and with DeepGeoloc's results as 'movies' and 'quarantine' can be mostly replaced by 'films' and 'isolation' respectively in the British English.

The second subset of Covid-large contains only published tweets from the U.S. At a more granular geographical level, we observe degradation in the performance of LIME when dealing with more than two classes. Given a set of 48 classes where each of which represents an American state, we observe three scenarios. In the third tweet, a match between LIM's output and our reasoning is noticed where the local word 'hella' is ranked with the highest importance. However, this agreement is not observed for the rest of instances. Precisely, the predicted location of the fourth tweet is Kansas whereas it should be California. This is due to the word 'BBQ' that is commonly used in Kansas which explains its high score of importance. The correct sense of this word is not captured in that tweet even with the presence of another local word of the correct class. Another example where LIME fails in generating an explanation that fits with DeepGeoloc results is illustrated in the fifth tweet. Contrarily to the third instance, the word 'hella' is not sufficient to define California as the correct location instead of Arizona. This can be explained by the similarity of writing styles in these two states.

To conclude, around 78% generated explanations match with DeepGeoloc results when dealing with both American and British tweets. At a state level, only around 39% allies with the geolocation model predictions. Thus, we find that LIME can be qualified as a faithful prediction explainer for binary classification. However, its performance is not guaranteed when dealing with multiple classes. In our case, this limitation is accentuated

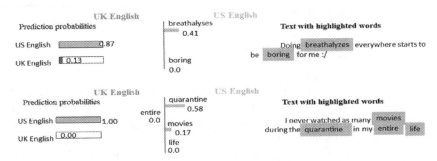

Fig. 2. Examples of local explanations for a binary classification

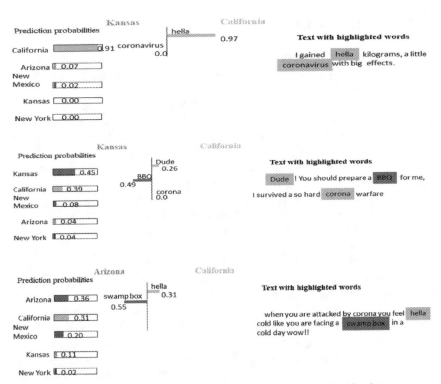

Fig. 3. Examples of local explanations for a multi-class classification

by the presence of neighboring regions that are marked by the use of common words and similar writing rules. At the light of these findings, proposing a prediction explainer that fills the gap between location granularity and explanation accuracy must be approached in order to take fully benefit from shared texts on social networks.

5   Conclusion

In this paper, we took advantage of LIME to explain predictions of a recently developed neural-network-based tweet geolocation model. For binary classification, generated explanations seem to be reasonable and interesting and they ally with human explanations and the model outputs. However, this performance is not guaranteed for multi-class classification and in the presence of common or multi-sense words. These results do not reflect the uselessness of LIME for determining local words per region. Instead, they motivate us to propose a prediction explainer in future works that meets the geolocation problem particularities. Otherwise, we seek to develop an applicable explainer on multi-geographical scale with preservation to explanation accuracy.

References

1. Hirose, H., Wang, L.: Prediction of infectious disease spread using Twitter: a case of influenza. In: 2012 Fifth International Symposium on Parallel Architectures, Algorithms and Programming, 17 December 2012, pp. 100–105. IEEE (2012)
2. Jin, F., Dougherty, E., Saraf, P., Cao, Y., Ramakrishnan, N.: Epidemiological modeling of news and rumors on Twitter. In: Proceedings of the 7th Workshop on Social Network Mining and Analysis, 11 August 2013, pp. 1–9 (2013)
3. Shin, S.Y., et al.: High correlation of Middle East respiratory syndrome spread with Google search and Twitter trends in Korea. Sci. Rep. 6(1), 1–7 (2016)
4. Paul, D., Li, F., Teja, M.K., Yu, X., Frost, R.: Compass: spatio temporal sentiment analysis of US election what Twitter says! In: Proceedings of the 23rd ACM SIGKDD International Conference on Knowledge Discovery and Data Mining, 13 August 2017, pp. 1585–1594 (2017)
5. Jiang, J., Chen, E., Yan, S., Lerman, K., Ferrara, E.: Political polarization drives online conversations about COVID-19 in the United States. Hum. Behav. Emerg. Technol. 2(3), 200–211 (2020)
6. Chen, E., Chang, H., Rao, A., Lerman, K., Cowan, G., Ferrara, E.: COVID-19 misinformation and the 2020 US presidential election. The Harvard Kennedy School Misinformation Review (2021)
7. Martín, Y., Cutter, S.L., Li, Z., Emrich, C.T., Mitchell, J.T.: Using geotagged tweets to track population movements to and from Puerto Rico after Hurricane Maria. Popul. Environ. 42(1), 4–27 (2020). https://doi.org/10.1007/s11111-020-00338-6
8. de Bruijn, J.A., de Moel, H., Jongman, B., Wagemaker, J., Aerts, J.C.: TAGGS: grouping tweets to improve global geoparsing for disaster response. J. Geovisual. Spat. Anal. 2(1), 2 (2018)
9. To, H., Agrawal, S., Kim, S.H., Shahabi, C.: On identifying disaster-related tweets: matching-based or learning-based? In: 2017 IEEE Third International Conference on Multimedia Big Data (BigMM), 19 April 2017, pp. 330–337. IEEE (2017)
10. Hawelka, B., Sitko, I., Beinat, E., Sobolevsky, S., Kazakopoulos, P., Ratti, C.: Geo-located Twitter as proxy for global mobility patterns. Cartogr. Geogr. Inf. Sci. 41(3), 260–271 (2014)
11. Priedhorsky, R., Culotta, A., Del Valle, S.Y.: Inferring the origin locations of tweets with quantitative confidence. In: Proceedings of the 17th ACM Conference on Computer Supported Cooperative Work & Social Computing, 15 February 2014, pp. 1523–1536 (2014)
12. Hasni, S., Faiz, S.: Word embeddings and deep learning for location prediction: tracking Coronavirus from British and American tweets. Soc. Netw. Anal. Min. 11(1), 1–20 (2021). https://doi.org/10.1007/s13278-021-00777-5

13. Evans, M.R., Oliver, D., Zhou, X., Shekhar, S.: Spatial big data. Big Data: Tech. Technol. Geoinform. **18**, 149 (2014)
14. Tjoa, E., Guan, C.: A survey on explainable artificial intelligence (XAI): toward medical XAI. IEEE Trans. Neural Netw. Learn. Syst. (2020)
15. Linardatos, P., Papastefanopoulos, V., Kotsiantis, S.: Explainable AI: a review of machine learning interpretability methods. Entropy **23**(1), 18 (2021)
16. Mueller, S.T., Hoffman, R.R., Clancey, W., Emrey, A., Klein, G.: Explanation in human-AI systems: a literature meta-review, synopsis of key ideas and publications, and bibliography for explainable AI. arXiv preprint arXiv:1902.01876, 5 February 2019
17. Ribeiro, M.T., Singh, S., Guestrin, C.: "Why should I trust you?" Explaining the predictions of any classifier. In: Proceedings of the 22nd ACM SIGKDD International Conference on Knowledge Discovery and Data Mining, 13 August 2016, pp. 1135–1144 (2016)
18. Sundararajan, M., Taly, A., Yan, Q.: Axiomatic attribution for deep networks. In: International Conference on Machine Learning, 17 July 2017, pp. 3319–3328. PMLR (2017)
19. Chen, J., Song, L., Wainwright, M., Jordan, M.: Learning to explain: an information-theoretic perspective on model interpretation. In: International Conference on Machine Learning, 3 July 2018, pp. 883–892. PMLR (2018)
20. Cheng, J., Dong, L., Lapata, M.: Long short-term memory-networks for machine reading. arXiv preprint arXiv:1601.06733, 25 January 2016
21. Li, J., Monroe, W., Jurafsky, D.: Understanding neural networks through representation erasure. arXiv preprint arXiv:1612.08220, 24 December 2016
22. Lampridis, O., Guidotti, R., Ruggieri, S.: Explaining sentiment classification with synthetic exemplars and counter-exemplars. In: Appice, A., Tsoumakas, G., Manolopoulos, Y., Matwin, S. (eds.) DS 2020. LNCS (LNAI), vol. 12323, pp. 357–373. Springer, Cham (2020). https://doi.org/10.1007/978-3-030-61527-7_24
23. Ribeiro, M.T., Singh, S., Guestrin, C.: Anchors: high-precision model-agnostic explanations. In: Proceedings of the AAAI Conference on Artificial Intelligence, 25 April 2018, vol. 32, no. 1 (2018)
24. Panigutti, C., Perotti, A., Pedreschi, D.: Doctor XAI: an ontology-based approach to black-box sequential data classification explanations. In: Proceedings of the 2020 Conference on Fairness, Accountability, and Transparency, 27 January 2020, pp. 629–639 (2020)

Removing Redundancies in Binary Images

Majid Banaeyan$^{(\boxtimes)}$, Darshan Batavia, and Walter G. Kropatsch

Pattern Recognition and Image Processing Group 193/03, TU Wien, Vienna, Austria
{majid,darshan,krw}@prip.tuwien.ac.at

Abstract. Every day a huge amount of digital data is generated. Processing such big data encourages efficient data structure and parallelized operations. In this regard, this paper proposes a graph-based method reducing the memory requirement of the data storage. Graphs as a versatile representative tool in intelligent systems and pattern recognition may consist of many nonessential edges accumulating memory. This paper defines the structure of such redundant edges in the neighborhood graph of a 2D binary image. We introduce a novel approach for contracting the edges that simultaneously assists in determining the structurally redundant edges. In addition, finding a set of independent edges, the redundant edges are removed in parallel with the complexity $\mathcal{O}(1)$. Theoretically, we prove that the maximum number of redundant edges is bounded by half of all edges. Practical results show the memory requirement decreases significantly depending on the input data in different categories of binary image data sets. Using the combinatorial map as the data structure, first the topological structure of the graph is preserved. Second, the method can be extended to higher dimensions (nD).

Keywords: Redundant edges · Connected component labeling · Binary image · Combinatorial map

1 Introduction

The amount of available data in intelligent systems has increased dramatically in recent years [19,20], and this situation will continue to become more extreme with the development of technologies [7,10]. Such circumstances necessitate the development of sophisticated schemes promoting better structural representation. The structure of the data helps to preserve the topology of the image and assists to achieve a compact representation of the data. This makes structure a crucial part of data analysis. The structure of data gives the information about the intrinsic relationships between the subset of the data. Helman et al. [9] stated that extraction of relevant structure helps to reduce the data storage and assists in better visualization. In their case the amount of storage required was approximately one-tenth of the actual storage required for the data. Elimination of the redundant data [18] plays a key role in achieving a compact representation of

Supported by Pattern Recognition and Image Processing Group (PRIP), Austria.

data and saving the storage memory. Besides, it largely depends upon the representation technique, the data structure used for storage of representation, the algorithm's compliance with parallel processing, etc. This paper covers the points related to a structure preserving algorithm for binary images. More specifically we will look into the elimination of the structurally redundant data (see Sect. 3) with a graph based representation (see Sect. 2.1) using the combinatorial maps (see Sect. 2.3) as the data structure.

2   Motivations and Definitions

2.1   Graph-Based Representation

Graphs have the capabilities to represent both structured data (like images, videos, grids) as well as unstructured data (like climate data, point cloud). Narrowing down to images, graphs based representation are simple and effective. A digital image can be easily represented using a 4-adjacent neighborhood graph. Let $G = (V, E)$ be the Region Adjacency Graph (RAG) of image P where V corresponds to the vertex set and E corresponds to the edge set. The vertex $v \in V$ associates with the pixels in image P and the edge $e \in E$ connects the corresponding adjacent vertices. Let the gray-value of vertex $g(v) = g(p)$ where $p \in P$ is a pixel in the image corresponding to vertex v. Let $contrast(e)$ be an attribute of an edge $e(u, v)$ where $u, v \in V$ and $contrast(e) = |g(u) - g(v)|$. Since we are working with binary images only, the pixels (and corresponding vertices can) have either of the two values 0 and 1. Similarly the edge contrast can have only two possible values 0 and 1. The edges in the neighborhood graph can be classified into the following two categories:

Definition 1 (Zero-edge). *An edge $e \in E$ is a **zero-edge**, e_0, iff the contrast between its two endpoints is zero.*

Definition 2 (One-edge). *An edge $e \in E$ is a **one-edge**, e_1, iff the contrast between its two endpoints is one.*

The set of edges classified as e_0 is denoted as E_0 and the set of edges classified as e_1 is denoted as E_1. The edge set $E = E_0 \cup E_1$.

2.2   Image Pyramid

Image Pyramids consist of a series of successively smaller images produced from a base image. They are efficient hierarchical structures which are able to propagate local information from the base level into a global one at the top of the pyramid. Generally, two types of the pyramid, namely regular and irregular pyramid exist.

In **regular pyramids** [12] the resolution is decreased in regular steps and therefore the size of the pyramid is fixed. On the contrary, in irregular pyramids the size of the pyramid is not fixed and it is adapted to the image data. In addition, unlike the regular ones, the irregular pyramids are shift- and rotation-invariant [16] that make them useful to use in a variety of tasks, such as image segmentation [6] and object recognition. It should be noticed that the irregular image pyramid is interpreted as the irregular graph pyramid when its pixels and the neighborhood relations between adjacent pixels correspond to the vertices and the edges of the graph, respectively.

Irregular Pyramids. [11,13–15] are a stack of successively reduced graphs where each graph is constructed from the graph below by selecting a specific subset of vertices and edges. For generation of irregular pyramids, we use the two fundamental operations on graphs: edge **contraction** and edge **removal** (Fig. 1). The edge contraction operation contracts an edge connecting two vertices, and the two vertices are merged into one. All edges that were incident to the merged vertices will be incident to the resulting vertex after the operation. The edge removal operation removes an edge from the graph, without changing the number of vertices or affecting the incidence relationships of other edges.

In each level of the pyramid, the vertices and edges that disappear in a level above are called *non-surviving* and those that appear in the upper level *surviving* ones.

Definition 3 (Contraction Kernel (CK)). *A spanning tree of a connected component.*

A contraction kernel contracts the non-surviving vertices to their corresponding surviving vertex such that each connected component indicated by one surviving vertex.

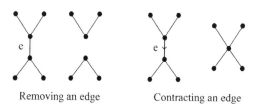

Removing an edge   Contracting an edge

Fig. 1. Two different operations on an edge.

There are different structures to build the irregular pyramid such as simple graphs [5], dual graphs [11] and combinatorial maps (CM) [4]. In the simple graph the produced region adjacency graph (RAG) cannot distinguish between different topological configurations [13], in particular between inclusion and multiple adjacency relationships of regions [5]. The problem with dual graphs is that they cannot unambiguously represent a region enclosed in another one on a local level [5]. Therefore, in this paper the CM, as a planar embedding of RAG, is used which not only solves the mentioned problems but also provides an efficient structure that preserves topological relations between regions and can be extended to higher dimensions (nD).

A *plane* graph is a graph embedded in the plane such that no two edges intersect. In the plane graph there are connected spaces between edges and vertices and every such connected area of the plane is called a *face*. The *degree* of the face is the number of edges bounding the face. In addition a face bounded by a cycle is called an *empty face*. In a non-empty face traversing the boundary would require to visit vertices or edges twice.

2.3   Combinatorial Pyramid

A combinatorial pyramid is a hierarchy of successively reduced combinatorial maps. A combinatorial map (CM) is similar to a graph but explicitly stores the orientation of edges around each vertex. The combinatorial map (G) is defined by a triple $G = (D, \alpha, \sigma)$ where the D is a finite set of darts. A dart is defined as the half edge and it is the fundamental element in the CM's structure. The α is an *involution* on the set D, provides a one-to-one mapping between darts forming the same edge such that $\alpha(\alpha(d)) = d$. The σ is a *permutation* on the set D and encodes consecutive darts around the same vertex while turning counterclockwise [17]. Note that the clockwise orientation is denoted by σ^{-1}.

Figure 2 left, shows a set of adjacent darts with their σ relations in a face of degree 4. Figure 2, right, shows the encoding of the darts. For instance, consider $e = (1, 2)$ where $\alpha(1) = 2$, $\alpha(2) = 1$, $\sigma(1) = 5$.

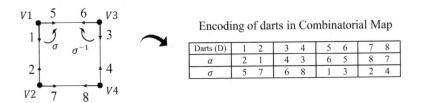

Fig. 2. Combinatorial map.

3   Structurally Redundant Edges

The definition of the term redundant edges differs depending on the application, the representation and the data structure used for the implementation. In our case, we are dealing with binary images. In order to obtain the structure of the binary image, the relevant edges consist of a tree that spans the connected components and the edges that interconnect the components. To detect the redundant edges, it is needed to define an efficient method for selecting the CK. Note that a connected component consists of edges with zero contrast (e_0) only, and the edges with contrast one (e_1) connect two different connected components together. Therefore, in a binary neighborhood graph, the contraction kernel is selected among only e_0s.

3.1   Selecting the Contraction Kernel

Selecting the contraction kernel (CK) has a key role in detecting the redundant edges in the neighborhood graph. To this aim, a totally ordered set is defined over the indices of vertices. Consider the binary image has M rows and N columns such that $(1, 1)$ is the coordinate of the pixel $(p \in P)$ at the upper-left corner and (M, N) at the lower-right corner. The corresponding 4-adjacent neighborhood graph of the binary image has MN vertices. An index $Idx(.,.)$ of each vertex is defined:

$$Idx : [1, M] \times [1, N] \mapsto [1, M \cdot N] \subset \mathbb{N} \tag{1}$$
$$Idx(r, c) = (c - 1) \cdot M + r \tag{2}$$

where r and c are the row and column of the pixel, respectively. Figure 3 shows the neighborhood graph of a 7 by 7 binary image where indices are from 1 to 49. Since the set of integers is totally ordered each vertex has a unique index. The important property of such totally ordered set is that every subset has exactly one minimum and one maximum member (integer number). This property provides a unique orientation between non-surviving and surviving vertices.

Consider a non-surviving vertex v. In order to find the surviving vertex, v_s, an incident e_0 must be found in its neighborhood. Such a neighborhood $\mathcal{N}(v)$ is defined as follows:

$$\mathcal{N}(v) = \{v\} \cup \{w \in V | e_0 = (v, w) \in E_0\} \tag{3}$$

if such neighborhood exists ($|\mathcal{N}(v)| > 1$) the surviving vertex is:

$$v_s = \operatorname{argmax}\{Idx(v_s)| v_s \in \mathcal{N}(v), |\mathcal{N}(v)| > 1\} \tag{4}$$

Definition 4 (Orientation of a e_0). *A $e_0 = (v, w) \in E_0$ is oriented from v to w if w has the largest index among the neighbors, $Idx(w) = \max\{Idx(u)|u \in \mathcal{N}(v)\}$. All edges to the other neighbors remain non-oriented.*

By such definition, a chain of oriented e_0s connects each non-surviving vertex to its corresponding survivor vertex. In Fig. 3 the oriented e_0s are identified by an arrow over each e_0. The three vertices (25, 33 and 49) are surviving vertices while the remaining vertices are non-surviving.

Proposition 1. *Selecting the CK partitions vertices into non-surviving and surviving vertices.*

Proof. If the $|\mathcal{N}(v)| = 1$, either there is no e_0s around v or the index of v is bigger than the indices of neighboring e_0s. Therefore the v is a surviving vertex. In case the $|\mathcal{N}(v)| > 1$, since the indices are totally ordered, there is a maximum in the neighborhood of v which is selected as survivor and the v becomes the nun-surviving vertex. □

Proposition 2. *Every non-surviving vertex has a unique surviving vertex.*

Proof. Each tree of oriented e_0s has one unique maximum as the index of the surviving vertex.   □

Property 1. With the choice of $Idx(.)$ and the coordinate axes in (1) a non-surviving vertex contracts either to its adjacent right vertex or to its down vertex where the right vertex has the higher priority.

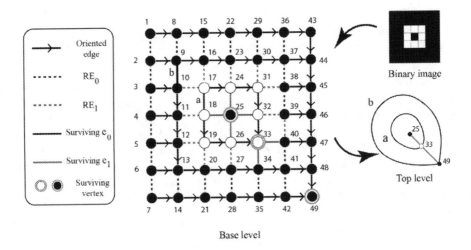

Fig. 3. Combinatorial map.

3.2 Redundant Edges

Connectivity is an essential property in the structure of a hierarchical graph pyramid. Nevertheless, there may be some edges the removal of which does not harm the connectivity. We define such edges as *redundant edges*.

Definition 5 (Redundant-Edge (RE)). *In an empty face, the non-oriented edge incident to the vertex with lowest Idx is redundant iff:*

– *The empty face is bounded by only non-oriented edges with the same contrast value.*
– *The empty face is bounded by non-oriented edges with the same contrast value and oriented edges.*

Based on the RE definition, an empty *self-loop* is redundant. In addition, in an empty face of degree 2 (*double edge*), one of the edges is redundant. Figure 4 illustrates an empty face of different degrees where in each empty face the redundant edge is indicated by RE.

Proposition 3. *The upper bound of the number of redundant edges (REs) is equal to half of the edges of the grid at the base level.*

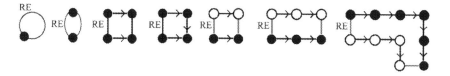

Fig. 4. Example of redundant edge (RE) in different empty faces.

Proof. In a grid M by N, the number of vertices is MN and the number of edges is $2MN - M - N$. To preserve the connectivity the smallest graph is a spanning tree of vertices with $MN - 1$ edges. Therefore, the maximum number of REs is:

$$Max|REs| = (2MN - M - N - (MN - 1)) = MN - M - N + 1 \quad (5)$$

$$\lim_{\substack{M \to \infty \\ N \to \infty}} (Max|REs|/E) = (MN - M - N + 1)/(2MN - M - N) = 1/2 \quad (6)$$

As the result, by growing M and N, the maximum number of REs becomes maximally half of all the edges (E) at the base level. □

Proposition 4. *In every face of degree n (n > 1) is bounded by only e_0s, one of the non-oriented e_0s is redundant.*

Proof. By contracting an edge, every face of degree $n > 2$ after $n - 2$ consecutive contractions becomes a face of degree 2 which has a RE (Definition 5). □

Proposition 5. *In every face of degree n (n > 1) is bounded by only e_1s and oriented e_0s, there is a redundant one-edge (RE_1).*

Proof. Contracting all oriented e_0s results in a face of degree 2 containing two e_1s between the same endpoints. Hence, one of the e_1s is redundant. □

Since edges classify into E_0 and E_1, the REs are partitioned into *Redundant Zero-Edges* (RE_0) and *Redundant One-Edges* (RE_1) as well:

$$REs = RE_0s \:\dot\cup\: RE_1s \quad (7)$$

In Fig. 3, the RE_0s are shown by black dashed-lines and the RE_1s are shown by red dashed-lines. Furthermore, the RAG at the top of the pyramid shows the connections between three different connected components. Using the combinatorial map structure, the inclusion relation is preserved because it is represented by the loop **a** aroundthe vertex 25.

It should be noted that a neighboring graph at the base level may not have any redundant edge. Consider a 4-connected graph that its vertices form a checkerboard pattern. In such the case, all edges have contrast one that it means there is no zero-edge and thus no RE_0. Furthermore, based on the Proposition 5, no two one-edges connect the same vertices and thus there is no RE_1 as well.

3.3   Removing Redundant Edges in Parallel

In order to remove the REs, a dependency between edges is considered. We define such dependency relation to detect a set of REs where by simultaneously removing, the combinatorial structure is not harmed. To this aim, first a set of dependent darts is defined as follows:

Definition 6 (Dependent Darts). *All darts of a σ-orbit sharing an endpoint are dependent darts.*

Next, by considering the corresponding edge of each dart, $e = (d, \alpha(d))$, the set of dependent darts results in the set of **dependent edges**. Consequently, two edges not sharing an endpoint are independent. In this manner, the only case of the dependency between REs occurs when the REs share an endpoint. In the grid at the base level the REs may be connected horizontally or vertically and thus are dependent. However, consider a horizontal edge in an odd row of the grid. This edge is independent to all other horizontal edges of other odd rows. Similarly, a vertical edge in an odd column is independent of all other vertical edges of other odd columns. Such independency exists between edges in even rows and even columns as well. Figure 5 shows the set of independent edges at the base. Therefore, all the edges in grid are classified to four independent classes of edges. Consequently, removing all edges belonging to each independence class (1, 2, 3 or 4) occurs simultaneously. This means, all the REs are removed in only four steps where each step has the complexity $\mathcal{O}(1)$. Therefore removing the redundant edges is performed in parallel.

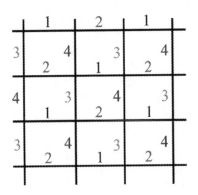

Fig. 5. The four independent classes of edges in the grid at the base.

4   Memory Consumption

The topological structure is well captured in the combinatorial map. A combinatorial pyramid is a hierarchy of successively reduced combinatorial maps [4]. The pyramid needs to store the combinatorial map of each level that results in high memory consumption. To avoid such expensive memory requirement, we use a *canonical encoding* [17] where the memory consumption of the pyramid is equal to the size of the base level.

In the canonical encoding of the combinatorial pyramid, all the darts are stored in a single array that preserves the history of pyramid construction. The number of darts at the base level is equal to $2 \cdot (2MN - M - N)$ in a binary image M by N. Since nearly half of the edges at the base level (Proposition 3) are redundant (RE), their removal decreases the memory requirements.

In addition, in the canonical pyramid, removing the darts performs in a sequential manner. In contrast, using the independent set of edges (Sect. 3.3) we are able to remove the independent set of corresponding darts in parallel. Therefore, in the canonical array such darts are removed in parallel. Fig. 6(a) illustrates the combinatorial map (CM) of a graph and Fig. 6(d) shows its canonical encoding. The REs are shown by dashed-lines. Four REs are corresponding to darts 1 to 8. The darts at the first row (1, 2, 5, 6) are removed in one step (Fig. 6(b, f)). Afterwards, darts at the second row (3, 4, 7, 8) are removed simultaneously (Fig. 6(c, g)). This results in, the smaller array of the canonical encoding shown in Fig. 6(h).

5   Comparisons and Results

To highlight the advantages of the proposed method, we compare the memory storage required with and without removing the REs. The comparison is done with the originally proposed canonical representation [17]. It was used by [1, 3, 6] for the implementation of topology preserving irregular image pyramids of gray scaled and RGB images. In addition, recently the canonical encoding was used in connected component labeling [2]. Since for our current research, the input images are restricted to binary images, it is easy to identify the connected components unlike the gray scale images. Considering the structure of the image, the number of REs that can be eliminated are significantly higher than that in a gray scale or RGB image.

In a combinatorial map, the involution α between the darts remain the same even after performing the contraction and/or removal operations. The α relations can be encoded into the even and odd numbering of darts for each edge. Thus all the modifications related to the contraction and the removal operation on the graphs are performed by modifying the σ-permutation. In the canonical representation, the minimum storage required to store and to modify the σ-permutation is equal to the number of darts i.e. twice the number of edges. By using the proposed method, we eliminate the edges that are structurally redundant and consequently reduce the storage space of darts and its permutation.

The algorithm was tested on several classes of images from the YACCLAB [8] dataset. Table 1 displays the outcome of the proposed method. The first column shows the name of the image class in the data set and an example from it, while the second column displays the 'size' of the image. The number of images ('#Images') from each class, on which the implementation was performed is

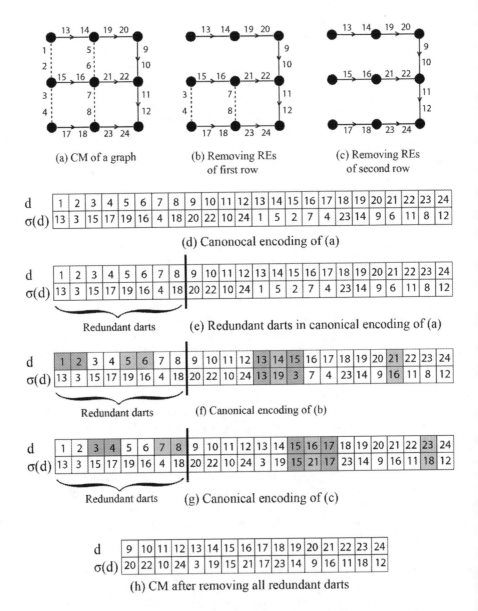

(a) CM of a graph

(b) Removing REs of first row

(c) Removing REs of second row

(d) Canonocal encoding of (a)

(e) Redundant darts in canonical encoding of (a)

(f) Canonical encoding of (b)

(g) Canonical encoding of (c)

(h) CM after removing all redundant darts

Fig. 6. Memory usage in the canonical encoding.

displayed in the third column. The forth column gives the percentage of vertices that survive ('$|V_s|/|V|$'). Since there is a significant variation in the size of the image, the number of REs are expressed in terms of percentage of the actual

Table 1. Results over images of different categories from (YACCLAB [8]).

Database	Example	Size	#Images	$|V_s|/|V|$	$|RE_{min}|$	$|RE_\mu|$	std($|RE|$)
Medical — Mitochondria		768×1024	495	0.33%	49.01%	49.44%	0.0073
Medical		890×886	189	2.74%	41.18%	46.87%	0.0145
Finger-print		300×300	962	3.50%	42.50%	46.05%	0.0108
MRI		256×256	1170	2.72%	44.42%	46.49%	0.0114
3dpes		704×576	2400	0.07%	49.81%	49.84%	0.0019
Hilbert		127×127	512	2.43%	41.31%	45.25%	0.0108
Random		64×64	89	18.90%	23.18%	27.66%	0.0407

number of edges. The last three columns display the lowest ('$|RE_{min}|$'), and the average number of REs ('$|RE_\mu|$') along with the standard deviation ('std($|RE|$)') over all images from each dataset.

The redundancy in the random images is notably lower than that in the other class of images. This can be observed in the number of surviving vertices as well. This happens due to the fact that the number of isolated vertices (vertices surrounded by e_1s only) are higher, making the connected component smaller in size. The worst case occurs in a checkerboard pattern where all the vertices are isolated making each region containing a single pixel. In such a case, none of the edges are redundant. In contrast, an image with only black (0) or only white (1) color will have 50% of the REs.

6   Conclusion and Future Works

The paper presents a new formalism to define redundant edges in the neighborhood graph of a 2D binary image. By proposing the new method for selecting the contraction kernels these redundant edges are efficiently detected and removed *before* the contraction operation. We prove that the amount of redundant edges may reach up to half of the edges at the base level with a grid like structure. The experiments show that most classes of images have 45%–49% of redundant edges (except for artificially generated random binary images). As a result, the memory consumption is reduced by 45%–49% while using combinatorial map as the data structure. Furthermore, all the redundant edges can be removed in parallel with a constant algorithmic complexity $\mathcal{O}(1)$. For the future work, we are going to develop the method for gray-scale images. Secondly, by using the combinatorial structure we will work on extending the redundant edges to higher dimensions (nD).

References

1. Banaeyan, M., Huber, H., Kropatsch, W.G., Barth, R.: A novel concept for smart camera image stitching. In: Čehovin, L., Mandeljc, R., Štruc, V. (eds.) Proceedings of the 21st Computer Vision Winter Workshop 2016, pp. 1–9 (2016)
2. Banaeyan, M., Kropatsch, W.G.: Pyramidal connected component labeling by irregular graph pyramid. In: 2021 5th International Conference on Pattern Recognition and Image Analysis (IPRIA), pp. 1–5 (2021). https://doi.org/10.1109/IPRIA53572.2021.9483533
3. Batavia, D., Gonzalez-Diaz, R., Kropatsch, W.G.: Image = structure + few colors. In: Torsello, A., Rossi, L., Pelillo, M., Biggio, B., Robles-Kelly, A. (eds.) S+SSPR 2021. LNCS, vol. 12644, pp. 365–375. Springer, Cham (2021). https://doi.org/10.1007/978-3-030-73973-7_35
4. Brun, L., Kropatsch, W.: Introduction to combinatorial pyramids. In: Bertrand, G., Imiya, A., Klette, R. (eds.) Digital and Image Geometry. LNCS, vol. 2243, pp. 108–128. Springer, Heidelberg (2001). https://doi.org/10.1007/3-540-45576-0_7
5. Brun, L., Kropatsch, W.G.: Hierarchical graph encodings. In: Lézoray, O., Grady, L. (eds.) Image Processing and Analysis with Graphs: Theory and Practice, pp. 305–349. CRC Press (2012)
6. Cerman, M., Janusch, I., Gonzalez-Diaz, R., Kropatsch, W.G.: Topology-based image segmentation using LBP pyramids. Mach. Vision Appl. **27**(8), 1161–1174 (2016). https://doi.org/10.1007/s00138-016-0795-1
7. Chen, L., Zheng, L., Xia, D., Cai, X., Sun, D., Liu, W.: Recognizing and analyzing private car commuters using big data of electronic registration identification of vehicles. IEEE Trans. Intell. Transp. Syst. pp. 1–15 (2022). https://doi.org/10.1109/TITS.2022.3142778

8. Grana, C., Bolelli, F., Baraldi, L., Vezzani, R.: YACCLAB - yet another connected components labeling benchmark. In: 2016 23rd International Conference on Pattern Recognition (ICPR), pp. 3109–3114. Springer (2016). https://doi.org/10.1109/ICPR.2016.7900112

9. Helman, J., Hesselink, L.: Visualizing vector field topology in fluid flows. IEEE Comput. Graph. Appl. **11**(3), 36–46 (1991). https://doi.org/10.1109/38.79452

10. Huang, W., et al.: A fast point cloud ground segmentation approach based on coarse-to-fine Markov random field. IEEE Trans. Intell. Transp. Syst. pp. 1–14 (2021). https://doi.org/10.1109/TITS.2021.3073151

11. Kropatsch, W.G.: Building irregular pyramids by dual graph contraction. IEE-Proc. Vision Image Signal Process. **142**(6), 366–374 (1995)

12. Kropatsch, W.G., Leonardis, A., Bischof, H.: Hierarchical, adaptive and robust methods for image understanding. Surv. Math. Ind. No. **9**, 1–47 (1999)

13. Kropatsch, W.G., Macho, H.: Finding the structure of connected components using dual irregular pyramids. In: Cinquième Colloque DGCI, pp. 147–158. LLAIC1, Université d'Auvergne (1995). ISBN 2-87663-040-0

14. Kropatsch, W.G., Reither, C., Willersinn, D., Wlaschitz, G.: The dual irregular pyramid. In: Chetverikov, D., Kropatsch, W.G. (eds.) CAIP 1993. LNCS, vol. 719, pp. 31–40. Springer, Heidelberg (1993). https://doi.org/10.1007/3-540-57233-3_4

15. Meer, P.: Stochastic image pyramids. Comput. Vision Graph. Image Process. **45**(3), 269–294 (1989)

16. Montanvert, A., Meer, P., Rosenfield, A.: Hierarchical image analysis using irregular tessellations. IEEE Trans. Pattern Anal. Mach. Intell. **13**(4), 307 (1991)

17. Torres, F., Kropatsch, W.G.: Canonical encoding of the combinatorial pyramid. In: Proceedings of the 19th Computer Vision Winter Workshop, pp. 118–125 (2014)

18. Wang, C., Wang, K., Liu, W.: Personalized recommendation via enhanced redundant eliminated network-based inference. In: 2019 First International Conference on Digital Data Processing (DDP), pp. 1–6 (2019). https://doi.org/10.1109/DDP.2019.00011

19. Wang, N., Haihong, E., Song, M., Wang, Y.: Construction method of domain knowledge graph based on big data-driven. In: 2019 5th International Conference on Information Management (ICIM), pp. 165–172 (2019). https://doi.org/10.1109/INFOMAN.2019.8714664

20. Zhang, D., Jiang, Y.: Design of urban intelligent traffic congestion situation monitoring system based on big data. In: 2020 International Conference on Intelligent Transportation, Big Data Smart City (ICITBS), pp. 12–15 (2020). https://doi.org/10.1109/ICITBS49701.2020.00011

Neural Machine Translation of Low Resource Languages: Application to Transcriptions of Tunisian Dialect

Abida Emna[✉], Saméh Kchaou, and Rahma Boujelban

ANLP Research Group, MIRACL Lab. FSEGS, University of Sfax, Sfax, Tunisia
abida.emna55@gmail.com

Abstract. With the evolution of speech technologies, the need to understand and process the poorly spoken language has gradually become a necessity. However, the lack of resources is the main computational processing challenge. We present, in this paper, an effort to create a Neural Machine Translation (NMT) model in order to translate the spoken language in Tunisia: The Tunisian Dialect (TD) into the Arabic Standard Language (MSA). Indeed, NMT tasks require an enormous amount of training data which represents a problematic for low resourced languages like TD. For this, two contributions will be presented in this paper, the first consists of the creating of a parallel corpus TD-MSA. Then, by exploiting the resulting corpus, we proposed a configuration of a neural translation model that achieved a BLEU score of 67.56%.

Keywords: Neural machine translation · Tunisian dialect transcriptions · Modern Standard Arabic

1 Introduction

The use of human-machine dialogue systems is beginning to spread in everyday life via the latest versions of smartphones. Oral communication with the machine makes it possible to retrieve information or solve problems related in particular to the blinds. In automatic speech understanding, particularly for standard languages, there are currently systems at google or apple for example, that work perfectly for English, Standard Arabic and French and we note currently that they start to cover even the poorly endowed languages. This work falls within this context, we focus on building a deep learning model to translate the spoken Arabic dialect into the standard language in order to take advantage of the potential of the models adapted for Modern Standard Arabic (MSA). However, dialects of the Arabic language are immensely varied from region to region where some of them are mutually unintelligible. Then, it is preferable to treat each dialect as a separate language. In this work, we are interested by the Tunisian Dialect (TD). The latter is little approached at the level of speech processing. In this context, there is the work of [11] who proposed a statistical model to translate

© Springer Nature Switzerland AG 2022
A. Bennour et al. (Eds.): ISPR 2022, CCIS 1589, pp. 234–247, 2022.
https://doi.org/10.1007/978-3-031-08277-1_20

TD written in social networks to MSA. The resulted model achieved a BLEU score of 15%. In addition, open access resources, in particular transcriptions have been proposed such as that of ([5] and [20]). But, to our knowledge, there ara no works dealing with oral translation. Thus, we propose, in this work, a pipeline to translate TD transcripts into MSA. We contribute at first, by a parallel corpus TD-MSA. Then, we compare through several experiments, different corpus configurations and neural architectures in order to define those which optimize the translation of the TD speech language.

2   Related Work

In computational linguistics, the machine translation arouses the interest of several researchers and research works in this area continues to progress. The early approach relied on rules and linguistic knowledge such as the work of [5] to create a bilingual Model (MSA - TD) and the study of [10] to translate verbs between Arabic standard and dialect Arabic by using morphological analysis. However, Linguistic Machine Translation (LMT) systems have quickly found their limits, especially for topologically rich languages where the construction of such systems demands a great amount of time and linguistic resources. The statistical approach (SMT) has solved this problem by abandoning the use of rules and dictionaries. The method was much more efficient and accurate than all the previous ones and also no linguists were needed. For example, the work of [11] applied this technique in order to augment their parallel corpus (TD-MSA). Moreover, in the study of [9], they used SMT to translate English sentences to Yoruba sentences. With the development of neural networks, neural machine translation (NMT) is a radical departure from previous machine translation approaches. NMT has emerged as a new paradigm which is based on neural networks [7]. In effect, several works have applied neural models to translate different dialects. [1] for example opted for this method to generate a translation model from Jordanian Dialect to MSA using Recurrent Neural Network model. They applied this model on two types of datasets : parallel word dataset and parallel sentence dataset. Results showed that this model has provided satisfactory results with an accuracy of 91.3 in word based dataset and 63.2 in sentence based dataset. We cite also the work of [3] where authors opted for BiLSTM (Bidirectional Long Short Term Memory) model to translate Arabic dialects (Levantine and Maghreb dialects) to Modern Standard Arabic. They used a POS tagging task (LA- MSA, MA-MSA and MSA-ENG) for the multitask NMT model which is reviewed on the translation task from MSA to AD and from MSA to English. Moreover, recent studies have focused on Transformer coupled in some work dealing with low resourced language, with the Byte Pair Encoding Model as pretreatment like in [18] and [8]. Transformer model has been proposed to translate in both ways English to Hungarian of [14]. To enhance their model performance , they proposed a data augmentation technique based on syntactic parsing. Their model achieved a BLEU score of 40.0 on Hungarian-English and 33.4 on English-Hungarian. In [15], authors investigate the utility of NMT on three low-resource similar language pairs: Spanish-Portuguese, Czech-Polish, and Hindi-Nepali using LSTM and transformer models. There are others contributions aiming to introduce NMT for different linguistic analysis tasks such as the work of [19], they applied Named Entity Recognition tool for Vietnamese sentences to determine the category of words in the tow ways English-Vietnamese and Vietnamese-English. The result obtained in NMT systems using NER for English in Vietnamese-to-English is better than the NMT system in the reverse dimension. BLEU and TER scores have been used to evaluate NMT models, They achieved (13.10%, 67.56%) for English-to-Vietnamese and (13.44%, 66.83%) for Vietnamese-to-English. To our knowledge, until now, there are no works that deal with the translation of the TD speech language.

3 PARASAR: PARAllel Speech Corpus of ARabic Language

3.1 PARASAR TD Data

The Arabic Tunisian Language is a spoken daily dialect by 12 million Tunisians; it belongs to the variety of Maghrebi Arabic and it differs from one region to another of the country. Indeed, it presents a morphology, a vocabulary, a pronunciation and a syntax considerably different from the MSA. Two levels of language can be distinguished in spoken TD. The popular dialect or known by the colloquial dialect that covers daily needs and the intellectualized dialect found in scholars conversations on radio and television programs [6]. The latter presents a mixture between MSA and TD. In the context of research on Arabic dialects, various types of dialect data collections have been proposed. Some works have used the web and social media to extract dialect data. Other works started from recordings of dialogues, radios, conversations and television broadcasts and transcribed them into written data. In fact, the collected oral data by researchers are not always freely accessible and available to the entire scientific community. In the literature, we noticed three available corpus which perfectly describe the different types of TD: *TARIC*[1], *STAC*[2] and *Transcriptions*. So, we explored them in order to build a parallel TD-MSA corpus.

TARIC: **T**unisian dialect **R**ailways **I**nteraction **C**orpus [13]: Corpus of Tunisian Dialect interactions in the railway domain recorded à la SNCFT: Tunisian National Railways Company. The corpus contains a collection of 20 h of audio recordings and transcriptions. It represents conversations between passengers and SNCFT agents using a colloquial dialect. The purpose of these conversations is to ask in Tunisian dialect for information on railway services in a train station. These requests correspond to the types of train, its timetables, its destination, the price and the reservation of tickets.

---

[1] https://www.researchgate.net/figure/presents-some-statistics-of-the-TARIC-corpus_tbl1_342420693.

[2] https://www.researchgate.net/figure/Some-annotations-used-in-STAC-corpus_tbl2_307583782.

STAC: **S**poken **T**unisian **A**rabic Corpus [22]. It contains transcriptions of five hours of recording of Tunisian Arabic speech from different TV channels and radio stations (Mosaique radio, Tunisian national TV, Ettounsiya TV and Sfax radio). These streams are generally radio and television talk shows, debates, and interactive programs where the general public is invited to participate in discussion by telephone on various fields such as politics, health, social issues, religion. STAC corpus is a mix between the colloquial and the intellectualized dialect.

Transcriptions [5]: It regroups 6 h of transcriptions about some television broadcasts in the political field. The dialect in these recordings is considered as an intellectualized dialect as the speakers often alternate between MSA and TD.

The collected transcription corpus is composed of 13648 sentences. The length of sentences varies between 3 to 556 words. More statistics on the corpus are described in Table 1. Figure 1 shows a sample of the corpus that explains the levels of dialectal language explained above, as we can see, MSA blocks are more common in news and talk shows than in STAC and TARIC. These transcriptions were written by different transcribers and since there was no orthographic standard, we noticed that there are different forms for certain words. There was an effort to create a spelling convention for the TD [21]. Based on the rules of this convention, [21] have developed an automatic transcription normalization model and they have made available the normalized version of the STAC corpus and the transcriptions of news and debates.

Table 1. Statistics of TD-MSA transcriptions.

Data	Resources	#Lines	#Tokens	#Vocabularies	Sequence length
TD data	TARIC	11943	49049	2525	[3..19]
	STAC	701	11610	4041	[32..233]
	Transcriptions	1004	18320	5412	[30..556]
MSA data	TARIC	11943	63777	4457	[3..22]
	STAC	701	11192	4578	[31..235]
	Transcriptions	1004	19052	5805	[30..550]

3.2   TD-MSA Parallel Corpus

In order to build a parallel corpus TD-MSA, we proposed to translate manually the TD transcription corpus by native speakers. Figure 1 shows some examples of the obtained corpus. As the TD is a variant of MSA, they partially share the same vocabulary. In order to explore the degree of similarity between the TD and MSA in the collected corpus, we generated the intersection set between the two vocabularies. Figure 2 shows the lexical similarity between these two languages. According to the Figure, we notice that TARIC shares with MSA 7% of vocabularies and this is due to the appearance of the colloquial dialect in this corpus. The addition of the STAC and Transcriptions corpus increases the shared vocabulary to 20%. This is explained by the existence of an intellectualized dialect in these corpus.

Resources	Transcriptions DT	Transcriptions MSA
TARIC	عَسْلَامَةْ بِاللاِّهِي يَعَيْشِكْ فِمَّةْ تَرَانَاتْ ثُوَّةْ لُسُوسَةْ	السلام عليكم بالله عليك هل هناك قطار الآن إلى سوسة؟
STAC	و تقرا بأسمي أنا ولِيت مشِيت إطّلَعت على الخبر إلى تنشر في تولوز عام ألفين و عشرة معناتها عندو سنتين التالي	هو نُثِر مرفوقا باسمي، فاطلعت في الحين على الخبر الأصلي، الذي كان قد نُثِر في تولوز سنة ألفين وعشر، أيّ ما يُقارب السنتين تقريبًا
Transcriptions	مرحبا بكم في نشرة الاخبار على قناة نسمة و نبداوا بالعناوين زعيم في تونس لزيارة ضريح المرحوم شكري بلعيد و تقديم التعازي لعايلته	مرحبا بكم في نشرة الأخبار على قناة نسمة ونبدأ بالعناوين زعيم في تونس يقوم بزيارة ضريح المرحوم شكري بلعيد وتقديم التعازي لعائلته

Fig. 1. Example of TD-MSA translated transcripts.

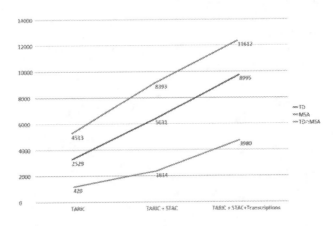

Fig. 2. Vocabularies evaluation of MSA and TD language.

3.3   Data Preprocessing

As we have mentioned above, TD is considered as a dynamic language due to the absence of an orthographic standard for its writing. For this, we proposed the following pre-treatment in order to guarantee a better application of the subsequent steps:

– Remove the diacritics: A part of the corpus has been mixed. The sentences do not have the same type of writing. This treatment allows getting a uniform presentation for the corpus. Figure 3 presents some examples of transcriptions before and after removing the diacritics.

- As the collected corpus is a mixture of intellectualized and colloquial dialect, in addition to the informal type of writing which characterizes the TD, we applied CODA-TUN (Conventional Orthography for Tunisian Arabic Dialect) of [20] in order to keep a simple representation of words. Application of CODA-TUN generates the reduction of vocabulary since certain words written differently have been normalized. Table 2 shows the statistics of non-normalized and normalized corpus.
- We choose to select long TD sentences whose length exceeds 30 words, then, we manually segment these sentences based on a few rules of links between the words such as conclusion link, cause link, alternative link, etc. Figure 4 depicts an example sentence before segmentation (Pre-condition) and after segmentation (Post-condition) and its corresponding MSA alignment.

Table 2. Statistics of normalized corpus.

Corpus type	TD words	TD vocabularies
Non Normalized-corpus	78986	10260
Normalized corpus	73647	9879

Resources	TD Transcriptions before remove diacritics	TD Transcriptions after remove diacritics
TARIC	عَسْلاَمَةٌ باللاَّهِي يَعَيْشِكْ فَقَّةُ تْرَانَاتْ تْوَّةْ لُسُوسَةْ	عسلامة باللاهي يعيشك فمة ترانات توة لسوسة
STAC	وي تقرا بأسمي أنا ولّيت مشيت إطّلعت على, الخبر إلِّي تنشر في تولوز عام ألفين و عشرة معناتها عندو سنتين التّال	وي تقرا بأسمي أنا وليت مشيت إطلعت على الخبر إلي تنشر في تولوز عام ألفين و عشرة معناتها عندو سنتين التالي
Transcriptions	هذاك علاش الواحد لازم يرد بالو وإنشاء اللّه, ماتتعاودش تتكرّر	هذاك علاش الواحد لازم يرد بالو وإنشاء الله ماتتعاودش تتكرر

Fig. 3. Example of TD transcriptions after and before the remove diacritics.

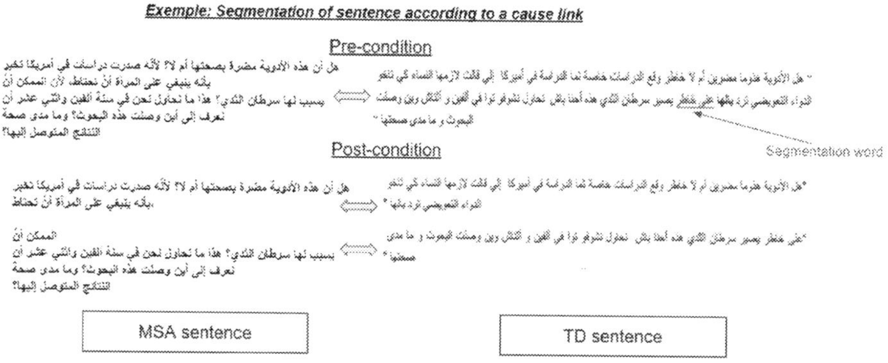

Example: Segmentation of sentence according to a cause link

Pre-condition

Post-condition   Segmentation word

MSA sentence   TD sentence

Fig. 4. Proposed pipeline for NMT of TD transcriptions.

3.4   TD-MSA Transcriptions Distribution

The PARASAR corpus is the first parallel TD speech corpus with MSA transcriptions. It will be published free to the committee of researchers[3]. This contributes to the availability of parallel data for poorly endowed languages and pushes forward the research in the field of speech translation for underfunded languages. The corpus package will be a CSV shape file consisting of the TD transcripts and its corresponding alignments in MSA.

4   TD-MSA NMT Models

We present, in this section, the different NMT models that we will try on the basis of different parameters for TD-MSA language pairs. Firstly, we test the Sequence to Sequence (Seq2Seq) learning architectures. Then, we test transformer architectures using two frameworks : Joey NMT and Tensor2Tensor.

4.1   Seq2seq Models

We train seq2seq learning architecture with both encoder and decoder implemented using:

- (1) Long Short Term Memory (LSTM): Long ShortTerm Memory in short is a special kind of RNN capable of learning long term sequences. LSTM has three gates: Input gate, forget gate and output gate.
- (2) Gated Recurrent Units (GRU): The workflow of GRU is a special kind of RNN, but the difference is in the operations inside the GRU unit. Inside GRU it has two gates: reset gate and update gate, each one has its own weights and biases.

Parameters Setting: We apply an attention mechanism between the decoder and the encoder in both models. In fact, attention mechanism show an improvement in the seq2seq architecture [2]. We use three dense layers. The sequence length is fixed to 30 words. We use a Batch size of 64, 3 epochs and an embedding_dim of 256. The ADAM optimizer [12] is applied with a constant learning rate of 0.0004 to update model weights.

4.2   Transformer Models

The Seq2seq models are generally based on the encoder-decoder architecture with an attention mechanism. The transformer model consists of handling the entire input sequence at once without an iteration of words. They differ from each other in the input representation and multi-head attention. We test, in this work, two structures of transformer models:

---

[3] https://github.com/sk-cmd/PARallel-Speech-Corpus-of-tunisian-Arabic-Dialect/ tree/main.

- **Classical Transformer:** The encoder layer consists of two sub-layers: a multi-head self-attention, which allows the model to jointly attend to information from different representation sub-spaces at different positions, followed by a position-wise fully connected feed-forward layer. The decoder layer consists of three sub-layers: a masked multi-head self-attention, encoder-decoder attention, and a position-wise feed-forward layer.
- **Joey NMT Transformer:** The input form of this transformer is a little different from the classical transformer. It is based on a coding model by pairs of bytes (BPE) to divide the words into sub-words according to their frequency in the corpus learning. BPE Model is a sub-word segmentation algorithm that encodes rare and unknown words as sequences of sub-word units. This particularly applies to different languages where the presence of many compound words can make it difficult to learn an otherwise rich vocabulary.

Parameters Settings: We use the following parameters to implement each transformer models: Batch size = 512, embedding_dim = 256, epochs = 30, num_heads= 4, sequence length = 30, num_layers= 6. The optimizer Adam is used for Joey NMT while rmsprop optimizer is used for classical transformer. Moreover, classical transformer is developed by Tensor2Tensor framework and Joey NMT is developed by Pytorch framework.

5   Experimental Results and Discussion

In this section, we present details adopted steps to build the NMT model for TD transcriptions. Figure 5 describes the proposed steps. We compare different NMT models with many versions of TD-MSA corpus in order to define the model that optimizes the translation. To implement the different models, we divide the corpus into two parts: the train part (75%) and the test part (25%). We extract from each corpus (TARIC, STAC, Transcriptions) a set of transcriptions to build our test corpus (25%). Each model will be evaluated,on the same test set, using the BlEU score

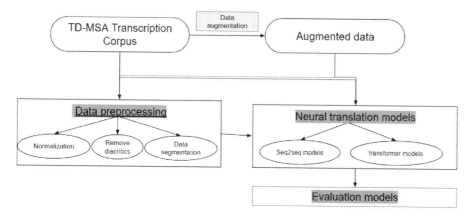

Fig. 5. Proposed pipeline for NMT of TD transcriptions.

5.1   Data Augmentation

In order to further increase the size of the corpus and to improve the quality of the model, we studied the impact of adding a parallel TD-MSA corpus of comments taken from social networks. So, we explore the **M**ulti **A**rabic **D**ialect **A**pplications and **R**esources (MADAR) [4] and **P**arallel **A**rabic **DI**alectal **C**orpus (PADIC) corpus to extract TD-MSA data. More details of these two corpora are described in [11]. Indeed, PADIC is a recording of different conversions from everyday life of the Annaba dialect and from recordings of television programs expressed in the dialect of Algeria. MADAR is created from the Corpus Basic Traveling Expression (BTEC) [17]. Table 3 presents the statistics of these corpora.

Table 3. Statistics of free corpus .

Corpus Name	#Lines	#Tokens	#Vocabularies
PADIC	6.4k	38.6k	10k
MADAR	1.8k	9.8k	3.8k

5.2   NMT Experiments

NMT_NONOR: NMT Models Using Non-normalized Corpus (EXP 1): The first experiment consists of training our models on the non-normalized corpus (without coda-TUN processing). We start to evaluate the NMT models using the first transcription corpus TARIC on the test corpus. Table 4 describes the obtained results on the same test set by the different models. The good BLEU score is obtained with the classical transformer model (28.88%). Subsequently, we add the other corpora of transcriptions (STAC and Transcriptions [5]). The best score is obtained with the LSTM model (23%). So, we can deduce that LSTM is suitable when the sequence length is longer since STAC corpus and Transcriptions [5] are made up of long sentences. Also, we add the used data for corpus augmentation. Similarly, LSTM model is the one that obtains the best score (22.40%) since MADAR and PADIC are formed from long sentences. For this, secondly, we choose to modify the sequence length parameter. We use different values (20, 10, 7) of sequence length to analyze sentence lengths. As shown in Table 4, classical transformer is the model that gives the best BLEU score (33.90) with sequence length of 10 using only TARIC corpus. We also notice from the Table that Joey NMT gives high scores on the sequence length of 30 for each corpus configuration.

Table 4. BLEU scores of NMT models using TD-MSA non-normalized corpus.

Resources	Models	Sequences Length			
		L = 30	L = 20	L = 10	L = 7
TARIC	LSTM	15,20	13.52	11.7	11.05
	GRU	25,85	22.14	24.93	23.14
	Joey NMT	13,75	14.52	12.26	10.91
	Classical transformer	28,88	31	33.90	33.01
All transcriptions data	LSTM	23	19,15	18.42	16.33
	GRU	22.78	20.19	18.12	15,62
	Joey NMT	11,73	9.40	9.12	8.78
	Classical transformer	21,92	20.55	18,78	16.42
All transcriptions data + Data augmentation	LSTM	22,40	21,59	20 ,92	18,78
	GRU	22	20,45	16	15,78
	Joey NMT	22.27	15,88	9,41	8,46
	Classical transformer	10,93	11,24	11,02	11,02

NMT_NORC: NMT Models Using NORmalized Corpus (EXP 2):

EXP 2 consists of analysing the normalized corpus. We apply the same principle as EXP 1 by modifying the version of the used corpus. Table 5 shows BLEU scores on the normalized corpus for each NMT models. We notice that almost all scores are improved for all models. Similarly, we notice the same result as EXP 1. For all sentences length values, Joey NMT is the model that gives the highest score with each corpus configuration. Moreover, the latter i.e. Joey NMT has obtained the best BLEU score (34.55) with sequence length of 30 on augmented data. Consequently, according to our results of EXP 2, we consider that the Joey NMT model is the most optimized for translating TD transcription. Indeed, Joey NMT shows brave results for low-resource machine translation with sufficient amounts of data [16].

Table 5. BLEU Scores of NMT Models Using TD-MSA Normalized Corpus.

Resources	Models	Sequences Length			
		L = 30	L = 20	L = 10	L = 7
TARIC	LSTM	15,20	13,52	11,70	11,05
	GRU	25,85	22,14	24,93	23,14
	Joey NMT	13,75	14,55	12,26	10,91
	Classical transformer	28,88	31	28	23,19
All transcriptions data	LSTM	22,98	22,5	21,08	19,15
	GRU	22	21,38	20,24	18,14
	Joey NMT	10,85	9,50	14	9,21
	Classical transformer	20,46	19,21	14	10,41
All transcriptions data + Data augmentation	LSTM	21,75	22	19,44	19,02
	GRU	16	19,72	18,52	15,5
	Joey NMT	**34,55**	29,21	25,40	29,11
	Classical transformer	15,15	17,25	16,88	14,31

NMT_COC: NMT Models Using COmbined Corpus (EXP 3):

Following the results of EXP 1 and EXP 2, we propose to combine the both of the non-normalized corpus with the normalized version in order to add samples data in the corpus. We only test the augmented corpus since for both experiments the high BLEU scores were obtained with the augmented corpus version. Table 6 describes BLEU scores on the combined corpus. As shown in the Table, the result of this experiment confirms the result of EXP2. Joey NMT is the model that shows the best score with a sentence length of 30 (BLEU score 46.99). Moreover, we notice that the data augmentation improves translation quality. For this, we choose the combined version of corpus (with and without normalization) to configure our models.

Table 6. BLEU scores of NMT models using TD-MSA corpus.

Resources	Models	Sequences Length			
		L = 30	L = 20	L = 10	L = 7
Non normalized corpus + Normalized Corpus	LSTM	23,11	21,79	19,52	16,33
	GRU	21,3	20,69	20,22	15,25
	Joey NMT	**46.99**	23,66	14,25	10,75
	Classical transformer	16,44	15,78	14	10,41

Model with Segmented Sentences (EXP 4):

According to previous experiments, we obtained the best scores with a sequence length equal to 30 using a combined corpus configuration (with and without normalization). For this, we choose to apply a segmentation method created above on the corpus (in MSA side and TD side) based on this value (L = 30). We test the different models using the new version of the segmented corpus. Table 7 summarizes the obtained BLEU scores. As shown in the previous experiments, Joey NMT is the model that achieves the obtained best score (46.99). Also, in this experiment, as shown in Table 7, Joey NMT gives the high score (67.56). For this, we deduce that the segmentation method improves the result (from 46.49 to 67.56).

Table 7. BLEU scores of NMT models using segmented corpus.

Resources	Models	Sequences Length L = 30
Segmented Corpus	LSTM	22.37
	GRU	23,96
	Joey NMT	**67,56**
	Classical transformer	19.74

5.3   Discussion

The highest BLEU score in EXP 1 (NMT_NONOR) is 33.90 with the classical transformer using the TARIC corpus only. While in EXP 2 (NMT-NORC), the highest score (34.55) was obtained by the Joey NMT transformer with the parameter of sequence length = 30 and using all transcript data including those obtained with data augmentation method. Similarly, in EXP 3 (NMT_COC), the best result is obtained by the Joey transformer using the same parameter (sequence length = 30). The mixture of normalized data with no normalized data leads to an increase in the BLEU score. This is explained by sample augmentation in the corpus. EXP 4 shows an improvement in results with the same model i.e. Joey transformer. According to these experiments, the configuration that shows the good translation is the one with the augmented and segmented corpus. Thus, almost every Joey transformer is the model that gives the high BLUE score for each experience. So, We deduce that the best model to translate TD transcription into MSA is the Joey transformer using the augmented data with a maximum sentence length of 30 words.

6   Conclusion

In this paper, we demonstrated whether NMT models are well adapted to translate speech TD into MSA. To achieve this goal, a state of the art corpus containing 3 varieties of spoken TD was explored. We used its transcriptions to create the first parallel corpus of transcriptions TD-MSA. We conducted different experiments dedicated to the analysis of the used corpus for the translation of TD using different neural architectures. Our experiences have shown that transformer model using Joey NMT outperform classical transformer, LSTM and GRU models. It achieved a BLEU score of 67.56%. This work will be pursued by exploring other augmentation methods to enlarge the size of data. We aim also to explore the end to end speech translation approach.

References

1. Al-Ibrahim, R., Duwairi, R.M.: Neural machine translation from Jordanian dialect to modern standard Arabic. In: 2020 11th International Conference on Information and Communication Systems (ICICS), pp. 173–178 (2020). https://doi.org/10.1109/ICICS49469.2020.239505
2. Bahdanau, D., Cho, K., Bengio, Y.: Neural machine translation by jointly learning to align and translate (2016)
3. Baniata, L.H., Park, S., Park, S.B.: A neural machine translation model for Arabic dialects that utilizes multitask learning (MTL). Comput. Intell. Neurosci. **2018**, 10 (2018)
4. Bouamor, H., et al.: The MADAR Arabic dialect corpus and lexicon. In: Proceedings of the 11th Language Resources and Evaluation Conference. Miyazaki, Japan (2018)

5. Boujelbane, R., Khemekhem, M.E, Belguith, L.H.: Mapping rules for building a Tunisian dialect lexicon and generating corpora. In: Proceedings of the Sixth International Joint Conference on Natural Language Processing, pp. 419–428. Asian Federation of Natural Language Processing, Nagoya, Japan (2013). https://www.aclweb.org/anthology/I13-1048
6. Boukadida, N.: Connaissances phonologiques et morphologiques dérivationnelles et apprentissage de la lecture en arabe (etude longitudinale) (2008)
7. Cho, K., van Merriënboer, B., Bahdanau, D., Bengio, Y.: On the properties of neural machine translation: encoder-decoder approaches. In: Proceedings of SSST-8, Eighth Workshop on Syntax, Semantics and Structure in Statistical Translation, pp. 103–111. Association for Computational Linguistics, Doha, Qatar (2014). https://doi.org/10.3115/v1/W14-4012. https://aclanthology.org/W14-4012
8. Fadaee, M., Bisazza, A., Monz, C.: Data augmentation for low-resource neural machine translation. In: Proceedings of the 55th Annual Meeting of the Association for Computational Linguistics (Volume 2: Short Papers), pp. 567–573. Association for Computational Linguistics, Vancouver, Canada (2017). https://doi.org/10.18653/v1/P17-2090. https://aclanthology.org/P17-2090
9. Folajimi, Y., Isaac, O.: Using statistical machine translation (SMT) as a language translation tool for understanding Yoruba language (2012). https://doi.org/10.13140/2.1.3522.8485
10. Hamdi, A., Boujelbane, R., Habash, N., Nasr, A.: The effects of factorizing root and pattern mapping in bidirectional Tunisian - standard Arabic machine translation. In: MT Summit 2013. p. pas d'édition papier. France (2013). https://hal.archives-ouvertes.fr/hal-00908761
11. Kchaou, S., Boujelbane, R., Hadrich-Belguith, L.: Parallel resources for Tunisian Arabic dialect translation. In: Proceedings of the Fifth Arabic Natural Language Processing Workshop, pp. 200–206. Association for Computational Linguistics, Barcelona, Spain (2020). https://www.aclweb.org/anthology/2020.wanlp-1.18
12. Kingma, D.P., Ba, J.: Adam: a method for stochastic optimization (2017)
13. Masmoudi, A., Khmekhem, M.E., Estève, Y., Belguith, L.H., Habash, N.: A corpus and phonetic dictionary for Tunisian Arabic speech recognition. In: Proceedings of the Ninth International Conference on Language Resources and Evaluation (LREC2014), pp. 306–310. European Language Resources Association (ELRA), Reykjavik, Iceland (2014). http://www.lrec-conf.org/proceedings/lrec2014/pdf/454_Paper.pdf
14. Nagy, A., Nanys, P., Konrád, B.F., Bial, B., Ács, J.: Syntax-based data augmentation for Hungarian-English machine translation (2022)
15. Przystupa, M., Abdul-Mageed, M.: Neural machine translation of low-resource and similar languages with backtranslation. In: Proceedings of the Fourth Conference on Machine Translation (Volume 3: Shared Task Papers, Day 2), pp. 224–235. Association for Computational Linguistics, Florence, Italy (2019). https://doi.org/10.18653/v1/W19-5431. https://aclanthology.org/W19-5431
16. Richburg, A., Eskander, R., Muresan, S., Carpuat, M.: An evaluation of subword segmentation strategies for neural machine translation of morphologically rich languages. In: Proceedings of the The Fourth Widening Natural Language Processing Workshop, pp. 151–155. Association for Computational Linguistics, Seattle, USA (2020). https://doi.org/10.18653/v1/2020.winlp-1.40. https://www.aclweb.org/anthology/2020.winlp-1.40
17. Takezawa, T., Genichiro, K., Masahide, M., Eiichiro, S.: Multilingual spoken language corpus development for communication research. In: Chinese Spoken Language Processing, pp. 781–791 (2006)

18. Tapo, A.A., et al.: Neural machine translation for extremely low-resource African languages: a case study on Bambara. In: Proceedings of the 3rd Workshop on Technologies for MT of Low Resource Languages, pp. 23–32. Association for Computational Linguistics, Suzhou, China (2020). https://aclanthology.org/2020.loresmt-1.3

19. Vu, V.H., Nguyen, P., Nguyen, H., Shin, J.C., Ock, C.Y.: Korean-vietnamese neural machine translation with named entity recognition and part-of-speech tags. IEICE Trans. Inf. Syst. **E103.D**, 866–873 (2020). https://doi.org/10.1587/transinf.2019EDP7154

20. Zribi, I., Boujelbane, R., Masmoudi, A., Ellouze, M., Belguith, L., Habash, N.: A conventional orthography for Tunisian Arabic. In: Proceedings of the Ninth International Conference on Language Resources and Evaluation (LREC2014), pp. 2355–2361. European Language Resources Association (ELRA), Reykjavik, Iceland (2014). http://www.lrec-conf.org/proceedings/lrec2014/pdf/219_Paper.pdf

21. Zribi, I., Kammoun, I., Ellouze, M., Hadrich Belguith, L., Blache, P.: Sentence boundary detection for transcribed Tunisian Arabic. In: Konvens-2016. RUHR-UNIVERSITAT BOCHUM, Bochum, Germany (2016), https://hal.archives-ouvertes.fr/hal-01462133

22. Zribi, I., Ellouze, M., Belguith, L., Blache, P.: Spoken Tunisian Arabic corpus "stac": transcription and annotation. Res. Comput. Sci. **90**, 123–135 (2015). https://doi.org/10.13053/rcs-90-1-9

SPIRAL: SPellIng eRror Parallel Corpus for Arabic Language

Shaimaa Ben Aichaoui, Nawel Hiri, and Mohamd Amine Cheragui[✉]

Mathematics and Computer Science Department, Ahmed Draia University, Adrar, Algeria
benaichaoui.shaimaa@gmail.com, hiri.01@gmail.com,
m_cheragui@univ-adrar.edu.dz

Abstract. Linguistic resources (corpus) have become a fundamental component in natural language processing over the last two decades, due to the role they play both in the testing and evaluation phase and in the development phase with the emergence of statistical and machine learning approaches. However, the development of such resources requires considerable time and effort.

In this paper, we present the steps to build our parallel corpus SPIRAL, which will be a useful resource for research in the field of spelling error detection and correction in Arabic texts. SPIRAL is the result of a study dedicated to the universe of spelling errors, where we exploited the different taxonomies dedicated to spelling error in Arabic texts, to generate automatically more than 248 million possible erroneous words from 420,000 correctly spelled words.

Keywords: Corpus · Spell-checker · Arabic language · Error generation

1 Introduction

The term Corpus has become during the last two decades a fundamental concept in natural language processing. Sinclair [1] defined the corpus as: a collection of pieces of language text in electronic form, selected according to external criteria to represent, as far as possible, a language or language variety as a source of data for linguistic research. The importance of corpora has increased with the emergence of stochastic or machine learning approaches, so several research fields have been taking advantage of corpora in order to develop new resolution techniques (Hidden Markov models, n-gram model, Neural networks, …etc.), In particular, spelling detection and correction has been considered since the 1960 s as one of the most important research fields in NLP [2].

It must be noted that in the age of digitalization huge amounts of the textual resources have been generated by different sources (OCR, machine translation, e-mails, ..etc.) [3]. This makes automatic spelling correction very advantageous compared to manual correction which consumes a lot of time and effort [4].

For Arabic, spelling correction still presents a real challenge, due to the complexity and morphological richness that this language presents compared to other languages such as English or French, especially through its flexion and derivation systems [5] which allow to generate a large number of words from a canonical unit (Stem). Despite

© Springer Nature Switzerland AG 2022
A. Bennour et al. (Eds.): ISPR 2022, CCIS 1589, pp. 248–259, 2022.
https://doi.org/10.1007/978-3-031-08277-1_21

this, several works and studies have been done in orthographic detection and correction in Arabic texts [6].

The objective of this paper is to present the main guidelines for building our SPIRAL[1] corpus (SPellIng eRror corpora for Arabic Language), by developing an automatic spelling error generator.

The remainder of the paper is organized as follows: Sect. 2 we discuss the importance of corpus in natural language processing. Section 3 overviews some of related works. Section 4 presents a taxonomy of spelling errors in Arabic texts. Our proposed approach to building SPIRAL corpus is detailed in Sect. 5. Section 6 presents our SPIRAL corpus. Finally, our conclusion and future work are in Sect. 7.

2 Why Building a Corpus is Important in NLP?

The importance of building a corpus can be summarised in two major points, which are:

- With the proliferation of natural language tools, it is clear that these tools need to be evaluated, in order to have an objective point of view about the performance of the developed system, which allows to improve the efficiency of the implemented system.
- With the emergence in the last two decades of new approaches such as statistical or machine learning approaches, the development of corpus has become a necessity due to the role played by corpus in the resolution phase. A corpus can be considered as a methodology to study the language, through the extraction of characteristics according to the studied field, in order to improve the performance of the generated models.

3 Related Work

Searching in literature about Arabic spelling detection and correction, we find a large number of works (and tools[2]) that vary in terms of approaches (Rule-Based Techniques, Similarity Distance Techniques, Morphology Techniques, Techniques relying on phonetics and Hybrid Techniques) [3], which allows for a progressive improvement in performance. However, in terms of building standard corpora, there is a lack of work, most researchers aim to build their own corpus during the development phase. In this section we present some corpora dedicated to spelling detection and correction (Table 1).

---

[1] Download SPIRAL: https://mega.nz/file/sa50BaKL#i9qjD52tt-QzLiKWM-rOQ9XrC1anyOwSOJ_kpzutN7M.

[2] Tools: Ghalatawi (http://ghalatawi.sourceforge.net/index.php?content=english), Arabic Spell checker (http://arabicspellchecker.com/), AyaSpell (http://ayaspell.sourceforge.net/).

Table 1. Specialized corpora in Arabic spelling error.

Corpus	Year	Size
QALB [7]	2013	+1 million words
Arabic wordlist for spell checking [8]	2015	9.2 million of words
Alkhatib et al. [5]	2020	15 million words
Al-jefri and Mahmoud [9]	2013	41,170,678 words
Abandah et al. [10]	2015	65,000 Words
Farwaneh and Tamimiin [11]	2012	50,000 Words
Mars [12]	2016	13.6 Million of words
CODA [13]	2020	10,000 Sentences

4   The Main Guidelines for Building the SPIRAL Corpus

To build our SPIRAL corpus, we split the process into two phases, which are: Collecting digital Arabic words and Process of error generation (Fig. 1).

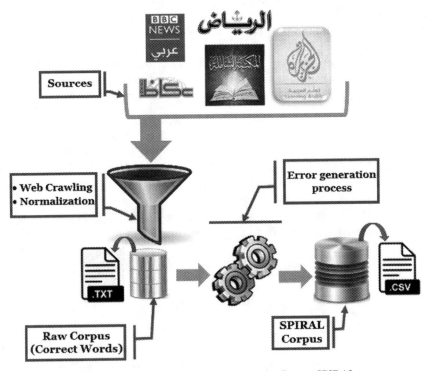

Fig. 1. General architecture of building the Corpus SPIRAL.

4.1 Collecting Digital Arabic Words

Sources of Extraction: The quality of the corpus is the most important feature in this field of research, in order to improve our corpus's quality we first collected the most common sites, newspapers and libraries that supports the MSA needed for the work, for this reason we opted for: the Riyadh newspaper[3] which is a very old paper since 1965, Okaz[4] and BBC[5] newspapers, also the Learning al-jazeera education website[6] for arabic and finally al-Maktaba al-shamela library[7].

Normalization: Once the extraction phase is completed, we move on to normalization, which mainly aims at unifying our raw corpus, through a number of 03 steps, which are:

- Step 1: delete non-Arab words (numbers, Latin alphabets, punctuation…etc.) as well as repeated words
- Step 2: We pass raw corpus to the Farasa[8] tool and extract the diacritical Arabic texts (Our corpus also has parallel side which is al-Mochakal corpus which will be used in a specific category of errors)
- Stap 3: converting files from the original "*.Txt" format to the "*.CSV" format with the heading [index,word] in both versions (Table 2).

Table 2. Different resources used for our corpus and their statistics.

Source	Number of Words (before Normalization)	Number of words (After Normalization)
Riyadh site	681.330	117.375
OKAZ site	135.101	37.018
BBC site	11.795	7.885
Learning el-jazeera site	26.899	24.778
El-maktaba el-shamila site	2.127.316	964.237
Total With Diacritization	2.982.441	1.130.237
Total without Diacritization	2.982.441	423.778

4.2 Process of Error Generation

A word spelled incorrectly can be classified as a non-word spell errors (which contains the types: Add, Delete, Replace, Permutate, Phonetic, Physical, Keyboard, Space-issues, Morphology, Hamza and Tachkil) or real word spell errors. In this section we present the mechanism of generation of each type of error.

---

[3] https://www.alriyadh.com/.

[4] https://www.okaz.com.sa/.

[5] https://www.bbc.com/arabic.

[6] https://learning.aljazeera.net/en/generallanguage/level/beginner.

[7] https://al-maktaba.org/.

[8] https://farasa.qcri.org/.

Add: This type of error happens when a character is added or duplicated in a word [14]. To generate incorrect words, the proposed method is based on two operations: the first one consists in adding each letter of "Abjd alphabetic" in every position of the correct word, while the second operation aims at duplicating the letters of the correct word (Fig. 2).

Fig. 2. Example of add Error.

Delete: This type of spelling error occurs when a character is omitted [15]. At each iteration, the proposed method consists of removing a character from the correct word (Fig. 3).

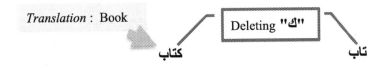

Fig. 3. Example of delete error.

Replace: This error is the result of substituting a character by another [15]. The idea of the proposed method is based on the substitution of each character of the correct word by every letter of the "Abjd alphabetic" (Fig. 4).

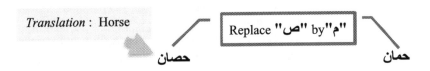

Fig. 4. Example of replace error.

Permutate: Such errors occur when the order of characters in the word is incorrectly written by typing one character before another [14]. The presented method works by permuting every two adjacent characters in the given correct word (Fig. 5).

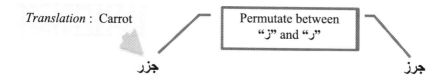

Fig. 5. Example of permutate error.

Phonetic: non-native speakers find some difficulty in choosing the right character, especially when two characters have almost the same phonetic pronunciation [16]. For this purpose, we have set up a classification grouping characters that are phonetically similar. Then via our algorithm we made a substitution between the characters of the same category ({ح،ه}, {ذ،ظ},{د،ض} , {س،ص} , {ت،ط})(Fig. 6).

Fig. 6. Example of phonetic error.

Physical: The recognition of handwritten characters can generate an error especially between those having the same shapes [16]. In the same way as the phonetic error, we have identified the letters that are similar and then we generate the words by making a substitution between the letters of the same category ({أ، آ، إ، ا}, {ض، ص}, {ط، ظ}, { ح، ج، خ }, {ي، ى}, { ر، ز}, {ف، ق}, {ع، غ}, {د، ذ},{ش، س})(Fig. 7).

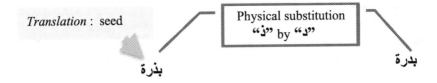

Fig. 7. Example of physical error.

Keyboard: This type of error results when a character is swapped with a neighbouring character in a keyboard [13]. Our method consists of replacing each character of the correct word with each letter adjacent to it on the keyboard. The basis of the neighbouring characters is shown in the figure below (Fig. 8) (Table 3):

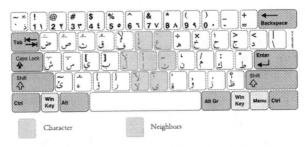

Fig. 8. Representation of neighbors in a keyboard.

Table 3. Example of keyboard error.

Correct word	Translation	Generated errors
كأس	Cup	case of replacing "ك "by his neighbors طأس، جأس، حأس، مأس، زأس، ظأس

Space-issues: This kind of error occurs when a space is added between the characters of one word [13]. The proposed method adds a space to each possible position in the given correct word (Table 4).

Table 4. Example of space-issues error.

Correct word	Translation	Generated error
مقتنع	Convinced	"مق تنع"، "مقتن ع"، "م قتنع"

Morphology: This type of error is due to the morphological structure of the Arabic language, where a non-native Arabic learner can easily make a mistake in the transcription, the morphological error can be divided into 03 forms, which are [17]:

- 1st form, Written without pronounced (تكتب ولا تنطق): This type of error refers to the pronunciation of the character " ل /Lam"in "ال"[9] (The), when it is followed by one of the following 14 Solar characters (ط, ل, ن, ت, ث, د, ذ, ر, ز, س, ش, ض, ص, ظ). In this case, it will not be pronounced. Our method consists of deleting the letter ("ل"/Lam)from the prefix if the correct word starts with a sun letter.
- 2nd form, pronounced without being written(تنطق ولا تكتب): In this part we have a limited list (38 words) of spell without written words (CL), and it's corresponding spell without being written error word list (EL). For example: "هاذا" → "هذا"and "الاكن" → "لكن". The method checks if the correct word is in the limited list CL. if yes, it replaces it by its corresponding error word from EL.
- 3rd form, is the one where we make a confusion when we write between ("ة" or "ه")and ("ا" or "ى")at the end of the word. So, the method generates an error word by replacing the last character by the one that has similar pronunciation (Table 5).

Table 5. Example of morphology error.

Morphological Error	Correct word	Translation	Generated Error
Written without pronounced	الشمس	The Sun	اشمس
Alif mAk-soUra	دعا	Invited	دعى
TaA error	مدفأة	Heater	مدفأت

Hamza: can generate two types of errors:

- The 1st, is due to a mis-typing between "Hamzah-QatA" and "Hamzah-wasl", so The proposed method permutates between "Hmazah-wasl" and "Hamzah-QatA".
- The 2nd, the supposed hamza (الهمزة المقدرة)in the middle of the correct word is replaced by the following variants: "ا, ئ, ء, و". we must note that the method treats the Agglutinated words as well (Table 6).

---

[9] Same observation for the prefixes: لل, بال, فال, وال, كال, فوال, فبال, وبال, وكال

Table 6. Example of hamzah error.

Hamza Error	Correct word	Translation	Generated Error
Wasl and QatA	أمن	Security	امن
Hamza wasathya	لبؤة	A lioness	لبأة، لبءة، لبنة

Tachkil (diacritization): This kind of spelling error occurs when learners write a letter instead of a diacritic [15]. The method proposed focus on 3 kinds, including:

- Vowel Errors: generates incorrect words by replacing the short vowels with the long vowels {(ا، فتحة), (و، ضمة), (ي، كسرة)}.
- Tanween Errors: replacing Tanween by adding an extra letter instead "ين، ان، تان، تين، تون ن، تن، ون،".
- Shadda Errors: duplicate the letter with the Shadda ("ّ")above (Table 7).

Table 7. Example of tachkil error.

Error Type	Correct word	Translation	Generated Error
Vowel Error	كُتِبَ	Has been written	كوتِبَ
Tanween Error	تَمْرٌ	Date	تَمْرن
	كُرَةٌ	Ball	كرتون
Shadda Error	سلّة	Basket	سللة

Real Word Error: These errors result when learners use correct Arabic words in the wrong context within a sentence [13], so our method is based on testing every error word returned from the previous categories and checking if it's correct using an Arabic dictionary. if it's correct, it will pass directly to the "real category file", else it will be passed to the "error category file" (Table 8).

Table 8. Example of real-word error.

Correct Word	Translation	Generated Errors	Translation
مع	With	عم (Permutation between two letters)	Uncle
فكّر	He thought	مفكّر (Add the letter "م")	Thinker

5   Results and Discussion

During the development process of our SPIRAL corpus, we focused on two fundamental characteristics, which are: the quality of the textual resources produced through the process of generating spelling errors, as well as the size (+248 million words) of the final corpus which will have an impact on the evaluation or the development of future spell checkers. In this section we present our SPIRAL corpus in numbers, and also some graphical interfaces of our Arabic spelling error generator, which is developed with PyQt5 (Table 9) (Fig. 9).

Table 9. Statistics about SPIRAL.

Category		Number of Words
Edit	Add	116.127.057
	Replace	95.784.610
	Permutation	2.015.801
	Delete	1.670.511
Similarity Errors		4.444.300
Keyboard Errors		15.558.089
Morphology Errors		171.852
Hamza Errors		306.714
Tachkil		3.771.834
Real words		8.591.124
Total		248.441.892

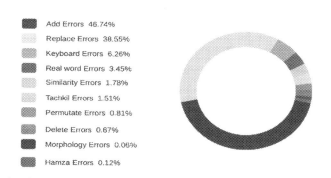

Add Errors 46.74%

Replace Errors 38.55%

Keyboard Errors 6.26%

Real word Errors 3.45%

Similarity Errors 1.78%

Tachkil Errors 1.51%

Permutate Errors 0.81%

Delete Errors 0.67%

Morphology Errors 0.06%

Hamza Errors 0.12%

Fig. 9. Graphical representation of the proportion of each error category in SPIRAL.

It is important to specify that for each category of error, we have developed a graphical interface, in order to be able to check the errors generated (Fig. 10).

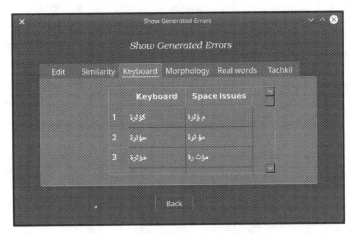

Fig. 10. GUI of SPIRAL Generator.

6   Conclusion

Building a corpus is not only a process of collecting texts from electronic resources; it consists in preparing and processing them, which requires a lot of time and effort. In this paper, we have presented the process of building our SPIRAL corpus, dedicated to spelling errors for the Arabic language. We have been able to generate over 248 million words, covering different categories of possible errors. This corpus can be very useful for the evaluation or development of spelling checkers.

As next steps, we will work on two perspectives, the first one concerning the generator that we will convert it into an API (Python) so that each researcher will be able to integrate it and generate the incorrect words by himself. The second perspective, we will move from the word to the sentence, working more on the agreement processing between the words composing the sentence, in order to generate incorrect sentences that have anomalies regarding morphological or grammatical features.

References

1. Sinclair, J.: Corpus and text-basic principles. In: Wynne, M., (ed.) Developing Linguistic Corpora: A Guide to Good Practice, pp. 1–16. Oxford, UK OxbowBooks (2005)
2. Kukich, K.: Technique for automatically correcting words in text. ACM Comput. Surv. **24**(4), 377–439 (1992)
3. Saty, A.A., Bouzoubaa, K., Si, L.A.: Survey of Arabic checker techniques. SUST J. Eng. Comput. Sci. (JECS) **21**(1), 34–41 (2020)

4. Alkanhal, M.I., Al-Badrashiny, M.A., Alghamdi, M.M., Al-Qabbany, A.O.: Automatic stochastic Arabic spelling correction with emphasis on space insertions and deletions. In: Proceeding of IEEE Transactions on Audio, Speech, and Language Processing, vol. 20, no.7, (2012)
5. Alkhatib, M., Azza, A., Shaalan, K.: Deep learning for Arabic error detection and correction. ACM Trans. Asian Low-Resour. Lang. Inf. Process. **19**(5), 1–13 (2020)
6. Nejja M., Yousfi A.: The vocabulary and the morphology in spell checker. In: The Proceeding of the First International Conference on Intelligent Computing in Data Sciences (2018)
7. Habash, N., Mohit, B., Obeid, O., Oflazer, k., Tomeh, N., Zaghouani, W.: QALB: Qatar Arabic language bank. In: Proceedings of Qatar Annual Research Conference (2013)
8. Attia, M., Pecina, P., Samih, Y., Shaalan, K., Van Ggenabith, J.: Arabic spelling error detection and correction. Nat. Lang. Eng. **22**(05), 751–773 (2015)
9. Al-Jefri, M.M., Mahmoud, S.A.: Context-sensitive Arabic spell checker using context words and N-gramlanguage models. In: Proceedings of the International Conference on Advances in Information Technology for the Holy Quran and Its Sciences, pp. 258–263 (2013)
10. Abandah, G.A, Graves, A., Al-Shagoor, B., Arabiyat, A., Jamour, F., Al-Taee, M.: Automatic diacritization of Arabic text using recurrent neural networks. Int. J. Doc. Anal. Recognit, **18**(2), 183–197 (2015)https://doi.org/10.1007/s10032-015-0242-2
11. Farwaneh, S., Tamimi, M.: Arabic learners written corpus: a resource for research and learning. The Center for Educational Resources in Culture, Language and Literacy (2012)
12. Eryani, F., Habash, N., Bouamor, H., Khalifa, S.: A spelling correction corpus for multiple Arabic dialects. In: Proceedings of the 12th Conference on Language Resources and Evaluation (2020)
13. Mars, M.: Toward a robust spell checker for Arabic text. In: Gervasi, O., et al. (eds.) ICCSA 2016. LNCS, vol. 9790, pp. 312–322. Springer, Cham (2016). https://doi.org/10.1007/978-3-319-42092-9_24
14. Shaalan, K., Allam, A., Gomah, A.: Towards automatic spell checking for Arabic. In: Proceedings of the 4th Conference on Language Engineering, Egyptian Society of Language Engineering (2003)
15. Shaalan, K., Aref, R., Fahmy, A.: An approach for analyzing and correcting spelling errors for non-native Arabic learners. In The Proceeding of 7th International Conference on Informatics and Systems (2010)
16. Brosh, H.: Arabic spelling: errors, perceptions, and strategies. Foreign Lang. Ann. **48**(4), 584–603 (2015)
17. Alamri, M., Teahan, W.J.: A new error annotation for dyslexic texts in Arabic. In: Proceedings of the Third Arabic Natural Language Processing Workshop, pp. 72–78 (2017)

Machine and Deep Learning

VMs Migration Mechanism for Underloaded Machines in Green Cloud Computing

Nassima Bouchareb[✉] and Nacer Eddine Zarour

LIRE Laboratory, Department of Software Technologies and Information Systems, Faculty of New Information and Communication Technologies, University of Constantine 2 - Abdelhamid Mehri, Constantine, Algeria
{nassima.bouchareb,nasro.zarour}@univ-constantine2.dz

Abstract. High cost of Cloud data centers' energy consumption have inspired numerous researches to provide more efficient virtual machine (VM) management approaches. Migration of VM is one of the important VM management solutions. However, inefficient VMs migration can also increase energy consumption. Thus, it must be handled very cautiously and at least as possible. In this work, a VMs migration mechanism is proposed, particularly the VMs migration of the underloaded machines. The suggested mechanism is founded on Minimum and Maximum thresholds to not have underloaded and overloaded machines, and to have stable hosts. The objective is to reduce the energy use. Finally, we present experimentation results on the simulator: CloudSim, to show the advantages of the adopted solution.

Keywords: Energy efficient · Cloud Computing · Green Computing · Virtual machine migration

1 Introduction

Energy consumption costs belong to the most Cloud provider total cost [1]. So, the Cloud Providers (CP) want to reduce these costs but still respecting the Service Level Agreements. For that, CP resort to using the virtualization concept, which is sharing one Physical Machine (PM) into several Virtual Machines (VMs) that can run simultaneously, transparently to users.

An inactive resource wastes 70% energy of the data centers [2]. So, on the one hand, the underloaded host consumes much energy to run few VMs. On the other hand, if we have overloaded machines, it may raise response time and minimize throughput, which can violate the SLA, and cause penalties to CP, that is why, we use two dynamic thresholds "Minimum/cold and Maximum/hot", like it was mentioned in [3, 4] to avoid having underloaded and overloaded resources, respectively.

If we obtain underloaded/overloaded resources, we will pass to optimize the VMs allocation "VMs reallocation process". This process is termed as *"migration of VMs"*. It is used to: *1) reduce power consumption*- because after migrating the VMs of the underloaded host to an activated machine, we can switch off the under loaded machine

© Springer Nature Switzerland AG 2022
A. Bennour et al. (Eds.): ISPR 2022, CCIS 1589, pp. 263–277, 2022.
https://doi.org/10.1007/978-3-031-08277-1_22

to economize energy. *2) for load balancing-* All resources are loaded between the Min and Max thresholds, because even the overload of an overloaded resource is migrated to other active resources.

We have two kinds of VM migration: *1) Hot (live) migration-* without shutting down of resources, transparently to users. *2) Cold (non-live) migration-* with interruption of service [5, 6].

To select VMs to migrate, we are interested in minimizing the migration rate and migrating small VMs instead of large ones, because migrating VMs needs also energy and time. So, a VM migration consumes also energy and may cause SLA violations.

In this paper; we treat the Virtual Machines migration in Cloud Computing, to minimize energy consumption, by using two thresholds "Minimum and Maximum" in order to avoid the underloaded and overloaded machines. A Min/Max thresholds strategy is previously proposed in [7], where the migration concerns the VMs of the overloaded resources. However in this work, we particularly deal with the migration of VMs of underloaded machines. The organization of this paper is as following: So, we present related work in the next section. In Sect. 3, we present our VMs migration mechanism. A comparison between related work and our mechanism is presented in Sect. 4. Then, experimental results are presented in Sect. 5. At the end, we give a conclusion and some perspectives in Sect. 6.

2   Related Work

We have noticed a great interest in the research community regarding power reduction and virtual machine migration in Cloud Computing systems. Several efforts have been made to build energy consumption models, develop energy efficiency costs, manage workload fluctuations and attempt to achieve an effective trade-off between system efficiency and energy cost. A survey of VM placement techniques is presented in [8]. These techniques are devised with and without VM migration. However, all the works presented bellow treat the VMs migration.

In [9], authors treated the Cloud VM allocation to economize energy and minimize the number of activated machines. In this work, migrations are only enforced if the host may be fully unloaded.

In [10], authors proposed an auction-based VM allocation which works by modeling agents as bidders and VMs as commodities. A negotiation based VM consolidation mechanism, which is designed for agents to exchange their assigned VMs to save energy cost and address system dynamics. A possible reason is that there are only a small number of profitable VM migrations.

Authors in [6] presented the different live VM migration techniques. They only treated the case of "hotspots". If a machine is overloaded, it may dynamically transfer certain amount of its load to another machine in a transparent way for the user, no threshold has been introduced.

In [5], a VM selection algorithm is proposed. They choose the adequate resource according the free memory in order to reduce the migrations. If the free memory is not sufficient, they look for a machine that has the min memory sufficient. However, what to proceed, if all free VMs are lower than requested memory?

In [10], a mechanism of VM consolidation based on negotiation is given to agents in order to exchange their VMs and economize power cost and address system dynamics with a small number of profitable VM migrations. In this work, authors did not give many details about the migration of VMs.

In [12], authors presented a technique of Machine Learning (ML) for live migrations of VMs founded on prediction of usage thresholds. The decision of migration will be taken after the prediction of the upcoming SLA violation.

Authors in [13] proposed a VM placement algorithm, and a power-aware algorithm. If there is a lot of underloaded machines, they switch off the one with higher power consumption and a lesser number of VMs. The number of the running VMs is a key indicator. However, in our work, our process depends on the VMs number and their time of execution, because it is possible to have one VM in a machine, with a long execution time. Here, it is preferable to migrate it and turn off the host. In addition to the lack of run time, authors in [13] did not explain how to choose the receiving machines.

In [14], again a Single Threshold based approach is proposed to keep the CPU utilization under this threshold. But the host is switched on even if the CPU utilization is much less than threshold. Other policies are also proposed in this paper, to select the adequate VMs for migration from the node. Authors in [15] proposed a lower threshold equal to 45% and an upper threshold equal to 81%. However, fixing thresholds is not suitable for dynamic systems. So, authors in [3] and [4] have proposed dynamic values of thresholds. However, there is no explanation about how to select VMs to migrate and which ones receive them.

After this study of related work, we have based our work on the latter "dynamic double thresholds", and we detail more the VMs migration. In [7], a VMs allocation and reallocation mechanism is first proposed and the proposed VMs migration protocol concerns the overloaded machines. In the current paper, we deal with VMs migration of the underloaded machines.

3 VMs Migration Mechanism

The load of each resource must $\in$ [Min, Max] but we can find overloaded resources which consume less energy than activating new ones. Besides, we may have underloaded resources due to few requests that are finished/set aside, what liberates few VMs on the host. Thus, if there is overloaded or underloaded hosts, their VMs will be migrated to liberated hosts (overloaded resources have been already treated in [7]). So, we treat the underloaded resources and we present the most frequently encountered cases. To fully explain these different cases, we follow each case by an example. We have fixed the minimum threshold = 20% and the maximum threshold = 80% (these are the most used values), to explain the mechanism. We use the symbols presented in Table 1 for the following cases.

3.1 Case 1: An Underloaded Resource

If we have one resource with a load < Min and there are other resources with load $\in$ [Min, Max], we migrate the VMs from the first resource to the one with a load close

Table 1. Denotations

Symbol	Significance
R	Physical resource (physical machine)
load	Load of resource VMs
OVM/FVM/SOVM	Occupied VMs/Free VMs/Shared VMs
nbr	Number of resources
Toverloaded	Overloaded resource time

to Max and which contains free VMs sufficient to accommodate the migrated VMs without exceeding the Max threshold, then the first machine is turned off (see Fig. 1). We summarize case 1 in the following algorithm:

If ($\exists R_n / load_{Rn} <$ Min) And ($\exists load_{Rm} \in$ [Min, Max]) Then
  Repeat
    Migrate OVM_{Rn} to $R_m / load_{Rm} \approx$ Max And $load FVM_{Rm} \geq loadOVM_{Rn}$
    Shut down R_n
  Until ($\nexists R_n / load_{Rn} <$ Min) Or ($loadFVM_{Rm} < loadOVM_{Rn}$)
Endif

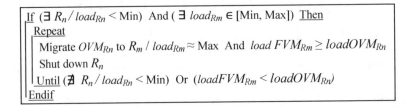

Fig. 1. Case 1

3.2 Case 2: All Resources are Underloaded

If all resources are underloaded and we have a limited number of resources ($<\lambda$). We migrate the VMs that have the lowest loads to the resource that has the maximum load, in order to shut them down. The principle here is to migrate small VMs, because the size of the VM affects the consumed energy during the migration (see Fig. 2). We summarize case 2 in the following algorithm:

If ($\forall R_i$: $load_{R_i}$ < Min) And (nbr_{R_i} < λ) <u>Then</u>
  <u>Repeat</u>
    Migrate OVM_{Rn} to R_m/ $load\ R_n$ = Min $load_{R_i}$ And $load\ R_m$ = Max $load_{R_i}$
    Shut down R_n
  <u>Until</u> load FVM_{Rm} < load OVM_{Rn}
Endif

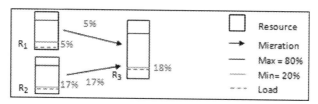

Fig. 2. Case 2

3.3   Case 3: Large Number of Underloaded Resources

We have a large number of resources (>λ) with a load less than the Min. We migrate the highest loads (unlike the 2nd case). This is to reduce migrations, which needs energy (see Fig. 3). We summarize case 3 in the following algorithm:

If ($\forall R_i$: $load_{R_i}$ < Min) And   (nbr_{R_i} > λ) <u>Then</u>
  <u>Repeat</u>
    Migrate OVM_{Rn} to R_m/ $load\ R_m$ = Max $load_{R_i}$ And $load\ R_n$ = Max $load_{(R_i\ Rm)}$
    Shut down R_n
  <u>Until</u> loadFVM_{Rm} > loadOVM_{Rn}
Endif

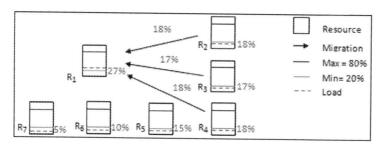

Fig. 3. Case 3

3.4   Case 4: Resources with Load = Max and Others with Loads < Min

We have resources with load = Max and others with loads < Min. We migrate the VMs from resources with minimal load to other underloaded ones, in order to minimize the number of activated machines (see Fig. 4). We summarize case 4 in the following algorithm:

> If ($\exists R_n$ / $load_{Rn}$ = Max) And ($\exists load_{Rm}$ < Min) Then
>> Repeat
>>> Migrate OVM_{Rx} to R_y / $load_{Rx}$ = Min $load_{Rm}$ and load $_{Ry}$ = Max $load_{(Rm -Rx)}$
>>> Shut down R_x
>>> Until ($\nexists R_n$ / $load_{Rn}$ < Min) Or ($loadFVM_{Rm}$ < $loadOVM_{Rn}$)
>
> Endif

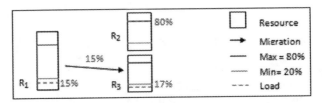

Fig. 4. Case 4

3.5   Case 5: Independent Requests

If the underloaded resource contains independent VMs and the other resources whose load is ∈ [Min, Max] do not have enough free VMs to accommodate these VMs (in a single resource). We do several migrations, placing each VM in a separate machine, starting with those with the maximum number of VMs, in order to maximize them (see Fig. 5). We summarize case 5 in the following algorithm:

> If ($\exists R_n$ / $load_{Rn}$ < Min) And (OVM_{Rn} = Independent) And ($\nexists R_m$ /
> $load_{Rm}$ = [Min, Max] And $FVM_{Rm} \geq$ load OVM_{Rn}) Then
>> Repeat
>>> Migrate $1OVM_{Rn}$ to R_m / $load_{Rm} \approx$ Max And $loadFVM_{Rm} \geq load1OVM_{Rn}$
>>> Until ($\nexists R_n$ / $load_{Rn}$ < Min) Or ($loadFVM_{Rm}$ < $load1OVM_{Rn}$)
>> Shut down R_n / $load_n$ = 0
> Endif

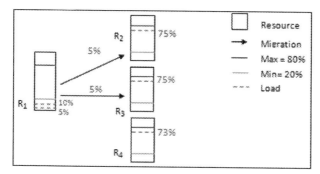

Fig. 5. Case 5

3.6 Case 6: Dependent Requests

If the VMs requests of the underloaded resource are dependent and their migration is highly desirable and all hosts cannot accommodate them. We share these requests on activated hosts (see Fig. 6). We summarize case 6 in the following algorithm:

If ($\exists$ R_n / $load_{Rn}$ < Min) And (OVM_{Rn} = Dependent) And ($\forall$ R_m/ $load_{Rm}$ = [Min, Max]
    And ($loadFVM_{Rm}$ < $loadOVM_{Rn}$) And (Σ $loadFVM_{Rm}$ $\geq$ $loadOVM_{Rn}$) Then
    Repeat
      Share OVM_{Rn}
      Migrate $SOVM_{Rn}$ to R_m / $load_{Rm}$ $\approx$ Max And $loadFVM_{Rm}$ $\geq$ $loadSOVM_{Rn}$
    Until ($\not\exists$ R_n / $load_{Rn}$ < Min) Or ($loadFVM_{Rm}$ < $loadSOVM_{Rn}$)
    Shut down R_n / $load_n$ = 0
Endif

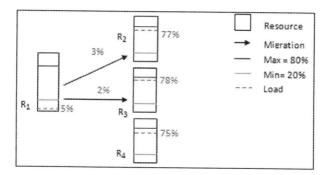

Fig. 6. Case 6

3.7 Case 7: Free Load not Available on the Activated Resources

The Cloud may receive a new request that requires free load not available on the activated resources. We prefer migrating VMs that occupy the minimum percentage in order to receive the new request. Sometimes we do not find small requests, so we share the requests that occupy the percentage that must be released. As in our example, the new request requires 25% load, the resource already has 10% free, then 15% is missing. It is assumed that there are no requests that occupy $<15\%$ to migrate them. So, we have to divide the VM of 15% in two (5% + 10%). Because sharing 15% in two is better than sharing 25% on the three resources (10% on R1, 10% on R2 and 5% on R3) (see Fig. 7). We summarize case 7 in the following algorithm:

If (New request received *Req*) And ($\forall R_n$ $load_{Req}$>$load$ FVM_{Rn} / $load_{Rn}$ = [Min, Max]) Then
   Migrate OVM_{Rx} / $load_{Rx}$ = Min ($load_{Rn}$) And (Σ migratedOVM_{Rx} + FVM_{Rx} $\geq$ $load_{Req}$)
   If ($\nexists$ R_n / $loadFVM_{Rn}$ $\geq$ $load_{Req}$ - $loadFVM_{Rx}$ Then Migrate $SOVM_{Rx}$
   Endif
Endif

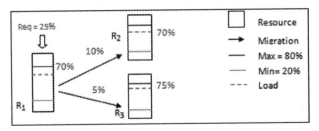

Fig. 7. Case 7

3.8 Case 8: Overloaded Resources After Migration

This is a specific case of the previous case. Sometimes all resources are not overloaded, but after migrating the VMs of the first resource, the loads of the other resources will exceed the Max. In this case, we choose the resource that will be unloaded as soon as possible. This is preferable when migration is desirable in order to shut down or to release the first resource in order to receive a new request having a large load (see Fig. 8). We summarize case 8 in the following algorithm:

If ($\exists$ R_n / $load_{Rn}$ < Min) And ($\forall R_m$ / $load_{Rm}$ = [Min, Max])
   And (Σ $loadFVM_{Rm}$ < $loadOVM_{Rn}$)   Then
   Migrate OVM_{Rn} to R_m / $Toverloaded(R_m)$ = Min ($Toverloaded$)
Endif

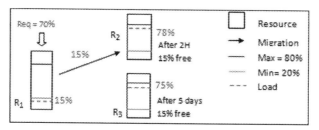

Fig. 8. Case 8

3.9 Case 9: Part of Load will be Released

If a part of load will be released, then we only migrate the remaining load to the adequate resource without exceeding the Max threshold (see Fig. 9). We summarize case 9 in the following algorithm:

If ($\exists R_n / load_{Rn} <$ Min) And ($\forall R_m / load_{Rm} =$ [Min, Max])
   And ($\Sigma loadFVM_{Rm} < loadOVM_{Rn}$) And (at $t_l load1OVM_{Rn} = 0$) Then
   Migrate $load\ OVM_{Rn} - load1OVM_{Rn}$ to $R_m / load_{Rm} \approx$ Max   And $load\ FVM_{Rm} \geq load1OVM_{Rn}$
   Shut down R_n
Endif

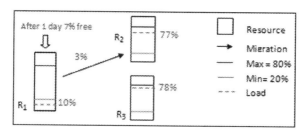

Fig. 9. Case 9

3.10 Case 10: The Resource will not be Underloaded

This case is when the resource will not be underloaded because of the reception of a new request which will start soon. Then, we avoid migrating the load of this resource (see Fig. 10). We summarize case 10 in the following algorithm:

If ($\exists R_n/load_{Rn}$< Min) And (New request Req) And ($\nexists R_m/loadFVM_{Rm} = load_{Req}$) Then
    Execute Req on R_n
Endif

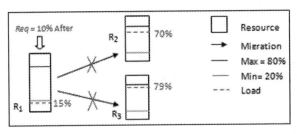

Fig. 10. Case 10

3.11   Case 11: VMs with Similar Execution Time

In this case, if there are VMs that have similar *execution time* (K) in different resources. So, we place them in the same resource as it was mentioned in [11], on condition that these VMs have the same *End Date (ED)*, to shut down the receiving resource at the end of the execution (see Fig. 11). We summarize case 11 in the following algorithm:

Repeat
    If $\exists$ $1OVM_{Rn}$ / $(K_{Rn} = X)$ And $(ED_{Rn} = Y)$ Then
        Migrate 1OVM to R_m
    Endif
Until ($\nexists$ $1OVM_{Rn}$ / $(K_{Rn} = X)$ And $(ED_{Rn} = Y)$) Or ($load_{Rm}$ = Max)

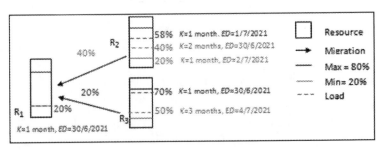

Fig. 11. Case 11

4 Comparison Between Related Work and our Mechanism

The main objective of all related works is to minimize energy consumption and accept the maximum of requests. Table 2 presents the most important differences between our proposed mechanism and the other works. These differences are the criteria that are taken into account when migrating VMs (see Table 2).

Table 2. Comparison between related work and our mechanism

	Min migrattions	Migrate the nearest	Place on the nearest	Min nbr of hosts	Min request sharing	Min coldspots	Min hotspots	Min Th	Max Th
[9]	×			×					
[5]	×	×	×			×	×		
[6]						×	×		
[13]	×			×		×	×	×	
[14]	×			×			×		×
[3, 4, 15]	×			×		×	×	×	×
[7]	×	×	×	×	×	×	×	×	×
Our mechanism	×	×	×	×	×	×	×	×	×

5 Experimentation

We have used the CloudSim simulator. We have considered the thresholds of the Dynamic Thresholds approach proposed in [3] (Max threshold = 80% and Min threshold = 20%), and we have estimated the simulation time equal to 60 min.

We have compared our mechanism with two other strategies:

1. *The Without Migration policy (WM).* This approach uses no energy optimization technique and all machines operate at 100% CPU utilization. This approach activate all the machines. WM policy is already implemented.
2. *The Single Threshold Policy* [4]. Only the Max threshold is used.

We have used 100 resources (physical machines). As shown in the Figs. 12, 13, and 14 we conclude that:

- In our approach, we initially used all the resources to satisfy the maximum of requests, but just at 5 min the number of the used resources decreased to 20 resources, and from 12 min this number stabilized at only 18 resources (see Fig. 12).
- In *WM* policy, all 100 resources are used for the entire simulation time (see Fig. 13).
- In *ST* policy, it was until 18 min that the number of resources started to decrease to just 75 resources. Then, continued to decrease to 40 resources used at 30 min. From 30 min, it stabilized at 40 resources (see Fig. 14).

We can conclude that the number of the used resources in our mechanism is lower than the number of the used resources in the other approaches, which minimizes power consumption. Therefore, our Min/Max Threshold approach is then a small step to Green Computing.

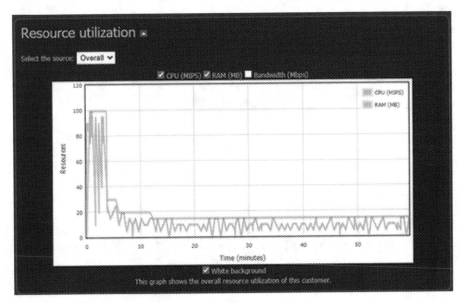

Fig. 12. Resource usage graph in our mechanism

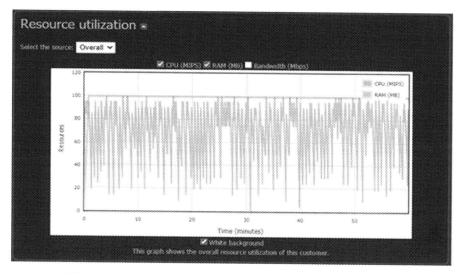

Fig. 13. Resource utilization graph in the *Without Migration* approach

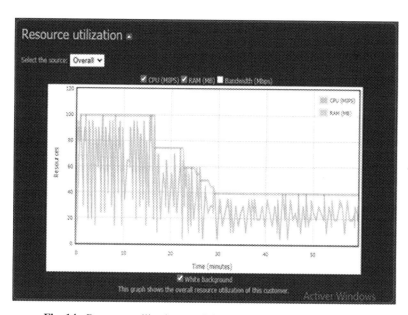

Fig. 14. Resource utilization graph in the *Single Threshold* approach

6 Conclusion

We propose in this work a mechanism for minimizing energy consumption in the Cloud data centers, thanks to VM migration with Min and Max thresholds, to not have underloaded and overloaded machines. We have treated the case of underloaded machines and we have presented the most frequently encountered cases. Our mechanism has been implemented in CloudSim and experimentally compared with the *WM* and *ST* strategies. Our mechanism gives the best results: minimum number of used resources, which consume minimum energy (Green Computing).

This work opens many perspectives: Apply this mechanism on real Cloud, with more machines, and more requests. We would like also to evaluate the SLAs violations. We also want to combine our two proposed mechanisms: the mechanism proposed in this paper which deals with migrations on underloaded resources and the mechanism proposed previously in [7] which deals with migrations on overloaded resources.

References

1. Guazzone, M., Anglano, C., Canonico, M.: Energy-efficient resource management for Cloud Computing infrastructures. In: Proceedings of the 3rd IEEE International Conference on Cloud Computing Technology and Science, pp. 424–431 (2011)
2. Yu, Y., Gao, Y.: Constraint programming-based virtual machines placement algorithm in datacenter. In: Shi, Z., Leake, D., Vadera, S. (eds.) IIP 2012. IAICT, vol. 385, pp. 295–304. Springer, Heidelberg (2012). https://doi.org/10.1007/978-3-642-32891-6_37
3. Sinha, R., Purohit, N., Diwanji, H.: Energy efficient dynamic integration of thresholds for migration at cloud data centers. Spec. Issue Int. J. Comput. Appl. Commun. Netw. (11), 44–49 (2011)
4. Maheshwari, D., Gandhi, P., Sinha, R.: Energy efficient threshold based approach for migration at cloud data center. Int. J. Eng. Res. Technol. (IJERT) 1(10) (2012)
5. Chandramouli, R., Suchithra, R.: Virtual machine migration in cloud data centers for resource management. Int. J. Eng. Comput. Sci. 5(9), 18029–18034 (2016)
6. Kaur, P., Rani, A.: Virtual machine migration in cloud computing. Int. J. Grid Distrib. Comput. 8(5), 337–342 (2015)
7. Bouchareb, N., Zarour, N.E.: Virtual machines allocation and migration mechanism in green cloud computing. In: Chikhi, S., Amine, A., Chaoui, A., Saidouni, D.E. (eds.) MISC 2018. LNNS, vol. 64, pp. 16–33. Springer, Cham (2019). https://doi.org/10.1007/978-3-030-054 81-6_2
8. Usmani, Z., Singh, S.: A survey of virtual machine placement techniques in a cloud data center. In: Proceedings of the International Conference on Information Security & Privacy, Nagpur, India (2015). Proc. Comput. Sci. 491–498 (2016)
9. Borgetto, D., Stolf, P.: An energy efficient approach to virtual machines management in cloud computing. In: Proceedings of the 3rd International Conference on Cloud Networking, Luxembourg, Luxembourg (2014)
10. Patel Hardikkumar, M.: Improve resource migration using virtual machine in cloud computing: a review. Multidisc. Int. Res. J. Gujarat Technol. Univ. 2(2), 81–88 (2020)
11. Li, Y., Wang, Y., Yin, B., Guan, L.: An energy efficient resource management method in virtualized cloud environment. In: Proceedings of the 14th IEEE International Conference on Network Operations and Management Symposium (APNOMS), Seoul, Asia-Pacific, pp. 1–8 (2012)

12. Hassan, M.K., Babiker, A., Amien, M.B.M., Hamad, M.: SLA management for virtual machine live migration using machine learning with modified Kernel and statistical approach. Eng. Technol. Appl. Sci. Res. **8**(1), 2459–2463 (2018)
13. Han, G., Que, W., Jia, G., Shu, L.: An efficient virtual machine consolidation scheme for multimedia cloud computing. J. Sens. **16**(2), 246 (2016)
14. Beloglazov, A., Buyya, R.: Energy efficient allocation of virtual machines in cloud data centers. In: Proceedings of the 10th IEEE/ACM International Conference on Cluster, Cloud and Grid Computing, Melbourne, Victoria, Australia, pp. 577–578 (2010)
15. VMware Inc: VMware distributed power management concepts and use (2010)

TunBERT: Pretrained Contextualized Text Representation for Tunisian Dialect

Abir Messaoudi[1(✉)], Ahmed Cheikhrouhou[2(✉)], Hatem Haddad[1(✉)],
Nourchene Ferchichi[2(✉)], Moez BenHajhmida[1(✉)], Abir Korched[2(✉)],
Malek Naski[1(✉)], Faten Ghriss[2(✉)], and Amine Kerkeni[2(✉)]

[1] iCompass, Tunis, Tunisia
{abir,hatem,moez,malek}@icompass.digital
[2] instaDeep, London, UK
{a.cheikhrouhou,n.ferchichi,a.korched,f.ghriss,ak}@instadeep.com
https://www.icompass.tn/, https://www.instadeep.com/

Abstract. Pre-trained models have accomplished high performances with the introduction of the Transformers like the Bidirectional Encoder Representations from Transformers known for BERT. Nevertheless, most of these proposed models have been trained on most represented languages (English, French, German, etc.) and few models target the under-represented languages and dialects.

This work introduces a feasibility study of pre-training language models based on Transformers on Tunisian dialect as an under-represented languages. The Tunisian language model is evaluated on dialect identification task, sentiment analysis task, and reading comprehension question-answering task. Results demonstrate that, instead of using datasets from traditional sources (Wikipedia, articles, etc.), noisy web crawled data is more convenient for a under-represented language such as the Tunisian dialect. Additionally, experiments show that a reasonably small-scale dataset conducts to similar or better achievements as when using a large-scale dataset and that TunBERT model performances reach or enhance the state of the art in all three downstream tasks. The pre-trained model named TunBERT and the used datasets for the fine-tuning step are publicly released.

Keywords: Transformers · Language models · Under-represented languages · TunBERT · BERT

1 Introduction

Recently, interest in Natural Language Processing (NLP) has increased due to the availability of data resources and hardware, and also to pre-trained contextualized text representation models that learn an powerful representation of a natural language. For instance, one of the first proposed approaches is Word2Vec [1] where words were represented according to their semantic property. Then, ELMO [2] combined the previous model with BiLSTM to address the polysemy

© Springer Nature Switzerland AG 2022
A. Bennour et al. (Eds.): ISPR 2022, CCIS 1589, pp. 278–290, 2022.
https://doi.org/10.1007/978-3-031-08277-1_23

problem. Afterwards, the pre-training models have been proposed with ULM-Fit [3] where they were fine-tuned for downstream tasks. These models have achieved good performances but they did not support long-term and multiple contexts of the words.

Since the introduction of the attention mechanism [4], pre-trained models has been developed accomplishing high performances owing to the introduction of the Transformers [5]. Besides, BERT [6] was released to become the cutting-edge model for contextualized embeddings and provide fresh inspiration for further development in the NLP field. BERT is conceived to pre-train deep bidirectional representations from unlabeled textual data by co-conditioning on the right and left context in all layers. Accordingly, most languages have their models based on BERT. In particular, the Arabic language has several language models: AraBERT [7], GigaBERT [8], and multilingual cased BERT model (hereafter mBERT) [9] which was simultaneously pre-trained on 104 languages.

The Arabic language has more than 300 million native speakers worldwide, and is spoken as a mother tongue in 25 countries. The formal and official Arabic language is known as Modern Standard Arabic (MSA). However, each Arabic-speaking country has one or more locally spoken Arabic languages, known as dialects. Tunisians (Tunisia's people) use the Tunisian arabic [10] in their everyday connections, in the majority of their media channels (TV shows, songs, radio, etc.), and on the social media platforms. However, Tunisian Arabic has no grammatical rules and there is multiple ways to write and speak. Furthermore, this dialect has its proprietary lexicon, phonetics, and morphological structure as shown in Table 1.

Table 1. Examples of Tunisian comments with their MSA and English translation.

Tunisian	MSA	English
محلاها هالغنانية	ما أحلى هذه الأغنية	How nice is this song
ماتعجبنيش كيفاش تتصرف	لا تعجبني تصرفاتها	I don't like how she behaves
وقتاه يبدا الماتش	متى تبدأ المباراة	When does the match start

The necessity for a strong language model for the Tunisian dialect has become essential to build NLP-based applications (sentiment analysis, translation, information retrieval, etc.). As far as we know, such a model does not yet exist in the literature.

In this work, we introduce the process of pre-training a Pytorch implementation of NVIDIA BERT language model[1], called TunBERT (Tunisian BERT), trained on only 67.2 MB Common-Crawl-based dataset. We compare our pre-trained Tunisian model on three NLP downstream tasks; that are of a different kind: (i) Sentiment Analysis (SA) task, (ii) Tunisian Dialect Identification (DI) task, and (iii) Reading Comprehension Question Answering (QA) task; against

---

[1] https://github.com/NVIDIA/DeepLearningExamples/tree/master/PyTorch/LanguageModeling/BERT.

mBERT [6], AraBERT [7], GigaBERT [8] and the state-of-the-art performances when available. We can summarise our contributions as follows:

- The first release of a pre-trained BERT-based model for Tunisian dialect trained on Common-Crawl-based Tunisian dataset.
- TunBERT application to 3 Natural Languafe Processing downstream tasks: Sentiment Analysis, Dialect Identification and Reading Comprehension Question-Answering.
- Empirical evaluations illustrate that a small-scale Tunisian training dataset can achieve alike or better performances compared to baselines such as monolingual models and multilingual models trained on large datasets.
- Publicly releasing TunBERT and the used datasets on popular Natural Language Processing hosting platform[2].

The remainder of this paper is organized as follows:

Sect. 2. provides a detailed literature review of previous work on monolingual and multilingual language representations.
Section 3 introduces our methodology to develop TunBERT.
In Sect. 4 presents the three downstream tasks for fine-tuning and the used datasets for evaluation.
Section 5 details the experiments, the results and the discussion.
Section 6 concludes and points to possible future work.

2   Related Works

Contextualized word representations, like BERT [6], RobBERTa [11] and more recently ALBERT [12], enhanced the word embeddings models representational power such as word2vec [1], GloVe [13] and fastText [14] by considering context into account. Following their success, the large pre-trained multilingual models were then applied such as mBERT [9]. In [15], authors have demonstrate that pre-trained multilingual models can achieve competitive results with pre-trained monolingual models. Nevertheless, these models have used large scale pre-training datasets and thus require high computational costs.

Recently, monolingual models based on different languages have been released: RobBERT for Dutch [16], FlauBERT [17] and CamemBERT for French [18], [19] for Spanish and [20] for Finnish. In [18], authors showed that their French model performances when trained on 4 GB are close to the performances of the same model trained on the 138 GB. They also concluded that a model trained on a Common-Crawl-based corpus achieved higher performances than the model trained on the French Wikipedia. They suggested that a sized 4 GB heterogeneous dataset in terms of genre and style is large enough as a pre-training dataset to achieve SOTA performances with the BASE architecture, better than those obtained with pre-trained mBERT on 60 GB. In [20], a Finnish

---

[2] https://github.com/iCompass-ai/TunBERT.

BERT model trained from scratch outperformed mBERT for three reference tasks (named entity recognition, part-of-speech tagging and dependency parsing). Authors suggested that language-specific deep transfer learning models for lower-resourced languages can outperform multilingual BERT models.

In comparison with the growing number of studies of contextualized word representations in Indo-European languages, similar researches in Arabic language are yet very limited. AraBERT [7], a BERT-based model was released with a pre-training dataset containing 70 million sentences, with a total size of 24 GB of text, covering news from different Arab media channels. Authors did not specify if Arabic dialects are included in the pre-training dataset. It achieved state of the art performances on three Arabic tasks: Sentiment Analysis, Named Entity Recognition, and Question Answering. Nevertheless, the pre-trained dataset is mostly MSA based. Authors concluded that there is a need for pre-trained models that can tackle a variety of Arabic dialects. Lately, GigaBERT [8], a customized bilingual language model for Arabic and English, has outperformed AraBERT in several downstream tasks.

3   TunBERT

In this section, we describe the training setup and pre-training data that were used for TunBERT.

3.1   Training Setup

TunBERT model uses the implementation of Pytorch of NVIDIA NeMo BERT[3]. Our model was pre-trained using 4 NVIDIA Tesla V100 GPUs for 1280K steps. The pre-trained model characteristics are shown in Table 3. Adam optimizer was used, with a batch size of 128, a learning rate (lr) of $1e-4$, a masking probability of 15% and 128 as max sequence length. We used cosine annealing for lr scheduling with a warm-up ratio of 0.01. Training took 122 h and 25 min for 330 epochs over all the tokens.

The model was trained on 2 unsupervised prediction tasks [6] using a Tunisian text corpus: The Masked Language Modeling (MLM) task and the Next Sentence Prediction (NSP) task.

For the Masked Language Modeling task, 15% of the tokens in every sequence are replaced with a [MASK] token. Then, the model tries to predict the original masked token based on the context of the non-masked tokens in this sequence. For the NSP task, pairs of sentences are provided to the model. The latter has to predict if the second sentence is the sub-sequent sentence in the original document. In this task, 50% of the pair sentences are sub-sequent to each other in the original document. The remaining random 50% sample sentences are chosen from the corpus to be added to the first sentence.

---

[3] https://github.com/NVIDIA/NeMo.

3.2   Pre-training Dataset

The pre-training process follows the existing literature on language model pre-training [11,17,18]. Due to a lack of Tunisian dialect data (wikipedia, books, etc.), we create a common-crawl-based dataset (500k sentences of text from different social media platforms such as Twitter and Youtube). The dataset was pre-processed by removing links, emojis and punctuation symbols, while keeping personal and sensitive information anonymous. Then, a dialect identification filter was applied to ensure that only Tunisian Arabic scripts are included. Pre-training dataset statistics are presented in Table 2. The training dataset size is 67.2 MB.

Table 2. Pre-training dataset statistics.

#Uniq Words	#Words	#Sentences
8,256K	48,233K	500K

Table 3. Pre-trained model configuration.

#Layers	Hidden Size	#self-attention heads
12	768	12

4   Evaluation

We measured the performance of TunBERT by evaluating it on three tasks: Sentiment Analysis, Dialect Identification and Reading Comprehension Question-Answering. The fine-tuning was done separately using the same configuration for all three tasks. We didn't run extensive grid-search to choose the best hyperparameters because of computational and time constraints. We applied a configuration usually used in the literature. And we used the splits provided by the datasets authors when available and the standard ratio of 80% and 20% when not.

4.1   Sentiment Analysis

For the Sentiment Analysis task, we used two manually annotated datasets:

- Tunisian Sentiment Analysis Corpus known as TSAC [21] collected from Facebook comments about Tunisian TV shows. It is composed of comments based on Latin scripts, Arabic scripts and emojis. We only used Arabic script comments.

- Tunisian Election Corpus known as TEC [22] collected from comments on tweeter about Tunisian elections in 2014. Besides the Tunisian dialect, the TEC dataset includes MSA content.

Statistics of the TSAC and TEC are shown in Table 4.

Table 4. TSAC and TEC sentiment analysis datasets statistics.

Dataset	TSAC	TEC
#Negative	4175	1799
#Positive	3277	1244
#Train	4680	1947
#Dev	1170	487
#Test	1516	609

4.2   Tunisian Dialect Identification

This task focuses on identifying and differentiating the Tunisian dialect of a given text from other Arabic dialects, especially on social media sources where there is no established standard orthography like MSA. First attempts to tackle the challenge identified 5 Arabic dialects categories in addition to MSA: Maghrebi, Egyptian, Levantine, Gulf, and Iraqi [23]. [24] proposed 4 Arabic dialects categories by merging the Iraqi with the Gulf. The Tunisian dialect was included in the Maghrebi dialect category along with the Algerian, Moroccan, and other dialects. Nevertheless, even if the Maghrebi vocabulary is pretty much similar throughout North African countries, many differences exist not only at the phonetic level [25] but also at the lexical, morphological and syntactic levels [26].

For evaluation, two sub-tasks were performed:

- Identification of the Tunisian dialect from other Arabic dialects (a dataset named TADI): this is a binary classification task. We used the Nuanced Arabic Dialect Identification (NADI) shared task dataset with 21,000 tweets, covering 21 Arab countries. NADI is an imbalanced dataset in which the training includes only 747 Tunisian tweets and the remaining tweets cover the other Arabic dialects. To solve this issue, we created a new dataset named TADI (Tunisian and Arabic Dialect Identification) by including a sub-set of the TSAC dataset as Tunisian comments to have the same number of tweets as the other dialects as shown in Table 5.
- Identification of the Tunisian dialect and the Algerian dialect (a dataset named TAD): for this sub-task we used the Multi-Arabic Dialect Applications and Resources (MADAR) dataset [27]. More specifically, we used the shared task dataset targeting a large set of dialect labels at country-level. We filtered the dataset of dialect labels at country level [28], to only keep Tunisian and Algerian labeled data as shown in Table 5. The newly created dataset is named TAD.

Table 5. TADI and TAD dataset statistics.

Dataset	TADI	TAD
#Train	40500	3200
#DEV	2396	400
#Test	7192	400

4.3 Reading Comprehension Question-Answering

Open-domain Question-Answering (QA) task has been intensively studied to evaluate contextualized embeddings' performances of the models. This task takes as input a textual question to look for correspondent answers within a large textual corpus. In [29], two MSA QA datasets have been proposed. However, as far as we know, no study was previously made for this kind of task for any Arabic dialect.

To do so, we create the first Tunisian Reading Comprehension Dataset (TRCD) as a Question Answering dataset dedicated for Tunisian dialect. We used a dialectal version of the Tunisian constitution based on the guideline in [30]. TRCD is composed of 144 documents containing 3 paragraphs and 3 Question-Answer pairs are assigned to each paragraph. Questions were formulated by 4 Tunisian speakers and each question should be paired with a single paragraph as shown in Fig. 1).

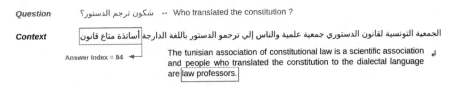

Fig. 1. TRCD dataset example with its corresponding English translation.

As far as we know, this is the first Tunisian dialect dataset for the Question-Answering task. The TRCD dataset statistics are presented in Table 6.

Table 6. TRCD statistics.

Dataset	#Document	#Paragraph	#QA
#Train	114	342	1026
#Dev	15	45	135
#Test	15	45	135

5   Experiments and Discussion

In this section, results for tasks under study are presented followed by results discussion.

5.1   Tunisian Sentiment Analysis

The efficiency of TunBERT was evaluated against mBERT, AraBERT and Giga-BERT language models and the state of the art performances when available. The obtained performances of Tunisian Sentiment Analysis using TunBERT were also compared against the state of the art systems that tackled these same datasets (word2vec for word embeddings, doc2vec for document embeddings, and Tw-StAR [31]) and listed in Table 7 and Table 8.

Table 7. Sentiment analysis results on TSAC.

Model	Accuracy	macro-F1
MLP [21]	78%	78%
word2vec [31]	77.40%	78.20%
doc2vec [31]	57.20%	61.70%
Tw-StAR [31]	86.50%	86.20%
mBERT [9]	92.21%	91.03%
GigaBERT [8]	94.92%	93.39%
AraBERT [7]	95.63%	94.91%
TunBERT	**96.98%**	**96.98%**

Table 8. Sentiment analysis results on TEC

Model	Accuracy	macro-F1
SVM [22]	71.10%	63%
word2vec [31]	61.90 %	58.40%
doc2vec [31]	62.20%	56.40%
Tw-StAR [31]	**88.20%**	**87.80%**
mBERT [9]	58.45%	36.89%
GigaBERT [8]	71.75%	65.32%
AraBERT [7]	79.14%	72.57%
TunBERT	81.20%	76.45%

The results in Table 7 illustrate the outperformance of the pre-trained contextualized text representation models over the previous techniques, namely word2vec and doc2vec. TunBERT achieved the best performance on the TSAC dataset. It reached 92.98% as macro-F1 which is a high result compared to

78.2%, 61.7% and 86.2% scored by word2vec, doc2vec and Tw-StAR, respectively. The results show that TunBERT also outperforms pre-trained language models: mBERT, GigaBERT and AraBERT.

Likewise, Table 8 illustrates the out-performance of BERT-based LM against other techniques with the TEC dataset. Nevertheless, the best performance was achieved by Tw-StAR because of its better fit to the evaluation data. For instance, the best achieved Tw-StAR macro-F1 was in TEC with a value of 87.8% compared to 76.45%, and 72.57% scored by TunBERT and AraBERT, respectively. This could be explained by the noisy nature of TEC dataset with a mixed Tunisian and MSA content and the better fit of Tw-StAR to the evaluation data. Results using mBERT achieved the worst performance, which could demonstrate that mBERT is not suitable for noisy data. The results showcase also the out-performance of TunBERT over the other pre-trained language models.

5.2   Tunisian Dialect Identification

For Tunisian Dialect identification, the results in Table 9 show that TunBERT outperforms other SOTA language models. Indeed, our model achieved a macro-F1 of 87.14% compared to 68.93% achieved by mBERT. TunBERT also outperforms AraBERT. Likewise, it has achieved a macro-F1 of 93.25% for the Tunisian-Algerian dialects identification task outperforming the other used language models as shown in Table 10.

Table 9. Tunisian dialect identification results on TADI.

Model	Accuracy	macro-F1
mBERT	75,21%	68.93%
AraBERT	79.57%	76.7%
GigaBERT	72.67%	65.30%
TunBERT	**87.46%**	**87.14%**

Table 10. Tunisian dialect identification results on TAD.

Model	Accuracy	macro-F1
mBERT	86.75%	86.4%
AraBERT	87.50% %	87.37%
GigaBERT	84.57%	84.14%
TunBERT	**93.30%**	**93.25%**

5.3   Reading Comprehension Question-Answering

Fine-tuning TunBERT on the Tunisian Reading Comprehension Dataset did not give impressive results (Exact match of 2.17%, F1 score of 13.66% and a Recall of 22.59%). Comparable results were obtained for GigaBERT (Exact match of 0.7%, F1 score of 14.02% and a Recall of 21.65%). MBERT gave slightly better results (Exact match of 4.25%, F1 score of 22.6% and a Recall of 31.3). Meanwhile, we noticed good results for AraBERT (Exact match of 26.24%, F1 score of 58.74% and a Recall of 63.96%).

Adding a pre-training step on an MSA reading comprehension dataset (in our case the Arabic-SQuAD dataset [29]) made great improvements in all of the models performances, especially for TunBERT. The strategy was to use the pre-trained language model, fine-tune it for a few epochs on the MSA dataset, then use the best checkpoint to train and test on the TRCD dataset. Following this strategy, TunBERT achieved great results with an exact match of 27.65%, an F1 score of 60.24% and a Recall of 82.36%, as shown in Table 11.

Table 11. TRCD results before and after pre-training on Arabic-SQuaD.

Finetuning datasets	TRCD dataset			Arabic SQuAD and TRCD		
Language models	Exact match	F1 score	Recall	Exact match	F1 score	Recall
mBERT	4.25	22.60	31.3	29.07	60.86	62.18
AraBERT	**26.24**	**58.74**	**63.96**	24.11	**63.53**	70.43
GigaBERT	0.70	14.02	21.65	**29.78**	62.44	66.34
TunBERT	21.27	13.665	22.597	27.65	60.24	**82.36**

5.4 Discussion

The experimental results indicate that the proposed pre-trained TunBERT model yields improvements, compared to mBert, Gigabert and AraBERT models in the studied tasks as shown in Tables 7 and 8 for the Sentiment Analysis sub-task, Tables 9 and 10 for Dialect Identification task, and Table 11 for the Question-Answering task.

Unsurprisingly, GigaBERT as customized BERT for English-to-Arabic cross-lingual transfer is not effective for the tackled tasks and should be applied for tasks using code-switched data as suggested in [8].

As AraBERT was trained on news from different Arab media, it shows good performance on the three tasks as the datasets contain some MSA text. TunBERT was trained on a dataset useful on casual text, such as Tunisian dialect in Social Media. For this reason, it performed better than AraBERT on all the performed tasks.

We show that pre-training the Tunisian model on a highly variable Common-Crawl-based dataset leads to better downstream performance compared to models trained on more uniform data. Moreover, results led to the conclusion that a relatively small Common-Crawl-based dataset (67.2M) leads to downstream performances as good as models pre-trained on datasets of larger magnitude (24 GB for AraBERT and about 10.4 B tokens for GigaBERT).

This is confirmed with the QA-task experiments where the created dataset contains a small amount of dialectal texts. The Arabic-SQuAD dataset was used to help with the missing embeddings of MSA and to permit the fine-tuned model to effectively learn the QA-task by providing more examples of question-answering. The TunBERT model has outperformed all other models in terms of exact match and recall.

6   Conclusion

This paper reported our attempt to build a robust Transformer-based language model for Tunisian dialect: TunBERT trained on a 67.2 MB Common-Crawl-based data consisting of 500k sentences of text. Our TunBERT model was fine-tuned on the different labeled datasets and reached a new state of the art on all tasks and datasets, except for the Reading Comprehension Question-Answering task where TunBERT outperformed SOTA models only for the Recall metric. Compared to larger models such as GigaBERT and AraBERT, our TunBERT model has better representation of the Tunisian dialect and yields better performances, besides using inferior computational cost at inference time.

Our immediate goal for the future are: (i) to evaluate our TunBERT model on more Arabic Natural Language Processing tasks and (ii) further pre-train it to improve its performances on the datasets where it is currently outperformed.

On social media, Tunisians tend to express themselves using an informal way called "TUNIZI" [10] that represents the Tunisian text written using Latin characters and numbers instead of Arabic letters. For instance, the word "sou2el"[4] is the Latin based characters of the word سؤال. An obvious future step would involve building a multi-script Tunisian dialect language model including Arabic script and Latin script based characters.

References

1. Mikolov, T., Chen, K., Corrado, G., Dean, J.: Efficient estimation of word representations in vector space. In: 1st International Conference on Learning Representations, Workshop Track Proceedings (2013)
2. Peters, M., Neumann, M., Iyyer, M., Gardner, M., Clark, C., Lee, K., Zettlemoyer, L.: Deep contextualized word representations. In: Proceedings of the 2018 Conference of the North American Chapter of the Association for Computational Linguistics: Human Language Technologies, Volume 1 (Long Papers), pp. 2227–2237 (2018). https://www.aclweb.org/anthology/N18-1202
3. Howard, J., Ruder, S.: Universal language model fine-tuning for text classification. In: Proceedings of the 56th Annual Meeting of the Association for Computational Linguistics (Volume 1: Long Papers), pp. 328–339 (2018). https://www.aclweb.org/anthology/P18-1031

---

[4] The word "Question" is the English translation.

4. Bahdanau, D., Cho, K., Bengio,Y.: Neural machine translation by jointly learning to align and translate. In: Proceedings of the 3rd International Conference on Learning Representations (2015)
5. Vaswani, A., et al.: Attention is all you need. Adv. Neural Inf. Process. Syst. **30**, 5998–6008 (2017). http://papers.nips.cc/paper/7181-attention-is-all-you-need.pdf
6. Devlin, J., Chang, M., Lee, K., Toutanova, K.: BERT: pre-training of deep bidirectional transformers for language understanding. In: Proceedings of the 2019 Conference of the North American Chapter of the Association for Computational Linguistics: Human Language Technologies, Volume 1 (Long And Short Papers), pp. 4171–4186 (2019)
7. Antoun, W., Baly, F., Hajj, H.: AraBERT: transformer-based model for Arabic language understanding. In: Proceedings of the 4th Workshop on Open-Source Arabic Corpora and Processing Tools, with a Shared Task on Offensive Language Detection, pp. 9–15 (2020)
8. Wuwei, L., Yang, C., Wei, X., Alan, R.: GigaBERT: zero-shot transfer learning from English to Arabic. In: Proceedings of the 2020 Conference on Empirical Methods on Natural Language Processing (EMNLP) (2020)
9. Pires, T., Schlinger, E., Garrette, D.: How multilingual is multilingual BERT? In: Proceedings of the 57th Annual Meeting of the Association for Computational Linguistics, pp. 4996–5001 (2019). https://www.aclweb.org/anthology/P19-1493
10. Fourati, C., Messaoudi, A., Haddad, H.: TUNIZI: a Tunisian Arabizi sentiment analysis dataset. In: AfricaNLP Workshop, Putting Africa on the NLP Map. ICLR 2020, Virtual Event. arXiv:3091079 (2020)
11. Delobelle, P., et al.: Computing research repository. arXiv:1907.11692 (2019)
12. Lan, Z., Chen, M., Goodman, S., Gimpel, K., Sharma, P., Soricut, R.: ALBERT: a lite BERT for self-supervised learning of language representations. In: Proceedings of the 8th International Conference on Learning Representations (ICLR) (2020)
13. Pennington, J., Socher, R., Manning, C.: GloVe: Global vectors for word representation. In: Proceedings of the 2014 Conference on Empirical Methods in Natural Language Processing (EMNLP), pp. 1532–1543 (2014)
14. Bojanowski, P., Grave, E., Joulin, A., Mikolov, T.: Enriching word vectors with subword information. Trans. Assoc. Comput. Linguist. **5**, 135–146 (2017)
15. Conneau, A., Lample, G.: Cross-lingual language model pretraining. In: Proceedings of the Advances in Neural Information Processing Systems, pp. 7059–7069 (2019)
16. Delobelle, P., Winters, T., Berendt, B.: RobBERT: a dutch RoBERTa-based language model. Computing Research Repository, version 2. arXiv:2001.06286 (2020)
17. Le, H., et al.: FlauBERT: unsupervised language model pre-training for French. In: Proceedings of the Eleventh International Conference on Language Resources and Evaluation (LREC), pp. 2479–2490 (2020)
18. Martin, L., et al.: CamemBERT: a tasty French language model. In: Proceedings of the 58th Annual Meeting of the Association for Computational Linguistics, pp. 7203–7219 (2020)
19. Canete, J., Chaperon, G., Fuentes, R., Ho, J., Kang, H., Pérez, J.: Spanish pre-trained BERT model and evaluation data. In: PML4DC @ ICLR 2020, p. 2020 (2020)
20. Virtanen, A., et al.: Multilingual is not enough: BERT for finnish. Computing Research Repository, version 1. arXiv:1912.07076 (2019)
21. Medhaffar, S., Bougares, F., Estève, Y., Hadrich-Belguith, L.: Sentiment analysis of Tunisian dialects: linguistic resources and experiments. In: Proceedings of the Third Arabic Natural Language Processing Workshop, pp. 55–61 (2017)

22. Sayadi, K., Liwicki, M., Ingold, R., Bui, M.: Tunisian dialect and modern standard Arabic dataset for sentiment analysis: Tunisian election context. In: Proceedings of the Second International Conference on Arabic Computational Linguistics, ACLING, pp. 35–53 (2016)

23. Zaidan, O., Callison-Burch, C.: The Arabic online commentary dataset: an annotated dataset of informal Arabic with high dialectal content. In: Proceedings of the 49th Annual Meeting of the Association for Computational Linguistics: Human Language Technologies, pp. 37–41 (2011)

24. El-Haj, M., Rayson, P., Aboelezz, M.: Arabic dialect identification in the context of bivalency and code-switching. In: Proceedings of the Eleventh International Conference on Language Resources and Evaluation (LREC), pp. 3622–3627 (2018)

25. Harrat, S., Meftouh, K., Smaïli, K.: Maghrebi Arabic dialect processing: an overview. J. Int. Sci. Gen. Appl. 1 (2018)

26. Horesh, S.: Languages of the Middle East and North Africa. In: The SAGE Encyclopedia of Human Communication Sciences and Disorders, vol. 1, pp. 1058–1061 (2019)

27. Bouamor, H., et al.: The MADAR Arabic dialect corpus and lexicon. In: The International Conference on Language Resources and Evaluation (2018)

28. Bouamor, H., Hassan, S., Habash, N.: The MADAR shared task on Arabic fine-grained dialect identification. In: Proceedings of the Fourth Arabic Natural Language Processing Workshop, pp. 199–207 (2019)

29. Mozannar, H., Maamary, E., El Hajal, K., Hajj, H.: Neural Arabic question answering. In: Proceedings of the Fourth Arabic Natural Language Processing Workshop, pp. 108–118 (2019). https://www.aclweb.org/anthology/W19-4612

30. Chen, D., Fisch, A., Weston, J., Bordes, A.: Reading Wikipedia to answer open-domain questions. ArXiv. abs/1704.00051 (2017)

31. Mulki, H., Haddad, H., Gridach, M., Babaoğlu, I.: Syntax-ignorant N-gram embeddings for dialectal Arabic sentiment analysis. Nat. Lang. Eng. 27, 1–24 (2020)

Road Recognition for Autonomous Vehicles Based on Intelligent Tire and SE-CNN

Runwu Shi[1] [ORCID], Shichun Yang[1], Yuyi Chen[1], Rui Wang[1], Jiayi Lu[1], Zhaowen Pang[2], and Yaoguang Cao[1](✉)

[1] Beihang University, Beijing, China
caoyaoguang@buaa.edu.cn
[2] Hainan University, Hannan, China

Abstract. High-level autonomous driving relies on the comprehensive perception of the environment. However, current perception research usually pays low attention to road recognition which is essential to the reliability and safety of autonomous driving. Even though existing vehicle sensors such as cameras, Lidars, and accelerometers can provide input for road recognition, recognition methods based on these sensors have challenges in balancing the needs of low cost, stability, and high accuracy. In this study, we proposed a low-cost piezoelectric sensor based intelligent tire system with a lightweight convolutional neural network (CNN) for accurate road surface recognition of autonomous vehicles. The time-frequency domain features of collected piezoelectric sensor signals are extracted by applying discrete wavelet transform (DWT). These features are input to the CNN embedded with the Squeezing-and-Excitation (SE) block. The SE block emphasizes valuable input information and improves road recognition accuracy. We perform experiments on the asphalt, marble, and painted roads using our test vehicle. The results show that the proposed SE-CNN achieves an accuracy of 99.14% in recognizing the road types, which enhances the environmental perception of autonomous driving.

Keywords: Road recognition · Convolutional neural network · Squeezing-and-Excitation (SE) · Intelligent tire · Autonomous driving

1 Introduction

With the development of autonomous driving technology, more and more people are concerned about its safety. Safe autonomous driving relies on accurate perception, reasonable behavior decisions, trajectory planning, and precise driving control. The perception capability determines the upper limit of decision-making and control technology level. Therefore, the sensing system should capture information about the surrounding traffic participants and driving environment as comprehensively as possible, of which the "road" information needs particular attention. Road conditions affect the comfort and smoothness of driving and cause many serious accidents. For autonomous vehicles, it is necessary to have the ability to recognize road conditions and adjust their driving

© Springer Nature Switzerland AG 2022
A. Bennour et al. (Eds.): ISPR 2022, CCIS 1589, pp. 291–305, 2022.
https://doi.org/10.1007/978-3-031-08277-1_24

strategies to improve safety and comfort [1, 5]. For instance, road recognition capabilities can assist the decision-making system in optimizing path planning [14] and the speed of autonomous vehicles for ride comfort and energy efficiency [8]. The obtained road information can also be input into the control systems such as semi-active suspension or the antilock brake system to improve driving comfort and braking performance [28, 29]. Additionally, road conditions significantly influence the vehicle ride quality, handling stability, fuel economy, and the life of critical components of the vehicle [23]. Apart from autonomous vehicles, road maintenance can also benefit from the road recognition capabilities of road cleaning vehicles [10]. Onboard road recognition systems can reduce the high cost of labor and time in monitoring road conditions. Both road users, such as autonomous vehicles, and road maintainers, are concerned about affordable and high-performance road recognition technology.

Several approaches for recognizing road conditions have been proposed based on vehicle sensors like cameras, lidars, ultrasonic sensors, and accelerometers. Cameras can predict the conditions of the road to be driven based on vision-based methods [6, 22, 26]. However, cameras are sensitive to changes in illumination and weather. It is difficult to provide reliable road recognition in various scenarios. Similarly, lidars are susceptible to rain and fog [32], and the high price of lidar also limits its practical application. For ultrasonic sensors, weather conditions and speed affect their performance [3, 4]. Accelerometers, wheel stroke sensors, etc., can measure sprung mass acceleration, unsprung mass acceleration, and suspension deflection caused by road excitation [2, 35]. These measured response parameters and road conditions can be correlated through vehicle dynamics or machine learning models [16, 20]. But tires filter out the high-frequency components of the actual road profile, blurring the details of the road surface, which means that the road surface information contained in the response of components of vehicles is partially lost [11, 15]. For more direct and accurate road recognition, the tires in contact with the road need to be considered. Measuring tire conditions to recognize road surfaces can be regarded as a "tactile method" to obtain more actual road surface information. Several sensors such as accelerometers, strain sensors, piezoelectric sensors, optical sensors, etc., can directly measure tire states for road recognition, and the technology utilizing tire sensors to estimate tire or road conditions is generally called "intelligent tire" or "smart tire" [9, 19]. The road recognition methods based on the intelligent tire have high accuracy, a simple system layout, and stable performance.

In this study, we designed an intelligent tire system to recognize road surfaces for safer autonomous driving. This intelligent tire system consists of a low-cost PVDF piezoelectric sensor and a lightweight network structure for recognition. The workflow contains several parts, including Discrete Wavelet Transform (DWT), Squeezing-and-Excitation (SE) block, and convolutional neural network (CNN). The DWT is performed on the sensor signals to obtain physical features containing time-frequency domain information. The physical features are input to the CNN embedded with the SE block for classification. The SE block can weigh each feature channel dynamically. Experiments on dry asphalt, marble, and painted roads demonstrate that the proposed SE-CNN achieves the highest accuracy rate of 99.14% in recognizing these road types compared with other machine learning methods. The main contribution of this paper is as follows.

1.   The state of the art evaluation of road recognition methods utilizing onboard sensors;

2. Intelligent tire system based on the cheap PVDF sensor that achieves accurate road recognition;

3. Propose a lightweight SE-CNN with an accuracy of 99.14% in recognizing road surfaces.

The remaining parts of this paper are organized as follows. Section 2 introduces the related works of road recognition methods. Section 3 presents the structure of the designed intelligent tire system. Section 4 describes the methods containing signal processing and the structure of the recognition network. Section 5 introduces the process of the experiments. Section 6 evaluates and discusses the performance of the proposed method. Section 7 concludes our work in this study and outlook on future research plans.

2 Related Works

Recently, several onboard road recognition methods have been proposed and divided into two main categories: non-contact recognition and response-based methods [16, 24, 25]. The non-contact recognition methods rely on cameras, lidars, and ultrasonic sensors to predict road conditions. The response-based methods measure vehicle responses such as unsprung mass acceleration and suspension displacement to recognize road conditions.

For the non-contact recognition methods, cameras are commonly used sensors in intelligent vehicles, and vision-based methods have been widely studied. These methods usually use road images as input to models for recognition [30]. Dewangan et al. proposed a CNN to classify images of dry, wet, ice, and rough roads [6]. Pereira et al. presented a paved and unpaved road image classification method based on CNN [22]. Rateke et al. used an in-vehicle camera and CNN to classify images of asphalt, paved and unpaved roads [26]. The vision-based methods can achieve satisfactory recognition accuracy when not being disturbed by the external environment. However, the actual illumination and weather conditions are diverse. It is challenging for vision-based methods to adapt to various scenarios. The lidar-based methods can reconstruct three-dimensional road surfaces for road recognition. Diaz-Vilarino et al. used lidar sensors combined with a K-means clustering method to classify asphalt and stone roads [7]. Wang et al. utilized a lidar sensor to recognize different road types, including asphalt, concrete, grass, and gravel roads [34]. Lidars are susceptible to fog and rain, and the high price of lidars also limits their application in road recognition [12]. Bystrov et al. used an ultrasonic sensor combined with a neural network to recognize asphalt, sand, gravel, and grass roads [3]. However, ultrasonic sensors are sensitive to weather conditions, limiting vehicle deployment [4].

Compared with non-contact recognition, which is sensitive to interference from the external environment or vehicle motion, the response-based methods are more stable because these methods are hardly affected by weather and light. Chris et al. [35] used suspension acceleration as input to a support vector machine to classify the road surfaces. Qin et al. collected the sprung mass acceleration, unsprung mass acceleration, and suspension deflection combined with neural network to identify road classes [25], and the method based on the deep neural network was also studied in [24]. However, the road profile input of the suspension system is not the actual road profile due to the filtering effect of tires [11, 36]. The road information contained in the dynamic response of the suspension and other vehicle components is partially filtered, which further affects the accuracy of road recognition. Thus, to directly recognize road conditions, it is necessary to consider the tires, the only part in contact with the road. The road recognition methods based on tire responses can retain the stability of response-based methods while also capturing more exhaustive road profile information. The "intelligent tire" containing sensors and recognition algorithms can recognize road conditions by establishing a correlation between the sensor signals and the expected parameters such as friction condition and road types, etc. Current road recognition research based on intelligent tires usually uses in-tire high-sensitive accelerometers. B. Singh et al. designed an accelerometer-based intelligent tire system. A fuzzy controller was used to classify the road surface type among rough, regular, smooth, and wet asphalt roads [28]. Kim et al. proposed an algorithm using fast Fourier transform (FFT) to extract features from the signals of the in-tire accelerometer. They applied a multi-Layer perception (MLP) neural network to classify three road conditions, including dry, wet, rough [18]. In [17], Seyedmeysam et al. designed an intelligent tire consisting of two accelerometers attached to the tire's inner liner. A fuzzy logic algorithm was developed to classify different road types into four categories: asphalt, sand, concrete, and grass. The high-precision accelerometers used in these studies are usually too expensive for practical applications. In addition, it is challenging for the mentioned methods to extract the hidden information in the signals, which limits the recognition accuracy. For more accurate road surface recognition and potential future deployment, intelligent tire systems with high-performance algorithms and cheap sensors are needed.

3   Intelligent Tire System

This section briefly introduces the structure of the designed intelligent tire system. As shown in Fig. 1(a), the intelligent tire system consists of a low-cost PVDF sensor, an AD conversion module, and a Raspberry Pi 4B. The PVDF sensor (DT1-028K) with the size of 16 × 41 mm is attached to the inner liner of a tire, as shown in Fig. 1(b).

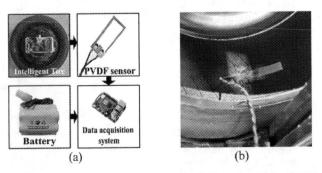

(a)   (b)

Fig. 1. (a) The proposed intelligent tire system, (b) Location of the PVDF sensor.

The sensor is flexible, lightweight, and needs no power supply, suitable for tire measurements. The road surfaces stimulate tire responses, so the PVDF sensor attached to the tread generates an electrical signal due to the piezoelectric effect [37]. The AD module converts analog voltage signals into digital data at the sample rate of 3000 Hz. The data is temporarily stored in the Raspberry Pi, which is later processed and analyzed on a PC. The PVDF signals are collected through the wired transmission to avoid delay and packet loss. The AD module and Raspberry pi are fixed to the tire and powered by a portable battery, and the intelligent tire system is deployed in the front left tire of the testing vehicle.

4   Methods

This section introduces the methods in the workflow of road recognition. The workflow contains three steps: contact patch signal detection, Discrete Wavelet Transform (DWT), and the recognition network (SE-CNN), as shown in Fig. 2. Firstly, we extract the tire-road contact patch signals from the continuous raw output voltage generated by the PVDF sensor. The contact patch signals are segment signals with the same length. Additionally, the DWT decomposes each segment signal into components at 9 level timescales. The higher-level components represent the lower frequency band of the signals. Finally, the SE-CNN receives all the 9 level components and outputs the road type classification.

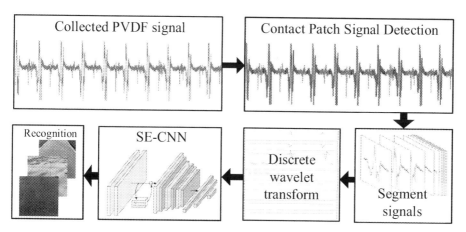

Fig. 2. Workflow of the proposed method.

4.1   Data Preprocessing

Contact Patch Signal Detection. Since the tire-road contact generates the piezoelectric response of the PVDF sensor, we extract the contact patch signal from the voltage signal of a complete rotation cycle based on the short-time energy method. This method can extract contact patch segment signals from the collected PVDF signal without manual selection. The short-time energy of the PVDF signals is defined as the sum of squares of the raw signal values in each frame,

$$E_n = \sum_{m=n-N+1}^{n} x^2(m) = x^2(n - N + 1) + \ldots + x^2(n) \tag{1}$$

where N is the window length, n is the frame-shift. The magnitude of short-time energy represents the degree of signal fluctuations. The contact patch signal that changes drastically corresponds to a high energy value so that the contact patch signal can be extracted according to the energy peak position.

Discrete Wavelet Transform. After extracting the contact patch segment signals from the original PVDF signal, the DWT is used to process the contact patch segment signals to obtain the time-frequency domain representation. Wavelet transform (WT) can decompose the signals at different timescales and represent them in the frequen-cy domain distribution state in the time domain. In addition, the WT has advantages in detecting abrupt changes in non-stationary signals and is appropriate for pro-cessing time-varying segment signals [27]. The commonly used WT contains Contin-uous Wavelet Transform (CWT) and the DWT. The CWT is defined by following the integral formula,

$$CWT(a, b) = \int_{-\infty}^{\infty} x(t) \frac{1}{\sqrt{|a|}} \psi \left(\frac{t-b}{a} \right) dt \qquad (2)$$

where $x(t)$ is the signal at time t, a and b are the scales and translational values, respectively, and ψ is the mother wavelet which is a continuous function with stretching and shifting parameters. For the CWT, wavelet coefficients are calculated at every possible scale to capture the hidden signal features, which occupies massive computing resource. Unlike the CWT, the DWT convolutes the signals with a series of low-pass and high-pass filters. It decomposes the signal hierarchically into approximation coefficients and detailed coefficients of different levels. With the proper selection of filters, the computation process of the DWT can save more resources. Thus, the DWT is more appropriate for real-time applications on vehicles. The principle of the DWT can be described as follows, where a and b in Eq. (2) are substituted with 2^j and $2^j k$ respectively [21],

$$DWT(j, k) = \frac{1}{\sqrt{|2^j|}} \int_{-\infty}^{\infty} x(t) \frac{1}{\sqrt{|a|}} \psi(\frac{t - 2^j k}{2^j}) dt \qquad (3)$$

4.2 Squeezing-and-Excitation Block

The decomposed signals at different time-frequency scales contain unequal road information. Therefore, each feature channel has different capabilities in representing the pattern of road surfaces. To weigh the importance of each feature channel, the channel attention, Squeeze-and-excitation (SE) block, is adopted in the network structure. The SE block is designed to adjust the weight of different channels adaptively [13]. This block recalibrates the input features, emphasizing the information-rich feature channels and suppressing the unimportant ones. The principle of the SE block is shown in Fig. 3. Given input with the size of $H \times W \times C$ is passed through a squeeze operation (F_{sq}), where H, W and C represent the number of height, width, and channels, respectively. Global average pooling is used to squeeze the feature maps of each channel into $1 \times 1 \times C$ feature maps. This process yields channel-level global features. The next step is the excitation operation (F_{ex}), which is achieved successively through the FC-layer, ReLU activation function, FC-layer, and Sigmoid activation function, with an output between 0 and 1 that can be used to weigh each channel. The original input is then reweighted by the scale operation (F_{scale}) to generate the output of the SE block.

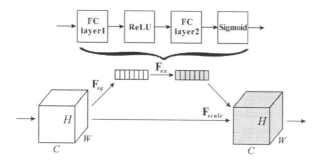

Fig. 3. Structure of squeezing-and-excitation block.

4.3 Proposed SE-CNN

In order to extract the implicit information from the physical features of the PVDF signals in time-frequency domains, we propose a network embedded with the SE block to enhance the valuable feature channels. The structure of the proposed network is shown in Fig. 4. The proposed approach comprises five modules: data preprocessing, 1D convolutional layers, SE block, 2D convolutional layers, and a classifier containing three fully connected layers.

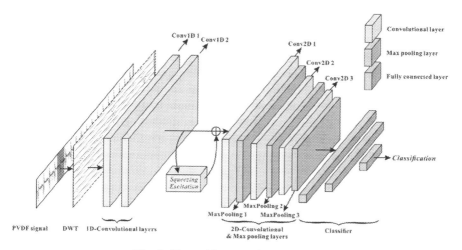

Fig. 4. The architecture of the SE-CNN.

The data preprocessing module includes segment signal detection and the DWT, which decomposes the collected PVDF signal at different time-frequency scales. The obtained wavelet coefficients of levels 1 to 9 that contain physical features are all input to the network as different channels. Two 1D convolutional layers are used to identify the local patterns in wavelet coefficients sequences and extract the hidden information in these physical features preliminarily. The output of the 1D-Convolutional layers contains the hidden representation pattern of the road surface. However, since each feature channel is given the same attention, their different ability to represent road patterns is ignored, and the obtained feature representation is inadequate. In order to improve the feature extraction capability of the proposed model for accurate road recognition, the SE block is embedded into the network structure. The SE block can adjust the weight of each channel, perform attention to important information and reduce redundant features. Three 2D convolutional layers, batch normalization, and three max-pooling layers are used to map the valuable physical features to hidden domains. The max-pooling layers can reduce the data dimension and make the network invariant to small offsets and distortions. Finally, the outputs are obtained using three fully connected layers with ReLU activation function, and Softmax is used as the final activation function. The input and output sizes of each module are shown in Table 1.

Table 1. Configuration specifications of the SE-CNN.

Module	Type	Input	Output
Preprocessing	Contact Patch signals detection	Original signal	1×950
	DWT	1×950	9×90
1D-CNN	Conv1D 1	9×90	32×88
	Conv1D 2	32×88	32×86
SE block	Recalibration	32×86	32×86
2D-CNN	Conv2D 1	$32 \times 86 \times 1$	$31 \times 85 \times 16$
	MaxPooling 1	$31 \times 85 \times 16$	$15 \times 42 \times 16$
	Conv2D 2	$15 \times 42 \times 16$	$14 \times 41 \times 32$
	MaxPooling 2	$14 \times 41 \times 32$	$7 \times 20 \times 32$
	Conv2D 3	$7 \times 20 \times 32$	$6 \times 19 \times 16$
	MaxPooling 3	$6 \times 19 \times 16$	$3 \times 9 \times 16$
Classifier	FC layer 1	1×432	1×256
	FC layer 2	1×256	1×128
	FC layer 3	1×128	1×3

5   Experiment

We conducted the experiments on three kinds of flat and dry road surfaces, including asphalt, marble, painted roads. The weather condition and the detail of the roads at the time of the experiments are shown in Fig. 5. From the close observation, it can be seen that the asphalt road is the roughest, the marble road is the second, and the painted road is the smoothest. The testing vehicle collects PVDF signals at different wheel speeds of 75 r/min, 100 r/min, 125 r/min, and 150 r/min on the three roads. The samples collected at different speeds are randomly scrambled, and all participated in the model's training. The purpose of not using vehicle speed as input data is to make the model adaptive to speed changes, which improves the robustness of the network.

Fig. 5. (a) Asphalt road, (b) Marble road, (c) Painted road.

6 Results and Discussion

6.1 Implementation Details

Data collected through experiments are analyzed and processed on a PC. The dataset contains 6409 PVDF segment signals with a length of 950, and the numbers of segment signals of asphalt road, marble road, and painted road are 2139, 2122, and 2148, respectively. Additionally, we select 80% of the total dataset (5127 samples) as the training dataset and the remaining (1282 samples) as the test dataset. In this paper, the cross-entropy function is used as the loss function, and the Stochastic Gradient Descent (SGD) optimizer is used to optimize the training with a learning rate of 0.01. The training and testing process is performed on a PC with Intel Xeon CPU@ 2.4 GHz, 32-GB main memory, and NVIDIA GeForce RTX 2080 Ti 12-GB GPU.

Table 2. Hyperparameters.

Optimizer	Stochastic Gradient Descent (SGD)
Loss function	Cross-entropy function
Learning rate	0.01
Momentum	0.9
Batch size	8

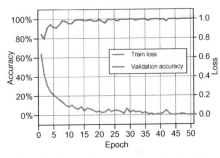

Fig. 6. The training process of the model.

6.2   Performance Evaluation and Comparison

This section analyzes the classification results and evaluates the performance of the proposed model by comparing it with other methods. Figure 6 shows the process of training and validation on the training dataset. The validation accuracy is defined as the ratio of correctly classification samples to the number of total samples in the validation dataset, and the validation dataset is composed of 50 samples randomly selected from the training dataset. The validation accuracy improves with the increase of training epochs, and the accuracy of recognizing road types achieves the best performance when the epoch is 50. To fairly verify the performance of the proposed model in this paper, we compare the model with existing machine learning methods, including 1D Resnet18, Resnet34, Resnet50, and K-Nearest Neighbor classifier (KNN) on the testing dataset.

Resnets and the proposed method are trained under the same hyperparameters listed in Table 2 and use the same nine levels detail coefficients as inputs. We train each model for 100 epochs and choose the one with the highest accuracy for comparison. For KNN, the number of the neighbor is set to 5, which can achieve the best performance after testing. Accuracy, precision, recall, and F1-score are the metrics for comparing and evaluating the performance of different methods. To reflect the overall performance of models, these metrics are macro-average scores defined as the arithmetic mean of the scores from different classes.

Table 3. Classification performance comparison.

Methods	Accuracy	Precision	Recall	F1Score
Our method	**99.14%**	**99.13%**	**99.15%**	**99.14%**
Resnet18	93.45%	93.41%	93.39%	93.40%
Resnet34	94.54%	94.46%	94.47%	94.46%
Resnet50	92.67%	93.35%	92.74%	92.58%
KNN	91.81%	92.21%	91.91%	91.83%

Table 3 presents the results of the testing dataset. The results show that the proposed network outperforms the other methods in all metrics. The accuracy and F1-score of our method is 99.14%, which proves that the proposed SE-CNN has an excellent performance in road recognition. Resnet34 achieves the highest accuracy rate of 94.54%. It should be noted that the proposed model without SE block is also compared. The decrease in accuracy shows the importance of the SE block, which can weigh or recalibrate different channels by considering the nonlinear interactions between the feature channels, finally improving the accuracy [33]. Figure 7(a) presents the testing confusion matrix and the evaluation metrics of classification. Our proposed model performs well in road recognition. The asphalt roads are accurately recognized without mistakes, while the recognition of painted and marble roads has slight errors. Asphalt road texture is rougher than the other two relatively smooth roads, so the model easily extracts recognition features. Meanwhile, there is less discrimination between the marble and painted roads, resulting in most errors occurring on these two types of roads. As shown in Fig. 7(b), the precision and recall of the same road are very high and reached a balance. The F1 scores of asphalt, marble, painted roads are 99.66%, 98.84%, and 98.91%, demonstrating the reliability of SE-CNN in recognizing each road.

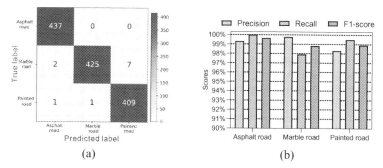

Fig. 7. (a) Confusion matrix and (b) Evaluation metrics.

6.3 Ablation Study

The ablation experiments are conducted to evaluate the contribution of different components of the SE-CNN, and the SE block and 1D convolutional layers are removed from the complete architecture. The results are shown in Table 4. The removal of the SE block results in a 1.02% decrease in accuracy, indicating that the emphasis on valuable features can enhance the recognition capability. Removing the 1D convolutional layers also reduces the recognition accuracy by 0.93%. The convolutional kernels of these layers are convolved in a single spatial dimension, which can be regarded as extracting local information hidden in the wavelet coefficients sequences in the temporal dimension. This information can further improve the performance of SE-CNN. Overall, the SE block and the 1D convolutional layers together improve the feature extraction ability of the network and ensure accurate road recognition.

Through the above experiment, we have proved the importance of the SE block in improving the performance of the recognition network. The effect of SE block at different

Table 4. Results of ablation experiment.

Method	Accuracy
Full architecture	**99.14%**
Without SE block	98.12%
Without Conv 1D layers	98.21%

locations also deserves further discussion. Since there are five convolutional layers in the network, a total of six locations are chosen for comparison. The results are shown in Table 5, and these locations imply that the SE block is placed between these two layers. It can be seen that the highest accuracy is achieved when the SE-CNN is placed between the Conv 1D 2 and Conv 2D 1. Meanwhile, the recognition accuracy shows a downward trend as the location of the SE block gradually becomes deeper, indicating that the ability of the SE block to recalibrate different feature channels is decreasing. The effect of the SE block highly relies on location in the model, and the placement should be considered from the perspective of overall performance.

Table 5. Comparison between the SE block at different locations.

Locations	Accuracy
Input, Conv 1D 1	98.51%
Conv 1D 1, Conv 1D 2	98.44%
Conv 1D 2, Conv 2D 1	**99.14%**
Conv 2D 1, Conv 2D 2	98.99%
Conv 2D 2, Conv 2D 3	98.67%
Conv 2D 3, Classifier	98.21%

6.4 Discussion

To demonstrate the feature discrimination ability at different layers in the model, we use the t-distributed stochastic neighbor (t-SNE) to dimensionally reduce the feature data to 3-D space [31]. Figure 8 presents the visualization of the high-dimensional features at three different layers of the proposed model, which illustrates the improvement in feature recognition.

Figure 8(a) shows the data distribution at the input layer containing the detail coefficients representing physical features calculated by the DWT. It can be observed that the original features of different road surfaces are highly overlapped and mixed, with almost no clustering. This reflects that there is little difference between the wavelet coefficients of these road surfaces, and these physical features need to be mapped into a more discriminative domain. Figure 8(b) presents the feature map at the Max-pooling 3. The

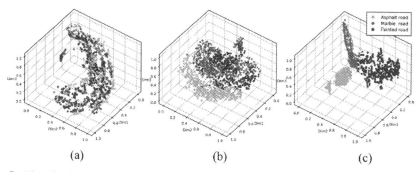

Fig. 8. Visualization using t-SNE at different layers: (a) input layer, (b) output of Max pooling layer 3, (c) output of the classifier.

boundary between the asphalt road and the other two types of roads becomes clearer, and the other two types of roads show a tendency to be distinguished, but there is still some overlap. This explains why most misrecognition occasionally occurs on painted and marble roads. These two types of roads are similar, making it more challenging to extract hidden information that can distinguish one from the other. Therefore, a classifier capable of extracting distinguishing features between similar roads is needed. As shown in Fig. 8(c), the output of the classifier is separable and presents apparent clustering. The classifier consisting of three fully connected layers with ReLU activation functions can map the feature data into a more discriminative domain. As the layer gets deeper, the overlapped input data becomes more separatable, which means that the proposed model can effectively map the indistinguishable physics features into the discriminative domain. Finally, an accurate road recognition is obtained.

7 Conclusion

Accurate recognition of the road surface conditions can assist autonomous vehicles in driving more safely. In this study, we design a PVDF sensor based intelligent tire system to recognize the road surface types. On this basis, we propose a network structure containing the DWT, SE block, and CNN to extract the hidden information from the collected PVDF signals. The physics features calculated by the DWT, which contains time-frequency domains information, are input to the convolutional layers and SE block to weigh each feature channel dynamically. Recognition results are obtained through the convolutional layers and a classifier. It is demonstrated that the proposed SE-CNN achieves the highest accuracy at 99.14% compared to the ResNet at different depths and the KNN. Our proposed method achieves the best performance in the road recognition task.

Our study proves the feasibility of accurate road recognition using the low-cost PVDF-based intelligent tire system. In the future, new intelligent tire systems containing different types of sensors and more accurate recognition models are going to be designed to discriminate complex road conditions accurately. Road recognition methods need to be further optimized to improve the adaptability of our intelligent tire system and realize the real-time recognition to match the perception demand of autonomous vehicles in different driving conditions.

References

1. Aron, M., Billot, R., Faouzi, N.-E.E., Seidowsky, R.: Traffic indicators, accidents and rain: some relationships calibrated on a french urban motorway network. Transp. Res. Procedia **10**, 31–40 (2015)
2. Bajic, M., Pour, S.M., Skar, A., Pettinari, M., Levenberg, E., Alstrøm, T.S.: Road roughness estimation using machine learning (2021). arXiv:210701199
3. Bystrov, A., Hoare, E., Tran, T.-Y., Clarke, N., Gashinova, M., Cherniakov, M.: Automotive surface identification system. In: 2017 IEEE International Conference on Vehicular Electronics and Safety (ICVES), pp. 115–120. IEEE, Vienna (2017)
4. Bystrov, A., Hoare, E., Tran, T.-Y., Clarke, N., Gashinova, M., Cherniakov, M.: Sensors for automotive remote road surface classification. In: 2018 IEEE International Conference on Vehicular Electronics and Safety (ICVES), pp. 1–6 (2018)
5. Dadashova, B., Ramírez, B.A., McWilliams, J.M., Izquierdo, F.A.: The identification of patterns of interurban road accident frequency and severity using road geometry and traffic indicators. Transp. Res. Procedia **14**, 4122–4129 (2016)
6. Dewangan, D.K., Sahu, S.P.: RCNet: road classification convolutional neural networks for intelligent vehicle system. Intel. Serv. Robot. **14**(2), 199–214 (2021). https://doi.org/10.1007/s11370-020-00343-6
7. Díaz-Vilariño, L., González-Jorge, H., Bueno, M., Arias, P., Puente, I.: Automatic classification of urban pavements using mobile LiDAR data and roughness descriptors. Constr. Build. Mater. **102**, 208–215 (2016)
8. Du, Y., Chen, J., Zhao, C., Liu, C., Liao, F., Chan, C.-Y.: Comfortable and energy-efficient speed control of autonomous vehicles on rough pavements using deep reinforcement learning. Transp. Res. Part C: Emerg. Technol. **134**, 103489 (2022)
9. Erdogan, G., Alexander, L., Rajamani, R.: Estimation of tire-road friction coefficient using a novel wireless piezoelectric tire sensor. IEEE Sens. J. **11**, 267–279 (2011)
10. Feng, J., Zhao, F., Ye, M., Sun, W.: The Auxiliary System of Cleaning Vehicle Based on Road Recognition Technology. SAE International, Warrendale (2021)
11. Guo, K., Liu, Q.: A Model of Tire Enveloping Properties and Its Application on Modelling of Automobile Vibration Systems, 980253 (1998)
12. Heinzler, R., Schindler, P., Seekircher, J., Ritter, W., Stork, W.: Weather influence and classification with automotive lidar sensors. In: 2019 IEEE Intelligent Vehicles Symposium (IV), pp. 1527–1534 (2019)
13. Hu, J., Shen, L., Sun, G.: Squeeze-and-Excitation Networks, pp. 7132–7141 (2018)
14. Hu, X., Chen, L., Tang, B., Cao, D., He, H.: Dynamic path planning for autonomous driving on various roads with avoidance of static and moving obstacles. Mech. Syst. Signal Process. **100**, 482–500 (2018)
15. Johnsson, R., Odelius, J.: Methods for road texture estimation using vehicle measurements, 10 (2012)
16. Kang, S.-W., Kim, J.-S., Kim, G.-W.: Road roughness estimation based on discrete Kalman filter with unknown input. Veh. Syst. Dyn. 1–15 (2018)
17. Khaleghian, S.: Terrain classification using intelligent tire. J. Terramech. **10** (2017)
18. Kim, H.-J., et al.: A road condition classification algorithm for a tire acceleration sensor using an artificial neural network. Electronics **9**, 404 (2020)

19. Lee, H., Taheri, S.: Intelligent Tires?a review of tire characterization literature. IEEE Intell. Trans. Syst. Mag **9**, 114–135 (2017)
20. Li, J., Zhang, Z., Wang, W.: New approach for estimating international roughness index based on the inverse pseudo excitation method. J. Transp. Eng. **13** (2018)
21. Ocak, H.: Automatic detection of epileptic seizures in EEG using discrete wavelet transform and approximate entropy. Expert Syst. Appl. **36**, 2027–2036 (2009)
22. Pereira, V., Tamura, S., Hayamizu, S., Fukai, H.: Classification of paved and unpaved road image using convolutional neural network for road condition inspection system. In: 2018 5th International Conference on Advanced Informatics: Concept Theory and Applications (ICAICTA), pp. 165–169 (2018)
23. Putra, T.E., Machmud, M.N.: Predicting the fatigue life of an automotive coil spring considering road surface roughness. Eng. Fail. Anal. **116**, 104722 (2020)
24. Qin, Y., Langari, R., Wang, Z., Xiang, C., Dong, M.: Road excitation classification for semi-active suspension system with deep neural networks. IFS **33**, 1907–1918 (2017)
25. Qin, Y., Xiang, C., Wang, Z., Dong, M.: Road excitation classification for semi-active suspension system based on system response. J. Vib. Control **24**, 2732–2748 (2018)
26. Rateke, T., Justen, K.A., von Wangenheim, A.: Road surface classification with images captured from low-cost camera - road traversing knowledge (RTK) dataset. Rev. de Informática Teórica e Aplicada **26**, 50–64 (2019)
27. Rhif, M., Ben Abbes, A., Farah, I., Martínez, B., Sang, Y.: Wavelet transform application for/in non-stationary time-series analysis: a review. Appl. Sci. **9**, 1345 (2019)
28. Singh, K.B., Ali Arat, M., Taheri, S.: An intelligent tire based tire-road friction estimation technique and adaptive wheel slip controller for antilock brake system. J. Dyn. Syst. Meas. Contr. **135**, 031002 (2013)
29. Singh, K.B., Taheri, S.: Estimation of tire–road friction coefficient and its application in chassis control systems. Syst. Sci. Control Eng. **3**, 39–61 (2015)
30. Slavkovikj, V., Verstockt, S., De Neve, W., Van Hoecke, S., Van De Walle, R.: Image-based road type classification. In: 2014 22nd International Conference on Pattern Recognition, pp. 2359–2364 (2014)
31. Van der Maaten, L., Hinton, G.: Visualizing data using t-SNE. J. Mach. Learn. Res. 9 (2008)
32. Vargas, J., Alsweiss, S., Toker, O., Razdan, R., Santos, J.: An overview of autonomous vehicles sensors and their vulnerability to weather conditions. Sensors **21**, 5397 (2021)
33. Wang, H., Xu, J., Yan, R., Gao, R.X.: A new intelligent bearing fault diagnosis method using SDP representation and SE-CNN. IEEE Trans. Instrum. Meas. **69**, 2377–2389 (2020)
34. Wang, S.: Road terrain type classification based on laser measurement system data, **13** (2012)
35. Ward, C.C., Iagnemma, K.: Speed-independent vibration-based terrain classification for passenger vehicles. Veh. Syst. Dyn. **47**, 1095–1113 (2009)
36. Yang, S., Lu, Y., Li, S.: An overview on vehicle dynamics. Int. J. Dyn. Control **1**(4), 385–395 (2013). https://doi.org/10.1007/s40435-013-0032-y
37. Yi, J., Tseng, E.H.: A "Smart Tire" system for tire/road friction estimation. In: ASME 2008 Dynamic Systems and Control Conference, Parts A and B, pp. 1293–1300. ASMEDC, Ann Arbor, Michigan (2008)

Malicious Packet Classification Based on Neural Network Using Kitsune Features

Kohei Miyamoto[1]([✉]), Hiroki Goto[1], Ryosuke Ishibashi[1], Chansu Han[2],
Tao Ban[2], Takeshi Takahashi[2], and Jun'ichi Takeuchi[1]

[1] Kyushu University, Fukuoka, Japan
miyamoto@me.inf.kyushu-u.ac.jp
[2] National Institute of Information and Communications Technology, Tokyo, Japan

Abstract. Network Intrusion Detection Systems (NIDSes) play an important role in security operations to detect and defend against cyberattacks. As artificial intelligence (AI)-powered NIDSes are adaptive to various kinds of attacks by exploring the knowledge presented in the data, they are in high demand to treat the cyberattacks nowadays with increasing diversity and intensity. In this paper, we present a feasibility study on neural networks (NNs) -based NIDSes aiming to solve the packet classification problem – distinguishing malicious packets from benign packets while specifying a class of anomaly to which a malicious packet belongs. We employ the features defined by Kitsune – a lightweight NN-based packet anomaly detector – as inputs to our classifier. A Kitsune feature vector is composed of statistics calculated from a single packet and its predecessors using a successive algorithm. We evaluate the proposed packet classification scheme using the CSE-CIC-IDS2018 open dataset. The experimental results show that our method can achieve good performance for particular attack types so that it can meet the requirement of a practical NIDSes.

Keywords: Network intrusion detection system · Packet classification · Neural networks

1 Introduction

The number and variety of devices connected to the Internet are growing exponentially in recent years, and so do the cyberattacks targeting these devices. In defending against these cyberattacks, network intrusion detection systems (NIDSes) help security operators by monitoring network traffic, detecting suspicious behaviors therein, and issuing alerts based on the detection results. So far, there have been many kinds of NIDSes proposed. Depending on the different detection mechanisms and implementations, these NIDSes have their own pros and cons. Generally, a proper aggregation of the outputs from multiple NIDSes is expected to realize better security protection than using a single appliance.

In this paper, we discuss effective ways to develop an AI-powered packet classifier that can predict a class name of cyberattacks for each attack packet.

© Springer Nature Switzerland AG 2022
A. Bennour et al. (Eds.): ISPR 2022, CCIS 1589, pp. 306–314, 2022.
https://doi.org/10.1007/978-3-031-08277-1_25

AI-powered NIDSes can be roughly divided into two categories: anomaly detectors and multi-class classifiers. An anomaly detector outputs values called anomaly scores to measure whether captured packets are benign or not. In contrast, a classifier outputs class labels of anomalies that the packets belong to. Both types use feature vectors extracted from monitored traffics as their input. Nevertheless, anomaly detectors can be trained in an unsupervised way: training data need not to be labeled; while classifiers have to be trained using labeled data.

We use Kitsune [5], a well-known AI-based packet anomaly detector, as a base of our development of AI-powered NIDS. The first step of our AI-powered NIDS is to extract the input features from monitored traffics. For that process, we utilize the feature extractor of Kitsune, which employs a successive algorithm to extract the statistical features that characterize the packet and the communication sessions the packet lies in. Exemplary features includes the length and protocol of the packet and frequencies of packet communication between two hosts, etc. Based on these features, Kitsune performs packet level anomaly detection based on the reconstruction error of auto-encoders.

The system framework proposed in Kitsune has proved to be effective and efficient as a packet anomaly detector. In this paper, we seek to further extend its application to solve the multi-class packet classification problem. To do so, we design a new packet classifier based on NNs that can explore the knowledge in Kitsune features to predict the attack types associated with the packet. We evaluate the proposed scheme using the CSE-CIC-IDS2018 open dataset [2,7]. The results of our experiment show that our classifier has good performance for many classes in the dataset.

In the rest of this paper, we explain the feature extraction in Kitsune and our scheme to classify packets using the Kitsune features. Finally, we explain the our experiments for evaluation of our scheme, show the results of the experiments and discuss them.

2 Related Work

Ishibashi et al. [3] proposed a method to generate labeled datasets using alerts from existing NIDSes, which we can use. Hwang et al. [1] proposed another packet classification method using features based on word embedding techniques. Takahashi et al. [8] proposed the integration of various methods for analysing cyberattacks. Trainable NIDSes like our work will be useful as a component of such products.

3 Preliminaries

In this section, we first introduce the problem setting of packet classification. Then, we provide a brief introduction of Kitsune and its feature extraction.

3.1 Problem Setting

When an NIDS is working, it monitors traffic in a specified network. The traffic can be represented as a sequence of packets. Let $\mathcal{P}$ be the set of all possible packets and $p_1, p_2, \ldots$ be a sequence of packets captured by the NIDS. We assume each packet to be timestamped when it is captured. When we have a finite set of classes $\mathcal{C}$, packet classifiers can be regarded as a mapping from $\mathcal{P}$ to $\mathcal{C}$. A NN for packet classification is also regarded as a mapping from some feature space to the set of probability vectors over $\mathcal{C}$. In this paper, we consider only simple feed-forward NNs. Therefore, the feature space is the real vector space $\mathcal{R}^D$ of fixed dimension D. Hence, a feature extraction method can be regarded as a mapping from $\mathcal{P}$ to $\mathcal{R}^D$. When a packet is captured, an NIDS extracts a feature vector from it. Then, the NIDS input the feature vector to the NN and obtain a probability vector over $\mathcal{C}$ as its output. As a classifier, the NIDS outputs a class which has the maximum probability in the distribution.

Labeled data for training of such classifiers are pairs of a packet and a class i.e. members of $\mathcal{P} \times \mathcal{C}$. Each class in $\mathcal{C}$ is one-hot encoded before we input it for a NN. A NN for classification is usually trained by minimizing categorical cross-entropy between output vectors and true labels. The categorical cross-entropy is a loss function commonly used in multi-class classification. When a given label is i-th class in the set of classes $\mathcal{C}$, this label is encoded into a one-hot vector $y = (y_1, \cdots, y_{|\mathcal{C}|})$ where $y_i = 1$ and other elements are 0. For an output probability vector $\hat{y}$ of the NN and an encoded label y, the categorical cross-entropy loss function for them is defined as $L(y, \hat{y}) = -\sum_{j=1}^{|\mathcal{C}|} y_j \log \hat{y}_i$. The optimization using the categorical cross-entropy loss leads to approximate the conditional probability of classes given input features. The data is usually split into 2 subsets, a train set and a test set. During the training phase, we optimize the weights of the NN by using the train set. During the testing phase, we evaluate the performance of the trained NN by using the test set. There are some kinds of measures of the performance of classifiers, e.g. precision, recall and F-measure of the prediction are commonly used.

3.2 Feature Extraction of Kitsune

Kitsune [5] is an NIDS based on a NN-based anomaly detector. A reference implementation of Kitsune is provided at [9]. The anomaly detector of Kitsune has a unique structure which consists of an ensemble of auto-encoders and a unique preprocessing method called feature mapper. However, in this paper, we use only the feature extractor from the structure of Kitsune. Therefore, we do not explain the detail of the anomaly detector of Kitsune.

The feature extractor of Kitsune is intended to be capable to process arriving packets successively without large memory consumption. Captured packets provide us a timestamp, a packet size, MAC addresses, IP addresses and TCP/UDP ports related to them. The feature extractor uses these information of a given packet to calculate a feature vector and update states for the calculation.

The feature extractor manages statistics called damped incremental statistics. For a parameter $\lambda > 0$, an incremental statistic is a 3-tuple of real values denoted as $IS_\lambda = (w, LS, SS)$. Each incremental statistic IS_λ is related to a data stream determined by MAC addresses, IP addresses and TCP/UDP ports. each packet is also related to some data streams. Data streams are divided into the following 4 types.

- srcIP: an IP address of source of packet
- srcMAC-IP: (srcMAC, srcIP), a pair of MAC address and IP address of source of a packet
- Channel: (srcIP, dstIP), a pair of srcIP and an IP address of destination of a packet
- Socket: (srcIP, srcPort, dstIP, dstPort), a 4-tuple of IP addresses and TCP/UDP ports used by a packet.

Therefore, for each packet, the Feature extractor updates 4 incremental statistics. Each incremental statistics is initialized by zero values. Let x be a packet size of a given packet for 3 types of incremental statistics except Channel-type and let x be a jitter value for Channel-type, where the jitter value is defined as the difference of the timestamp from the timestamp of the last packet observed between the same IP addresses. For a packet with a timestamp t, each incremental statistics are updated by the followings.

$$\gamma = 2^{-\lambda(t - t_{\text{last}})}, \tag{1}$$

$$(w, LS, SS) \leftarrow (\gamma w + 1, \gamma LS + x, \gamma SS + x^2), \tag{2}$$

where t_{last} means the timestamp of the last packet related to the same stream and $\leftarrow$ mean updates of variables in the left side. These updates can be done successively without keeping information of packets processed in the past except the timestamp t_{last}. The parameter λ determines the intensity of time decay done by multiplying γ. The feature extractor uses multiple values of λ. It extracts features based on each of them and concatenates these features. Then, it output the concatenated feature vector.

From an incremental statistic, we obtain statistics, $\mu = LS/w$ and $\sigma = \sqrt{|SS/w - (LS/w)^2|}$. They reflect approximations of a mean value and a standard deviation of x observed in some period respectively. Since each of them depends on single data stream, these features are called as 1D statistics in [5]. For Channel and Socket type streams, other 4 kinds of statistics called as 2D statistics are defined. They depend on 2 data streams, for example 2 streams related to different source IP addresses. They reflect characteristics like covariance and correlation between 2 streams.

The feature extractor extracts 20 statistics from a packet for each λ. The extracted statistics consist of $4 \times 3 = 12$ 1D statistics and $2 \times 4 = 8$ 2D statistics. In [5], $\lambda = 5, 3, 1, 0.1, 0.01$ are employed. The extracted feature vectors used for anomaly detection are $5 \times 20 = 100$ dimensional vectors consisting of 60 1D statistics and 40 2D statistics.

4   Methodology

In this section, we propose a new packet classification method based on NN and Kitsune features.

Suppose we have a dataset consisting of packets and labels that indicate which class each packet belongs to. Using the relationship between packets and labels in the dataset, we can construct a packet classifier in a supervised learning way. NN is a powerful model capable of learning such relationship between inputs and outputs. Packet classifiers using NN can adapt to various characteristics of attacks and traffics by learning appropriate data.

We propose using Kitsune features as inputs for a NN-based packet classifier. Kitsune uses features extracted from its feature extractor for anomaly detection. However, we can use them as input also for packet classification based on a NN. Although Kitsune features are originally 100-dimensional vectors, we use only the 60-dimensional subset consisting of 1D statistics. The reason for this is that the extraction of 2D statistics has difficulty on computational time for large datasets.

In this paper, we use a simple feed-forward NN as classifiers. Our classifier has a 60 dimensional input layer and a softmax layer as an output layer. An output for each input is regarded as a probability vector over a set of classes to predict. Our classifier takes an argmax of the output probability vector and output the class corresponding to it as the prediction.

Using Kitsune features as inputs of a NN has the following benefit. After the training, we can use the NN for online processing, because the feature extraction is done in an online manner.

5   Experiment

In this section, we show the experimental results using an open dataset CSE-CIC-IDS2018 [2]. First, we provide an introduction to the dataset. Then, we introduce the setting of the experiments and show its results.

5.1   CSE-CIC-IDS2018 Dataset

CSE-CIC-IDS2018 dataset [2,6] is an open dataset of traffics of cyberattacks. This dataset is provided by the Communications Security Establishment (CSE) and the Canadian Institute for Cybersecurity (CIC) and distributed at [7].

CSE-CIC-IDS2018 dataset was generated by simulating a network with benign traffic and running some tools to attack the simulated network. This dataset contains raw data of captured traffics per day and information of the attacks. The attacks' information includes the kinds of each attack, periods of each attack, and IP addresses of attackers/targets of each attack. Therefore, we can label packets in the captured traffics by using the information of the attacks.

This dataset consists of data of 10 days. The traffics in the data were captured per day and per machine in the network. Each day includes traffics of 1 to 3 kinds of attacks and all days include benign traffics. All kinds of attacks have no overlapping of their periods. This dataset contains 14 kinds of attacks in total. Therefore, including benign class, we use 15 classes for our experiments.

5.2 Labeling and Feature Extraction

We label the data by the following procedure. For each packet, we see the timestamp of capture and IP addresses of it. If the timestamp is in a period of a kind of attack and the packet was transmitted from the attackers to the targets, we label the packet the attack's name. If no kinds of attacks contain the timestamp of the packet in their periods or the packet is not from attackers to targets, we label the packet "BENIGN".

Since the number of benign packets is usually much larger than the number of anomaly packets, for each day, we use only packets captured at target IP addresses of attacks to ease the imbalance of labels.

We use the reference implementation of the extractor in [9]. The extraction was done in the temporal order of captures.

5.3 Experiments and Results

We did two types of experiments. The first type is experiments using data per day. Since each day's data contain labels at most four-classes, we performed at most four class classification in this type of experiment. We separated the last 20% of all the packets in each attack duration, which were used as the test data. We used the rest of the packets in attack duration and the packets captured from 30 min before the attack duration as the training data. As an exception, for data from 2018/02/21, we used only sub-sampled 25% of such training data, because the total number of packets of this date is too large to use in our experiments. The sub-sampling was done with stratification.

The second type is an experiment using the data from all the days. We did stratified sampling of 20000 packets from each day's training data used in the previous experiments and merged them into a sub dataset. We call this sub dataset mixture data. We performed a 15 classes classification with this mixture data. We used the same test data as the first type of experiments in the test phase.

In all experiments, we used NNs consisting of an input layer, 3 hidden layers and a softmax layer. All of hidden layers have 16 units. We used hyperbolic tangent activation functions in the hidden layers. We implemented NNs using Tensorflow and used Adam [4] as the optimizer. The initial learning rate was 0.001. The training batch size was 1024. We enabled the training to early stop when the validation loss does not update its minimum for 5 epochs.

In each experiment, we did the following procedure 5 times and calculated mean values of evaluation metrics we obtained. First, we initialize a model. Then, we randomly split the training data into train/validation sets with a ratio of 3:1. Finally, we train the model and evaluate it with the test data. All features are standardized based on the train set in the training and evaluation.

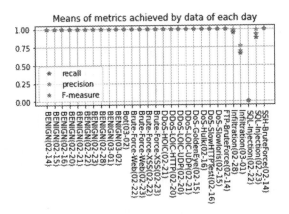

Fig. 1. Experimental results per day

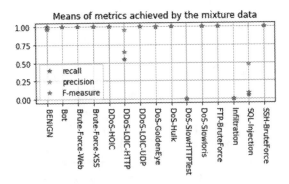

Fig. 2. Experimental results for the mixture data

The metrics we employed to evaluate a classifier were precision, recall and F-measure. Let $\mathcal{T}$ be a test set of pairs of a feature vector and a label. Let $p(x)$ be a class predicted by the classifier for the input feature vector x. The metrics are defined for each class c, as precision$(c) = \text{TP}(c)/(\text{TP}(c) + \text{FP}(c))$, recall$(c) = \text{TP}(c)/(\text{TP}(c) + \text{FN}(c))$ and F$(c) = 2\text{precision}(c) \cdot \text{recall}(c)/(\text{precision}(c) + \text{recall}(c))$, where $\text{TP}(c) = \sum_{(x,y)\in\mathcal{T}} I(p(x) = c, y = c)$, $\text{TN}(c) = \sum_{(x,y)\in\mathcal{T}} I(p(x) \neq c, y \neq c)$, $\text{FP}(c) = \sum_{(x,y)\in\mathcal{T}} I(p(x) = c, y \neq c)$, $\text{FN}(c) = \sum_{(x,y)\in\mathcal{T}} I(p(x) \neq c, y = c)$ and $I(\cdot)$ is the indicator function. All of these metrics take values in $[0, 1]$ and larger values mean better performance.

We show the results for experiments using data per day in Fig. 1. The horizontal axis shows the names of classes and the dates. The vertical axis shows the mean values of each metric. We also show the results for the experiment using mixture data in Fig. 2.

6 Discussion

Figure 1 shows that our classifiers for each day have good performance except for classes "Infiltration" and "SQL-Injection". However, Fig. 2 shows that our classifier for mixture data has lower performance for some classes than the classifiers for each day. In particular, the performance for the DDoS-LOIC-HTTP class and the DoS-SlowHTTPTest show significant decreases. This implies that our classifier may not classify these classes in practical situations. Since Kitsune features originally are designed to be used in anomaly detection, they may not contain sufficient information to discriminate some attacks.

7 Conclusion

We propose a new packet classifier based on NN using Kitsune features as inputs. We evaluate the proposed classifier by experiments using CSE-CIC-IDS2018 open dataset. Our experiments show that Kitsune 1D features can be used for packet classification with some performance for many kinds of attacks. However, it also shows that the performance is not good when we should discriminate a large number of classes of attacks.

Acknowledgments. This research was conducted under a contract of "MITI-GATE" among "Research and Development for Expansion of Radio Wave Resources (JPJ000254)", which was supported by the Ministry of Internal Affairs and Communications, Japan.

References

1. Hwang, R.H., Peng, M.C., Nguyen, V.L., Chang, Y.L.: An LSTM-based deep learning approach for classifying malicious traffic at the packet level. Appl. Sci. 9(16), 3414 (2019)
2. Iman, S., Arash, H.L., Ali, A.G.: Toward generating a new intrusion detection dataset and intrusion traffic characterization. In: 4th International Conference on Information Systems Security and Privacy (ICISSP), January 2018
3. Ishibashi, R., Goto, H., Han, C., Ban, T., Takahashi, T., Takeuchi, J.: Which packet did they catch? Associating NIDS alerts with their communication sessions. In: The 16th Asia Joint Conference on Information Security, August 2021
4. Kingma, D.P., Ba, J.: Adam: a method for stochastic optimization. arXiv preprint arXiv:1412.6980 (Dec 2014)
5. Mirsky, Y., Doitshman, T., Elovici, Y., Shabtai, A.: Kitsune: an ensemble of autoencoders for online network intrusion detection. In: 2018 Network and Distributed System Security Symposium, February 2018
6. Online: CSE-CIC-IDS2018 on AWS. https://www.unb.ca/cic/datasets/ids-2018.html. Accessed 31 Dec 2021
7. Online: A realistic cyber defense dataset (CSE-CIC-IDS2018). https://registry.opendata.aws/cse-cic-ids2018/. Accessed 31 Dec 2021

8. Takahashi, T., et al.: Designing comprehensive cyber threat analysis platform: can we orchestrate analysis engines? In: 2021 IEEE International Conference on Pervasive Computing and Communications Workshops and other Affiliated Events (PerCom Workshops) (2021)
9. ymirsky: Kitsune-py. https://github.com/ymirsky/Kitsune-py. Accessed 31 Dec 2021

An Hybrid Deep Learning Approach for Prediction and Binary Classification of Student's Stress

Nesrine Kadri[1,2(✉)], Sameh Hbaieb Turki[3], Ameni Ellouze[1,4], and Mohamed Ksantini[1]

[1] CEM Lab, ENIS, University of Sfax, Sfax, Tunisia
kadrinesrine2@gmail.com, amani.ellouze@isimg.tn,
mohamed.ksantini@ipeis.usf.tn
[2] ISITCom, University of Sousse, Sousse, Tunisia
[3] MIRACL Lab, FSEGS, University of Sfax, Sfax, Tunisia
[4] ISIMG, University of Gabes, Gabes, Tunisia

Abstract. Nowadays, Stress has repercussions on the mental, physical and psychological health for many persons in life especially students in universities. Stressful life has many negative consequences such as anxiety disorders and depression. The negative influences of stress can be seen in several areas such as mental health.

The prediction of stress can compensate for the negative effects and does not lead to an advanced state. This prediction can be made through smartphones.

In this paper, we aim to classify psychological students state on two classes "stressed" and "not stressed" using smartphones by analyzing extracted features from heterogenous smartphone sensors input information. Indeed, we suggest hybrid deep learning method using both attentional model and Long Short-Term Memory (LSTM) recurrent network. The obtained result achieves 93% accuracy on the test set and comparing to other studies.

Keywords: Deep learning · LSTM · Mental health · Students · Stress · Smartphone · Sensors · Attentional model

1 Introduction

Stress represents a factor that causes well-being disorders. It's bad influences on everyone.

Stress, as in [1], is the consequence of moving from a quiet situation to a change of situation. This change can be either negative or positive. The negative influences of stress can be seen in several areas such as mental health, physical health, productivity, decision-making capacities and situational awareness [2].

Stress is known to worsen the outcome of conditions such as sickness of Parkinson [3] and disorder of heart [4]. This has a negative impact on personal well-being. However, academic and professional pressures are among the major factors of stress that increase

© Springer Nature Switzerland AG 2022
A. Bennour et al. (Eds.): ISPR 2022, CCIS 1589, pp. 315–326, 2022.
https://doi.org/10.1007/978-3-031-08277-1_26

with modern life [5]. In later a long time, the discovery of mental push has pulled in increasingly consideration.

There are different methodologies for detecting stress including clinical tests, traditional methods and various sensors and systems developed using either a smartphone, wearable devices or sensors connected to the human body.

Several recent projects have investigated the potential use of mobile technologies for monitoring stress, depression and other mental disorders.

Indeed, mobile phones are ubiquitous and highly personal devices, equipped with sensing capabilities, which are carried by their owners during their daily routine [6]. Subsequently, there is an opportunity to research the relationship among the telephone's detecting facts and the people's intellectual state and use it to create a mastering show for intellectual push discovery [7].

However, predicting the stress using sequential data with time series characteristics represents a classification problem.

The commitment of this paper lies within the taking after three perspectives: To begin with, we extricate highlights from heterogeneous smartphone detecting information which help to discriminant between two populations states, as stressed or not stressed. In this step, we use an auto-encoder model for feature extraction. These extracted features will be used for classification. Second, a deep learning method is introduced to recognize student's stress, which uses an LSTM predictive model with a softmax layer for "stressed" and "not stressed" binary classification.

At last, we assess our technique primarily based on an open dataset containing both heterogeneous smartphones detecting information and intellectual stretch tiers of forty-eight college understudies amid ten weeks. The exploratory comes about legitimize the points of interest of our approach over a few baselines. Our framework achieves 93% accuracy on the test set.

The stay of this paper is distributed as takes after; the taking after segment exposes the related works, contribution is explained in Sect. 3. Section 4 discusses the experimental results, and the document concludes in Sect. 5.

2 Related Works of Stress Prediction

In recent years and since students are always accompanied by mobile phones which are sources of stress, several research works on cell phones are carried out, from recognition of mental health to finding solutions to prevent increased stress with different algorithms.

Moreover, alongside smartphones, deep learning algorithms are used to predict stress with its classification. Typically, deep learning models consisted of three layers, a to begin with (input), a moment (covered up), and a third (yield). As the number of layers' increments, the arrange gets to be more complex or more profound. Each layer recognizes particular characteristics. The repetitive neural organize (RNN), programmed autoencoders (AE) are a few of the most profound learning techniques.

Machine Encoders (AEs) with its encoder and decoder are useful to reduce in size input instruction. Redo Error (L) is a basic execution metric of AE [8, 9].

Repetitive Neural Arrangement (RNN) could be a type of neural organization where relinquishment of past situation acts as enter to modern-day situation. Not like other powerful learning models, this is a memory-based example that tests metrics.

LSTM is a version of recurrent networks that helps to solve the problem of the leakage gradient [10].

For example, in [11] authors provide multidimensional characteristics of the StudentLife database from smartphones. They adopt straight relapse to interpret the relation with assortment of mental markers, inclusive of the person's behavior and mental weight amid the practice period. This study translates the connection between the detecting facts and the long-time period mental markers instead of the short-term markers.

There is also contemporary research such as [12] and [13] that predict student 'mental health as the rate of stress from smart mobile data.

Additionally, using the data collected from the StudentLife application, the authors in [14] were able to classify students as depressed or not in a binary classification problem.

With the advent of smartphones, researchers have used different data modalities to predict stress such as behavioral metrics like call and text logs and location data from GPS [15, 16], application usage models [17], voice recordings [18] and video recordings [19].

Additionally, other works have focused on the use of sensor-based smartphone data, including touchscreen data and accelerometer data [19, 20].

Recently, in [21], the authors conducted a study on the smartphone and showed that typing pressure increases during stressful situations.

Also, [22] has shown that the number of text errors is related to stress and typing performance.

In [23], the authors present a framework to predict academic person' rate of mental instability using automatic encoders on passive sensor smartphone data.

In [24], the authors demonstrate that LSTM outperforms Convolutional Neural Network (CNN) and CNN-LSTM algorithms, which accept sequence data as input can also work in passive mobile phone sensor data to predict human mental stress.

In [25], the authors built forecast models utilizing inactively detected information from wearable sensors, portable phones, and climate API, and profound learning strategies and assessed the models with the information from unused clients. The differentiations are based totally at the profound lengthy brief-time period memory arrange and the combination of convolutional neural organize (CNN) and the LSTM show. It is shown that their profound LSTM show given exhibitions.

Most of the existing approaches for stress prediction used two classes 'stressed' and 'Not stressed' [15, 16, 18] or three classes 'Low stress', 'Mid stress' and 'High stress' [26].

However, all the works above showed that the task of predicting the stress using sequential data with time series characteristics represents a classification problem.

3 Proposed Stress Prediction Framework

There are often cases where university students undergo stress and early detection of the symptoms can prove to be very useful to prevent this type of mental health.

The objective is to analyze the user's mental health like stress using smartphone sensor and usage data, and predict whether a particular user is experiencing any mental instability.

The target variable is the state of stress faced by the student, which is obtained using various data taken at regular intervals from Student life dataset [5].

In this section, we represent our approach (Fig. 1) of stress prediction. It is composed by three components/layers: (i) Data pre-processing layer, (ii) autoencoder feature extraction layer, (iii) LSTM predictive model with softmax layer for stress binary classification.

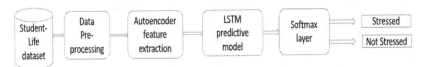

Fig. 1. Steps of the proposed framework

3.1 Data Pre-processing

The data pre-processing (Fig. 2) was composed by: Data integration, Data cleaning, Data visualization, Data transformation (normalization) and Data splitting.

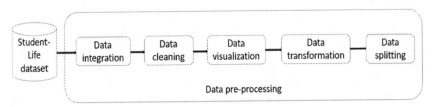

Fig. 2. Data pre-processing

- **Data integration**

StudentLife [3] is the primary take a look at that makes use of automated sensing facts from the telephones of a category of forty-eight Dartmouth college students over a ten-week term to evaluate their intellectual health, academic overall performance and behavioral trends.

The dataset has various types of data spanning from app usage, to sensing data, and finally to user survey response data.

To give a rough estimate, the dataset consists of about 300 CSV files, 150 JSON files and 60 TXT files.

We have integrated all of these data into a single table with 36 features and 1 target variable:

We divided these 36 features into 9 groups as in the below table (Table 1):

In Table 1, it is shown that the features used in this work belong into different groups as:

Table 1. Features of this work

Groups	Descriptions	Features
Application	Application data refers to the total number of times a user uses an application belonging to each category in the given interval	'Academic', 'Books', 'Dating', 'Games', 'Health and Fitness', 'Mail', 'Maps', 'News', 'Puzzle', 'Travel', 'Movies and TV'
Social	Social determines the daily number of messages, calls and conversations interactions done by each user	'SMS', 'Call duration', 'Conversation duration'
GPA (Grade Point Average)	GPA gets each user's grades: Cumulative GPA, Current Spring Term's GPA and CS 65 class GPA	'Cumulative GPA', 'Spring GPA', 'CS65 GPA'
Restaurant	Restaurant calculates the total number of times which a user visits each restaurant and cafe in the given time interval	'King Arthur Flour Coffee Bar', '53 Commons', 'Collis Cafe', 'Courtyard Cafe', 'Collis Market', 'Novack Cafe'
Sleep	Sleep gets each user's following average sleep data: sleep time per night, sleep rating for that night and several times the user had trouble staying awake during the following day	'Sleep Time', 'Sleep Rating', 'Times Drowsy'
Piazza_activity	Piazza_activity gets all the user's activity details	'Days online', 'Views', 'Contributions', 'Questions', 'Notes', 'Answers'
Depression	Depression calculates the depression frequency of each user	'Depression frequency'
Comments	Comments retrieves all the comments given by each user and calculates their total count	'Total Comments' 'Comments positivity'
Deadlines	Deadlines retrieves the total number of deadlines for each user in the given interval	'Deadlines'

Application = ['Academic', 'Books', 'Dating', 'Games', 'Health and Fitness', 'Mail', 'Maps', 'News', 'Puzzle', 'Travel', 'Movies and TV']

Social = ['SMS', 'Call duration', 'Conversation duration']

GPA = ['Cumulative GPA', 'Spring GPA', 'CS65 GPA']

Restaurant = ['King Arthur Flour Coffee Bar', '53 Commons', 'Collis Cafe', 'Courtyard Cafe', 'Collis Market', 'Novack Cafe']

Sleep = ['Sleep Time', 'Sleep Rating', 'Times Drowsy']

Piazza_activity = ['Days online', 'Views', 'Contributions', 'Questions', 'Notes', 'Answers']

Depression = ['Depression frequency']

Comments = ['Total comments', 'Comments positivity']

Deadlines = ['Deadlines']

- **Data cleaning**

The data is cleaned by filling the missing values. The most logically and accurate way seems to fill the missing values with mean of that feature.

- **Data visualization**

Correlation coefficients are used to measure how strong a relationship is between two variables. There are several types of correlation coefficient, but the most popular is Pearson's. So, for data visualization (Fig. 3), we have used Pearson correlation method to plot the correlation heatmaps between smartphone data and user's stress:

$$\text{Correlation: CORR }(X, Y) = (COV(X, Y)/\sigma X \sigma Y) \tag{1}$$

with

$$\text{Covariance: COV }(X, Y) = \left(\sum (Xi - \overline{X})(Yi - \overline{Y})/N\right) \tag{2}$$

wherein:

Xi: The X-variable 'values'

Yi: The Y-variable 'values'

$\overline{X}$: the imply (common) of the X-variable

$\overline{Y}$: the suggest (common) of the Y-variable

N: the range of records factors

σX: the usual deviation of the X-variable

σY: the usual deviation of the Y-variable

In Fig. 3, it is shown that people who engage in long duration phone calls, read books, and/or watch Movies & TV are least stressed. Also, stressed people do not sleep for longer duration and are dissatisfied with their sleep.

- **Data transformation: normalization**

Min-max normalization is one of the most common ways to normalize data. For every feature, we have transformed the minimum value of that feature into a 0 and the maximum value gets transformed into a 1.

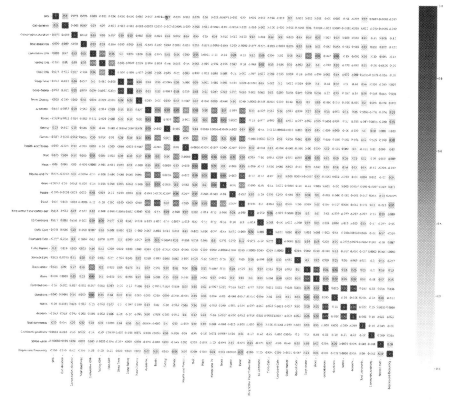

Fig. 3. Correlation heatmaps between smartphone data and user's stress

- **Data Splitting**

In this work, as final step of data pre-processing, we have splitted the StudenLife database into 80% for training and 20% for testing.

3.2 Autoencoder Element Extraction for Classification

In this segment, we created an autoencoder to memorize a compressed representation of the input highlights for a classification prescient modeling issue (Fig. 4): To begin with, let's characterize a classification prescient modeling issue: We characterized a engineered double (2-class) classification assignment (focused or no) with 36 input highlights. Another, we created a Multilayer Perceptron (MLP) autoencoder show. The show had all the highlights as input, at that point outputted the same values. It learned to reproduce the input design exactly. The autoencoder comprises of two parts: the input form named encoder and the output form named decoder. The input form determines how to decipher the input information and reduce in size it to an inner reproduction for the decoder. The last takes the output of the encoder and endeavors for reproducing the input features.

We characterize the encoder to have two covered up layers and the decoder to have also two covered up layers.

A batch normalization and leaky Relu activation are used to assure the perfect learning of the model.

This architecture is fitting with the application of the efficient algorithm of stochastic slope plunge and minimizes the cruel squared blunder (epochs: 200 and batch size: 16).

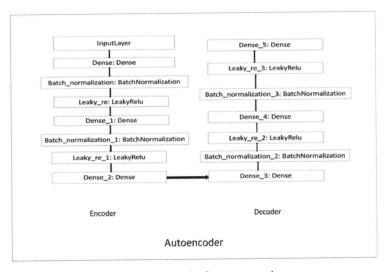

Fig. 4. Autoencoder feature extraction

3.3 LSTM Anticipating Architecture

We utilized the prepared encoder from the over autoencoder to reduce in size input information for multi-layers LSTM predictive model (Fig. 5).

The functioning of the LSTM unit can be represented by the following set of equations:

$$z_t = \tanh\left(W_z x_t + R_z h_{t-1} + b_z\right) \text{ (Input)} \tag{3}$$

$$i_t = \text{sigmoid}(W_i x_t + R_i h_{t-1} + b_i) \text{ (Input gate)} \tag{4}$$

$$f_t = \text{sigmoid}(W_f x_t + R_f h_{t-1} + b_f) \text{ (Forget gate)} \tag{5}$$

$$o_t = \text{sigmoid}(W_o x_t + R_o h_{t-1} + b_o) \text{ (Output gate)} \tag{6}$$

$$s_t = z_t.i_t + s_{t-1}.f_t \text{ (Cell state)} \tag{7}$$

$$h_t = \tanh\left(s_t\right).o_t \text{ (Output)} \tag{8}$$

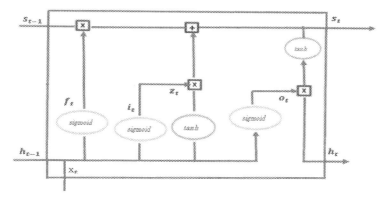

Fig. 5. LSTM cell

With the W represent input weights, the R are recurrent weights, b are the biases.

As the final step in the proposed framework is the prediction, we have used the softmax layer with an additional output layer with two neurons, representing 'stressed' or 'Not stressed'.

4 Experimental Outcomes

In this segment, experimental outcomes are presented. Also we compare this work with others on the same StudentLife dataset.

The results of this work were presented in table below (Table 2).

Table 2. Accuracy of our work

Accuracy LSTM with encoded features	Accuracy LSTM without encoded features
93%	86%

In Table 2, the proposed framework achieves 86% accuracy when the features were not encoded, but with encoded features, the accuracy increases and reaches 93%.

To show the performance of the proposed framework on the same dataset StudentLife, we compare this work with others (Table 3).

In Table 3, we can see that the proposed framework with encoded features in LSTM reached 93% accuracy and without encoded features in LSTM reached 86%. These results present better results than the others as LSTM [24] which reached only 62,83% of accuracy.

Table 3. Comparison with other works

Model	Accuracy
CNN [24]	60.43%
CNN-LSTM [24]	60.00%
LSTM [24]	62,83%
Our work: LSTM without encoded features	86%
Our work: LSTM with encoded features	93%

5 Conclusion

Stress has negative effects on the day-to-day course of our lives and if left untreated it can lead to serious situations. The prediction of this disease is not easy and requires the intervention of a doctor.

At universities, students are always accompanied by smartphones which can help detect stress.

For this type of mental health, many works focus on finding solutions to prevent increased stress.

In this approach, a framework was constructed to anticipate and classify student's stress. This framework is based on StudentLife dataset that has many informations about students from smartphones and used autoencoder with LSTM to predict and classify the stress in two states.

Comparing with other works, we can say that this framework achieves best results and outperforms CNN and CNN-LSTM.

But this work was presented only for students, so we create a Framework more general than this work in the future and we focus on classification of level of stress: low, medium and high.

References

1. Shoumy, N.J., Ang, L.M., Seng, K.P., Rahaman, D.M., Zia, T.: Multimodal big data affective analytics: a comprehensive survey using text, audio, visual and physiological signals. J. Netw. Comput. Appl. **149**, 1–26 (2020). https://doi.org/10.1016/j.jnca.2019.102447
2. Politou, E., Alepis, E., Patsakis, C.: A survey on mobile affective computing. Comput. Sci. Rev. **25**, 79–100 (2017). https://doi.org/10.1016/j.cosrev.2017.07.002
3. Hemmerle, A.M., Herman, J.P., Seroogy, K.B.: Stress, depression and Parkinson's disease. Exp. Neurol. **233**(1), 79–86 (2012). https://doi.org/10.1016/j.expneurol.2011.09.035
4. Pushkarev, G.S., Kuznetsov, V.A., Fisher, Y.A., Soldatova, A.M., Enina, T.N.: Depression and all-cause mortality in patients with congestive heart failure and an implanted cardiac device. Turk Kardiyoloji Dernegi arsivi: Turk Kardiyoloji Derneginin yayin organidir **46**(6), 479–487 (2018). https://doi.org/10.5543/tkda.2018.04134
5. Weiten, W., Dunn, D.S., Hammer, E.Y.: Psychology applied to modern life: adjustment in the 21st century (2014)

6. Lane, N., Miluzzo, E., Lu, H., Peebles, D., Choudhury, T., Campbell, A.: A survey of mobile phone sensing. IEEE Commun. Mag. **48**(9), 140–150 (2010). https://doi.org/10.1109/mcom. 2010.5560598

7. Wang, F., Wang, Y., Wang, J., Xiong, H., Zhao, J., Zhang, D.: Assessing mental stress based on smartphone sensing data: an empirical study. In: 2019 IEEE SmartWorld, Ubiquitous Intelligence and Computing, Advanced and Trusted Computing, Scalable Computing and Communications, Cloud and Big Data Computing, Internet of People and Smart City Innovation (SmartWorld/SCALCOM/UIC/ATC/CBDCom/IOP/SCI) (2019). https://doi.org/ 10.1109/smartworld-uic-atc-scalcom-iop-sci.2019.00200

8. Voulodimos, A., Doulamis, N., Doulamis, A., Protopapadakis, E.: Deep learning for computer vision: a brief review. Comput. Intell. Neurosci. (2018). https://doi.org/10.1155/2018/706 8349

9. Bengio, Y.: Learning deep architectures for AI. Found. Trends Mach. Learn. **2**(1), 1–27 (2009). https://doi.org/10.1561/2200000006

10. Khan, S., Yairi, T.: A review on the application of deep learning in system health management. Mech. Syst. Sig. Process. (2018). https://doi.org/10.1016/j.ymssp.2017.11.024

11. Wang, R., et al.: StudentLife: assessing mental health, academic performance and behavioral trends of college students using smartphones. UbiComp (2014). https://doi.org/10.1145/263 2048.2632054

12. Sano, A., Picard, R.W.: Stress recognition using wearable sensors and mobile phones. In: Humaine Association Conference on Affective Computing and Intelligent Interaction, vol. 24, pp. 386–396 (2013). https://doi.org/10.1109/ACII.2013.117

13. Sano, A., et al.: Recognizing academic performance, sleep quality, stress level and mental health using personality traits, wearable sensors and mobile phones. Draft Body Sens. Netw. **24**, 386–396 (2015). https://doi.org/10.1109/BSN.2015.7299420

14. Wang, R., et al.: Tracking depression dynamics in college students using mobile phone and wearable sensing. Proc. ACM Interact. Mob. Wear. Ubiquit. Technol. **2** (2018). https://doi. org/10.1145/3191775

15. Bauer, G., Lukowicz, P.: Can smartphones detect stress-related changes in the behaviour of individuals? In: IEEE International Conference on Pervasive Computing and Communications Workshops. IEEE (2012). https://doi.org/10.1109/PerComW.2012.6197525

16. Bogomolov, A., Lepri, B., Ferron, M., Pianesi, F., Pentland, A.S.: Daily stress recognition from mobile phone data, weather conditions and individual traits. In: Proceedings of the 22nd ACM International Conference on Multimedia, New York, NY, USA. ACM (2014). 10.1145/ 2647868.2654933

17. Osmani, V., Ferdous, R., Mayora, O.: Smartphone app usage as a predictor of perceived stress levels at workplace. In: Proceedings of the 9th International Conference on Pervasive Computing Technologies for Healthcare (2015). https://doi.org/10.4108/icst.pervasivehealth

18. Lu, H., et al.: StressSense: detecting stress in unconstrained acoustic environments using smartphones. In: Proceedings of the ACM Conference on Ubiquitous Computing. ACM (2012). https://doi.org/10.1145/2370216.2370270

19. Carneiro, D., Carlos Castillo, J., Novais, P., Fernández-Caballero, A., Neves, J.: Multimodal behavioral analysis for non-invasive stress detection. Expert Syst. Appl. **39**(18), 13376–13389 (2012). https://doi.org/10.1016/j.eswa.2012.05.065

20. Garcia-Ceja, E., Osmani, V., Mayora, O.: Automatic stress detection in working environments from smartphones' accelerometer data: a first step. IEEE J. Biomed. Health Inform. **20**(4), 1053–1060 (2016). https://doi.org/10.1109/jbhi.2015.2446195

21. Exposito, M., Hernandez, J., Picard, R.W.: Affective keys: towards unobtrusive stress sensing of smartphone users. In: Proceedings of the 20th International Conference on Human-Computer Interaction with Mobile Devices and Services Adjunct. ACM (2018). https://doi. org/10.1145/3236112.3236132

22. Sarsenbayeva, Z., et al.: Measuring the effects of stress on mobile interaction. Proc. ACM Interact. Mob. Wear. Ubiquit. Technol. (2019). https://doi.org/10.1145/3314411
23. Shaw, A., Simsiri, N., Deznaby, I., Fiterau, M., Rahman, T.: Personalized Student Stress Prediction with Deep Multitask Network. ArXiv (2019)
24. Acikmese, Y., Alptekin, S.E.: Prediction of stress levels with LSTM and passive mobile sensors. Pro. Comput. Sci. **159**, 658–667 (2019). https://doi.org/10.1016/j.procs.2019.09.221
25. Yu, H., Sano, A.: Passive sensor data based future mood, health, and stress prediction: user adaptation using deep learning. In: 2020 42nd Annual International Conference of the IEEE Engineering in Medicine & Biology Society (EMBC) (2020). https://doi.org/10.1109/embc44109.2020.917624
26. Maxhuni, A., Hernandez-Leal, P., Sucar, L.E., Osmani, V., Morales, E.F., Mayora, O.: Stress modelling and prediction in presence of scarce data. J. Biomed. Inform. **63**, 344–356 (2016). https://doi.org/10.1016/j.jbi.2016.08.023

A Novel Deep Convolutional Neural Network Architecture for Customer Counting in the Retail Environment

Almustafa Abed[1,2], Belhassen Akrout[1,3]([✉]), and Ikram Amous[1,2]

[1] Multimedia Information Systems and Advanced Computing Laboratory (MIRACL), Sfax University, 3021 Sfax, Tunisia
Ikram.amous@enetcom.usf.tn
[2] ENET'COM, University of Sfax, National School of Electronics and Telecommunications of Sfax, Road Tunis City El Ons, 3018 Sfax, Tunisia
[3] Department of Computer Science, College of Computer Engineering and Sciences, Prince Sattam Bin Abdulaziz University, Alkharj 11942, Saudi Arabia
b.akrout@psau.edu.sa

Abstract. Machine-learning and feature-based approaches have been developed in recent years to count shoppers in retail stores utilizing RGB-D sensors without occlusion in a top-view configuration. Since entering the era of large-scale media, deep learning approaches have become very popular and are used for a various variety of applications like the detection and identification of people in crowded scenes. Detecting and counting people is a difficult task especially in cluttered and crowded environments like malls, airports, and retail stores. Understanding the behavior of humans in a retail store is crucial for the efficient functioning of the business. We present an approach to segment and count people heads in a heavy occlusion environment by using a convolutional neural network. We present a novel semantic segmentation approach to detect people heads using top-view depth image data. The goal of our approach is to segment and count the human heads where the datasets are acquired by depth sensors (ASUS Xtion pro). For semantic segmentation, RGB images are used, but here in this case we are going to use depth images to segment human heads. The proposed architecture begins with ResNet50 as the pre-trained encoder and is then followed by the decoder network. The framework is assessed using the publicly available TVHeads Dataset, which contains depth images of people collected using an RGB-D sensor positioned in a top-view configuration. The results show good accuracy and prove that our approach is efficient and appropriate.

Keywords: People counting · Computer-vision · Deep-learning · Intelligent retail environment · Convolutional neural networks

1 Introduction

Detecting and counting individuals for various interactive and intelligent retail systems, are significant and important tasks. This has been an important subject of extensive

© Springer Nature Switzerland AG 2022
A. Bennour et al. (Eds.): ISPR 2022, CCIS 1589, pp. 327–340, 2022.
https://doi.org/10.1007/978-3-031-08277-1_27

research in recent years and robust techniques for counting people [1]. However, the tracking of people in more crowded circumstances such as in retail stores, where there are numerous people, remains substantially a difficulty because of several major problems such as occlusion, dynamic and complicated background and variation of aspect, [2]. All of these limitations and issues make it more difficult for traditional cameras to deal with, since conventional cameras have difficulty comprehending the image [3]. Sensors which are viable in these conditions are the RGB-D cameras because they are reliable, available and affordable. Researchers have shown the excellent value of depth sensors in efficiency as well as accuracy [3]. Addressing extreme human occlusions and complex background [4, 8]. Combining high resolution depth image and visual information provides new difficulties and possibilities for counting and tracking people for retail applications. Depth images can present crucial information to enhance counting and detecting outcomes considerably [5]. The semantic segmentation is the high-level task in handling 2D, video, and also 3D images. It sets the way for significant and full understanding of the scene and its currently being tackled by using deep-learning networks (CNNs) generally overcome other techniques by a broad margin of accuracy and even efficiency [4]. We describe an approach for detecting and counting individuals in crowded and cluttered environment and at the present of temporary occlusion using CNNs for semantic image segmentation on top-view RGB-D images dataset named Top-View Heads (TvHeads) [6].

This paper is organized as follows: Sect. 2 provides a detailed description of the related works and techniques that were implemented with RGB-D cameras configured in a Top-View setup. Section 3 explains the proposed approach methods in details and illustrates the model's architectures. In Sect. 4 the dataset used to train and test the model and data-augmentation techniques are described. In Sect. 5, our models results and discussion are explained. Finally, in Sect. 6, the conclusion and discussion of future works of our research are illustrated.

2   Related Work

Detecting, counting and analyzing persons behaviors in image and video sequences has been receiving a lot of attention in computer vision [7, 28, 29] and deep learning research community, with a lot of applications, especially in security monitoring and intelligent retail environments [1]. Notable research has been performed on developing solid techniques for counting single and small groups of individuals, for whom only temporary occlusion exists [9]. Two types of people counting: Counting the number of people at a certain location and counting the number of people entering a passageway or a line [5, 10, 11].

This work focuses on the second category, which is counting persons who pass through a passage, line or corridor. In this subject, the majority of research are vision-based, employing radio-frequency (RF) signals like WiFi, UWB, and Zig-Bee [12].

The primary difficulties of people detection and counting in a particular region have concentrated on the features and detection of the individual, moreover, they have attempted to establish index that change with the number of persons, as well as quantifying the total number of persons based on these index values.

Alternatively, when the aim is to count individuals going through a passage or a line, the binary direction, as well as the detection, must be considered [13].

Recent research has shown that CNN may be used to estimate density maps in single images for crowd people counting. Wang et al. [14] and Fu et al. [15] were the first to use approaches based on CNNs to estimate the crowd density. Concurrently, the researchers offer a cross scene crowd people counting method in [16]. The main concept is to convert images into crowd numbers. and then for cross-scene mapping, adapt that mapping to new target scenes counting. The necessity for perspective maps for both training and testing scenarios, is a disadvantage of this technique.

Noh et al. 2015 [17] built a deep deconvolution network to create a new semantic segmentation method. The VGG 16-layer net's convolutional layers serve as the foundation for the new network's learning. The de-convolution model is made up of deconvolution and un-pooling layers that identifies pixel wise class labels and predict the segmentation mask. The network performed admirably on the PASCAL-VOC (2012) data set, with the highest accuracy (72.5%) of all techniques trained without utilizing the Microsoft COCO dataset through ensemble with the fully convolutional network.

Badrinarayanan et al. 2016 [18] Seg-Net is a unique and effective deep fully convolutional neural network architecture for semantic segmentation. This main trainable semantic segmentation model is made up of an encoder-decoder network, and a pixelwise classification layer. The encoder-network is topologically equivalent to the 13 convolutional layers of the VGG16 network [19]. The Seg-Net decoder's novelty is in the way it up-samples its lower resolution input feature maps.

He et al. 2016 [20] presented a framework for residual learning that can be used to assist in the training of networks that are much deeper than previously used networks. Rather than learning unreferenced functions, they redefined the layers as learning residual functions with respect to the layer inputs. Additionally, they show substantial empirical evidence proving that these residual networks are easier to adjust and can gain accuracy as the depth of the network increases. They evaluate residual networks with up to 152 layers of depth on the ImageNet dataset—eight times the depth of VGG nets. [19], but with lesser complexity. On the ImageNet test set, an ensemble of these residual nets achieves 3.57% error.

Del Pizzo et al. 2016 [10] proposed a method based on vision for calculating the numbers of people who pass a virtual-line They analyzed the video-flow recorded by a sensor positioned in a zenithal configuration with respect to the counting line, in their study, allowing them to clearly identify the number of people who crossed the virtual-line and provide the crossing direction for every individual.

Chen et al. 2018 [21] proposed an architecture, DeepLabv3+, which extends DeepLabv3 by adding a basic yet useful decoder module for refining segmentation results, particularly at object boundaries Building on this concept, they propose using DeepLabv3 [22] as the encoder module, and a basic yet effective decoder module to provide better segmentations.

Shami et al. 2019 [23] Proposed a method which is based on the notion that the person head is the most visible component of a person in a crowded environment. They used cutting-edge convolutional neural networks to detect sparse heads in a dense crowd. The method was tested against three publicly accessible datasets for highly dense crowds:

UCF CC 50, Shanghai-Tech, and AHU Crowd. The technique achieves equivalent results on these difficult datasets as other state of the art methods.

Nogueira Jr et al. 2019 [24] Have developed a cheap deep learning technique for real-time estimation of the number of persons in retail businesses, as well as detecting and visualizing hot areas. They use a supervised-learning technique based on a Convolutional Neural Network (CNN) regression-model to tackle the people counting problem. The results show that the technique is extremely resilient to be utilized in real-world scenarios and surpasses simple CNN approaches.

The authors in [25] present a novel two-stream CNN architecture for semantic segmentation that directly wires shape information as a distinct processing branch, referred to as shape stream, that analyzes data concurrently with the classical stream. A novel kind of gate that connects the intermediary levels of the two streams is key to this architecture. This allows the shape stream, which functions at the image-level resolution, to employ a very shallow architecture.

By scanning the literature for gaps and by searching for advantages and disadvantages we have concluded that the Top-View configuration is a better configuration to use for this research due to its occlusion free and privacy compliance in developed countries.

We utilized transposed convolution instead of up-sampling due to the fact that it implements the up - sampling operation while also interpreting the coarse input data to fill in the details and another advantage is the extra learnable parameters in transposed convolution. It's similar to a layer that combines the UpSampling2D and Conv2D layers. We used dilated convolution because it expands the field of view without increasing the computation and number of parameters. The advantage of using attention mechanism is because it focuses on specific parts of the image that is more important than other parts according to the required task and this reduces the complexity of the model and reduce training time.

All of these advantages that we used in our approach made it possible to obtain accurate results. In the following section we describe our proposed approach and the methods used that includes the solution for some problems in the literature.

3   Proposed Approach

In this section we present our proposed approach. The proposed approach as depicted in Fig. 1 is based on encoder-decoder architecture in which the encoder is ResNet50 by utilizing transfer learning. The encoder takes the input images dataset, encodes it and output a feature tensor, this feature map contains the information and features of the input data, and then passes the output to the decoder which was built as a novel contribution. The decoder takes the feature tensor from the encoder as input and tries to map this input to the closest result of the actual input or the required output.

In fact, the proposed architecture begins with a pre-trained ResNet50 as the encoder described in Fig. 2, which is trained on the Image-Net dataset. We have used the ResNet50 as feature extractor and we removed the last two layers which is the average pooling and the softmax layer because we don't need the classification and fully connected layers, we only need the convolutional layers.

The ResNet50 is a variant of the ResNet model [20], which begins with a 7×7 convolution with a stride value of 2 and 64 number of feature channels. After that it is followed by a 3×3 maxpooling with a stride value of 2.

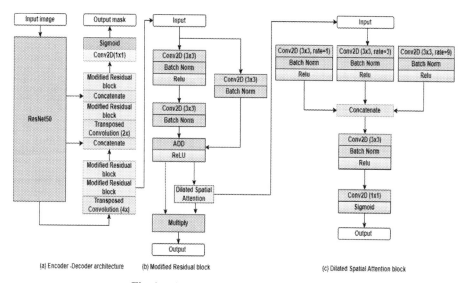

Fig. 1. The proposed approach architecture

Next, it consists of a number of residual blocks. The output of the pre-trained ResNet50 acts as the input for the decoder network as illustrated in the approach architecture shown in Fig. 1(a).

The decoder network which is also described in Fig. 1(a), begins with a transpose convolution that increases the spatial dimensions of the feature maps by a factor of 4. Then it is followed by two modified residual blocks which is illustrated in Fig. 1(b) consisting of the Dilated Spatial Attention which is illustrated in Fig. 1(c). The output of the residual block is then concatenated with the skip connection feature maps from the encoder. The concatenated feature maps are then followed by a transpose convolution, which increases the spatial dimensions of the feature maps by a factor of 2. Then comes the modified residual blocks consisting of the Dilated Spatial Attention. Again, it is concatenated with a skip connection feature map from the encoder. These skip connections assist in obtaining the features from the encoders by avoiding redundant information and enhancing the semantic relevance of the feature maps, which helps in better semantic feature learning in the decoder. These skip connections also act as a shortcut during the backpropagation, which helps in the better flow of the gradients.

At last, the network is followed by a 1×1 convolution and then a sigmoid activation function. The sigmoid activation function generated the binary mask.

In the following sub-sections, we will discuss the decoder part and the methods used in our model in details.

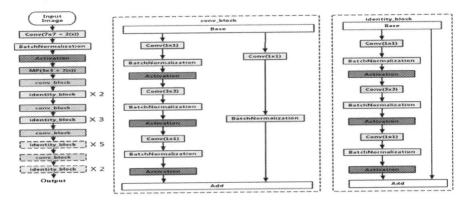

Fig. 2. Resnet50 encoder architecture

3.1 Modified Residual Block

The modified residual block is one of the main building blocks of the proposed architecture as shown in Fig. 3. It mainly consists of two parts, first the main convolution path and second the shortcut connection or the identity mapping. The input feature maps are first passed through a 3 × 3 convolution, batch normalisation and then A ReLU activation function.

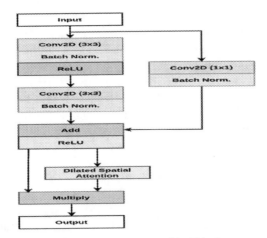

Fig. 3. The modified residual block

Next, again comes a 3 × 3 convolution and a batch normalization layer. Now we apply an element-wise addition between the output of the batch normalization and the shortcut connection. The shortcut connection consists of the 1 × 1 convolution and the batch normalization layer. After the addition, we use a ReLU activation function and then followed by the Dilated Spatial Attention block. The modified residual block further refines the concatenated feature maps. The identity mapping is multiplied by a linear projection W to enlarge the shortcut channels used to fit the residual. And we can apply linear projection W_s by the shortcut connection. This enables the inputs x and $F(x)$ to be combined as the input to the subsequent layer. Where x and y denote the input and output vectors, respectively, and the function "$F(x, \{W_i\})$" represents the residual mapping to be learned [20]. As illustrated by the following equation:

$$y = F(x, \{W_i\}) + W_s x \tag{1}$$

3.2 Transposed Convolution

The transposed convolution is utilized in the decoder part described in Fig. 1. Transposed convolution is mostly used in semantic segmentation architecture for increasing the resolution of the feature maps. It consists of a kernel matrix which learns how to increase the feature maps' resolution. The learning of the transpose convolution makes it more efficient than the nearest neighbor or bilinear up sampling. The following equation defines the size of the output feature map (o) produced by normal convolution for a given input (i), kernel (k), padding (p), and stride (s):

$$o = ((i + 2p - k)/s) + 1 \tag{2}$$

The following equation defines the size of the output feature map (o) produced by transposed convolution given a specified input (i), kernel (k), padding (p), and stride (s):

$$o = i - 1 \times s + k - 2p \tag{3}$$

3.3 Dilated Spatial Attention Block

The Dilated Spatial Attention as shown in Fig. 4 is an attention mechanism which uses the power of dilated convolution to generate a spatial attention map to enhance the feature representation, its used to increase the feature representation by suppressing the irrelevant features and highlighting the important ones.

The Dilated Spatial Attention begins with three parallel dilated convolutions layers with dilation rate 1, 3 and 9 respectively. These dilated convolution helps to enlarge the receptive field, which helps it to capture a broader range of features. Next, these convolutions are followed by the batch normalization and a ReLU activation function. Now the output of the three activation functions is concatenated together to get a single feature map. Now this concatenated feature map is preceded by a 3×3 convolution layer, which is further preceded by a batch normalization and a ReLU activation function. And then a 1×1 convolution with one filter is followed by a sigmoid activation. The output of the sigmoid contains values between 0 and 1, which acts as a soft-attention. A value near to zero indicates less important features and while a value near to one indicates a more important feature map. So, the Dilated Spatial Attention basically suppresses the less-relevant features while retaining the more important features. Our proposed Dilated

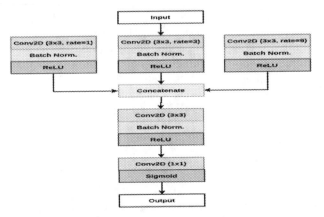

Fig. 4. Dilated spatial attention

Spatial Attention uses dilated convolution to generate an attention map. And the equation for dilated convolution is described in the equation below:

$$y[i] = \sum_{k=1}^{K} x[i + r \cdot k]w[k] \tag{4}$$

1D Dilated (Atrous) Convolution($r > 1$: dilated convolution, $r = 1$: standard convolution), where r corresponds to the stride with which we sample the input. Where the input is x[i] and the output of atrous convolution is y[i] and with a filter w[k] of length K [26].

3.4 Implementation Details

Our suggested architecture is implemented in TensorFlow framework using Python 3.8 and trained on a windows 10 OS with RTX2060 GPU. We have used categorical cross entropy as the loss function in the experiment with the Adam optimiser having a learning rate of 1e−4 (0.0001). We also used ReduceLROnPlateau to reduce the learning rate when the validation loss stops decreasing for a certain number of consecutive iterations which is called epochs. To make sure that the system resources are not wasted we have used the EarlyStopping callback. It is utilized to halt the training when the model stops improving.

4 Experimental Corpus and Data Augmentation

The TV-Heads (Top-View Heads) [6] dataset provides top-view depth data of people. The aim of this dataset is to identify persons whose heads are visible below the camera. It includes 1815 depth images (16 bit) with a 320 × 240-pixel resolution. Moreover, following image pre-processing, the depth data are converted and scaled appropriately, to generate an (8 bit) image that highlights the silhouette of the head by enhancing the image brightness and contrast. Six human annotators manually labeled the ground truth. Figure 5 illustrates an instance of the dataset containing the two images shown below.

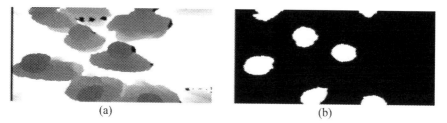

Fig. 5. A sample of Tv-Heads dataset [6]. (a) 8-bit scaled depth image, (b) ground-truth

We propose a data augmentation on the dataset which is illustrated in Fig. 6, we applied VerticalFlip, HorizontalFlip, GaussNoise, and CoarseDropout to Tv-Heads images to improve our model training and results. We increased the dataset from 1815 depth images to 9080 8bit depth images, we have split the dataset to 80:10:10 ratio where 80% data is used for the training which consists of 8718 depth images and masks pair and the rest is 10% which is 181 depth images and masks pair for validation and 10% for testing as well.

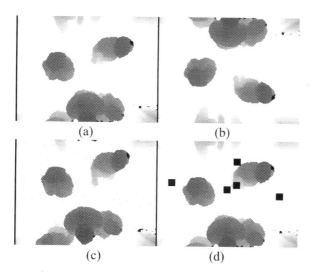

Fig. 6. Data augmentation. (a) Vertical-Flip (b), Horizontal-Flip (c), Gaussian-Noise, (d) Coarse-Dropout

5   Experimentation and Discussion

This work focuses specifically on people counting in a super market. The results of the tests performed with the TVHeads dataset are given in this section. The model is trained using depth images to highlight heads silhouettes with 8-bit (scaled images). During the training phase, we divided the dataset into 80:10:10 ratios for training, validation, and testing. The learning process is repeated 100 times with a learning rate of 0.0001 and for optimization we utilized Adam optimization algorithm. The best results were acquired by primarily using the 8 bits scaled images. Table 1 shows the outcomes of semantic segmentation, as well as the Jaccard [27] indices, and also the accuracy, precision, recall, and F1 score. As can be seen, the existing network performed admirably in terms of the Jaccard indices, as well as accuracy. Because their outcomes are adequate, it implies that the segmentation is accurate and precise. Hence showing the efficiency of the proposed approach.

Table 1. Model test results

Accuracy	0.99879
F1	0.80052
Jaccard	0.79054
Recall	0.79836
Precision	0.80413

As we can see in Table 2 our model has the highest accuracy compared with other state of the art models and is relatively similar or slightly lower in terms of Jaccard index and precision, and its acceptable when comparing the models in regards of training time and the GPU necessary for training and also the number of epochs the model trained until convergence, our model was trained on a rtx2060 GPU and the model converged after 15 epochs only. Compared to SegNet which runs 33 epochs on a NVIDIA Titan GPU, and the dual GPU for ResNet and a K80 GPU for deeplabv3. For gated CNNs it took 230 epochs for the model to reach its best results and was trained on a NVIDIA DGX Station equipped with eight GPUs.

Table 2. State of the art for semantic segmentation comparison

Metrics	Accuracy	Jaccard	Precision
Our approach	0.99879	0.79054	0.80413
Seg-Net [18]	0.9927	0.6010	0.9463
Res-Net [20]	0.9938	0.7382	0.9684
DeepLabv3 [22]	NA	0.8132	NA
Gated-SCNN [25]	NA	0.8280	NA

As shown in Fig. 7, the segmentation is accurate and nearly identical to the ground truth mask, and thus the model can work in crowded and congested environment where there 6 people per square meter and can perform admirably in terms of the segmentation accuracy.

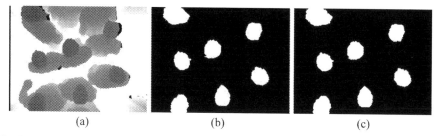

Fig. 7. Example results of our approach. (a) input image from TV-Heads dataset [6], (b) ground truth mask, (c) the predicted output

For counting the heads in the last step, we generated bounding boxes for the segmentation mask. After that we may simply use an image processing method to identify and count the contours of the segmented areas to count persons from the mask of the predicted segmentation. The scikit-image, region props, and find contours techniques were utilized. Then we can easily count the number of head which are labeled each with a number as illustrated in Fig. 8.

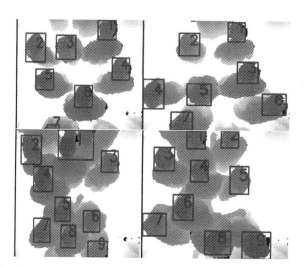

Fig. 8. An example of Head count results using TV-Heads dataset.

6 Conclusion and Future Work

Human detection and tracking in a retail environment with a high number of individuals present and continuous occlusion is a difficult but rewarding endeavor. This work introduces a model for semantic heads segmentation utilizing depth pictures collected from an RGB-D camera mounted in top-view mode. Our approach is based on CNN which shifts the entire technique from a feature and geometric based approach to entirely deep learning approach that utilizes a CNN model processing the same frame to accurately segment and count individuals even in crowded scenarios. Our method can learn a high-level representation of picture content while achieving excellent accuracy and recall. For future work we will collect a larger and more complex dataset in other retail and supermarket environment to build a more challenging test environment and integrate more complex architectures to build a better model and be able to improve performance for real time application.

References

1. Paolanti, M., Liciotti, D., Pietrini, R., Mancini, A., Frontoni, E.: Modelling and forecasting customer navigation in intelligent retail environments. J. Intell. Rob. Syst. **91**(2), 165–180 (2017). https://doi.org/10.1007/s10846-017-0674-7

2. Liu, J., Liu, Y., Zhang, G., Zhu, P., Chen, Y.Q.: Detecting and tracking people in real time with RGB-D camera. Pattern Recogn. Lett. **53**, 16–23 (2015). https://doi.org/10.1016/j.patrec.2014.09.013

3. Liang, B., Zheng, L.: A survey on human action recognition using depth sensors. In: 2015 International Conference on Digital Image Computing: Techniques and Applications (DICTA), Adelaide, Australia, pp. 1–8, November 2015. https://doi.org/10.1109/DICTA.2015.7371223

4. Paolanti, M., Sturari, M., Mancini, A., Zingaretti, P., Frontoni, E.: Mobile robot for retail surveying and inventory using visual and textual analysis of monocular pictures based on deep learning. In: 2017 European Conference on Mobile Robots (ECMR), Paris, pp. 1–6, September 2017. https://doi.org/10.1109/ECMR.2017.8098666

5. Liciotti, D., Paolanti, M., Frontoni, E., Zingaretti, P.: People detection and tracking from an RGB-D camera in top-view configuration: review of challenges and applications. In: Battiato, S., Farinella, G.M., Leo, M., Gallo, G. (eds.) New Trends in Image Analysis and Processing – ICIAP 2017. LNCS, vol. 10590, pp. 207–218. Springer, Cham (2017). https://doi.org/10.1007/978-3-319-70742-6_20

6. Liciotti, D.: TVHeads (Top-View Heads) Dataset, vol. 1, January 2018. https://doi.org/10.17632/nz4hy7yrps.1

7. Akrout, B.: A new structure of decision tree based on oriented edges gradient map for circles detection and the analysis of nano-particles. Micron **145**, 103055 (2021). https://doi.org/10.1016/j.micron.2021.103055

8. Akrout, B., Mahdi, W.: A novel approach for driver fatigue detection based on visual characteristics analysis. J. Ambient Intell. Hum. Comput. 1–26 (2021). https://doi.org/10.1007/s12652-021-03311-9

9. Bondi, E., Seidenari, L., Bagdanov, A.D., Del Bimbo, A.: Real-time people counting from depth imagery of crowded environments. In: 2014 11th IEEE International Conference on Advanced Video and Signal Based Surveillance (AVSS), Seoul, South Korea, pp. 337–342, August 2014. https://doi.org/10.1109/AVSS.2014.6918691

10. Del Pizzo, L., Foggia, P., Greco, A., Percannella, G., Vento, M.: Counting people by RGB or depth overhead cameras. Pattern Recogn. Lett. **81**, 41–50 (2016). https://doi.org/10.1016/j.patrec.2016.05.033

11. Liciotti, D., Paolanti, M., Pietrini, R., Frontoni, E., Zingaretti, P.: Convolutional networks for semantic heads segmentation using top-view depth data in crowded environment. In: 2018 24th International Conference on Pattern Recognition (ICPR), Beijing, pp. 1384–1389, August 2018. https://doi.org/10.1109/ICPR.2018.8545397

12. Mrazovac, B., Bjelica, M.Z., Kukolj, D., Todorovi, B.M.: A human detection method for residential smart energy systems based on Zigbee RSSI changes. IEEE Trans. Consum. Electron. **58**(3), 6 (2012)

13. Garcia, J., Gardel, A., Bravo, I., Lazaro, J.L., Martinez, M., Rodriguez, D.: Directional people counter based on head tracking. IEEE Trans. Ind. Electron. **60**(9), 3991–4000 (2013). https://doi.org/10.1109/TIE.2012.2206330

14. Wang, C., Zhang, H., Yang, L., Liu, S., Cao, X.: Deep people counting in extremely dense crowds. In: Proceedings of the 23rd ACM International Conference on Multimedia, Brisbane, Australia, pp. 1299–1302, October 2015. https://doi.org/10.1145/2733373.2806337

15. Fu, M., Xu, P., Li, X., Liu, Q., Ye, M., Zhu, C.: Fast crowd density estimation with convolutional neural networks. Eng. Appl. Artif. Intell. **43**, 81–88 (2015). https://doi.org/10.1016/j.engappai.2015.04.006

16. Zhang, C., Li, H., Wang, X., Yang, X.: Cross-scene crowd counting via deep convolutional neural networks. In: 2015 IEEE Conference on Computer Vision and Pattern Recognition (CVPR), Boston, MA, USA, pp. 833–841, June 2015. https://doi.org/10.1109/CVPR.2015.7298684

17. Noh, H., Hong, S., Han, B.: Learning deconvolution network for semantic segmentation. In: 2015 IEEE International Conference on Computer Vision (ICCV), Santiago, Chile, pp. 1520–1528, December 2015. https://doi.org/10.1109/ICCV.2015.178

18. Badrinarayanan, V., Kendall, A., Cipolla, R.: SegNet: a deep convolutional encoder-decoder architecture for image segmentation, October 2016. arXiv:1511.00561, http://arxiv.org/abs/1511.00561. Accessed 01 Apr 2021

19. Simonyan, K., Zisserman, A.: Very deep convolutional networks for large-scale image recognition, April 2015. arXiv:1409.1556, http://arxiv.org/abs/1409.1556. Accessed 02 Apr 2021

20. He, K., Zhang, X., Ren, S., Sun, J.: Deep residual learning for image recognition. In: 2016 IEEE Conference on Computer Vision and Pattern Recognition (CVPR), Las Vegas, NV, USA, pp. 770–778, June 2016. https://doi.org/10.1109/CVPR.2016.90

21. Chen, L.-C., Zhu, Y., Papandreou, G., Schroff, F., Adam, H.: Encoder-decoder with atrous separable convolution for semantic image segmentation, August 2018. arXiv:1802.02611, http://arxiv.org/abs/1802.02611. Accessed 26 Jan 2022

22. Chen, L.-C., Papandreou, G., Schroff, F., Adam, H.: Rethinking atrous convolution for semantic image segmentation, December 2017. arXiv:1706.05587, http://arxiv.org/abs/1706.05587. Accessed 22 Sep 2021

23. Shami, M.B., Maqbool, S., Sajid, H., Ayaz, Y., Cheung, S.-C.S.: People counting in dense crowd images using sparse head detections. IEEE Trans. Circ. Syst. Video Technol. **29**(9), 2627–2636 (2019). https://doi.org/10.1109/TCSVT.2018.2803115

24. Nogueira, V., Oliveira, H., Augusto Silva, J., Vieira, T., Oliveira, K.: RetailNet: a deep learning approach for people counting and hot spots detection in retail stores. In: 2019 32nd SIBGRAPI Conference on Graphics, Patterns and Images (SIBGRAPI), Rio de Janeiro, Brazil, pp. 155–162, October 2019. https://doi.org/10.1109/SIBGRAPI.2019.00029

25. Takikawa, T., Acuna, D., Jampani, V., Fidler, S.: Gated-SCNN: gated shape CNNs for semantic segmentation, July 2019. arXiv:1907.05740, http://arxiv.org/abs/1907.05740. Accessed 06 Dec 2021

26. Chen, L.-C., Papandreou, G., Kokkinos, I., Murphy, K., Yuille, A.L.: DeepLab: semantic image segmentation with deep convolutional nets, atrous convolution, and fully connected CRFs, May 2017. arXiv:1606.00915, http://arxiv.org/abs/1606.00915. Accessed 26 Jan 2022

27. Jaccard, P.: Étude comparative de la distribution florale dans une portion des Alpes et du Jura (1901). https://doi.org/10.5169/SEALS-266450

28. Akrout, B., Fakhfakh, S.: Three-dimensional head-pose estimation for smart Iris recognition from a calibrated camera. Math. Prob. Eng. **2020** (2020). https://doi.org/10.1155/2020/9830672

29. Mahdi, W., Akrout, B., Alroobaea, R., Alsufyani, A.: Automated drowsiness detection through facial features analysis. Computación y Sistemas **23**, 511–521 (2019). https://doi.org/10.13053/cys-23-2-3013

Transfer Learning for the Classification of Small-Cell and Non-small-Cell Lung Cancer

Mohamed Gasmi[1]([⊠]), Makhlouf Derdour[2], and Abdelatif Gahmous[3]

[1] Department of Science and Technology, LAMIS Laboratory Larbi Tebessi University, Tebessa, Algeria
Mohamed.gasmi@univ-tebessa.dz
[2] Department of Computer Science, Larbi Ben Mhidi University, Oum El Bouaghi, Algeria
[3] Department of Computer Science, Larbi Tebessi University, Tebessa, Algeria

Abstract. Lung cancer is a disease caused by abnormal lung cell growth. The number of people of all ages and sexes with lung tumors is constantly increasing. Classical classification of lung tumors can be sometimes misleading and time-consuming. Consequently, automated diagnosis is becoming a necessity to avoid the occurrence of errors and increase the survival rate of patients with lung tumors. However, deep learning and transfer learning are effective tools for the early detection and classification of lung tumors on the basis of anatomopathological slides of the lung. This work presents a Deep learning/Transfer learning implementation for lung tumor classification using a six-class database (LUAD, LUSC, SCLC, PTB, OP, NL). In order to reach the average accuracy of 98.9%, the implementation was trained using three convolutional neural network models: VGG19, ResNet50, and InceptionV3.

Keywords: Deep learning · Transfer learning · CNN · Lung cancer · Slide · Classification

1 Introduction

According to the American Cancer Society (ACS) and the International Agency for Research on Cancer's publication "Global Cancer Statistics 2020." Lung cancer remained the leading cause of cancer death in 2020, with an anticipated 1.8 million fatalities (18% of all cancer deaths) (IARC). According to the mentioned analysis, the world will witness a significant raise in cancer cases of about 28.4 million additional cases by 2040, which is a 47% increase from 2020.

Experts are warning from the ramifications of rising lung cancer cases, which, if left uncontrolled, might overwhelm health-care systems. The global fight against lung cancer entails preventing it through establishing efficient measures, as well as early and precise diagnosis in all countries, especially among patients in transition.

The diagnosis, which takes a long time and often results in errors, is one of the key issues doctors confront when dealing with this disease. This will have a direct impact on

© Springer Nature Switzerland AG 2022
A. Bennour et al. (Eds.): ISPR 2022, CCIS 1589, pp. 341–348, 2022.
https://doi.org/10.1007/978-3-031-08277-1_28

therapeutic management, putting patients' lives in danger. Meanwhile, artificial intelligence had established itself in the medical field with success in the detection and classification of tumors. Whereas, deep learning based on convolutional neural networks is one of the AI techniques that had recently been utilized to improve diagnosis.

In order to determine the kind, nature, and stage of the malignancy in the field of oncology, an anatomopathological investigation is required following the radiographic discovery of pulmonary nodules. The diagnosis is based on a microscopic examination of lung anatomopathological slides. This study is crucial and is considered an outstanding alternative to diagnosing lung tumors.

By extracting information from pictures acquired by electron microscopes, deep learning, namely the convolutional neural network (CNN), has shown to be particularly effective for the classification of lung cancers. Deep learning, in fact, offers a lot of potential for analyzing medical imagery. That is why we use transfer learning to assist pathologists in diagnosing tumors using CNN-based pathology classification in this study.

The remainder of this paper is arranged as follows: Sect. 2 introduces some concepts of lung cancer. Section 3 present recent related works. Methodologies are detailed in Sect. 4. The methodology of this approach was explained and contextualized. In Sect. 5 results and evaluation are illustrated. Finally, in Sect. 6, we reach a conclusion.

2 Lung Cancer

Lung cancers are malignant tumors that develop in the bronchial structures and/or the lung parenchyma in rare cases. They might be either primary or secondary in nature [2]. Also, Anatomopathology is used to determine the certainty of bronchopulmonary cancers.

There are two histological categories that make up primary lung cancer:

- NSCLC, which includes adenocarcinoma, undifferentiated carcinoma, squamous cell carcinoma, and more rarely sarcomatoid or large cell carcinoma,
- Neuroendocrine tumors, which includes small cell bronchial cancer (SCC), large cell neuroendocrine carcinoma, typical, and atypical carcinoid tumors (3).

The most frequent histological category (80–85% of PBCs) is NSCLC (4).

Histological diagnosis is based not only on morphological characteristics, but also on immunohistochemical criteria (IHC).

3 Related Works

There are numerous papers in the literature that use deep learning to classify lung cancer anatomopathologically. As indicated in Table 1, these works are based on daily or weekly supervised learning through convolutional neural network (CNN) models. Tools for visualizing, annotating, and exploring anapath slides have been developed. Notably, QuPath [5] by Bankhead for tumor detection, biomarker assessment, batch processing, and scripting is one of the most popular tools for visualizing, annotating, and studying anapath slides. DeepFocus [6] by Senaras is similarly interested in detecting out-of-focus regions in WSIs. Wang [7] created ConvPath for Cell Type Classification and TME Analysis. Janowczyk's HistQC [8] is a tool for digitizing tissue slides, and Zheng's ACD Model [9] is a color normalization tool for H&E-stained WSIs. Furthermore, several major research have been conducted to investigate the relationship between molecular genotypes and morphological genotypes [10, 11]. However, previous breakthroughs were restricted to "non-small cell lung carcinoma," a single cohort, or a small number of cases, and there are still more paths to clinical impact.

Additionally, several major researches have been conducted to investigate the relationship between molecular genotypes and morphological genotypes [10, 11]. However, previous breakthroughs were restricted to "non-small cell lung carcinoma," a single cohort, or a small number of cases, and there are still more paths to clinical impact.

Table 1. Recent related work

Year	Research	Title	Objective
2018	Coudray et al. [10]	Classification and mutation prediction from non-small cell lung cancer histopathology images using deep learning	3 outputs LUAD, LUSC and NL classification; With prediction of (STK11, EGFR, FAT1, SETBP1, KRAS and TP53)
2019	Gertych et al. [12]	Convolutional neural networks can accurately distinguish four histologic growth patterns of lung adenocarcinoma in digital slides	5 Histological subclassification of lung adenocarcinoma
2019	Wei et al. [13]	Pathologist-level classification of histologic patterns on resected lung adenocarcinoma slides with deep neural networks	6 kind of Histological subclassification of lung adenocarcinoma
2020	Yu et al. [11]	Classifying non-small cell lung cancer types and transcriptomic subtypes using convolutional neural networks	Identification of gene expression subtypes of non-small cell lung carcinoma
2020	Kriegsmann et al. [14]	Deep Learning for the Classification of Small-Cell and Non-Small-Cell Lung Cancer	Classification model for outputs (LUAD, LUSC, SCLC and NL)
2021	Huan Yang et al. [15]	Deep learning-based six-type classifier for lung cancer and mimics from histopathological whole slide images: a retrospective study	Developed a deep learning-based six-type classifier for histopathological WSI classification

4   Method

Our work begins with the most important task, which is to prepare the dataset that contains several classes. We followed image segmentation of questionable regions, feature extraction, and classification to utilize three CNN models for learning to perform image classification and lung tumor detection from digitized slides.

4.1   Dataset

The dataset used in our work is composed of 741 slides of lung tissue processed with hematoxylin and eosin for 6 diagnostic classes (with 298 slides for LUAD, 111 for LUSC, 103 for SCLC, 64 for PTB, 66 for OP, or 99 for NL). Each of the slides in the dataset has a type of lesion indicating a diagnostic class. As a result, the dataset included immunohistochemistry and histochemical staining slides that were scanned with a KF-PRO-005-EX electron microscope at an equivalent zoom of 40 (0.25 μm per pixel). The lung tumor classification criteria of the World Health Organization (WHO) were used to classify this dataset [16] Fig. 1.

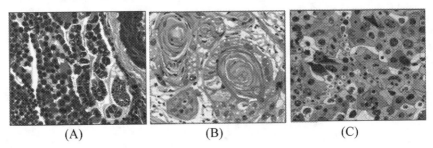

(A)   (B)   (C)

Fig. 1.   Lung cancer types. (A) LUAD. (B) LUSC. (C) SCLC.

4.2   Data Augmentation

By applying image transformations in terms of orientation, size, zoom, and other factors, numerous strategies for data augmentation can be used to generate new samples from existing ones. It is worth noting that one of the most effective ways to improve the accuracy of deep learning algorithms is to use data augmentation. Indeed, this enhancement can greatly expand the variety of data available for model training and can also be useful when working with an unbalanced dataset. The ImageDataGenerator class technique of the Keras library was used to enhance the number of pathological images of lung tumors in this study. This class contains a variety of quick and simple augmentation techniques including normalization, rotation, shift, flip, picture alteration, and so on.

4.3   Proposed Approach

In our experiments, we divided our work into two steps.: the first one is using existing architectures like VGG, ResNet, and Inception (trained with the ImageNet dataset with more than one million images) by modifying just the last layer so that the outputs are equivalent to the number of lung tumor classes and by freezing all the other layers while the second step is using transfer learning to re-train the models used in the first step by unfreezing all the layers of the models.

Step 1. Before starting to employ transfer learning techniques on the pre-trained model (by removing or adding new layers, or by training or fixing other layers) the model must be trained using the new database.

VGG19: VGG is a convolutional neural network proposed by K. Simonyan and A. Zisserman of Oxford University and gained notoriety by winning the ImageNet Large Scale Visual Recognition Challenge (ILSVRC) in 2014. The model achieved an accuracy of 92.7% on Imagenet, which is one of the highest scores achieved. It marked an improvement over previous models by proposing smaller convolution kernels (3 × 3) in the convolution layers than had been done previously. The model was trained over weeks using state-of-the-art graphics cards [17].

ResNet: Residual Network (ResNet) is one of the famous deep learning models introduced by Shaoqing Ren, Kaiming Il, Jian Sun, and Xiangyu Zhang. Their paper was titled "Deep Residual Learning for Image Recognition." In 2015, The ResNet [18] model is one of the most popular and successful deep learning models to date.

Inception: Inception is a complex DNN which was designed and built by Google to improve the performance in terms of speed and accuracy. Its evolution has led to the creation of several versions of the network. The Inception architecture [19] aims to reduce the resource consumption of Deep Convolutional Neural Networks (DCNN), which is common for Network in Network models.

Firstly, we have to load the model each time with the help of the Keras "load model" class, then we launch the learning task with a single modification of the output layer using stochastic gradient descent as an optimization algorithm to correct the predictions and guide the network towards accurate weights.

Step 2. In the second step, we used transfer learning, which allows us to reuse the pre-trained model on a large dataset and adjust its parameters to better fit our dataset.

We ran several types of experiments to see if employing Transfer learning makes the pre-trained network more efficient for our dataset:

- Fix the weights of all layers of the pre-trained model, and train the last layer (dense_)
- Fix the weights of all the top layers of the pre-trained model, and replace the last two layers of the model (dense_2, flatten 2) by new trainable layers.
- Fix a set of surface layers, and unfreeze the rest of the model.

5   Results and Evaluation

We used three different neural networks on the dataset (six classes) to perform pathology slide classification and lung tumor detection. In this section, we will illustrate the various outcomes of learning three models (VGG19, ResNet50, and InceptionV3). The evaluation of each model will be done by different metrics, as well as a comparison between the different results.

The evaluation metrics used are:

– Accuracy $= \frac{number\ of\ correct\ predictions}{total\ number\ of\ predictions}$
– precision $= \frac{TP}{TP+FP}$
– Recall $= \frac{TP}{TP+FN}$
– F1-score $= 2 * \frac{precision*Recall}{Precision+Recall}$

In our work, we used the pre-trained models VGG19, ResNet50, and Inception V3, which are characterized by a very high accuracy rate and a very acceptable number of parameters despite the number of layers used. Our work consists of freezing and training the layers of the models, as well as removing and adding layers in order to classify our dataset into (LUAD, LUSC, SCLC, PTB, OP, and NL) classes. The model parameters were initialized with pre-trained weights optimized for the ImageNet dataset with a high accuracy rate.

The first step is to freeze all layers of the three models so that the "gradient descent" does not modify them when learning the new model and, most importantly, to train only the last fully connected layer. We launched the training with several values of the batch-size and a different number of epochs. Table 2 shows the collected results that indicate that despite the Resnet model's had the best results, they were not satisfactory when compared to previous works.

Table 2. Results after training last fully connected layer

Model	Accuracy	Precision	Recall	F1-score
VGG19	0.524	0.408	0.431	0.415
ResNet50	0.839	0.873	0.792	0.834
Inception V3	0.687	0.761	0.679	0.717

After a number of trainings iterations, we obtained the following results: (Table 3).

Table 3. Results after training all layers

Model	Accuracy	Precision	Recall	F1-score
VGG19	0.811	0.829	0.869	0.850
ResNet50	0.989	0.985	0.953	0.968
Inception V3	0.856	0.844	0.917	0.879

The best rate was obtained in the Resnet, which had an accuracy rate of 98.9%, precision of 98.5%, recall of 95.3%, and f1-score with a rate of 96.8%, as shown in the table. This is the best outcome of the group's previous efforts with this dataset. When comparing the accuracy of this work to the accuracy of Huan Yang's paper published in 2021 under the title "Deep learning-based six-type classifier for lung cancer and mimics from histopathological whole slide images: a retrospective study," our work accuracy is 98.9%, while Huan Yang's had 98.6%.

6 Conclusion

The challenge we faced was that obtaining classification results necessitated a big amount of data (pictures). To overcome the shortage of training data, we used the "data augmentation" and transfer learning techniques to produce a classification model for anapaths slides of lung cancer tissues. The obtained model is created from a Resnet model that has achieved better prediction performance and is pre-trained on a large dataset of images. The new model is in turn re-trained on our histopathological image dataset. Results are very satisfactory, whether it is on the accuracy rate or the precision rate, as well as the recall rate and the f1-score, where we reached a rate of 98.9%.

References

1. Sung, H., et al.: Global cancer statistics 2020: GLOBOCAN estimates of incidence and mortality worldwide for 36 cancers in 185 countries. CA Cancer J. Clin. (2021). https://doi.org/10.3322/caac.21660
2. Barlesi, F., Mazieres, J., Merlio, J.-P., Debieuvre, D., Mosser, J., Lena, H., et al.: Routine molecular profiling of patients with advanced non-small-cell lung cancer: results of a 1-year nationwide programme of the French Cooperative Thoracic Intergroup (IFCT). Lancet **387**(10026), 1415–1426 (2016)
3. Travis, W.D., Brambilla, E., Nicholson, A.G., Yatabe, Y., Austin, J.H.M., Beasley, M.B.: The 2015 World Health Organization classification of lung tumors. J. Thorac. Oncol. **10**(9), 1243–1260 (2015)
4. Travis, W.D., Colby, T.V., Corrin, B., Shimosato, Y., Brambilla, E., Sobbin, L.H., et al.: Histological Typing of Lung and Pleural Tumours. Springer, Berlin (1999)
5. Bankhead, P., Loughrey, M.B., Fernández, J.A., Dombrowski, Y., McArt, D.G., Dunne, P.D., et al.: QuPath: open source software for digital pathology image analysis. Sci. Rep. **7**, 16878 (2017)
6. Senaras, C., Niazi, M.K.K., Lozanski, G., Gurcan, M.N.: DeepFocus: detection of out-of-focus regions in whole slide digital images using deep learning. PLoS ONE **13**, e205387 (2018)
7. Wang, S., Wang, T., Yang, L., Yang, D.M., Fujimoto, J., Yi, F., et al.: ConvPath: a software tool for lung adenocarcinoma digital pathological image analysis aided by a convolutional neural network. EBioMed. **50**, 103–110 (2019)
8. Janowczyk, A., Zuo, R., Gilmore, H., Feldman, M., Madabhushi, A.: Histoqc: an open-source quality control tool for digital pathology slides. JCO Clin. Cancer Inform. **3**, 1–7 (2019)
9. Zheng, Y., Jiang, Z., Zhang, H., Xie, F., Shi, J., Xue, C.: Adaptive color deconvolution for histological WSI normalization. Comput. Methods Prog. Biomed. **170**, 107–120 (2019)
10. Coudray, N., Ocampo, P.S., Sakellaropoulos, T., Narula, N., Snuderl, M., Fenyö, D., et al.: Classification and mutation prediction from non-small cell lung cancer histopathology images using deep learning. Nat. Med. **24**, 1559–1567 (2018)

11. Yu, K.H., Wang, F., Berry, G.J., Ré, C., Altman, R.B., Snyder, M., et al.: Classifying non-small cell lung cancer types and transcriptomic subtypes using convolutional neural networks. J. Am. Med. Inform. Assoc. **27**, 757–769 (2020)

12. Gertych, A., Swiderska-Chadaj, Z., Ma, Z., Ing, N., Markiewicz, T., Cierniak, S., et al.: Convolutional neural networks can accurately distinguish four histologic growth patterns of lung adenocarcinoma in digital slides. Sci. Rep. **9**, 1483 (2019)

13. Wei, J.W., Tafe, L.J., Linnik, Y.A., Vaickus, L.J., Tomita, N., Hassanpour, S.: Pathologist-level classification of histologic patterns on resected lung adenocarcinoma slides with deep neural networks. Sci. Rep. **9**, 3358 (2019)

14. Kriegsmann, M., Haag, C., Weis, C.A., Steinbuss, G., Warth, A., Zgorzelski, C., et al.: Deep learning for the classification of small-cell and non-small-cell lung cancer. Cancers **12**, 1604 (2020)

15. Yang, H., Chen, L., Cheng, Z., et al.: Deep learning-based six-type classifier for lung cancer and mimics from histopathological whole slide images: a retrospective study. BMC Med. **19**, 80 (2021)

16. Travis, W.D.: The 2015 WHO classification of lung tumors. Pathologe **35**(2), 188 (2014). https://doi.org/10.1007/s00292-014-1974-3

17. Simonyan, K., Zisserman, A.: Very deep convolutional networks for large-scale image recognition. In: Proceedings of the IEEE Conference on Computer Vision and Pattern Recognition (2015)

18. He, K., Zhang, X., Ren, S., Sun, J.: Deep residual learning for image recognition. In: Proceedings of the IEEE Conference on Computer Vision and Pattern Recognition (2015)

19. Szegedy, C., Liu, W., Jia, Y., et al.: Going deeper with convolutions. In: Proceedings of the IEEE Conference on Computer Vision and Pattern Recognition, pp. 1–9 (2015)

Attentional Conditional Generative Adversarial Network for Ambient Occlusion Approximation

Fayçal Abbas[1]([⊠]), Mehdi Malah[2], and Mohamed Chaouki Babahenini[3]

[1] LESIA Laboratory, Computer Science Department,
University of Abbes Laghrour Khenchela, Khenchela, Algeria
abbas_faycal@univ-khenchela.dz

[2] ICOSI Laboratory, Computer Science Department,
University of Abbes Laghrour Khenchela, Khenchela, Algeria
malah.mehdi@univ-khenchela.dz

[3] LESIA Laboratory, Computer Science Department,
University of Mohamed Khider Biskra, Biskra, Algeria

Abstract. Ambient occlusion is a method that increases the realism of computer generated images by estimating the reflected illumination in areas where light fails to illuminate them due to occlusions imposed by surrounding objects. In this paper, we introduce a new approach able to generate an approximation of the ambient occlusion, thus estimating the location of soft shadows. Our approach is based on using a conditional generative adversarial network with an attention mechanism to perform a space translation from the input data to the output data space by enforcing the conditioning with an attention mechanism. Our attention module is integrated into the generator architecture and the discriminator to allow the neural network to pay more attention to relevant areas to estimate the location of soft shadows and generate a good approximation of the ambient occlusion. Our method generates images with a satisfactory similarity with the reference method and does not require any pre-processing of the generated image, so it does not perform any computation in the three-dimensional space of the 3D scene.

Keywords: Ambient occlusion · Generative adversarial network · Attention mechanism

1 Introduction

The demand for realistic 3D scenes in video games continues to grow with the evolution of GPUs. Producing photo-realistic images encourages programmers to simulate direct and indirect light diffusion using global illumination algorithms. The indirect illumination component increases the realism of rendered scenes. On the other hand, the computation of the indirect illumination component dramatically reduces the performance of the rendering, especially for complex scenes.

© Springer Nature Switzerland AG 2022
A. Bennour et al. (Eds.): ISPR 2022, CCIS 1589, pp. 349–361, 2022.
https://doi.org/10.1007/978-3-031-08277-1_29

Ambient occlusion is a widespread technique in the field of computer graphics that offers an approximate solution for the calculation of indirect illumination indeed the effects of ambient illumination increase the realism of the synthesized images are principle consists in estimating the quantity of light occulted by the objects around a point and that by adding soft shadows. Different techniques, in particular Ray tracing AO, have been introduced [1] and offer good results in terms of realism and precision, but with a considerable execution time, so they do not allow dynamic scenes to be rendered. In order to remedy this problem, another generation of techniques [2–4] whose principle is to perform these calculations in the screen space based on the scene data contained in the G-Buffer. The latter offers a real-time solution; however, they suffer from artifacts, noise, and false occlusion limitations. Recent models whose architecture is based on neural networks have appeared indeed generative neural networks offer good results in terms of realism and accuracy, especially in different areas such as image synthesis, computer vision, medical imaging. In this paper, we propose an approach able to generate an approximation of the ambient occlusion, thus estimating the location of soft shadows. Our approach is based on using a conditional generative adversarial network with an attention mechanism to perform a space translation from the input data to the output data space by enforcing the conditioning with a spatial attention module. Our attention module is integrated into the architecture of the generator and the discriminator to allow the neural network to focus on relevant areas. The images generated by our method are of satisfactory quality compared to reference images (see Fig. 1). Our contribution can be summarized as follows:

- We introduce a new approach based on generative neural networks with an attention mechanism for approximating ambient occlusion.
- We propose a spatial attention mechanism in the generator and discriminator that allows our model to pay more attention to relevant areas to estimate the location of soft shadows.
- Creation of a large dataset composed of synthetic images to train and validate the model.
- We present a comparison of our approach to existing methods.

Fig. 1. Complex scene with ambient occlusion generated by our approach. The left image represents RGB map without AO, the middle image represents the reference image, the rightimage represents our result.

2   Related Works

Improvements in graphics processors mark the birth of a new generation of techniques to calculate the amount of ambient illumination in the screen space. For example, the SSAO (Screen Space Ambient Occlusion) method [2] has been proposed to approximate the ambient occlusion in real-time. This method appeared for the first time in the video game Crysis. Its principle is to evaluate the occlusion in the screen space by using the information in the depth buffer to determine the distance between the point of view and the scene. Several variants are proposed around this idea [5, 6]. [7] present a new HBAO (Horizon Based Ambient Occlusion) approach to solve the problem of noise appearing around the pixel sampled by the SSAO method. Its principle is to approximate the ambient occlusion by evaluating the horizon angle. The algorithm uses the depth buffer and the normal vector to determine the free angle. Indeed, the HBAO offers promising results in terms of realism; however, it requires computational resources to render complex and dynamic scenes. Other approaches propose an analytical solution by reformulating the directional ambient occultation integration formula [8] into a volumetric formula that offers efficient processing on GPU. The latter allows rendering scenes in real-time. An extension based on the improvement and optimization of the previous method VAO++ has been introduced by [9] by adopting adaptive sampling. This method offers good results in terms of rendering quality and performance.

Recent methods are based on neural networks to build new models whose principle is to perform learning on the data. These models produce photorealistic images [10–12]. [13] present an approach based on a neural network to approximate the ambient occlusion. The latter takes as input both the depth and the depth around a pixel and, as output, predicts the ambient occlusion around this pixel. [14] propose a model whose principle is to deduce the appearance from the attributes by performing learning on a large data set of images. The architecture of the model is based on convolutional neural networks. Indeed, the model can reproduce the effect of ambient occlusion in the screen space as well as other effects such as blur, indirect lighting, light diffusion, depth-of-field in a reduced time [15] using a multi-layer perceptron to better capture the non-linearity characterizing the values of the ambient occlusion, in fact, the model proceeds in two steps. A learning step on the dataset and a rendering step. Using a neural network implemented through a shader allows a calculation of the ambient occultation in real-time. In [16] the case of the RGB image, a generative neural network is used to generate an approximation of the ambient occultation. The model produces good results in terms of accuracy and performance.

3   Preliminaries

3.1   Adversarial Neural Network

Our solution uses a generative neural network [17] composed of a generator and a discriminator. Indeed, these two are trained in competition. The generator will have as a task to generate a synthetic image as realistic as the reference images in order to deceive the discriminator. On the other hand, the discriminator has a task to carry out a classification of the input images in order to determine if the input image has a satisfactory similarity compared to the training images, in this case, this image is classified as real, on the contrary case the image is classified as a dummy. During the learning stage, each neural network (discriminator or generator) tries to maximize its gain. The objective function min-max GAN is given by the following equation:

$$min_G mix_D V(D, G) = E_{x \sim P_{data}(x)} [log D(x|y)] + E_{z \sim P_z(z)} [log(1 - D(G(z|y)))]$$
(1)

where G is the generator network, while D is the discriminator network. $G(z|y)$ represents the distribution as a function of z and y. z is a noise distribution. $log D(x|y)$ is the discriminator's loss. $log(1 - D(G(z|y)))$ is the generator's loss.

3.2   Attention Mechanism

Attention mechanisms have played an important role in the last three years to revolutionize the state of the art of deep learning in different fields such as machine translation, image synthesis, computer vision. The first use of attention mechanisms was in natural language processing (NLP) by [18]. The idea of the authors is to endow the decoder with the ability to focus its attention on specific words during each temporal step. [19] uses an attention mechanism to build a model able to generate a caption for an image. Its principle consists in using two neural networks: a convolutional network CNN and a recurrent network RNN. The CNN generates feature maps while the RNN generates the legend based on the relevant part of the image. Some works based on generative neural networks have taken advantage of integrating the attention mechanism to generate high-quality images [20–22]. This mechanism allows to model local and global features and to model long dependencies between feature maps.

4   Proposed Method

4.1   Architecture

The Generator. Our generator is an auto-encoder (see Fig. 2). Its task is to generate samples of ambient occultation images whose distribution tends to the distribution of reference images. Its architecture is based on convolution layers whose number is seven layers. A normalization layer follows each layer by batch and LeakyRelu. We designed a new architecture of the generator based on an attention mechanism. We introduce an attention layer in the middle between the encoder and the decoder in order to improve the performance of the generator and allow the generator to focus on the relevant areas of the image. The generator takes as input three images an RGB image without AO, Normal map and depth map. The size of the input images is $256 \times 256 \times 9$. Connections are used to link the encoder and the decoder layers to recover the spatial resolution. The output of the generator is an image of size 256×256 pixels.

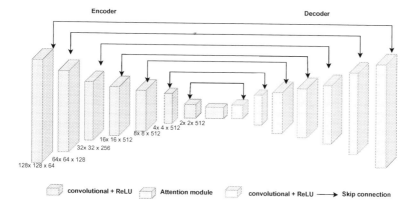

Fig. 2. Architecture of the generator.

The Discriminator. The discriminator is illustrated in Fig. 3 Based on the convolutional architecture. In this paper, we introduce a spatial attention mechanism in the discriminator. Indeed our idea is to insert an attention layer before the last output layer. The discriminator comprises seven convolution layers, where each block is composed of a convolution layer followed by a normalization and ReLU batch. The discriminator takes as input the set of input images and an image generated by the generator or a reference image. In fact, the output of the discriminator is a binary classification with a sigmoid cost function.

4.2   Attention Mechanism for Ambient Occlusion

In our architecture, we have proposed introducing an attention mechanism in the generator and the discriminator to obtain a dynamic feature extraction. Indeed the network starts by focusing on local features, and as the data passes through the network, our architecture will have the ability to focus on global features, allowing the network to focus on relevant parts difficult to reach by a simple architecture. Our attention module illustrated in Fig. 4 is based on the attention formula inspired by the work [20]. First, we generate three layers of convolutions Queries (q), keys (k), and values (v) after a multiplication operation between the generated weights (1×1 convolution) matrices and the input feature map $Input_f$ as illustrated in the following formula:

$Q = Input_f * w_q$ in a similar manner $K = Input_f * w_k$ and $V = Input_f * w_v$
The attentional feature maps is calculated by the following formula:

$$Att = softmax(Q.K^T) \qquad (2)$$

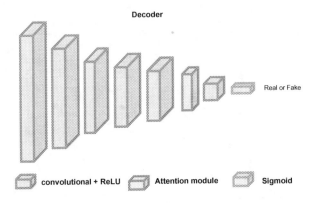

Fig. 3. Architecture of the discriminator.

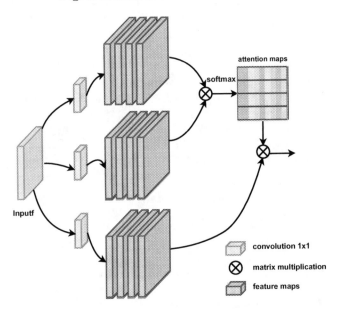

Fig. 4. The attention module.

$Q.k$ has the objective to locate the important regions of the image, where it compares the key of all the regions with the query of a well-defined position of the feature map. In other words, we try to measure the similarity between each query and the set of keys for each feature. Then we use the softmax function to convert these similarity values into weights between 0 and 1. These weights are used to generate the attention map by multiplying their contents with V and performing multiplication by the element of the value.

Where the final formula is:

$$g_i = \gamma(Att)V + x_i \tag{3}$$

The factor γ is initialized to 0 is as the network learns. This value will allow the network to focus not only on local features but also on global features, which increases the performance of our architecture Fig. 5.

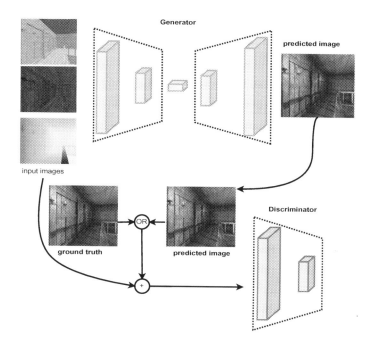

Fig. 5. Overview of the architecture of our approach.

4.3 Loss Function

In order to generate images that resemble the input images, The similarity index has been used in several works [23,24]. Whose goal is to ensure an efficient reconstruction between the input and output spaces. We introduce the structural similarity index SSIM [25] in the formula of the cost function in order to minimize the error between the generated image and the reference image to have a satisfactory structural similarity with the latter. The following formula defines the similarity index:

$$SSIM = \frac{2(\mu_x\mu_y + C_1)(\sigma_{xy} + C_2)}{(\mu_x^2 + \mu_y^2 + C_1)(\mu_x^2 + \mu_y^2 + C_2)} \tag{4}$$

where x, y: are patches (window) of the image. μ_x, μ_y correspond to the average of the patch x and y respectively. μ_x^2, μ_y^2: the variance of the patch x and y respectively. σ_{xy} is the covariance of x and y. $C1$, $C2$: Are constants.

Our final goal is given by the following formula:

$$min_G mix_D V(D,G) = l_{GAN}(G,D) + \beta l_{ssim}(I_{reference}, I_{predict}) \qquad (5)$$

5   Experiments

In this section, we present results obtained by our model as well as an evaluation of our model through a quantitative and qualitative comparison with the state-of-the-art methods. In order to show the efficiency of our generative model with an attention module for the approximation of ambient occlusion and the estimation of soft shadow locations for complex 3D scenes. Indeed our algorithm was implemented in TensorFlow and tested on an i5 processor and an Nvidia gtx 1060ti graphics card.

5.1   Data Preparation

The generation of the dataset images was performed using the Unity rendering engine [27]. For each viewpoint position, we retrieve three image depth maps, normal map, RGB image without AO, and RGB with AO. Indeed we have created two datasets, the first one to train our model on reference images with AO only without texture and the second one with AO with texture. We used 20 scenes for training and five scenes for validation. The generated images are of resolution 256×256 pixels. Indeed the images are taken by rotating through the three axes X, Y, Z. At each iteration, we increase the rotation angle by $15°$.

5.2   Qualitative and Quantitative Evaluation

In this section, we present in the Fig. 6. a qualitative comparison between the results obtained by our method and the methods HBAO [7], NNAO [13], VAO [8] of state of the art on the two datasets (with AO only Fig. 6 and AO with texture Fig. 7), we observe that the HBAO method produces an intense shadow in the different areas of the geometry. Hence, the result produced depends on the number of samplers in the hemisphere as well as the position of the normal. A blur step is necessary to remedy the noise problem. The NNAO method produces images with apparent noise, which implies the use of a pre-processing step on the output image. We note that the VAO produces less accurate images, which requires increasing the number of samples. Indeed we observe that our model with a Attention mechanism produces images with high similarity with the reference images. Thus, our model can generate images with a good approximation of the ambient occultation in the appropriate areas. Our method offers an excellent alternative to render complex scenes in the presence of ambient cloaking without performing calculations in the 3d space of the scene.

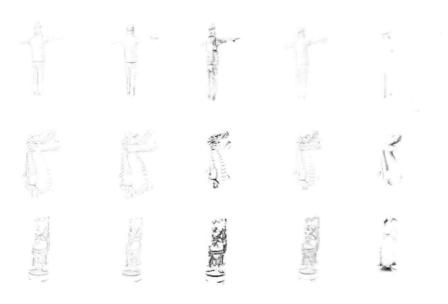

Fig. 6. Qualitative comparison: the first column represents the ground truth images with AO only, the second column represents our result, the third column HBAO [7], and the last two columns represent NNAO [13] and VAO [8].

Figure 8 presents an evaluation of our model by varying the dataset size. As the number of samples in the dataset increases, the mean square error value decreases. This means that the size of the dataset affects the ability of our model to produce images with a good approximation of the ambient occlusion. In other words, by increasing the size of the network, the error decreases, and the image generated will be of a satisfactory similarity with the reference image conversely, if the number of samples is small, the network over-adjusts, and the error starts to increase.

Table 1 presents a quantitative comparison using two metrics: the mean square error RMSE [25] and structural similarity index SSIM [26]. Indeed the RMSE allows evaluating the error between the pixels of the predicted image and those of the reference image; consequently, the SSIM calculates the error by focusing on the changes of structure between the image generated by the generator and the reference image.

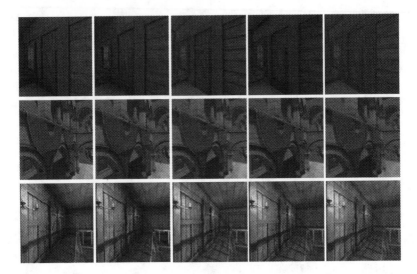

Fig. 7. Qualitative comparison: the first column represents the ground truth images with AO and texture, the second column represents our result, the third column HBAO [7], and the last two columns represent NNAO [13] and VAO [8].

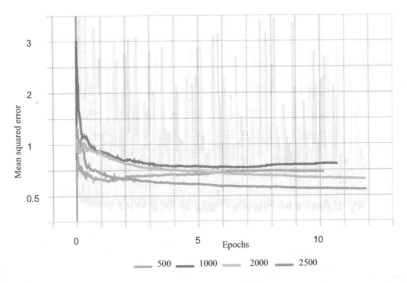

Fig. 8. Different curves of the mean square error over training epochs by varying the size of dataset.

We can see that our method outperforms the state-of-the-art methods in terms of similarity and visual quality. Furthermore, our method allows to generate images with an approximation of the ambient occlusion close to those generated by the reference method without performing calculations in the three-

Table 1. Quantitative comparison in terms of average RMSE and SSIM with HBAO [7], NNAO [13] and VAO [8].

	Dataset AO with texture		Dataset AO without texture	
	RMSE	SSIM	RMSE	SSIM
HBAO [7]	0.098	0.72	0.035	0.84
NNAO [13]	0.067	0.75	0.010	0.893
VAO [8]	0.12	0.73	0.011	0.896
Our	**0.038**	**0.79**	**0.0068**	**0.93**

dimensional space, so it does not require any step of pre-processing of the output image.

5.3 Ablation Stady

In this paper, we present a study ablation to show the attention module's efficiency through three combinations. The first one consists in using a simple gan architecture without an attention mechanism. The second one consists in using the attention mechanism in the generator and the discriminator. The Table 2 shows that our architecture with an attention mechanism capable of extracting local and global features and focusing on relevant areas of the images, unlike A simple CGAN architecture.

Table 2. The effectiveness of our attention module.

	CGAN without attention	CGAN without attention
RMSE	0.070	0.038

6 Conclusion and Future Works

In this paper we have presented a generative model with an attention mechanism for approximating ambient occlusion. Our idea is to integrate an attention mechanism in the generator architecture and the discriminator, this will allow to focus on the local features, and as the data passes through the network, our architecture will have the ability to reach the global features. We prove its efficiency in order to ensure a translation between the input space and the output space through a qualitative and quantitative comparison. Our model produces images whose quality is close to the reference images. Indeed, our method is simple to implement and does not require any further processing of the output image. We will consider improving our architecture in order to have more control over the approximation of the amount of ambient cloaking and to converge towards a more accurate solution.

References

1. Landis, H.: Production-ready global illumination. SIGGRAPH Course Notes **16**, 11 (2002)
2. Mittring, M. : ACM SIGGRAPH 2007 courses (2007)
3. McGuire, M., Osman, B., Bukowski, M., Hennessy, P.: The alchemy screen-space ambient obscurance algorithm. In: Proceedings of the ACM SIGGRAPH Symposium on High Performance Graphics, pp. 25–32 (2011)
4. McGuire, M., Mara, M., Luebke, D.P.: Scalable ambient obscurance. In: High Performance Graphics, pp. 97–103 (2012)
5. Klehm, O., Ritschel, T., Eisemann, E., Seidel, H.P.: Bent normals and cones in screen-space. In VMV, pp. 177–182 (2011)
6. Seidel, H.P.: Screen-space bent cones: a practical approach. In: GPU PRO, vol. 3, 207–224 (2012)
7. Bavoil, L., Sainz, M., Dimitrov, R.: Image-space horizon-based ambient occlusion. In: ACM SIGGRAPH 2008 Talks, p. 1 (2008)
8. Szirmay-Kalos, L., Umenhoffer, T., Tóth, B., Szécsi, L., Sbert, M.: Volumetric ambient occlusion for real-time rendering and games. IEEE Comput. Graph. Appl. **30**(1), 70–79 (2009)
9. Bokšanský, J., Pospíšil, A., Bittner, J.: VAO++: practical volumetric ambient occlusion for games. In: Eurographics Symposium on Rendering: Experimental Ideas Implementations; EGSR, vol. 17, pp. 31–39 (2017)
10. Albahar, B., Lu, J., Yang, J., Shu, Z., Shechtman, E., Huang, J.B.: Pose with style: detail-preserving pose-guided image synthesis with conditional StyleGAN. ACM Trans. Graph. (TOG) **40**(6), 1–11 (2021)
11. Richardson, E., et al.: Encoding in style: a StyleGAN encoder for image-to-image translation. In: Proceedings of the IEEE/CVF Conference on Computer Vision and Pattern Recognition, pp. 2287–2296 (2021)
12. Werhahn, M., Xie, Y., Chu, M., Thuerey, N.: A multi-pass GAN for fluid flow super-resolution. Proc. ACM Comput. Graph. Interact. Tech. **2**(2), 1–21 (2019)
13. Holden, D., Saito, J., Komura, T.: Neural network ambient occlusion. In: SIGGRAPH ASIA 2016 Technical Briefs, pp. 1–4 (2016)
14. Nalbach, O., Arabadzhiyska, E., Mehta, D., Seidel, H.P., Ritschel, T.: Deep shading: convolutional neural networks for screen space shading. In: Computer Graphics Forum, vol. 36, no. 4, pp. 65–78 (2017)
15. Erra, U., Capece, N.F., Agatiello, R., Peytavie, A., Bosch, C.: Ambient occlusion baking via a feed-forward neural network. In: Eurographics (Short Papers), pp. 13–16 (2017)
16. Inoue, N., Ito, D., Hold-Geoffroy, Y., Mai, L., Price, B., Yamasaki, T.: RGB2AO: ambient occlusion generation from RGB images. In: Computer Graphics Forum, vol. 39, no. 2, pp. 451–462 (2020)
17. Goodfellow, I., et al.: Generative adversarial nets. Adv. Neural Inf. Process. Syst. **27** (2014)
18. Bahdanau, D., Cho, K., Bengio, Y.: Neural machine translation by jointly learning to align and translate (2014)
19. Xu, K., et al.: Show, attend and tell: neural image caption generation with visual attention. In: International Conference on Machine Learning, pp. 2048–2057 (2015)
20. Zhang, Y., Zheng, Z., Hu, R.: Super resolution using segmentation-prior self-attention generative adversarial network (2020)

21. Chen, R., Zhang, H., Liu, J.: Multi-attention augmented network for single image super-resolution. Pattern Recogn. **122**, 108349 (2022)
22. Vaswani, A., et al.: Attention is all you need. In: Advances in Neural Information Processing Systems, pp. 5998–6008 (2017)
23. Zhang, R., Dong, S., Liu, J.: Invisible steganography via generative adversarial networks. Multimedia Tools Appl. **78**(7), 8559–8575 (2018). https://doi.org/10.1007/s11042-018-6951-z
24. Mahapatra, D., Antony, B., Sedai, S., Garnavi, R.: Deformable medical image registration using generative adversarial networks. In: 2018 IEEE 15th International Symposium on Biomedical Imaging, pp. 1449–1453 (2018)
25. Girod, B.: What's wrong with mean-squared error? Digit. Images Hum. Vis. 207–220 (1993)
26. Wang, Z., Bovik, A.C., Sheikh, H.R., Simoncelli, E.P.: Image quality assessment: from error visibility to structural similarity. IEEE Trans. Image Process. **13**(4), 600–612 (2004)
27. Unity: Unity technologies (2022). https://unity.com/

An Improvement of CNN Model for Traffic Sign Recognition and Classification

Tahar Mekhaznia$^{(\boxtimes)}$ ⓘ and Imtiez Fares

LAMIS Laboratory, University of Tebessa, Tebessa, Algeria
Tahar.mekhaznia@univ-tebessa.dz

Abstract. The recognition of traffic signs could be used as assistant for drivers; it maintains the traffic flexibility and reduces road accidents. The related works addressed the problem from different angles and found solutions for the most issues, especially the recognition of signs with bad appearance and the right classification within wide databases. The used methodologies achieved acceptable results but seem greedy in processing time, which seems inappropriate for use in real time. In this work, a deep neural network (CNN) is used to elaborate a lightweight model of recognition and classification of traffic signs with less processing time. In order to improve such fact, the proposed model is processed throw various distinct scenarios using different parameters. The experimental results show an accuracy of 99,49% within less than 15 epochs and without any additional modules or artificial data augmentation.

Keywords: Convolutional Neural Network · Machine learning · Traffic Sign Recognition

1 Introduction

Traffic signs are illustrative symbols, erected at the road's sides, dedicated to guide the traffic flow and advice car drivers and pedestrians about their movement. They represent a fundamental part of the road system which make easy and safe the traffic flow [1]. Traffic signs are grouped in several classes, including direction, warning, prohibition, road state information and so on. Usually, compliance with the road signs guidelines is achieved by their visual recognition. Road users are then advised to follow signs meaning in real time. Such fact cannot be often accomplished properly due to user late reaction, his wrong assimilation or lack of visibility. It should then be necessary to retain the services of an autonomous system of *traffic sign detection and recognition* (TSDR), avoiding then a part of the driver's failing.

Hence, a TSDR is a collection of intelligent units by which a vehicle is able to identify and interpret road's signs in order to comply to traffic general terms. It is then desirable for driver's assistance since it compensates his possible inattention and tiredness. A TSDR may be embedded in the vehicle dashboard and keeps users informed about the road environment in real time. It prevents invisible dangers and provides a significant vital purpose leading to traffic convenience [2]. TSDR has been object of use for road users

© Springer Nature Switzerland AG 2022
A. Bennour et al. (Eds.): ISPR 2022, CCIS 1589, pp. 362–376, 2022.
https://doi.org/10.1007/978-3-031-08277-1_30

assistance as the adaptative cruise control [3], ignition interlock devices [4], forward collision [5] and various other applications [6].

The main TSDR components are a visual sensor and an image processing unit. The first, captures the information from the wild environment whereas the second involves the segmentation of the image and extracts its characteristics. The collected data is then broken down according to traffic signs' categories and made available to drivers [7]. In general, the TSDR uses a vast body of segmentation and classification algorithms, built based on artificial intelligence and computer vision concepts. Their effectiveness depends on the used processing tools and the significance of the data collected from the surrounding environment. It involves, in general, the machine learning-based techniques [8] which seem fruitful but require often huge amount of training data, intensive resources and labor.

Machine Learning techniques (ML) are a methodology built on artificial intelligence; it allows programs and, during their processing, to acquire new environment experience and consequently, enriches the knowledge base without explicitly be programmed for this purpose. It involves a hierarchical cascading layers of functions called *neurons*, denoted for information transformation and extraction. The mostly known related architectures are the *Artificial Neural Networks* (ANN), the *Conventional Neural Networks* (CNN) and the *Spiking Neural Networks* (SNN). Related algorithms raised for the first time during 1950s [9] where the best known is none other than Perceptron [10], followed by other alternatives dedicated especially to image recognition and speed analysis [9]. ML are effective in accuracy and speed when they carried out joint with big data and data mining. They are inspired from social networks and CRM platforms and offer significantly results better than traditional alternatives. Hence, a machine learning algorithm alter its strategy based on experience extracted from available data and environment parameters. If the data intended for learning is predefined and tagged, we refer to supervised learning; then the algorithm knows in advance what elements to look for and be able to find the same within untagged data. It is suitable for resolution of classification and regression problems. The unsupervised algorithms involve training within any available data. They take more time but seem useful in clustering and cipher keys recovery. ML is behind various up-to-date services as natural language recognition and translation. It goes same for web search engines, social media feeds and for voice assistants.

By another side, the TSDR has received much interest from the computer vision community. Numerous related works involving the problem were accomplished [8], leading to a variety of classification algorithms but the challenge remains open due to that, the proposed solutions are designed in particular for drivers assistance [3] and autonomous vehicles systems [11]. They always use dedicated benchmarks with reduced amount of data and distinct appearance of signs and seem to be ignoring categories with text that differs the instances signification of a same class.

In order to overcome some of the mentioned issues, a lightweight recognition and classification model is proposed in this paper. It detects a waste part of traffic signs; including disfigured and obscured ones with less recognition errors. Its principle consists in adjusting the traffic sign image size, pinpoints its features and then, assign it to the appropriate category. The process takes advantages from the Convolutional Neural Networks resources to some extent. Experiments were accomplished throw several test scenarios, using the *German Traffic Sign Recognition Benchmark* (GTSRB). Results achieved a recognition accuracy of more than 99% and predicts the unknown traffic sign classes within less than 3 ms on an ordinary PC. The proposed approach, which proved its efficiency throw a comparative study, can be adopted as a driver assistant system in real world environment.

The five sections of the paper are illustrated as follows: After a background introduction and recent trends of related works in Sects. 1 and 2, the proposed idea is exposed in Sect. 3. Section 4 sum up various experiments and results analysis and the Sect. 5 constituted the paper conclusion.

2   Literature Survey

The TSDR problem remains, over more two decencies, an active research field. Accordingly, and for its resolution, the scientific community establish a common methodology that encloses two main phases (a) the sign's detection, that identify the sign geometry and extracts its features from a data source (natural scene or a predefined image) and (b) segregate the sign to an appropriate reference class according to its features. Therefore, and depending on the traffic signs segmentation, the detection process is achieved by one of two main approaches: the color-based and shape-based methods.

The *color-based* detection method relies on color to segment areas belong to the traffic signs. It consists, and after converting the image to specific color space RGB [12], HSV [13], HSI [14] or others [15] to split it into classes of adjacent pixels with similar color range. The method is widely implemented [13, 16–18]; it characterized by its robustness to distortion and low computing resources. However, it seems sensitive to light reflection especially when using low-resolution or grayscale input images. Actually, various related alternatives have been emerged and used for the pre-processing purposes [19], the resolution of the illumination variation or the poor lighting.

The geometry-based method or more commonly, the *shape-based* method focus on the object behavior and attempt to locate its contours. In this context, various approaches have been proposed (a) the shape detection approaches, effectives for recognition of objects with standard geometrical form; (b) the shape analysis and matching, allow recognizing complex shapes based on their convex arcs; (c) the Fourier transform, express traffic signs behavior based on local segmented contours and (d) the key point detection, which detects shapes based on their corners and angular edges. Shape based methods are unaffected by the light variation: it reduces the search space to the objects' contours. However, their performance is less quiet for large, obscured or damaged images; So, they are suitable only to deal with traffic signs dotted of distinct and clear edges [8]. To notice also that experiments of the cited methods deliver sometimes, unintended outcome especially when dealing with databases from different countries due to the lack of standard content significance.

About implementation tools, the TSDR problem often involves ML algorithms, especially the *Neural Networks* (NN), characterized by their ability in retention of just the essential of the input data information and then, reducing the classifiers size. The related literature offers a diversity of models that exhibit acceptable outcome in some circumstances [20]. The CNN are addressed by various researchers: on a private database [21], by using a mask R-CNN for wide of traffic sign categories manipulation [22] or by the Hough transform [23]. Experiments provide high accuracy and less error rate. The *Deep Neural Network* model (DNN) has been used for TSDR on real time data reliability. Researchers adopted the model for diverse angle views: heterogeny environment conditions [24] [25], multiscale object features [26], to make use of contextual information in order to recover the missed detection region [27], on different classifiers [28]. Experiments studies validate the effectiveness of the model and its accuracy in regard of similar works. By another way, the ANN for TSDR took part of the literature; they have been adopted for interpretation of road signs, using vision-based information [29], applied using various datasets [30], for improvement of speed and accuracy [31] and by using the Wasserstein metric [32]. Experimental studies show the robustness of the proposed alternatives, their stability and reliability.

About the evaluation of experimental works, authors use often samples images of public datasets or acquired from real scenes. The public datasets are abundant and enclose a variety of traffic signs images, generally spread across multiple categories. The most common widespread datasets is the GTSRB [33] with more than 50 thousand images, split in 43 categories, the Tsinghua–Tencent 100K TT100K [34] with its 30 thousands traffic-sign instances, The European Traffic Sign dataset (ETSD), with its 82 hundred signs [35], gathers public available datasets of numerous European countries. Other datasets, less important, have also been object of use as the German Traffic Sign Detection Benchmark (GTSDB) [36], the Russian Traffic Sign Dataset (GTSRB) [37] or the Indian Traffic sign Detection (ITSD) [38], whereas, certain other authors use their own traffic signs datasets [39–41].

The implementation environment involves a set of tools known for their aptitude for dealing with image recognition and classification: The *TensorFlow*, an integrated platform for ML applications doted of an extensive library [42–44]. It provides the integration of other software that improve the training databases [45]. Certain similar tools are also available: the *Speeded Up Robust Features* (SURF) that allows the images comparison using filters [46, 47] or the *You Only Look Once* software (YOLO) which detect objects throw once step [48, 49]. Such tools allow leading to acceptable results, nerveless, certain other issues still obscure and unresolved: the difference between signs geometry, the detection within low illumination, the bad sign position or the superimposition appearance. These issues still tackled by researchers in regard of experiments accuracy. The problem complexity increases when considering traffic signs interpretation among countries where they have distinct appearance and same signification. In addition, the classification by neural networks disclose difficulties lies to the distinguish between closed classes and training overhead especially when using multilayer architecture.

3 The Proposed Model

The proposed model carries out a fine-grained segmentation and unsupervised classification of a set traffic sign images extracted from the GTSRB database and processed through the CNN methodology. Experimental components are achieved with the Python programming language, using Keras and Tensorflow libraries on the Spyder environment and thus, on a CPU I5, 20 GHz, doted of a GPU GeForce 4 Go and a RAM of 8 Go. In term of conception, the model is built upon four stages as illustrated in Fig. 1:

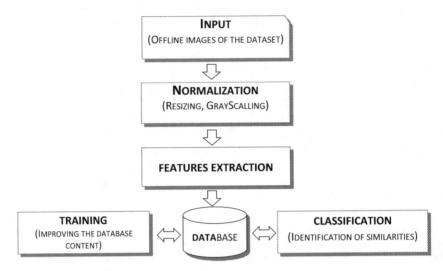

Fig. 1. The various stages of the proposed model.

The model works in two ways simultaneously (a) The training mode, where a given traffic sign, if accepted, is stored in the database and (b), the classification mode, where the model can recognize the traffic sign based on a similar object within the database content and then, split it to the adequate class.

3.1 Data Acquisition

Input data consists on a set of RGB images, with variable resolution 15×15 pixels to 250×250 pixels and distinct variation of color, visibility and shape, extracted from the GTSRB database. The GTSRB a public image classification database. It encloses about 50 thousand images spread throw 43 classes. The number of images per class varies in range of [220–2260] and each image has its own label.

3.2 The Model Description

The proposed model takes advantage of the CNN for the TSDR problem. The CNN is doted of the convolution technique: it is an operation on two functions, each one represents a matrix of pixels of a given image, the result expresses another matrix, represents the common behavior of the two basic ones. The CNN considers various convolutional layers doted of 2D trainable filters (known also as kernels) handled by the convolution function. Practically, each input image, depicted by its features, will cross through layers where it experiences changes by filters functions in view to produces an *activation map*, leads the image to be moved toward the right class.

The proposed model architecture consists of two phases (Fig. 2).

a. The feature learning phase, built on a combination of Conv2D, MaxPool and Dropout layers; it is processed multiple times with different filters sizes for distinguishing between traffic sign features themselves. Within this phase, a part of the model parameters are updated with specified values for minimizing the loss rate. The convolutional output layer Conv2D is handled by a stride and a filter which are respectively a couple of integers (high and width of frame) that specify the output stride and size according to Eq. (1).

$$Output = \frac{(Input - filter + 1)}{Stride} \qquad (1)$$

Within the training mode and where the model encloses a large number of layers as the case, the Conv2D layers provide the *Rectified linear unit function* (Eq. 2) that discards negative values and consequently, avoids the vanishing gradient problem.

$$Relu(x) = 0 \ if \ x \leq 0 \ and \ x \ elswere \qquad (2)$$

The normalization layer adjusts the image behavior, so that the average output value and the output standard deviation lean respectively towards zero and one. It is applied for either training and validation processes for reducing the epochs number. The maxpool layer decreases the spatial output size and retains a summarization of each image patch. It works similar to conv2D layer but instead of dot it takes the max value. It seems suitable when dealing with high dimension databases. The dropout layer, and during the training phase, ignores randomly a certain set of neurons for preventing the over-fitting effect. The retained neurons values are scaled up by a value less to 1 avoiding any changes over inputs.

b. The Classification phase is charged with labelling traffic signs and affecting them to the appropriate classes. During this phase, the dense layer is processed twice. It is used first with 500 neurons. The associated Relu function removes neurons providing negative values. In second, the same layer is used with 43 neurons which corresponds to the output classes. According to the Softmax function probability, the model predicts the candidate class of the available feature map. The flatten layer, as its name implies, merges the visible 2D layers to 1D feature map in order to be used by the dense layer. This last, with a given size, implements the outputs from its previous layer weights. The model uses two dense layers, the first is activated by the same function as the conv2D layer, the second uses the Softmax function which classify images with probabilistic values between 0 and 1. It also normalizes the previous layer output leading the original input image to the right class.

3.3 Data Preprocessing

As mentioned in Sect. 3.1, the GTSRB content is imbalanced in term of features and classes number; it is then mandatory to adjust image characteristics so that the model manages properly the training process and achieves suitable results. Hence, the data processing is accomplished throughout the following steps:

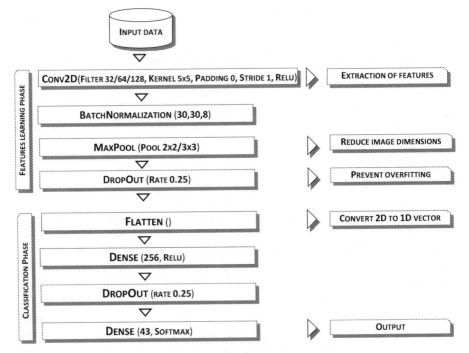

Fig. 2. The proposed model architecture.

a. Acquisition and standardization of images: The validation set is built based on a training set of 30 images for each class picked randomly from the database, for a total of 1290 images. This step was repeated twice in order to ensure an optimal accuracy of image's features. Then, the *regions of interest* (ROI) of each image are rescaled by stretching vertically or horizontally in order to keep a unified format while preserving as much as possible their characteristics. Various sizes have been experimented: 16 × 16, 20 × 20 and 64 × 64 pixels. We opted for 30 × 30 pixels, ignoring aspect ratio. It seems adequately identifiable by human eye and frequently used by the research community.

b. Grayscaling: It consists in reducing the channels number while preserving characteristics. Such fact reduces the data size leading to a fast processing.

c. Normalizing: consists in rescaling the pixel intensity value x in range from x_{min} to x_{max} according to the dataset mean and its standard deviation (Eq. 3). The boundary values x_{min} and x_{max}, are affected respectively with 0.1 and 0.9 constants.

$$x' = \frac{x - x_{min}}{x_{max} - x_{min}} \tag{3}$$

d. Shuffling the data set: it randomly rearranges objects in order to make data representative and ensures its variety in training dataset.

3.4 Compilation

The compilation process [50] leads the model to the training phase, configure the learning process and set the various related metrics. The Loss function detects errors throughout the training phase. It is affected by both the *crossentropy* and the *Mean Squared Error* (MSE) parameters and thus, to give more weight to experiments. The first, suitable for multiclass model, evaluates the model performance, whereas, the second, reduces the loss effect. The Adam optimizer parameters are set to the most common values.

3.5 Train and Evaluation of the Model

During this phase, images 'dataset are split into training and test modes with the proportion 80/20 ratio. During the train process, input data is randomly split over batches so that they fit into memory and make easily the execution control. Each train iteration refers to an *epoch*. An epoch is built upon one or more batches and denotes a single pass over all training set for one iteration. The model is then processed using various filters dimension and batches sizes of training set where the effective metrics (accuracy and lost rate) are kept for each epoch. The *accuracy* function, reflects the model performance is evaluated according to Eq. 4, where Id, In denote respectively the correct detection/no detection of image with traffic sign and Ifd, Ifn respectively the detection/no detection of an image without traffic sign. The *loss rate* function evaluates the mean difference between labels and predictions probability.

$$accuracy = \frac{(Id + In)}{(Id + Id + Ifd + Ifn)} \tag{4}$$

The training process should continue until both the loss and accuracy values become stable. The effective training metrics depict the model performance. The related input parameters will be used as start element for the model experimentation. As example, and by using a batch_size = 512, and a kernel_size = (5,5) and after 50 epochs of training, an extract of the model metrics is showed as follows:

```
Epoch 1/50
62/62 [==============] – 212s 4s/step - loss: 3.9761 - accuracy: 0.1596 - val_loss: 2.0819 - val_accuracy: 0.4699
...
Epoch 22/50
62/62 [==============] – 223s 4s/step - loss: 0.1304 - accuracy: 0.9596 - val_loss: 0.0705 - val_accuracy: 0.9767
...
Epoch 50/50
62/62 [==============] – 230s 4s/step - loss: 0.0615 - accuracy: 0.9808 - val_loss: 0.0337 - val_accuracy: 0.9808
```

It seen, that the model achieves an accuracy value of approximatively 98% in less than 4 min by using the hardware configuration illustrated in Sect. 3.

3.6 Evaluation of the Model

Experiments were carried on various data scenarios (Table 1). Each scenario is conducted using a set of parameters (batch size, epochs number and filters size) distinctly from others, collected during the training phase among values that exhibit the best results. As Example, the scenario #1 uses respectively 32 and 64 filter sizes for the first and the second conventional layers, 32 neurons for the first dense layer, etc. Within the same scenario, the database (with its 39209 samples) is split into 1226 batches of 32 samples within each one. The maxpolling layers allow leading to a final feature map of 12 × 12. The trailing convolution layers are doted of 30 × 30 filters size which leads to the last maxpolling layer with a 4 × 4 size of features map which corresponds to a vector of 480 pixels.

Table 1. Optimal training parameters.

Scenario #	Batch size	Loss	Filter 1	Filter 2	Kernel size 1	Kernel size 2	Pool size 1	Pool size 2	Dense 1
1	512	Cross entropy	32	64	5,5	3,3	2,2	2,2	256
2	256								
3	32								
4	8								
5	32								
6	1024	mse							
7	1024	Cross entropy							
8	512		64	128					512

To the best performance of experiments, each test is performed over an average of 10 runs' results. The representative curves of the accuracy/lost rate related to the considered scenarios are showed in Figs. 3a to h.

Figure 3 shows a gradually increasing of accuracy and a decreasing of loss rate while increasing the number of epochs. Results become stable after approximatively 5 epochs for scenarios b, c, e and after 15 epochs for other ones.

4 Discussion

In terms of performance, the experimental results of the accurate recognition rate and lost values are illustrated in Table 2. They are respectively in range of [12,1%–99,49%] and [0,029–3,48]. This is due to tests sensibility against the input parameters values, in particular the batches and filters sizes. The best result is achieved by the scenario #6 with an accuracy of 99,49% and a lost value of 0,023. This result is achieved within 81 s as overall processing time, which denotes a 3 s per epoch (approximatively 2,6 ms per frame). Hence, the model performs well with a wide batch size which reduces the number of iterations and then, leading to a moderate processing time.

Compared to the aforementioned literature works, the proposed model acquires a comfortable position based on its overall performance when using similar hardware and the same dataset [13, 20, 29, 51–55]. Besides that, the model results become stable within a reduced number of epochs as scenarios #2, #5 and #8 where results still unchanged after respectively 2, 1 and 9 epochs, instead of 40, 30 and 50 as defined in

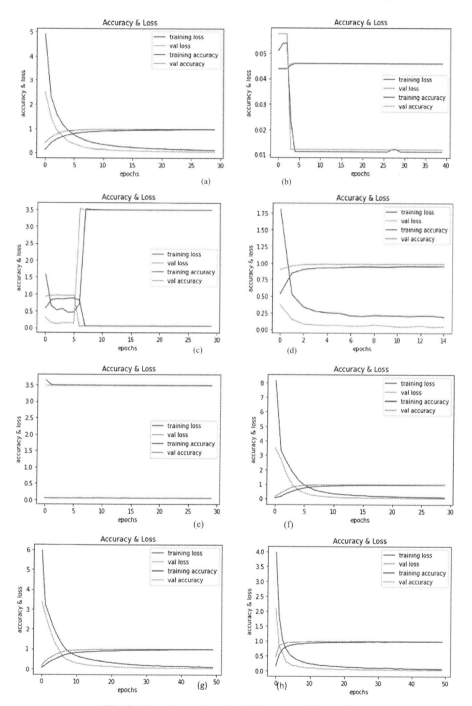

Fig. 3. Experimental results of the proposed scenarios.

Table 2. Optimal experiment results.

Scenario #	Epochs	Overall test time (s)	Loss value	Accuracy recognition rate (%)	Number of epochs that achieved stable results	Time/epoch (s)	Time/frame (ms)
1	30	81	0.034	99.04	15	1	1,9
2	40	112	0.0459	12.10	5	0.91	3,5
3	15	141	0.044	98.91	6	9,4	0.045
4	30	128	3.488	57.59	7	0.032	0.04
5	30	94	3.478	57.43	1	3,2	0.03
6	30	81	0.0233	99.49	11	3	2,6
7	50	87	0.029	99.17	16	3	2,9
8	50	230	0.0337	99.08	9	4,6	8,9

the training process. Such fact allows reducing considerably the processing time if the training process have been redesigned. Also, the proposed model uses just the CNN architecture without any other form of artificial data augmentation or additional tools that allow boosting the classification as the Modified Residual Networks [56], Small Scale CNN [57], ConvNETS [58], etc. Anyway and, given that the aim of the relevant research is dedicated to build an assistant driver tool, handled by a hardware device, generally with reduced resources, the proposed model achieved the above experiments, using a computer with similar resources as well.

5   Conclusion

In this paper, a lightweight model for recognition and classification of traffic signs is presented. The methodology is processed based on the CNN Deep learning methodology. This is due to its success in objects detection, results precision and easiness of implementation. To meet out the appropriate CNN architecture, various empirical experiments are achieved within the GTSRB. The optimal prediction exhibits an accurate recognition of 99.49% and a lost value less than 0.02, which outperforms the most similar state-of-the-art works.

Moreover, the model allow handling distorted and partially occluded traffic signs within a relatively reduced processing resource. It then can be included as a basis component of driver assistant systems.

References

1. He, J.Y., et al.: Road traffic injury mortality and morbidity by country development status, 2011–2017. Chin. J. Traumatol. – Engl. Ed. **24**, 88–93 (2021). https://doi.org/10.1016/j.cjtee.2021.01.007

2. Vokhidov, H., Hong, H.G., Kang, J.K., Hoang, T.M., Park, K.R.: Recognition of damaged arrow-road markings by visible light camera sensor based on convolutional neural network. Sensors (Switz.) **16**, 2160 (2016). https://doi.org/10.3390/s16122160
3. Reis, L.A., Pereira, S.L., Dias, E.M., Scoton, M.L.D.: Adaptative optimal control of nonlinear systems simulation to support hazardous materials traffic management. J. Control Autom. Electr. Syst. **32**, 1143–1152 (2021). https://doi.org/10.1007/s40313-021-00751-8
4. Scherer, M., et al.: Typologies of drivers convicted of driving under the influence of alcohol as predictors of alcohol ignition interlock performance. Alcohol. Treat. Q. **39**, 96–109 (2021). https://doi.org/10.1080/07347324.2020.1830734
5. Yang, W., Wan, B., Qu, X.: A forward collision warning system using driving intention recognition of the front vehicle and V2V communication. IEEE Access **8**, 11268–11278 (2020). https://doi.org/10.1109/ACCESS.2020.2963854
6. Krishnarao, S., Wang, H.-C., Sharma, A., Iqbal, M.: Enhancement of advanced driver assistance system (ADAS) using machine learning. In: Yang, X.-S., Sherratt, R.S., Dey, N., Joshi, A. (eds.) ICICT 2020. AISC, vol. 1183, pp. 139–146. Springer, Singapore (2021). https://doi.org/10.1007/978-981-15-5856-6_13
7. Martí, E., De Miguel, M.Á., García, F., Pérez, J.: A review of sensor technologies for perception in automated driving. IEEE Intell. Transp. Syst. Mag. **11**, 94–108 (2019). https://doi.org/10.1109/MITS.2019.2907630
8. Liu, C., Li, S., Chang, F., Wang, Y.: Machine vision based traffic sign detection methods: review, analyses and perspectives. IEEE Access **7**, 86578–86596 (2019). https://doi.org/10.1109/ACCESS.2019.2924947
9. Emmert-Streib, F., Yang, Z., Feng, H., Tripathi, S., Dehmer, M.: An introductory review of deep learning for prediction models with big data. Front. Artif. Intell. **3**, 4 (2020). https://doi.org/10.3389/frai.2020.00004
10. Rosenblatt, F.: The perceptron: a probabilistic model for information storage and organization in the brain. Psychol. Rev. **65**, 386 (1958). https://doi.org/10.1037/h0042519
11. Liu, S., Li, L., Tang, J., Wu, S., Gaudiot, J.L.: Creating autonomous vehicle systems. Synth. Lect. Comput. Sci. **8**, i–216 (2018). https://doi.org/10.2200/S00787ED1V01Y20170 7CSL009
12. Surinwarangkoon, T., Nitsuwat, S., Elvin, J.: A traffic sign detection and recognition system. Int. J. Circuits Syst. Signal Process. **7**, 58–65 (2013)
13. Cao, J., Song, C., Peng, S., Xiao, F., Song, S.: Improved traffic sign detection and recognition algorithm for intelligent vehicles. Sensors (Switz.) **19**, 4021 (2019). https://doi.org/10.3390/s19184021
14. Ellahyani, A., El Ansari, M., El Jaafari, I.: Traffic sign detection and recognition based on random forests. Appl. Soft Comput. J. **46**, 805–815 (2016). https://doi.org/10.1016/j.asoc.2015.12.041
15. Wu, X., Wei, Z., Hu, Y., Wang, L.: Traffic sign detection method using multi-color space fusion (2020). https://doi.org/10.1109/ICAICA50127.2020.9182603
16. Kaplan Berkaya, S., Gunduz, H., Ozsen, O., Akinlar, C., Gunal, S.: On circular traffic sign detection and recognition. Expert Syst. Appl. **48**, 67–75 (2016). https://doi.org/10.1016/j.eswa.2015.11.018
17. Huang, H., Hou, L.-Y.: Traffic road sign detection and recognition in natural environment using RGB color model. In: Huang, D.-S., Bevilacqua, V., Premaratne, P., Gupta, P. (eds.) ICIC 2017. LNCS, vol. 10361, pp. 345–352. Springer, Cham (2017). https://doi.org/10.1007/978-3-319-63309-1_32
18. Gubbi, C.: Automatic tracking of traffic signs based on HSV. Int. J. Eng. Res. Technol. **3**, 914–917 (2014)

19. Vaidya, B., Paunwala, C.: Traffic sign recognition using color and spatial transformer network on GPU embedded development board. In: Nain, N., Vipparthi, S.K., Raman, B. (eds.) CVIP 2019. CCIS, vol. 1147, pp. 82–93. Springer, Singapore (2020). https://doi.org/10.1007/978-981-15-4015-8_8
20. Santos, A., Abu, P.A., Oppus, C., Reyes, R.: Real-time traffic sign detection and recognition system for assistive driving. Adv. Sci. Technol. Eng. Syst. **5**, 600–611 (2020). https://doi.org/10.25046/AJ050471
21. Alghmgham, D.A., Latif, G., Alghazo, J., Alzubaidi, L.: Autonomous Traffic Sign (ATSR) Detection and Recognition using Deep CNN. Proc. Comput. Sci. **163**, 266–274 (2019). https://doi.org/10.1016/j.procs.2019.12.108
22. Tabernik, D., Skocaj, D.: Deep learning for large-scale traffic-sign detection and recognition. IEEE Trans. Intell. Transp. Syst. **21**, 1427–1440 (2020). https://doi.org/10.1109/TITS.2019.2913588
23. Sun, Y., Ge, P., Liu, D.: Traffic sign detection and recognition based on convolutional neural network (2019). https://doi.org/10.1109/CAC48633.2019.8997240
24. Alhabshee, S.M., Bin Shamsudin, A.U.: Deep learning traffic sign recognition in autonomous vehicle (2020). https://doi.org/10.1109/SCOReD50371.2020.9251034
25. Abdi, L., Meddeb, A.: Deep learning traffic sign detection, recognition and augmentation (2017). https://doi.org/10.1145/3019612.3019643
26. Tai, S.K., Dewi, C., Chen, R.C., Liu, Y.T., Jiang, X., Yu, H.: Deep learning for traffic sign recognition based on spatial pyramid pooling with scale analysis. Appl. Sci. **10**, 6997 (2020). https://doi.org/10.3390/app10196997
27. Li, D., Zhao, D., Chen, Y., Zhang, Q.: DeepSign: deep learning based traffic sign recognition (2018). https://doi.org/10.1109/IJCNN.2018.8489623
28. Arcos-García, Á., Álvarez-García, J.A., Soria-Morillo, L.M.: Deep neural network for traffic sign recognition systems: an analysis of spatial transformers and stochastic optimisation methods. Neural Netw. **99**, 158–165 (2018). https://doi.org/10.1016/j.neunet.2018.01.005
29. Islam, K.T., Raj, R.G., Mujtaba, G.: Recognition of traffic sign based on bag-of-words and artificial neural network. Symmetry (Basel) **9**, 138 (2017). https://doi.org/10.3390/sym9080138
30. Park, D.-C.: Classification of traffic signs using artificial neural networks. Contemp. Eng. Sci. (2017). https://doi.org/10.12988/ces.2017.7327
31. Avramović, A., Sluga, D., Tabernik, D., Skočaj, D., Stojnić, V., Ilc, N.: Neural-network-based traffic sign detection and recognition in high-definition images using region focusing and parallelization. IEEE Access **8**, 189855–189868 (2020). https://doi.org/10.1109/ACCESS.2020.3031191
32. Shakhuro, V.I., Konushin, A.S.: Image synthesis with neural networks for traffic sign classification. Comput. Opt. **42**, 105–112 (2018). https://doi.org/10.18287/2412-6179-2018-42-1-105-112
33. Stallkamp, J., Schlipsing, M., Salmen, J., Igel, C.: Man vs. computer: benchmarking machine learning algorithms for traffic sign recognition. Neural Netw. **32**, 323–332 (2012). https://doi.org/10.1016/j.neunet.2012.02.016
34. Zhu, Z., Liang, D., Zhang, S., Huang, X., Li, B., Hu, S.: Traffic-sign detection and classification in the wild. In: 2016 IEEE Conference on Computer Vision and Pattern Recognition (CVPR), June 2016, pp. 2110–2118 (2016). https://doi.org/10.1109/CVPR.2016.232
35. Gamez Serna, C., Ruichek, Y.: Classification of traffic signs: the European dataset. IEEE Access **6**, 78136–78148 (2018). https://doi.org/10.1109/ACCESS.2018.2884826
36. Houben, S., Stallkamp, J., Salmen, J., Schlipsing, M., Igel, C.: Detection of traffic signs in real-world images: the German traffic sign detection benchmark (2013). https://doi.org/10.1109/IJCNN.2013.6706807

37. Shakhuro, V.I., Konushin, A.S.: Russian traffic sign images dataset. Comput. Opt. **40**, 294–300 (2016). https://doi.org/10.18287/2412-6179-2016-40-2-294-300
38. Rituparna, S.: ITSD (2018). https://www.mapsofindia.com/my-india/government/traffic-signs-and-road-safety
39. Larsson, F., Felsberg, M.: Using fourier descriptors and spatial models for traffic sign recognition. In: Heyden, A., Kahl, F. (eds.) SCIA 2011. LNCS, vol. 6688, pp. 238–249. Springer, Heidelberg (2011). https://doi.org/10.1007/978-3-642-21227-7_23
40. Brkić, K., Pinz, A., Šegvić, S.: Traffic sign detection as a component of an automated traffic infrastructure inventory system. In: 33rd Annual Workshop of the Austrian Association for Pattern Recognition (2009)
41. Ertler, C., Mislej, J., Ollmann, T., Porzi, L., Neuhold, G., Kuang, Y.: The mapillary traffic sign dataset for detection and classification on a global scale. In: Vedaldi, A., Bischof, H., Brox, T., Frahm, J.-M. (eds.) ECCV 2020. LNCS, vol. 12368, pp. 68–84. Springer, Cham (2020). https://doi.org/10.1007/978-3-030-58592-1_5
42. Staravoitau, A.: Traffic sign classification with a convolutional network. Pattern Recognit. Image Anal. **28**, 155–162 (2018). https://doi.org/10.1134/S1054661818010182
43. Shustanov, A., Yakimov, P.: CNN design for real-time traffic sign recognition. Proc. Eng. **201**, 718–725 (2017). https://doi.org/10.1016/j.proeng.2017.09.594
44. Burleigh, N., King, J., Braunl, T.: Deep learning for autonomous driving (2019). https://doi.org/10.1109/DICTA47822.2019.8945818
45. Sabirov, A.I., Katasev, A.S., Dagaeva, M.V.: A neural network model for traffic signs recognition in intelligent transport systems. Comput. Res. Model. **13**, 429–435 (2021). https://doi.org/10.20537/2076-7633-2021-13-2-429-435
46. Alam, A., Jaffery, Z.A.: Indian traffic sign detection and recognition. Int. J. Intell. Transp. Syst. Res. **18**(1), 98–112 (2019). https://doi.org/10.1007/s13177-019-00178-1
47. Guo, S., Yang, X.: Fast recognition algorithm for static traffic sign information. Open Phys. **16**, 1149–1156 (2018). https://doi.org/10.1515/phys-2018-0135
48. Sichkar, V.N., Kolyubin, S.A.: Real time detection and classification of traffic signs based on YOLO Version 3 algorithm. Sci. Tech. J. Inf. Technol. Mech. Opt. **127**, 418–424 (2020). https://doi.org/10.17586/2226-1494-2020-20-3-418-424
49. Dewi, C., Chen, R.C., Liu, Y.T., Jiang, X., Hartomo, K.D.: Yolo V4 for advanced traffic sign recognition with synthetic training data generated by various GAN. IEEE Access **9**, 97228–97242 (2021). https://doi.org/10.1109/ACCESS.2021.3094201
50. Kingma, D.P., Ba, J.L.: Adam: a method for stochastic optimization (2015)
51. Kherarba, M., Abbes, M.T., Boumerdassi, S., Meddah, M., Benhamada, A., Senouci, M.: Road sign identification with convolutional neural network using TensorFlow. In: Renault, É., Boumerdassi, S., Mühlethaler, P. (eds.) MLN 2020. LNCS, vol. 12629, pp. 255–264. Springer, Cham (2021). https://doi.org/10.1007/978-3-030-70866-5_17
52. Narejo, S., Talpur, S., Memon, M., Rahoo, A.: An automated system for traffic sign recognition using convolutional neural network. 3C Tecnol. innovación Apl. a la pyme **9**, 119–135 (2020). https://doi.org/10.17993/3ctecno.2020.specialissue6.119-135
53. Zaibi, A., Ladgham, A., Sakly, A.: A lightweight model for traffic sign classification based on enhanced LeNet-5 network. J. Sens. (2021). https://doi.org/10.1155/2021/8870529
54. Velamati, A., et al.: Traffic sign classification using convolutional neural networks and computer vision. Turkish J. Comput. Math. Educ. **12**, 4244–4250 (2021). https://doi.org/10.17762/turcomat.v12i3.1715
55. Islam, K.T., Raj, R.G.: Real-time (vision-based) road sign recognition using an artificial neural network. Sensors (Switz.) **17**, 853 (2017). https://doi.org/10.3390/s17040853
56. Wen, L., Jo, K.H.: Traffic sign recognition and classification with modified residual networks (2018). https://doi.org/10.1109/SII.2017.8279326

57. Chaudhari, T., Wale, A., Joshi, A., Sawant, S.: Traffic sign recognition using small-scale convolutional neural network. SSRN Electron. J. (2020). https://doi.org/10.2139/ssrn.364 5805

58. Sermanet, P., Lecun, Y.: Traffic sign recognition with multi-scale convolutional networks (2011). https://doi.org/10.1109/IJCNN.2011.6033589

Social Media Sentiment Classification for Tunisian Dialect: A Deep Learning Approach

Mehdi Belguith[1](✉), Nesrine Azaiez[1](✉), Chafik Aloulou[1](✉), and Bilel Gargouri[2](✉)

[1] ANLP-RG, MIRACL Laboratory, FSEGS, University of Sfax, Sfax, Tunisia
belguith.mehdi2017@gmail.com, nesrine.azaiez90@gmail.com,
chafik.aloulou@fsegs.usf.tn
[2] MIRACL Laboratory, FSEGS, University of Sfax, Sfax, Tunisia
bilel.gargouri@fsegs.usf.tn

Abstract. Social media becomes nowadays a valuable resource for posting and expressing opinions about services or products. Sentiments about a product or a service offered to companies are too valuable in this era than ever before. Indeed, knowing whether their customers are expressing positive, neutral or negative sentiments toward their products can be of a high importance for these companies. Hence, extracting the sentiments from comments (or reviews) in Tunisian dialect and written with Tunisian Arabizi script is a challenge compared to other languages. Although, we are getting better with each passing year, but it is still a long way to go to handle Tunisian dialect.

In this paper, we focus on sentiment analysis of Tunisian dialect comments posted on social media. More precisely, we propose an interesting deep learning approach for sentiment classification. Thus, we used three corpora, experimented and evaluated four deep learning models: CNN, LSTM, Bi-LSTM and GRU. Our deep neural networks have achieved good results for Tunisian dialect sentiment classification. Best results are obtained based on GRU model.

Keywords: Sentiment analysis · Deep learning · Tunisian dialect · Arabizi script · Social media

1 Introduction

Nowadays, internet is growing exponentially and users get more opportunities to post their opinions, express their feelings and share their experiences about different products or services. Sentiment classification is an automated process that identifies the opinions expressed in texts (i.e., in our case comments posted on social media) and labelling them as positive, negative, or neutral. Thus, sentiment classification is very helpful for companies since it allows them to know the opinions of the customers about their products, services, or brands. Hence, managers can make better decisions regarding their products or services.

Most prior studies on sentiment analysis have focused on Indo-European languages, mainly on English, French, etc. However, few research works have been done for Arabic in general, and for its dialects in specific.

© Springer Nature Switzerland AG 2022
A. Bennour et al. (Eds.): ISPR 2022, CCIS 1589, pp. 377–393, 2022.
https://doi.org/10.1007/978-3-031-08277-1_31

In this research work, we are interested in Tunisian Arabic Dialect. We propose an original approach for sentiment classification to determine opinions (positive, neutral or negative) expressed in Tunisian comments scrapped from social networks, mainly YouTube and Facebook.

This paper is organised as follows. We present in Sect. 2 the recent literature review on sentiment analysis. Then, we describe in Sect. 3, the Tunisian dialect and focus on its varieties and main difficulties of its processing. In Sect. 4, we propose our original approach for Tunisian sentiment classification. Experimental results are then discussed in Sect. 5. At the end, we conclude by recalling our major contributions and presenting some interesting perspectives.

2   Related Work

Sentiment Analysis (SA) is a recent study topic for extracting semantics and detecting the polarity (positive/none/negative) from a document, a text or a sentence.

Sentiment Classification (SC) is the process of determining opinions in texts (e.g., reviews, comments, etc.) and labelling them with corresponding polarities (i.e., positive, negative, or neutral). These opinions are identified based on the sentiments or emotions expressed by the customers. Hence, sentiment classification can help understand how customers feel about the company products, services or brands based on Natural Language Processing (NLP) techniques to interpret subjective data.

Many researchers confuse "Sentiment Analysis" and "Sentiment Classification", but the main differences between them is the idea that classification is objective but sentiment is subjective. Moreover, Sentiment analysis may involve classification, depending on the applied technique. Hence, when machine learning is used (i.e. classifiers) one would talk about sentiment classification.

We present in the following the main approaches proposed for sentiment analysis including sentiment classification, to give a better idea about related work done on sentiment (or opinion) classification.

There are mainly three approaches for sentiment analysis: the lexicon based approach, the learning based approach and the hybrid approach.

2.1   The Lexicon Based Approach

The knowledge based approach, also named lexicon-based approach, usually relies on a sort of lexicon in which one count and weigh the words related to the sentiments.

The lexicon or the predefined list of words is used to define word semantic polarity, namely positive, negative or neutral (i.e., without any sentiment expression).

The study presented in [1] proposed a sentiment analysis method based on a lexicon related to football domain. The dataset was collected from Twitter microblogging platform. It consists of 10 000 tweets related to the 10 top-level football matches. The sentiments of the tweets were annotated both manually by human annotators and automatically based on available sentiment analysis tools. Based on a test Dataset of 1 000 tweets, an accuracy of 95% was achieved.

A lexicon-based method for Chinese sentiment analysis is proposed in [2]. First, the authors introduced a method to automatically construct the FCP-Lex sentiment lexicon, which is based on CP-chunks. Then, they experimented their lexicon for the text sentiment classification task. Evaluation results show that the FCP-Lex lexicon seems to be more powerful, for sentiment classification, than other available lexicons. Indeed, it reached high performance with an accuracy of 82%.

2.2 Machine Learning Based Approach

Machine learning based approach proposed for sentiment analysis tasks could be classified into two sets according to the applied models (i.e., machine learning models or deep learning ones).

- **Machine learning models**

Machine learning is a branch of Artificial Intelligence (AI) that relies on algorithms to parse data, learn from that data, and then apply what has been learned to take decisions or propose previsions, etc.

Sayed et al. [3] have proposed an Arabic sentiment analysis model. They collected a corpus of 6 318 reviews that have different writing forms of Arabic. These reviews were extracted from "Booking.com" Website. They implemented nine machine learning models which are the Logistic Regression (LR), the Gradient Boosting (GB), the Support Vector Machine (SVM), the Decision Tree (DT), the Ridge Classifier (RC), the K-Nearest Neighbour (KNN), the Multilayer Perceptron (MLP), the Naive Bayes (NB) and the Random Forest (RF).

The Ridge model reached the best performance among the nine classifiers and obtained a high accuracy of 95.21%.

Medhaffar et al. [4] suggested applying a sentiment analysis method for Tunisian Dialect (TD). They first collected their corpus called TSAC (Tunisian Sentiment Analysis Corpus)[1]. This corpus contains 17 000 comments extracted from Facebook. The comments deal with Tunisian TV shows. TSAC has been annotated manually by the authors. Then, they experimented three classifiers as training models, which are the SVM, the Bernoulli NB (BNB) and the Multi-Layer Perceptron (MLP).

The MLP classifier reached the best evaluation results (i.e., the best accuracy measure is 78% and the best F1-score measure is 78%).

Aljabri et al. [5] introduced machine learning techniques to implement Arabic tweet sentiment analysis. Their domain of interest is distance learning in Saudi Arabia.

---

[1] https://github.com/fbougares/TSAC.

They proposed a feature extraction approach, which uses unigram, TF-IDF and machine learning classification algorithm based on LR. The highest achieved accuracy is 0.899.

- **Deep learning models**

Deep Learning (DL) represents an evolution of Machine Learning (ML). It is based on programmable neural networks that enable computers to take better decisions or make good predictions with no human aid. Note that deep learning techniques are technologies that can make machines learn from previous experiences and data. They are one of the ways to lead to artificial intelligence [6]. They have proven an important role in many systems of sentiment analysis [7].

Zhang et al. [8] have proposed a method for conversational sentiment classification. This method is based on an interactive Long Short-Term Memory (LSTM) model. to model speaker interactions in conversations by adding a confidence gate before each LSTM hidden unit to (i) estimate the previous speakers credibility and (ii) to combine the output gate with the learned influence scores in order to incorporate the influences of the previous speakers. They obtained an accuracy of 68.2% for the LSTM interactive model with speaker A and 78% for the LSTM model with speaker B.

Masmoudi et al. [9] applied Sentiment analysis system for Tunisian dialect. They have manually annotated a corpus extracted from Facebook (dealing about Tunisian Supermarkets). The authors used two corpora. The first one is written with Tunisian Arabizi and contains 42 000 comments. The second one is written with Arabic Tunisian and contains 17 000 comments.

They experimented and evaluated three deep learning models, which are the Long Short-Term Memory (LSTM), the Convolution Neural Networks (CNN) and the Bi-directional Long-Short-Term-Memory (Bi-LSTM). One note that LSTM and Bi-LSTM models represent two major types of RNNs.

To conduct their experiments, the dataset was annotated according to twenty categories of aspects and five polarities namely very negative, negative, neutral, positive and very positive.

Their experimental study shows that the considered features enhanced the performance results when applying CNN and Bi-LSTM neural networks [9]. Indeed, they obtained the following F1-score measures: 86% for the Convolution Neural Network model and 87% for the Bi-directional Long-Short-Term-Memory model.

The TSAC dataset [4] is also used by Jerbi et al. [10] for sentiment classification of Tunisian code-switching. The authors proposed a model with five types of RNNs which are Deep Bi-LSTM, deep LSTM, LSTM and Bi-LSTM. The highest accuracy (90%) was achieved by the deep LSTM classifier.

Srinivas et al. [11] proposed Simple Berber Neural Network, LSTM model and CNN network classifiers for sentiment classification of Tweets. The highest accuracy of 87% was reached based on LSTM model.

AlBadani et al. [12] suggested a new deep learning method to analyze sentiments on Twitter. Their method combines the Universal Language Model Fine-Tuning (ULMFiT) with the SVM model to enhance the classification results. The authors experimented the Twitter US airlines corpus and they obtained an accuracy of 99.78%.

2.3 The Hybrid Approach

The hybrid approach combines the lexicon-based approach and the machine learning approach.

A method within the hybrid approach is proposed by Altaher Taha [13]. This method is based on a combination of a neural network model and other learning models mainly SVM and decision tree. The highest accuracy and precision measures, obtained by this method, are respectively 90% and 93.7%. Dang et al. [14] suggested a hybrid deep learning method in order to analyse sentiments in social media. They tested the performance of combining three models, which are SVM, CNN, and LSTM, using two-word embedding techniques (i.e., BERT and Word2vec). Their test corpus is composed of eight textual datasets of tweets and reviews.

Evaluation results showed that for all datasets, hybrid models outperformed single models when using Word2vec. With BERT, they reported a small improvement since the models reached an accuracy that exceeds 90%.

Dang et al. [14] proposed an hybrid method for sentiment analysis classification which combines SVM, LSTM and CNN classifiers. They showed that hybrid models outperformed the single models.

3 Tunisian Dialect Description

We briefly describe below the Tunisian Dialect (TD) and present its specificities and difficulties of processing, comparing to other languages.

3.1 Description

Tunisian Dialect is a subset of the Arabic dialects of the Western group and belongs to the Maghrebi dialects. TD is also known as "al-Tounsi" or "al-Darija".

Tunisian dialect is mainly composed of Standard Arabic vocabulary (i. actually a part of it) spiced with many Berber and French words and expressions. It also contains some borrowed words from Latin languages such as Spanish and Italian. One note that TD also contains some Turkish loanwords. Thus, TD is highly influenced by foreign languages.

Moreover, one note that Tunisia is divided into 24 administrative areas and there are mainly four regional varieties of Tunisian dialect covering these areas. These regional varieties are mainly located in Tunis, Sfax, Souse and Tataouine [15].

Difficulties in data collection were especially faced with the regions of Tataouine and Sousse. This could be explained on the one hand by the lack of available online resources from Tataouine region, and on the second hand by the phenomenon of dialects continuum that exists in the Tunisian coast and among it the region of Sousse.

It is interesting to note that the sub-dialect of Tunis is the one used in Television and radio programs, formal interviews, political debates and news broadcasts.

For Sfax, mainly people originating from this region and speaking in their regional dialect were found to be speaking the Sfaxian dialect [15].

Moreover, the diversity of the Tunisian dialect from one region to another has created the distinction between the tone of the cities and the tone of the countryside. Thus, according to the geographical map, there are mainly two dominant linguistic areas of Tunisia which are the South and the North [16].

3.2 Difficulties and Challenges

The Tunisian dialect (independently of its four varieties presented above) is characterised by two linguistic registers: the familiar dialect and the intellectualised dialect. The colloquial dialect (i.e. familiar dialect) is the one used in the daily oral communication of Tunisians. However, the intellectualised dialect is considered as a mixture between the Modern Standard Arabic (MSA) and the Tunisian dialect. It is often used in conversations on shows, radios and televisions.

Note that Tunisian dialect, which is an unstandardized variety, differs from MSA in terms of phonological, lexical and morphological variations.

- **Lexical differences**

As mentioned above, the Tunisian dialect is a mixture of Arabic, Berber and some other foreign languages (e.g., French, Italian and Spanish). Hence, TD is characterised by the use of several borrowed words.

In Table 1, we present some Tunisian words borrowed from foreign languages mainly French, Italian, Berber, and Spanish.

Table 1. Some foreign words used in TD

Tunisian word	Foreign word	English Translation
برسانة /bersane	Italian (Persienne)	Window
تلفون / tlfwn	French (Téléphone)	Phone
قرنيط / qrnyt	Berber (Quarnit)	Octopus
كنسترو/ Kenastro	Spanish (Canastro)	Basket

- **Morphological differences**

At the morphological level, there are distinction between the Tunisian regions. For example, unlike the dialect of southern regions, in the Nordic dialect, people use the same pronunciation and writing for both masculine and feminine of the second person singular. Table 2 presents an example of the verb جاء (to arrive) conjugated with the 2nd person singular feminine, according to the dialects of the North and the South.

- **Lack of diacritics**

Diacritics help the reader to read, analyse and understand the text. Tunisian dialect writings are generally written without diacritics. This often leads to increasing the layer

Table 2. Example of differences between the North and the South

Pronouns	Nordic dialect	Southern dialect	Translation
2nd Singular feminine pronoun	جيت/jyt	جيتي/jyty	You arrived

of semantic ambiguities in the TD. For example, the word معلم//mElm without any diacritic could have two different part of speech (i.e., grammatical categories) and hence two meanings. Since it could be a noun (a teacher) or an adjective (expert).

4 Our Proposed Approach

We propose in this section, our approach for sentiment classification, which is based on deep learning. Our main objective is to determine the sentiment of social media comments written in TD and related to many fields.

These comments could be written using Arabic or Arabizi scripts, since the latter is very used on social media. For handling Arabizi, we propose a transliteration step in order to convert Arabizi script into Arabic one. Then, we can apply the pre-processing steps on our corpus and annotate it. Note that the corpus annotation is realised manually.

We present in Fig. 1 the main steps of our proposed approach, which are transliteration from Arabizi to Arabic Tunisian dialect, dataset pre-processing, dataset annotation, vectorization and sentiment classification based on four deep learning models (i.e. LSTM, Bi-LSTM, GRU and CNN).

4.1 Dataset Description

In this work, we used three datasets, which consist of Tunisian comments extracted from social media (Mainly Facebook and YouTube) and related to various domains.

The first one is our own dataset that we collected for this work and called YCTSA (YouTube Corpus for Tunisian Sentiment Analysis). It consists of Tunisian comments scrapped from YouTube and related to different domains (i.e. Mobile phones, Food, Tunisian election and TV Programs). The dataset scrapping is based on Selenium[2] (a suite of tools for automating Web browsers). Our YCTSA corpus contains 23275 Tunisian comments written in Tunisian Arabic, Tunisian Arabizi or both.

In addition to our YCTSA dataset, we also used two other available datasets. So, the second dataset we used in this work is the one collected by [9] from the social network "Facebook" and which is related to the supermarket field in Tunisia. The authors focused on five official Tunisian supermarkets (i.e., "Magasin general", "Monoprix", "Carrefour", "Aziza" and "Geant"). To collect the data they used two well-known tools (i.e. Facepager[3] and Export Comments[4]).

---

[2] https://www.selenium.dev/.

[3] https://github.com/strohne/Facepager.

[4] https://exportcomments.com/.

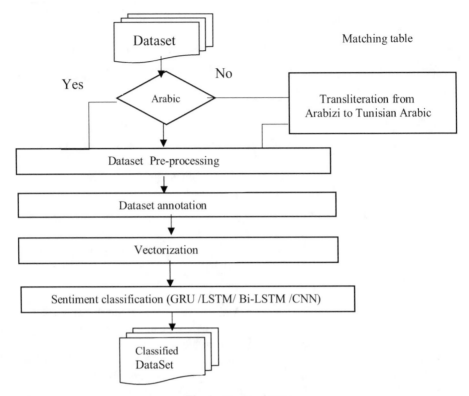

Fig. 1. Proposed steps

The third Dataset we used in this work is constructed by [4] and is available on internet[5]. This Dataset represents comments collected from official pages of Tunisian radios and television channels mainly "Mosaique FM", "Jawhara FM", "Shams FM", "Hiwar Ettounsi TV" and "Nessma TV". These comments cover a period extending from January 2015 to June 2016. The dataset is called TSAC (Tunisian Sentiment Analysis Corpus) and is composed of 17 000 Tunisian comments and is manually annotated using positive and negative polarities [4].

Table 3 shows some details about the three datasets described in this section and that we used for our experiments. In particular, we present for each dataset, the numbers of sentences, words and unique words.

4.2 Transliteration from Tunisian Arabizi to Tunisian Arabic

The transliteration consists of converting comments written with Tunisian Arabizi (i.e. using Latin letters and numbers) into comments written with Tunisian Arabic (i.e. using Arabic letters only). For the transliteration, we rely on a matching table (see Table 4) which gives the corresponding of each Arabizi letter to Arabic letters.

---

[5] https://github.com/fbougares/TSAC.

Table 3. Some statistics on the three used datasets

Dataset	# sentences	# words	# Unique words
YCTSA	23 275	273 979	39 487
Corpus [9]	17 810	127 990	29 995
TSAC[4]	17 060	112 596	42 129

Table 4. Matching table

Arabizi	Arabic	Arabizi	Arabic
a	ا,ى,ة,أ	p	ب
b	ب	q	ك
c	ك,س	r	ر
d	ظ, ض,د	s	ص ,س
e	ا	t	ط,ت
f	ف	u	و,ا
g	ق	v	ف
h	ح,ه	w	و
i	ي	x	كس
j	ج	y	ي,ا
k	ق,ك	z	ز
l	ل	3	ع
m	م	5	خ
n	ن	7	ح
o	ا,و	9	ق

As mentioned in Sect. 3, there are specific aspects for Arabizi Tunisian dialect. Therefore, some Tunisian people, mainly (young people) use Latin characters, to refer to Arabic letters that they pronounce almost the same. For instance, the Latin letters "b", "s" and "l" are respectively used for the Arabic letters ب, سand ل. In addition, some numbers (e.g. 3, 4, 5, 6, 7 and 9) replace the letters that do not have equivalents in the Latin alphabet. The idea is to use numbers that are graphically somehow similar to the corresponding Arabic letters. For instance, the number "7" is used instead of the Arabic letter ح//H since it is graphically close to it. Moreover, a single Arabic letter may be replaced by a couple of letters in Latin script as for example the letter ض//D which is represented by "dh" [16].

4.3 Dataset Pre-processing

We applied some pre-processing techniques on the three used datasets. The aim of these techniques is to handle the unstructured sentences, orthographic mistakes, etc.

Indeed, data pre-processing is very crucial and must be done in order to make data ready for further steps.

We present in the following subsections the main techniques used for the data pre-processing namely the light stemming and the data cleaning.

4.3.1 Light Stemming

The light stemming consists of eliminating both prefixes and suffixes of the comment words. Thus, words with similar meaning will be considered as the same unit (or word). In the literature, many researchers have proved that light stemming for Arabic language and its dialects improve the results for sentiment classification [17].

Table 5 shows the list of prefixes and suffixes for Tunisian dialect. Note that the pre-fixes represent both definite articles and conjunctions. However, the suffixes correspond to the words endings and indicate the gender, the number or the personal pronoun.

Table 5. List of prefixes and suffixes [17]

Prefixes	Suffixes
ال، وال، بال، كال، فال، لل، و	ها،ان،ات،ون،ين،هن،هم،ته،تي،ني،يه،يت،ة،ة،ي

Table 6 presents an example of comment before and after applying the light stemming.

Table 6. Example of light stemming

Before light stemming	After light stemming	English translation
مبروك عليكم الديموقراطية	مبروك عليك ديموقراطية	Congratulations on democracy

4.3.2 Dataset Cleaning

The dataset cleaning consists in removing foreign sentences or words (e.g. French or English comments). It also consists in removing the URLs, user mentions, punctuation signs, redundant letters (e.g. نموووووووت/I liiiike will be replaced by نموت/I like). The aim of the data cleaning is to remove words, letters or signs that have no interest for sentiment analysis and that could make the learning process a time consuming task.

4.4 Dataset Annotation

We manually annotated our YCTSA dataset according to three polarities: positive, neutral and negative. Table 7 presents some examples of comments extracted from our YCTSA Dataset. Note that the two other datasets, which we have used in this work, are already annotated by their corresponding authors.

Table 7. Examples of annotated comments

Examples of comments	Polarities
سوم مناسب و تستاهل حتى اكثر	Positive
صحافي فاشل يسال ويجاوب وحدو	Negative
بلاهي ياسين كان فما امكانية نوت10 لايت	Neutral
تصميم تلفون ناقص شوي	Negative

4.5 Vectorization

In order to apply the learning models, we have to transform the textual comments into numerical vectors. Word embedding is a technique of vectorization that enables to transform the comments (i.e word representation) into numeric vectors. Thus, words having similar meanings and contexts are represented by similar vectors. Embeddings are used by many researchers for sentiment classification and also for some Natural Language Processing (NLP) systems [18]. In our case, we use them as the input layers for our deep learning models. Indeed, we used GloVe[6] (i.e., word vectorization technique) to represent the words of the comments into vectors. Thus, similar words cluster together and different words repel. One note that GloVe is an open-source project of Stanford University [19]. It is based on a combination of two model features, namely the global matrix factorization and the local context windows.

4.6 Sentiment Classification with Deep Learning Techniques

In this section, we propose to experiment four deep learning models, which are CNN, LSTM, Bi-LSTM and GRU for sentiment classification. In the following, we briefly present these four models and then we present the result of our experiments.

4.6.1 CNN

The Convolutional Neural Networks (CNNs), also called ConvNets, are among the most popular deep neural networks. CNNs have multiple layers, including the Convolution Layer, the Correction Layer, the Pooling Layer, and the Fully Connected Layer.

CNN has a strong performance in machine learning issues. Indeed, it is widely used in image data processing, image classification, computer vision, and Natural Language Processing (NLP) [20].

Figure 2 shows the CNN model architecture. It consists of an input layer, an embedding layer, a convolutional layer, a pooling layer, a fully connected layer and an output layer. The output layer generates the polarity of each input comment.

---

[6] https://nlp.stanford.edu/projects/glove/.

388   M. Belguith et al.

Input vector   Feature vectors   Convolution layer   Pooling layer   Fully connected layer   Output layer

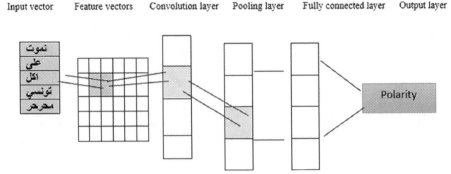

Fig. 2. The CNN model architecture

4.6.2   LSTM

The Long Short Term Memory (LSTM) network handles the problem of vanishing gradient commonly found in the Recurrent Neural Network (RNN) by means of gating functions incorporation into their dynamic state.

LSTMs are special RNNs that are convenient for learning long-term dependencies. They are characterized by a component called memory block that represents its key part allowing to enhance modelling long-term dependencies [21].

Figure 3 presents the architecture of the LSTM classifier. This model is mainly composed of an input layer, an embedding layer, an LSTM layer, a Hidden layer, a fully connected layer and an output layer, which generates the polarity of each given comment in the input layer.

Input vector   Feature vectors   LSTM layer   Hidden layer   Fully connected layer   Output

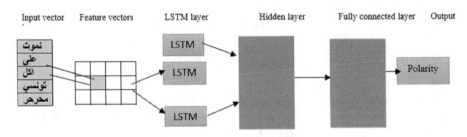

Fig. 3. The LSTM model architecture

4.6.3   Bi-LSTM

The Bi-LSTM neural networks represent LSTM units operating in forward and reverse directions in order to incorporate both past and future context information. Thus, Bi-directional Long-Short-Term-Memory model can learn long-term dependencies without retaining duplicate context information [22]. The Bi-LSTM network has two parallel layers that operate in two directions (i.e., forward and reverse passes) in order to handle dependencies in both contexts [23]. One note that Bi-LSTM model is widely used for text classification [24].

Figure 4 shows the Bi-LSTM model architecture which consists of an input layer, an embedding layer, a forward layer, a backward layer, a fully-connected layer and an output layer. The output layer generates the polarity (positive, negative or neutral) of each input comment.

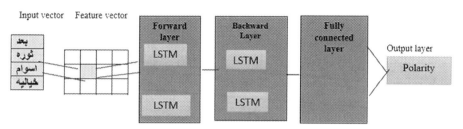

Fig. 4. The Bi-LSTM model architecture.

4.6.4 GRU

The Gated Recurrent Unit (GRU) model was first introduced by [25] in 2014. It aims to solve the vanishing gradient problem, which comes with a standard recurrent neural network.

Figure 5 shows the GRU model architecture. One note in this architecture, the input layer, the embedding layer, the hidden layer, the fully-connected layer and the output layer which generates the comment sentiment (i.e., positive, neutral or negative).

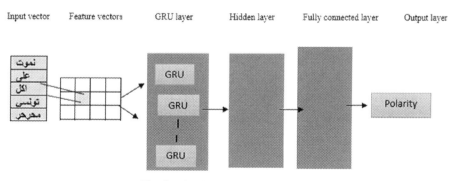

Fig. 5. The GRU model architecture

5 Experiments and Discussion

As mentioned in previous section, we are interested on four deep learning models namely LSTM, Bi-LSTM, CNN and GRU.

We experimented these models on the three datasets detailed in Table 8. We present in this table the number of negative, neutral and positive comments for each dataset. One note that each comment was manually annotated with one polarity (positive, negative or neutral).

Table 8. Statistics on datsets polarities

Corpus	#Comments	#Positive	#Neutral	#Negative
YCTSA	23 275	10 349	9 009	3 917
Corpus [9]	17 810	2 285	8 380	7 145
TSAC [4]	17 060	8 215	0	8 845
Total	58 145	20 739	17 389	19 907

Table 9 shows some statistics about the training and test datasets, that we experimented on our classifiers. It details for each dataset, the number of comments and the number of positive, negative and neutral comments.

Note that for the four training models, we used 80% of each dataset for training. For the test, we used the remaining comments (i.e., 20% of each dataset). All neural networks were implemented using the TensorFlow library.

We conduced three experiments. The first, second and third experiments used respectively the training datasets of the three mentioned corpora.

Table 9. Training and test datasets

	Dataset of [9]	YCTSA	TSAC [4]
Training dataset	14 248	18 620	13 648
Test dataset	3 562	4 655	3 412

5.1 Setting Parameters

For our deep learning models, there are a number of parameters to be fine-tuned. More precisely, we have to define the epochs and the batch parameters. Thus, we have tried different values for these two parameters. The values that perform the best results are the following. The number of epochs is 10 and the dropout rate is equal to 0.2 (i.e. the dropout mainly allows to avoid the over-fitting problem). One note that we adopted Adam's optimizer [26].

5.2 Experiments

In this work, we have conducted an overall of twelve experiments. Indeed, for the three Datasets (i.e. YCTAS, Dataset [9] and TSAC [4]) we have experimented four deep learning models (i.e., CNN, LSTM, Bi-LSTM and GRU). Our deep neural networks have achieved good results for Tunisian dialect sentiment classification. Results of all experiments are presented in Table 10.

Table 10. Obtained results for the 12 experiments

DataSet	Model	Accuracy	F-measure
YCTAS	LSTM	0.79	0.79
	GRU	0.86	**0.86**
	Bi-LSTM	0.76	0.77
	CNN	0.56	0.60
Dataset [9]	LSTM	0.79	0.80
	GRU	0.80	**0.80**
	Bi-LSTM	0.79	0.79
	CNN	0.60	0.60
TSAC [4]	LSTM	0.91	0.91
	GRU	0.91	**0.92**
	Bi-LSTM	0.91	0.91
	CNN	0.49	0.60

One note that the best performances have been achieved with the GRU model for the three datasets. Indeed, the F_measure for YCTAS Tunisian Dataset is 0.86. For the dataset of [9], the F_measure is equal to 0.80 and for the Tunisian Dataset TSAC it is equal to 0.92.

We also note that the best results are obtained based on TSAC Dataset. This could be explained by the fact that this dataset is balanced. Indeed, the number of positive and negative comments are almost the same (i.e., respectively 8 215 and 8 845).

Moreover, we think that it is important to note that our obtained results are very interesting since we achieved better performances than [4] who experimented TSAC on SVM, BNB and MLP models and obtained respectively an accuracy of 77%, 58 % and 78%.

6   Conclusion and Perspectives

In this research work, we have proposed an original approach for Tunisian Dialect Sentiment classification. Our approach allows to classify the comments into positive, neutral or negative polarities based on deep learning models. It is also able to handle comments in different scripts (Tunisian Arabizi and Tunisian Arabic).

We have experimented four deep learning models (CNN, LSTM, Bi-LSTM and GRU) and used three datasets collected from social media (our YCTAS dataset, the dataset of [9] and the TSAC dataset [4]) to train our models.

Best results were obtained by the GRU model. Indeed, the F_measure for YCTAS Tunisian Dataset is 0.86. For the dataset of [9], the F_measure is 0.80 and for the Tunisian Dataset TSAC it is equal to 0.92. These results are very interesting and outperformed previous works done on TSAC dataset [4].

As perspectives, we would like to enhance the results by experimenting other deep learning models and by applying other word embedding techniques such as Fasttext and Bert. We also intend to propose a method for fine-grained aspect sentiment analysis based our YCTAS corpus.

References

1. Wunderlich, F., Memmert, D.: Innovative approaches in sports science—Lexicon-based sentiment analysis as a tool to analyze sports-related Twitter communication. Appl. Sci. **10**, 431 (2020). https://doi.org/10.3390/app10020431
2. Yin, F., Wang, Y., Liu, J., Lin, L.: The construction of sentiment lexicon based on context-dependent part-of-speech chunks for semantic disambiguation. IEEE Access. **8**, 63359–63367 (2020). https://doi.org/10.1109/ACCESS.2020.2984284
3. Sayed, A.A., Elgeldawi, E., Zaki, A.M., Galal, A.R.: Sentiment analysis for Arabic reviews using machine learning classification algorithms. In: 2020 International Conference on Innovative Trends in Communication and Computer Engineering (ITCE), pp. 56–63. IEEE, Aswan, Egypt (2020). https://doi.org/10.1109/ITCE48509.2020.9047822
4. Medhaffar, S., Bougares, F., Estève, Y., Hadrich-Belguith, L.: Sentiment analysis of Tunisian dialects: linguistic ressources and experiments. In: Proceedings of the Third Arabic Natural Language Processing Workshop, pp. 55–61. Association for Computational Linguistics, Valencia, Spain (2017). https://doi.org/10.18653/v1/W17-1307
5. Aljabri, M., et al.: Sentiment analysis of Arabic tweets regarding distance learning in Saudi Arabia during the COVID-19 pandemic. Sensors **21**, 5431 (2021). https://doi.org/10.3390/s21165431
6. Li, R., et al.: Deep learning based imaging data completion for improved brain disease diagnosis. In: Golland, P., Hata, N., Barillot, C., Hornegger, J., Howe, R. (eds.) MICCAI 2014. LNCS, vol. 8675, pp. 305–312. Springer, Cham (2014). https://doi.org/10.1007/978-3-319-10443-0_39
7. Nassif, A.B., Shahin, I., Attili, I., Azzeh, M., Shaalan, K.: Speech recognition using deep neural networks: a systematic review. IEEE Access **7**, 19143–19165 (2019). https://doi.org/10.1109/ACCESS.2019.2896880
8. Zhang, Y., et al.: Learning interaction dynamics with an interactive LSTM for conversational sentiment analysis. Neural Netw. **133**, 40–56 (2021). https://doi.org/10.1016/j.neunet.2020.10.001
9. Masmoudi, A., Hamdi, J., Hadrich Belguith, L.: Deep learning for sentiment analysis of tunisian dialect. CyS **25**, 129–148 (2021). https://doi.org/10.13053/cys-25-1-3472
10. Jerbi, M.A., Achour, H., Souissi, E.: Sentiment analysis of code-switched Tunisian dialect: exploring RNN-based techniques. In: Smaïli, K. (ed.) ICALP 2019. CCIS, vol. 1108, pp. 122–131. Springer, Cham (2019). https://doi.org/10.1007/978-3-030-32959-4_9
11. Srinivas, A.C.M.V., Satyanarayana, Ch., Divakar, Ch., Sirisha, K.P.: Sentiment analysis using neural network and LSTM. IOP Conf. Ser.: Mater. Sci. Eng. **1074**, 012007 (2021). https://doi.org/10.1088/1757-899X/1074/1/012007
12. AlBadani, B., Shi, R., Dong, J.: A novel machine learning approach for sentiment analysis on twitter incorporating the universal language model fine-tuning and SVM. ASI **5**, 13 (2022). https://doi.org/10.3390/asi5010013

13. Altyeb, A.T.: Hybrid approach for sentiment analysis of Arabic tweets based on deep learning model and features weighting. Int. J. Adv. Appl. Sci. **4**, 43–49 (2017). https://doi.org/10.21833/ijaas.2017.08.007

14. Dang, C.N., Moreno-García, M.N., De la Prieta, F.: Hybrid deep learning models for sentiment analysis. Complexity **2021**, 1–16 (2021). https://doi.org/10.1155/2021/9986920

15. Abdallah, N.B., Kchaou, S., Bougares, F.: Text and speech-based Tunisian Arabic sub-dialects identification, vol. 7 (2020)

16. Dammak, A.M.: Approche hybride pour la reconnaissance automatique de la parole en langue arabe, 28 November 2019, p. 168 (2019). https://doi.org/10.1145/3364319

17. Atwan, J., Wedyan, M., Al-Zoubi, H.: Arabic text light stemmer, vol. 8, p. 8 (2019)

18. Yu, T., Hidey, C., Rambow, O., McKeown, K.: Leveraging sparse and dense feature combinations for sentiment classification. arXiv:1708.03940 [cs] (2017)

19. Pennington, J., Socher, R., Manning, C.: GloVe: global vectors for word representation. In: Proceedings of the 2014 Conference on Empirical Methods in Natural Language Processing (EMNLP), pp. 1532–1543. Association for Computational Linguistics, Doha, Qatar (2014). https://doi.org/10.3115/v1/D14-1162

20. Albawi, S., Mohammed, T.A., Al-Zawi, S.: Understanding of a convolutional neural network. In: 2017 International Conference on Engineering and Technology (ICET), pp. 1–6. IEEE, Antalya (2017). https://doi.org/10.1109/ICEngTechnol.2017.8308186

21. Hochreiter, S., Schmidhuber, J.: Long short-term memory. Neural Comput. **9**, 1735–1780 (1997). https://doi.org/10.1162/neco.1997.9.8.1735

22. Liang, D., Zhang, Y.: AC-BLSTM: asymmetric convolutional bidirectional LSTM networks for text classification. arXiv:1611.01884 [cs] (2017)

23. Zhou, P., Qi, Z., Zheng, S., Xu, J., Bao, H., Xu, B.: Text classification improved by integrating bidirectional LSTM with two-dimensional max pooling. arXiv:1611.06639 [cs] (2016)

24. Huang, Z., Xu, W., Yu, K.: Bidirectional LSTM-CRF models for sequence tagging. arXiv:1508.01991 [cs] (2015)

25. Chung, J., Gulcehre, C., Cho, K., Bengio, Y.: Empirical evaluation of gated recurrent neural networks on sequence modeling. arXiv:1412.3555 [cs] (2014)

26. Reddi, S.J., Kale, S., Kumar, S.: On the convergence of adam and beyond. arXiv:1904.09237 [cs, math, stat] (2019)

Soil Moisture Prediction Based on Satellite Data Using a Novel Deep Learning Model

Amina Habiboullah$^{(\boxtimes)}$ and Mohamed Abdellahi Louly

GTI International, Nouakchott, Mauritania
{a.habiboullah,ma.louly}@gti-intl.com

Abstract. Predicting soil moisture plays a key role in precision agriculture development and wildfires prevention. In this paper, we designed and implemented a novel deep learning architecture to predict soil moisture content (SMC) from satellite images using vegetation index (NDVI). The architecture combines a **set of U-Net** semantic segmentation model with a sequence-to-sequence **ConvLSTM layers** in order to capture both the pixel-wise satellite image content as well as taking into account the spatial correlation property of SMC. The model was trained on data collected from European Sentinel-2 and NASA SMAP satellites for an agricultural area in the Senegalese-Mauritanian river valley. We deployed the model with an **end-to-end ML-Ops** pipeline using **KServe** on Google Cloud platform and Microsoft Azure with a production-ready Json-API. The model shows predictions close to ground truth data with a Mean Absolute Error of **0.0325**, a RMSE of 0.0447 and an unbiased RMSE of 0.0435.

Keywords: Soil moisture · Satellite imagery · Precision agriculture · Deep learning

1 Introduction

In its 2018 edition report called *Agriculture 4.0 - The Future of Farming Technology*, the World Government Summit states that global population is expected to reach 11.2 billion by 2100. Furthermore, according to the United Nations Food and Agriculture Organization (FAO), as demand is continuously growing, farmers will have to produce 70% more food by 2050. To achieve this challenge, governments need innovative agricultural technologies. Thus, precision agriculture has the potential to considerably enhance efficiency and manageability of farms.

As soil moisture is one of the most important variables to control in agriculture in order to maintain high crop yields, an interesting application of precision agriculture is the estimation of soil moisture content. In 2010, the World Meteorological Organization lists it among 50 Essential Climatic Variables. In addition,

A. Bennour et al. (Eds.): ISPR 2022, CCIS 1589, pp. 394–408, 2022.
https://doi.org/10.1007/978-3-031-08277-1_32

soil moisture anomalies in under-populated areas can be an indicator of wildfire risk [1,2]. Thus, large number of researches have introduced methods to retrieve soil moisture content using remote sensing data as listed by Ahmad et al. [3], namely active, passive and a combination of both active and passive remote sensing methods.

As addressed in Sect. 2, numerous machine learning architectures have been used to predict soil moisture content using high spectral remote sensing satellite imagery. Deep learning architectures are, particularly, used for both SMC forecasting and inference using historical and spectral data. Several researches used CNN or ConvLSTM architectures to predict SMC since in the real world soil moisture level is **both** affected by the pixel position in the remote sensed image as well as by spatial correlation.

The main contributions/novelties of this work are:

- A new model to predict SMC by taking into account its semantic segmentation nature (based on U-Net architecture [4]) and spatial correlation between adjacent images leveraging ConvLSTM layers [5] and Encoder-Decoder framework as detailed in Sect. 3.2.
- End-to-end production-ready pipeline leveraging MLOps tools is implemented (Sect. 3.4) and deployed on both Google Cloud Platform as well as Microsoft Azure. The deployed system exposes a simplified API for applications (Web, Mobile, IoT devices).
- 14,960 960 m × 960 m surface areas in West Africa (Mauritania, Senegal) region were collected from both NASA SMAP satellite (soil moisture) and Sentinel-2 European Space Agency satellite (vegetation index) to train and validate the model (Sect. 3.1 and Sect. 4.2).

2   Related Work

In recent years, deep neural networks encountered a large success in many research areas, including remote sensing as elaborated by Zhu et al. [6]. However, due to the lack of labeled remote sensing data, there is a performance gap between state-of-the-art methods and satellite imagery [7]. A wise approach would, then, be to combine deep learning methods and satellite observed data to retrieve some helpful information about disaster prediction and environmental monitoring.

As remote sensing images present spatiotemporal correlations, Shi et al. [5] introduces the brilliant idea to create an LSTM variant with convolution named ConvLSTM. ConvLSTM allows to use the strength of convolution to extract features from images while taking into account spatiotemporal dependencies. Hong et al. [8] uses a convolutional encoder-decoder architecture with satellite imagery data to predict future satellite data in order to avoid possible environmental disasters. This paper introduces an interesting approach of selecting the best skip connection configuration between the encoder and the decoder. Some other papers use semantic segmentation architectures with satellite data either to identify snow and cloud on images (non-symmetric encoder-decoder framework) [9] or to classify land coverage [10].

In a narrower context, several research papers propose to use machine learning to retrieve soil moisture content from remote sensed data. Adab et al. [11] compares between four different machine learning models (Random Forest, SVM, ANN and Elastic Net regression) performances on soil moisture prediction using in-situ soil moisture data, Landsat 8 Satellite data, CHIRPS and SMAP datasets. As LSTMs proved an undeniable ability to extract contextual information from sequenced data, Fang et al. (2017) [12] and Fang et al. (2020) [13] propose to use it in order to forecast soil moisture based on SMAP data. Several other papers combine CNN and RNN(using LSTM or GRU cells) architectures to retrieve soil moisture either with a forecasting approach or by considering the correlation between soil moisture and spectral data [14–18].

In this work, we propose to predict soil moisture content using NDVI data as the correlation between these two variables has been demonstrated by several researches [19–21]. To build the proposed network, we thought the soil moisture prediction task as a soil segmentation task while introducing a regression loss to simulate the correlation between soil moisture and the NDVI. As U-NET network [4] achieves very good performance on segmentation applications, U-NET structure is introduced in an encoder-decoder framework to highlight spatial dependencies in soil moisture data.

3   Methods

3.1   Data

In order to train and validate the neural network presented in this paper, we propose to use satellite imagery from the European Space Agency Sentinel 2 [22] Level-1C product to calculate NDVI and NASA SMAP SPL2SMAP_S [23,24] product to retrieve soil moisture. SMAP/Sentinel-1 L2 Radar/Radiometer Soil Moisture (Active/Passive) Data Product [23,24] combines both active and passive remote sensing data. Soil moisture data is retrieved as follows. It uses native 36 km SMAP footprint, Sentinel-1 radar backscatter data and ancillary data including soil texture, vegetation opacity and daily precipitation forecast, as detailed in [25], to produce 3 km resolution soil moisture retrievals. In another note, Sentinel 2 ESA satellite has a MultiSpectral Instrument (MSI) that measures reflectances in twelve spectral bands. R, G, B and NIR bands used to calculate NDVI are resampled with a constant Ground Sampling Distance (GSD) of 10 m [22]. For the purpose of this research, a matrix expansion method is used to match between NDVI and soil moisture data.

We have collected data of a 135 squared kilometers agricultural area based in West Africa with 2 days tolerance between Sentinel 2 data [22] and SMAP data [23,24]. This data has been sensed between November 2015 and September 2021 and only Sentinel 2 images with a cloud coverage less than 10% have been used. Further, we sequenced this data to sequences of four 96 × 96 sized images.

Thereby, 3740 instances have been created and split with a ratio of 0.8:0.2 for training and validation purposes. Collected data statistics are illustrated in Fig. 1 and Fig. 2.

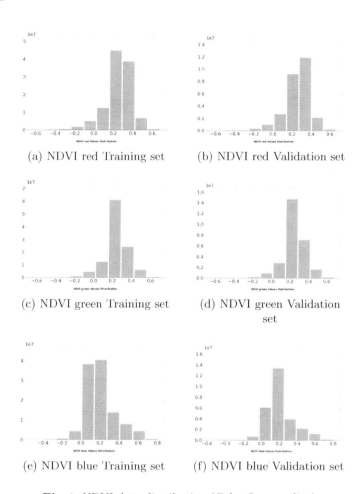

(a) NDVI red Training set

(b) NDVI red Validation set

(c) NDVI green Training set

(d) NDVI green Validation set

(e) NDVI blue Training set

(f) NDVI blue Validation set

Fig. 1. NDVI data distribution (Color figure online)

3.2 Model Architecture

In this section, we present the architecture illustrated in Fig. 3 used to predict soil moisture content. To predict soil moisture content, we used an encoder-decoder framework combined with a U-Net architecture [26]. The architecture consists of two major components.

The first component is an encoder that receives a sequence of four 96×96-sized NDVI data with 3 channels (NDVI red, NDVI green and NDVI blue). Each image in the sequence goes through an Encoder block and each encoder block is composed of five downsampling blocks. Each downsampling block consists of

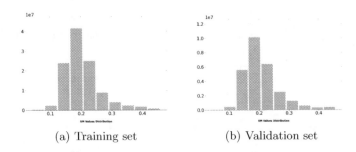

(a) Training set   (b) Validation set

Fig. 2. Soil moisture data distribution

two 3×3 convolutional layers followed by a Rectified Linear Unit (ReLU) and a 2×2 max pooling. By passing from one downsampling block to another, the number of filters is multiplied by 2, starting with 32 filters. A dropout with a rate of 0.6 is applied at the end of the last convolutional block.

Then, two ConvLSTM layers [5] are applied on the encoded sequence, the second one receives the output of the first one and the hidden state of the encoder.

The second part of the architecture, namely the decoder, receives the output of the last ConvLSTM layer and thus decodes the previously encoded useful information by using five upsampling blocks for each image of the sequence. Each upsampling block consists of a 2-strided 3×3 transpose convolutional layer. When the skip connection's flag is activated, the output is concatenated with the corresponding convolutional block output, otherwise only the transpose convolutional layer output is considered. Afterwards, two 3×3 convolutional layers with the same number of filters as the transpose convolutional layer are applied. By passing from an upsampling block to another, the number of filters is halved, starting with 512 filters. The upsampling operation allows to recover the initial size of data images (96×96). At last, a pointwise convolution is used in order to retrieve 1-channel 96×96 soil moisture content data.

3.3   Evaluation Metrics

As soil moisture content prediction is considered as a regression problem, we used the Mean Squared Logarithmic Error as a loss function. It is defined as the relative difference between the log-transformed predicted soil moisture and the log-transformed ground truth.

$$L(y,\hat{y}) = \frac{1}{N}\sum_{i=0}^{N}(\log(\hat{y}_i + 1) - \log(y_i + 1))^2 = \frac{1}{N}\sum_{i=0}^{N}(\log(\frac{\hat{y}_i + 1}{y_i + 1}))^2 \quad (1)$$

As shown by the second part of Eq. 1, this loss measures the relative error between each point of the soil moisture image and its prediction. It splits soil moisture image into equally weighted values which allows to treat the soil moisture prediction task as independent one-dimensional regression problems.

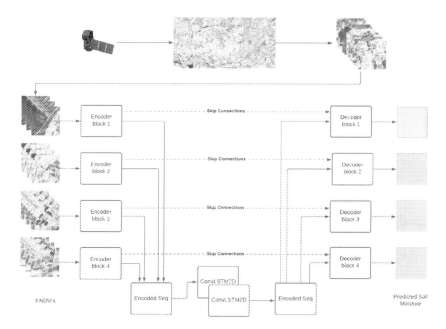

(a) Model Architecture. In order to apply encoding blocks and decoding blocks on the images of the sequence in a parallel way, TimeDistributed Tensorflow[27] layer has been used.

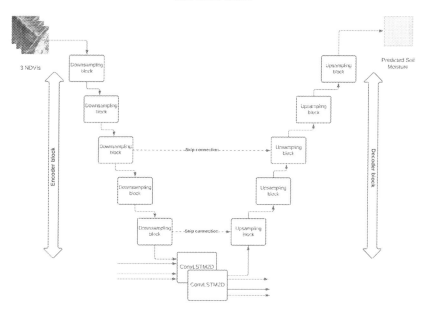

(b) Processing applied on each image of the sequence.

Fig. 3. Soil moisture content prediction model

Furthermore, thanks to logarithmic function, outliers points, where correlation between NDVI and soil moisture is not obvious, will not penalize the learning.

Quadratic performance metrics are often used to evaluate satellite measurements performance. Particularly for soil moisture retrievals, Root Mean Squared Error (RMSE) is quite convenient as discussed by Entekhabi et al. [28]. However, this metric is severely compromised if there are biases in soil moisture data. Hence, the unbiased RMSE (ubRMSE) is used to estimate soil moisture anomalies more reliably by removing the mean-bias [28]. These two metrics are, then, used for evaluating performance and tuning hyper-parameters.

$$RMSE = \sqrt{\frac{1}{N} \sum_{i=0}^{N} (\hat{y}_i - y_i)^2} \tag{2}$$

$$ubRMSE = \sqrt{RMSE^2 - MBE^2} \tag{3}$$

where Mean Bias Error (MBE) is defined by Eq. 4.

$$MBE = \frac{1}{N} \sum_{i=0}^{N} (\hat{y}_i - y_i) \tag{4}$$

In order to evaluate absolute differences between predicted soil moisture content and ground truth, we have monitored the Mean Absolute Error.

$$MAE = \frac{1}{N} \sum_{i=0}^{N} |\hat{y}_i - y_i| \tag{5}$$

3.4   Deployment

The system has been deployed using KServe version 0.7.0 which is a serverless machine learning inference solution [29] based on Kubernetes. KServe proposes three components for each endpoint: predictor, explainer and transformer. For our service, we have used transformer and predictor components. The transformer component enabled us to define a preprocessing and postprocessing steps before and after the prediction. The service has been deployed using an inference pipeline illustrated in Fig. 4 as a web application. To be served, the user chooses a date and geographic coordinates of the region of interest. The first module consists of checking the geometry of the area in question and its compatibility with the prediction model input. The updated coordinates are then sent to the downloading module which tries to find the closest date with less than 10% cloud coverage images. It downloads R, G, B and NIR bands from Sentinel-hub to calculate the three NDVIs. These three NDVI images are ingested into a sequencing module in order to sequence them into n 96 × 96 sized images. Finally, these images are ingested into the predictor component as a batch of four-sized sequences. At the output of the predictor component, soil moisture sequences of 4 × 96 × 96 are then assembled and returned to the user with the same geometry as requested.

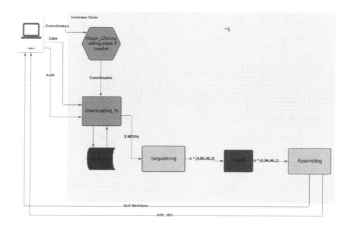

Fig. 4. Inference pipeline

The deployment has been validated on two cloud service providers, namely Google Cloud Platform and Microsoft Azure. A cluster of 3 nodes (each node having 4 CPUs and 16 GB of RAM) has been used for inference purposes.

4   Experiments

4.1   Optimization

Adam optimizer [30] is used for gradient optimization with an initial learning rate of 10^{-4} (obtained through a learning rate scheduling). Since, soil moisture values are between $0\,\mathrm{cm}^3/\mathrm{cm}^3$ and $0.45\,\mathrm{cm}^3/\mathrm{cm}^3$ (Fig. 2), the MSLE loss described in Sect. 3.3 is quite low and decreases quickly. To avoid a *vanishing gradients* problem, we have tried to scale up the loss function by scheduling $\hat{\epsilon}$ parameter defined by Adam optimizer [30].

Figure 5 shows convergence curves of different metrics on the training set for 30 first Epochs. As we can see, the model has more time to learn features on images for $\hat{\epsilon} = 10^{-11}$ and eventually converges well. This parameter value is,

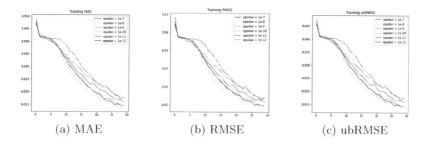

| (a) MAE | (b) RMSE | (c) ubRMSE |

Fig. 5. Epsilon parameter scheduling

therefore, used in Sect. 4.2 to tune hyper-parameters and to train the proposed architecture.

To improve the learning, a gradient centralization technique [31] has been embedded into Adam optimizer.

4.2   Model Training

Deep learning models used in this paper are created using Tensorflow framework [27]. In order to get the optimal configuration of the soil moisture content prediction neural network, we have tuned several hyper-parameters presented in Table 1. Firstly, as proposed by Hong et al. [8], seven different skip connection configurations have been tested with Max Pooling after each convolutional layer and a batch size of 16. As Exponential linear unit (ELU) [32] increases non-linearity and is largely used with satellite imagery, it has been, initially, used after each convolutional layer and each ConvLSTM layer. L2/4 skip connection configuration showed divergence on the validation set and, therefore, has been removed. L3/5 skip connection shows the best result on the validation set. In order to improve the accuracy of the model, we have tested four different batch sizes with the best skip connection configuration. Then, by comparing between ELU and ReLU activation functions on this particular task, we have noticed that ReLU activation function reduces overfitting and allows the network to have a much more better performance.

Table 1. Model Tuning. Results on the validation dataset. L0 is a vanilla configuration where no skip connection is activated. Numbers 2 and 4 in L2/4, for example, refer to upsambling blocks where skip connections are activated.

Configuration	Search space	Loss ($\times 10^{-3}$)	MAE	RMSE	ubRMSE	Epoch
Skip connections	L0	1.618	0.0371	0.0486	0.0465	29
	L2/4	1.818	0.0379	0.0513	0.0501	13
	L3/5	**1.535**	**0.0347**	**0.0468**	**0.0455**	**47**
	L1/3/5	1.587	0.0353	0.0483	0.0472	22
	L2/3/5	1.808	0.0374	0.0511	0.0498	18
	L1/2/3/4/5	1.738	0.0366	0.0503	0.0493	28
Batch size	4	1.897	0.0400	0.0497	0.0436	43
	8	1.671	0.0363	0.0482	0.0456	47
	16	**1.535**	**0.0347**	**0.0468**	**0.0455**	**47**
	32	1.799	0.038	0.0522	0.0513	13
Activation function	**ReLU**	**1.358**	**0.0325**	**0.0447**	**0.0435**	**35**
	ELU	1.535	0.0347	0.0468	0.0455	47

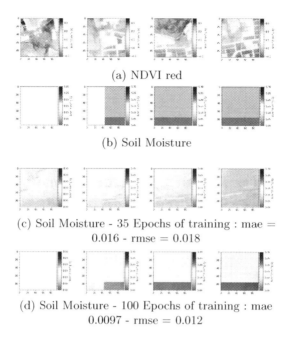

(a) NDVI red

(b) Soil Moisture

(c) Soil Moisture - 35 Epochs of training : mae = 0.016 - rmse = 0.018

(d) Soil Moisture - 100 Epochs of training : mae 0.0097 - rmse = 0.012

Fig. 6. Example 1 of validation set

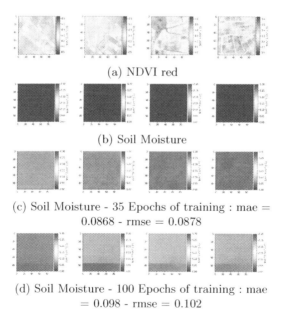

(a) NDVI red

(b) Soil Moisture

(c) Soil Moisture - 35 Epochs of training : mae = 0.0868 - rmse = 0.0878

(d) Soil Moisture - 100 Epochs of training : mae = 0.098 - rmse = 0.102

Fig. 7. Example 2 of validation set

4.3   Results and Discussion

As shown in Fig. 6, after only 35 Epochs of training, the model prediction shows a low overall error compared to the ground truth. We can notice that when the model is overtrained to 100 Epochs, it can detect soil moisture variation accurately. Figure 7 shows an example where the model presents a weak performance. This particular case presents an average soil moisture value of $0.341\,\mathrm{cm^3/cm^3}$. As shown in Fig. 2, this range of values is under-represented in the training set, which may explain the poor performance of the model.

In order to test the whole implemented system on an unknown landscape, we have collected 12 images from a $132\,\mathrm{km^2}$ sahelian region of Africa located $2000\,\mathrm{km}$ km away from the training and validation dataset area. Each image has been sequenced to 36 instances of 4-sized sequences, resulting in a total of 432 sequences. Pipeline inference described in Fig. 4 has been used to predict the corresponding soil moisture. As explained earlier in Sect. 3.1, soil moisture target data provided by NASA SMAP SPL2SMAP_S [23,24] product has a spatial resolution of 3 km and NDVI data is computed using bands from Sentinel 2 [22] with a spatial resolution of 10 m. As an expansion matrix computation has been used to match these two resolutions, a block averaging technique is integrated with a window size of 300×300 at the output of the assembling module (Fig. 4) to simulate target soil moisture distribution. As shown in Table 2 and Fig. 8, this averaging technique improves the system performance uniformly across the region of interest.

Table 2. Performance on a sahelian region in Africa. The block averaging technique improves the overall system performance with either the 35 Epochs trained model or the 100 Epochs trained model.

Inference pipeline	MAE	RMSE	ubRMSE	Epoch
Without block averaging	0.089	0.100	0.055	35
	0.087	0.099	0.056	100
With block averaging	0.088	0.099	0.053	35
	0.086	0.097	0.053	100

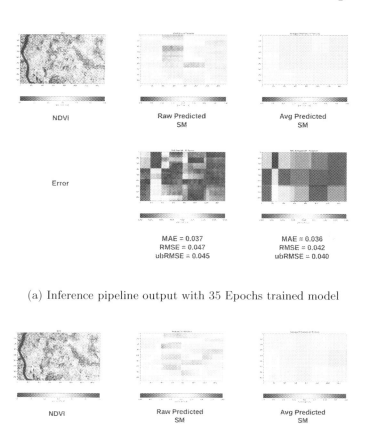

(a) Inference pipeline output with 35 Epochs trained model

(b) Inference pipeline output with 100 Epochs trained model

Fig. 8. Example of test dataset. Sentinel 2 data sensed on 07/23/2020 and SMAP data sensed on 07/21/2020.

5   Conclusion and Further Work

In this work, we studied how combining a segmentation-oriented architecture and RNN's strength in correlating contextual information can be used to predict soil moisture content. We have trained the proposed model on data collected from a poor zone of Africa where relevant agricultural solutions are of great need. The solution allows to retrieve soil moisture using low-cost and high resolution NDVI data. The system has taken a first step in the challenge of bringing Machine learning solutions to production as it has been deployed within an accommodated inference pipeline on two cloud service providers.

Nevertheless, our proposed model still needs improvement in order to better generalize to different landscapes. We have planned to collect more data with a larger range of soil moisture and NDVI values to better train the model. Furthermore, *in situ* measurements can be used to have a higher resolution on soil moisture data. As stated in Sect. 3.1 and Sect. 3.4, only Sentinel 2 satellite images with a cloud coverage less than 10% have been used for both training and inference. Yet, this can generate a large temporal gap on NDVI data and can penalize choice of dates by the end user. Therefore, we plan to implement a NDVI forecasting architecture to fill these gaps.

As a complete and sustainable solution in the agricultural field, the trained model can be embedded into an automatic irrigation IoT system. This solution will allow a considerable decrease in irrigation costs.

Acknowledgment. R, G, B and NIR bands are collected from Sentinelhub. The authors wish to thank the European Space Agency for sponsoring the access to Sentinelhub. We wish also to thank the National Snow and Ice Data Center Distributed Active Archive Center (NSIDC DAAC) and NASA Earthdata Search for providing free access to SMAP data.

References

1. Ambadan, J.T., Oja, M., Gedalof, Z., Berg, A.A.: Satellite-observed soil moisture as an indicator of wildfire risk. Remote Sens. **12**, 1543 (2020). https://doi.org/10.3390/rs12101543
2. Sungmin, O., Hou, X., Orth, R.: Observational evidence of wildfire-promoting soil moisture anomalies. Sci. Rep. **10**, 11008 (2020). https://doi.org/10.1038/s41598-020-67530-4
3. Ahmad, A., Zhang, Y., Nichols, S.: Review and evaluation of remote sensing methods for soil-moisture estimation. SPIE Rev. **2**, 028001 (2011)
4. Ronneberger, O., Fischer, P., Brox, T.: U-Net: convolutional networks for biomedical image segmentation (2015)
5. Shi, X., Chen, Z., Wang, H., Yeung, D.-Y., Wong, W.K., Woo, W.-C.: Convolutional LSTM network: a machine learning approach for precipitation nowcasting. In: CVPR (2015)
6. Zhu, X.X., et al.: Deep learning in remote sensing: a comprehensive review and list of resources. IEEE Geosci. Remote Sens. Mag. **5**(4), 8–36 (2017)
7. Yuan, X., Shi, J., Gu, L.: A review of deep learning methods for semantic segmentation of remote sensing imagery. Expert Syst. Appl. **169**, 114417 (2021)
8. Hong, S., Kim, S., Joh, M., Song, S.-K.: PSIque: next sequence prediction of satellite images using a convolutional sequence-to-sequence network. In: Workshop on Deep Learning for Physical Sciences, NIPS 2017 (2017)

9. Zheng, K., Li, J., Ding, L., Yang, J., Zhang, X., Zhang, X.: Cloud and snow segmentation in satellite images using an encoder-decoder deep convolutional neural networks. ISPRS Int. J. Geo-Inf. **10**(7), 462 (2021)

10. Ulmas, P., Liiv, I.: Segmentation of satellite imagery using u-net models for land cover classification (2020)

11. Adab, H., Morbidelli, R., Saltalippi, C., Moradian, M., Ghalhari, G.A.F.: Machine learning to estimate surface soil moisture from remote sensing data. Water **12**(11), 3223 (2020)

12. Fang, K., Shen, C., Kifer, D., Yang, X.: Prolongation of SMAP to spatiotemporally seamless coverage of continental US using a deep learning neural network. Geophys. Res. Lett. **44**(21) (2017)

13. Fang, K., Shen, C.: Near-real-time forecast of satellite-based soil moisture using long short-term memory with an adaptive data integration kernel. J. Hydrometeorol. **21**(3), 399–413 (2020)

14. ElSaadani, M., Habib, E., Abdelhameed, A.M., Bayoumi, M.: Assessment of a spatiotemporal deep learning approach for soil moisture prediction and filling the gaps in between soil moisture observations. Front. Artif. Intell. **4**, 11 (2021)

15. Masrur Ahmed, A.A., et al.: Deep learning forecasts of soil moisture: convolutional neural network and gated recurrent unit models coupled with satellite-derived MODIS, observations and synoptic-scale climate index data. Remote Sens. **13**(4) (2021)

16. Yu, J., Zhang, X., Xu, L., Dong, J., Zhangzhong, L.: A hybrid CNN-GRU model for predicting soil moisture in maize root zone. Agric. Water Manag. **245**, 106649 (2021)

17. Zhang, F., et al.: Predicting soil moisture content over partially vegetation covered surfaces from hyperspectral data with deep learning. Soil Sci. Soc. Am. J. **85**, 989–1001 (2020)

18. Efremova, N., Zausaev, D., Antipov, G.: Prediction of soil moisture content based on satellite data and sequence-to-sequence networks (2019)

19. Zhang, H., Chang, J., Zhang, L., Wang, Y., Li, Y., Wang, X.: NDVI dynamic changes and their relationship with meteorological factors and soil moisture. Environ. Earth Sci. **77**(16), 1–11 (2018). https://doi.org/10.1007/s12665-018-7759-x

20. West, H., Quinn, N., Horswell, M., White, P.: Assessing vegetation response to soil moisture fluctuation under extreme drought using sentinel-2. Water (2018). https://doi.org/10.3390/w10070838

21. Sharma, M., Bangotra, P., Gautam, A.S., Gautam, S.: Sensitivity of normalized difference vegetation index (NDVI) to land surface temperature, soil moisture and precipitation over district Gautam Buddh Nagar, UP, India. Stochast. Environ. Res. Risk Assess. (2021). https://doi.org/10.1007/s00477-021-02066-1

22. ESA Standard Document. Sentinel-2 User Handbook. European Space Agency (2015)

23. Das, N., et al.: SMAP/Sentinel-1 L2 Radiometer/Radar 30-Second Scene 3 km EASE-Grid Soil Moisture, Version 2. SMAP a.m only. Boulder, Colorado USA. NASA National Snow and Ice Data Center Distributed Active Archive Center (2018). https://doi.org/10.5067/KE1CSVXMI95Y

24. Das, N., et al.: The SMAP and Copernicus Sentinel 1A/B microwave active-passive high resolution surface soil moisture product. Remote Sens. Environ. **233**, 111380 (2019). https://doi.org/10.1016/j.rse.2019.111380

25. Das, N.N., Entekhabi, D.: Algorithm Theoretical Basis Document SMAP-Sentinel L2 Radar/Radiometer Soil Moisture (Active/Passive) Data Products: L2_SM_SP. National Aeronautics and Space Administration (2019)

26. Ronneberger, O., Fischer, P., Brox, T.: U-Net: convolutional networks for biomedical image segmentation. In: Navab, N., Hornegger, J., Wells, W.M., Frangi, A.F. (eds.) MICCAI 2015. LNCS, vol. 9351, pp. 234–241. Springer, Cham (2015). https://doi.org/10.1007/978-3-319-24574-4_28
27. Abadi, M., et al.: TensorFlow: large-scale machine learning on heterogeneous systems (2015). Software http://tensorflow.org/
28. Entekhabi, D., Reichle, R.H., Koster, R.D., Crow, W.T.: Performance metrics for soil moisture retrievals and application requirements. J. Hydrometeorol. (Notes and Correspondence) (2009)
29. Cox, C., Sun, D., Tarn, E., Singh, A., Kelkar, R., Goodwin, D.: Serverless inferencing on kubernetes (2020)
30. Kingma, D.P., Ba, J.L.: Adam: a method for stochastic optimization. In: International Conference on Learning Representations, pp. 1–15 (2015)
31. Yong, H., Huang, J., Hua, X., Zhang, L.: Gradient centralization: a new optimization technique for deep neural networks. In: Vedaldi, A., Bischof, H., Brox, T., Frahm, J.-M. (eds.) ECCV 2020. LNCS, vol. 12346, pp. 635–652. Springer, Cham (2020). https://doi.org/10.1007/978-3-030-58452-8_37
32. Clevert, D.-A., Unterthiner, T., Hochreiter, S.: Fast and accurate deep network learning by exponential linear units (ELUs) (2016)

Author Index

Abbas, Fayçal 349
Abed, Almustafa 327
Adoux, Jérémy 3
Aichaoui, Shaimaa Ben 248
Akrout, Belhassen 327
Al-A'araji, Nabeel 107
Al-Kababji, Ayman 204
Al-Khamees, Hussein A. A. 107
Aloulou, Chafik 377
Al-Shamery, Eman S. 107
Amine, Aouatif 119
Ammar, Sourour 78
Amous, Ikram 327
Amri, Saber 51
Atif, Dalia 165
Azaiez, Nesrine 377
Azizi, Nabiha 65

Babahenini, Mohamed Chaouki 349
Ban, Tao 306
Banaeyan, Majid 221
Batavia, Darshan 221
Belguith, Mehdi 377
Bellafkir, Hicham 189
BenHajhmida, Moez 278
Benhamza, Karima 19
Benleulmi, Maroua 65
Bensaali, Faycal 204
Bentagine, Amel 19
Bouchareb, Nassima 263
Boujelban, Rahma 234

Cao, Yaoguang 291
Cheikhrouhou, Ahmed 278
Chen, Yuyi 291
Cheragui, Mohamd Amine 248
Cheriguene, Soraya 65

Dakua, Sarada Prasad 204
Derdour, Makhlouf 341

Echi, Afef Kacem 93
Ellouze, Ameni 315
Emna, Abida 234

Faiz, Sami 213
Fares, Imtiez 362
Feki, Ines 78
Ferchichi, Nourchene 278
Freisleben, Bernd 189
Frieß, Nicolas 189

Gader, Takwa Ben Aïcha 93
Gahmous, Abdelatif 341
Gargouri, Bilel 377
Gasmi, Mohamed 341
Ghriss, Faten 278
Gidey, Habtom Kahsay 146
Goto, Hiroki 306
Gottwald, Jannis 189
Guerziz, Ines 19

Habiboullah, Amina 394
Haddad, Hatem 278
Han, Chansu 306
Hasni, Sarra 213
Hillmann, Peter 146
Hiri, Nawel 248
Houzet, Dominique 3

Ishibashi, Ryosuke 306

Kaddachi, Med Lassaad 51
Kadri, Nesrine 315
Karcher, Andreas 146
Kazar, Okba 132
Kchaou, Saméh 234
Kerdvibulvech, Chutisant 29
Kerkeni, Amine 278
Kesseler, Mario 146
Kessentini, Yousri 78
Khyara, Hamza 119
Korched, Abir 278
Korfhage, Nikolaus 189
Kropatsch, Walter G. 221
Ksantini, Mohamed 315

Laallam, Fatima Zohra 132
Lagrini, Samira 65

Lampe, Patrick   189
Layeb, S. Nadine   65
Louly, Mohamed Abdellahi   394
Lu, Jiayi   291

Malah, Mehdi   349
Mayer, Helmut   43
Mekhaznia, Tahar   362
Meksumphun, Kawin   29
Messaoudi, Abir   278
Miyamoto, Kohei   306
Mühling, Markus   189

Nagaraj, Naik   139
Naski, Malek   278
Nassih, Bouchra   119
Nauss, Thomas   189

Pang, Zhaowen   291

Rahmani, Kujtim   43

Salmi, Mabrouka   165
Seridi, Hamid   19

Shi, Runwu   291
Siagh, Asma   132
Stangl, Patrick   146

Takahashi, Takeshi   306
Takeuchi, Jun'ichi   306
Thisse, Quentin   3
Turki, Sameh Hbaieb   315

Vikranth, B. M.   139
Vogelbacher, Markus   189

Wang, Rui   291
Wu, Jie   180

Xu, Huigang   180

Yang, Shichun   291
Yogesh, N.   139

Zarour, Nacer Eddine   263
Zhu, Peiyi   180
Zoghbi, Abderraouf   65